ALSO BY JAMES S. KUNEN

The Strawberry Statement: Notes of a College Revolutionary

Standard Operating Procedure

"How Can You Defend Those People?":
The Making of a Criminal Lawyer

RECKLESS DISREGARD

Corporate Greed,

Government Indifference, and

the Kentucky School Bus Crash

JAMES S. KUNEN

SIMON & SCHUSTER
New York London Toronto Sydney Tokyo Singapore

95-   37520

SIMON & SCHUSTER
Rockefeller Center
1230 Avenue of the Americas
New York, New York 10020

SIMON & SCHUSTER and colophon are registered trademarks
of Simon & Schuster Inc.

Designed by Liney Li
Manufactured in the United States of America

10 9 8 7 6 5 4 3 2 1

Library of Congress Cataloging-in-Publication Data

Kunen, James S.
    Reckless disregard : corporate greed, government indifference, and the Kentucky school bus
crash / James S. Kunen.
        p.   cm.
    Includes bibliographical references and index.
    1. Ford Motor Company—Trials, litigation, etc.   2. Trials (Murder)—Kentucky—
Carrollton.   3. Criminal liability of juristic persons—United States.   4. School buses—Safety
regulations—United States.   5. Corporations—United States—Corrupt practices.   6. Drinking
and traffic accidents—United States.   I. Title.
KF224.F67K86   1994
346.7303′22—dc20
[347.306322]   94-21297
                                                                                                                   CIP

ISBN: 0-671-70533-4

PHOTO CREDITS:

1, 17 courtesy of Janey and Lawrence Fair; 2 courtesy of Jim and Karolyn Nunnallee; 3 by Bill
Luster, Louisville *Courier-Journal;* 4 courtesy of George Murgatroyd III; 5 Associated Press; 6, 9
National Transportation Safety Board; 7, 10, 11 by Steve Durbin, Louisville *Courier-Journal;* 8 by
Paul Schumann, Louisville *Courier-Journal*; 12 Exhibit, *Commonwealth of Kentucky* v. *Larry
Wayne Mahoney;* 13 by Ed Reinke/AP, print courtesy TIME INC. PICTURE COLLECTION; 14
Nixon Presidential Materials, National Archives; 15, 16 by Keith Philpott.

AUTHOR'S NOTE

The 1988 Kentucky school bus crash gained instant infamy as the worst drunk driving disaster in the nation's history. I was an associate editor at *People* magazine in New York City when I learned that two military families, who had each lost a daughter in the fire, were insisting that the design of the school bus, as much as the drunk driver, was to blame for the deaths of twenty-seven aboard. The Fairs and Nunnallees had turned down a big settlement offer and were instead pressing Ford Motor Company to improve the safety of its school bus chassis. I asked Jim Gaines, then *People*'s managing editor, to send me out to report on their battle with the auto maker. Ford was a huge advertiser in the magazine, but Gaines put me on the story and published it. That act of journalistic integrity deserves recognition.

I was dispatched to cover the murder trial of the drunk driver, Larry Mahoney, as well. Armed with my two articles, I asked Lieutenant Colonel Lawrence and Janey Fair if they would allow me to follow them closely as they pursued their lawsuit against the bus manufacturers, so I could write a book about it. After characteristically extensive deliberation, the Fairs agreed. They did not ask for or receive either monetary compensation or editorial control. Over the past five years they have submitted again and again to laborious, sometimes agonizing, often tearful interviews. They did it to spread the word about the dangers of drunk driving and unsafe school buses and perhaps save some other child from their daughter, Shannon's, fate. And they did it so that Shannon might be remembered.

Major Jim Nunnallee had been reassigned to Cannon Air Force Base in New Mexico, or else I would have asked him and his wife, Karolyn, to play an equal part. As it was, they spent many hours talking with me, despite the pain entailed in discussing the loss of their beloved Patty.

I have never met more honest, upstanding people than the Fairs and Nunnallees, and I thank them not only for helping with the book, but for showing me a model of dignity and courage to which I can only aspire.

Reckless Disregard represents my best effort to provide a detailed and accurate account of a horrific event, and our justice system's subsequent efforts to fix blame, administer punishment and restore the world to equilibrium. Words enclosed in quotation marks come from my interviews, the notes that I took at the criminal and civil trials, transcripts and tapes of legal proceedings, and tapes of broadcasts. The occasional description of someone's thoughts is based on an interview with that person, or his published remarks. Accounts of any scenes or actions that I did not see are derived from interviews with people who were there. Descriptions of chaotic scenes, such as those on the bus and at the church, represent a consensus view based on points of congruity among interviews of numerous people who lived through those events.

This book could not have been written without the help of a very large number of people. Only a few can be named here; others are credited in the notes to the text.

I am especially grateful to the survivors of the crash who relived their ordeal with me; and to the parents, spouses and friends of those who died, for taking out their photo albums and sharing their memories in the hope that by doing so they could help spare some other family a phone call in the night. Janet Kytta and Bill and Maddy Nichols gave me many hours. The indomitable Lee Williams—whose life is a testimony to the power of faith—shared not only his story but his wisdom, assuring me early on, "Buddy, I don't care who you are or what you write, you're gonna get people who say you've got it wrong."

Among those who went to particularly great lengths were Katrina, LuAnn and Kevin McNickle, and Janey Fair's sisters, Patty and Gloria. The Fairs' lawyers, John Coale, Skip Murgatroyd, Ann Oldfather and Mark Robinson, gave me all the information legal ethics allowed, and no more. The Nunnallees' attorneys, Larry Franklin and Mike Hance, helped, too. I am a lawyer, not an engineer, and so am indebted to former Ford engineer Larry Bihlmeyer and, especially, fuel system expert Neva Johnson, for patiently answering my questions. Barry Felrice of the National Highway Traffic Safety Administration contributed to my understanding of the regulatory process. Ernest Farmer, Tennessee's director of pupil transportation, steered me through the history of the industry's national standards. I had the assistance as well of attorneys Mark Arnzen, Dana Deering and Jacqueline Sawyers, who defended the bus body builder, Sheller-Globe. Ford Motor Company's defense lawyers Bill Grubbs, Bill King and Grace den Hartog also sat down with me, as did Ford's design analyst Robert Pelkey.

Paul Richwalsky, Jr., prosecutor in the murder case against the drunk driver, Larry Mahoney, was generous with his time, as was the leader of Kentucky's investigation, State Trooper Sonny Cease. Mahoney's lawyer, Bill Summers, prevailed upon his client to talk to me during the trial, and later in prison, in the belief that a fair portrayal of Mahoney could only help him; and I appreciate Mahoney's doing so.

Any writer on the subject of the bus crash is standing on the shoulders of the *Courier-Journal* of Louisville, whose Pulitzer Prize–winning coverage added luster to that award. The *News-Enterprise* of Hardin County and the *News-Democrat* of Carroll County also did yeoman work. My own research was assisted by Robert and Charlene Myles and Deirdre Cossman, and facilitated by Carroll County Circuit Court Clerk Bill Wheeler. Thanks for providing a place to work are owed first to Joyce Sparrow, and then to the three fine gentlemen Victor, John and Tony Scarpati, who sustained me in every way.

Finally, I am immeasurably grateful to my beautiful wife, Lisa Karlin, who despite her own demanding job took up the slack on the home front for *three years,* and then critiqued the manuscript; and to our children, Halley and Johnny, whose willingness to climb and fall and climb again will forever inspire me.

JAMES S. KUNEN
Brooklyn 1994

"If we could protect our children from every danger, then surely we would do so."
—Governor Wallace Wilkinson of Kentucky

❑

This book is dedicated to the memory of the twenty-seven people who lost their lives aboard a burning school bus near Carrollton, Kentucky, on May 14, 1988.

Jennifer Arnett, 13

Cynthia Atherton, 13

Sandy Brewer, 12

Joshua Conyers, 14

Mary Daniels, 14

Julie Earnest, 12

Kashawn Etheredge, 14

Shannon Fair, 14

Dwailla Fischel, 12

Richard Gohn, 19

Lori Holzer, 11

Chuck Kytta, 34

Anthony Marks, 15

April Mills, 15

Phillip Morgan, 13

Tina Mustain, 14

William Nichols, Jr., 17

Patty Nunnallee, 10

John Pearman, 36

Emillie Thompson, 13

Crystal Uhey, 13

Denise Voglund, 13

Amy Wheelock, 14

Joy Williams, 34

Kristen Williams, 14

Robin Williams, 10

Chad Witt, 14

CONTENTS

Prologue 9

PART I *The End* 15

PART II *The Beginning* 133

PART III *Judgment* 189

Epilogue 339

Notes 349

Index 367

PROLOGUE

Carroll County Coroner James Dunn and his wife, Cheryl, were driving south on Interstate 71, that May Saturday night, from one of Cheryl's just-about-weekly shopping excursions to the Lazarus department store and Florence Mall, up near Cincinnati. Cheryl remarked that they were passing an awful lot of school buses. They didn't know that it had been Church Day at Kings Island amusement park, and all those buses were hauling youth groups home.

It was smooth sailing, the forty-five miles back to Carrollton, Kentucky, and Dunn pulled his wife's Lincoln Continental into the car port just in time to catch the eleven o'clock news. Dunn usually headed for bed after the weather, before the sports, and he was still up when the phone rang —must have been about 11:10. It was the Campbellsburg dispatcher. The woman's voice on the phone calmly said that there'd been a traffic accident out on I-71 and the coroner was needed, by mile marker 39,* on the southbound side of the divided highway, about four miles below the Carrollton interchange. Dunn went out and loaded a stretcher into his station wagon, thinking he was likely headed for a single-car accident.

Dunn settled into the plush maroon seat of the big gray Mercury Marquis and drove out toward the highway, his emergency lights blazing. Below the glove compartment the red light of his scanner radio, blinking from left to right across four channels, froze in its tracks again and again as police cars and fire trucks and ambulances tersely announced their arrival at the scene. The state police were calling for "every available ambulance." Dunn couldn't imagine what was going on.

* The wreck was actually at mile 40.3.

A licensed funeral director and embalmer, Dunn was as familiar with death as a man could be. Death, after all, was how he made his living, always had been. It was as a junior in high school, back in December 1960, that Dunn was enlisted in his remarkable profession by Carroll Graham, a family friend who owned a local funeral home. ("He phoned and said they were busy, and would I go to Cincinnati and help them pick up a body at a hospital. It turned out to be a high school friend of mine who'd been killed in a car accident. I still don't know why he picked me.")

Whatever Carroll Graham had seen in him or sensed about him, he picked right, for Dunn took a part-time job in the funeral home immediately, signed on full-time after high school, did a three-year apprenticeship under Graham, completed a year of study at the Kentucky School of Mortuary Science, passed his state boards, and ultimately bought the business. Now his every pore exuded the same sweet smell that permeated the deeply carpeted rooms of the two white clapboard houses on Fifth Street that comprised the Graham-Dunn Funeral Home.

Dunn had augmented his stature in the community by becoming county coroner, first by appointment and then three times by election. The $700 a month job required him to determine (with the help of the state medical examiner's pathologists, if necessary) the cause of death whenever someone died in the county unattended by a physician, as in murders, suicides, and accidents. He was not infrequently called to the highway, and was so obviously inured to blood and gore that he'd take pains to assure you that morticians are not without feelings: "We are human beings too," he'd say. But nothing he had ever seen had prepared him for what he was about to encounter this night on a quiet country stretch of I-71.

Traffic was stopped dead, so he drove down the median until a distant glow condensed into a riot of flashing blue emergency lights just his side of the Henry County line. It was about 11:25. He got out of his car and saw a whole lot of children lying in the median. Up ahead stood the blackened husk of what must have been a school bus. Not far away rested the remains of a pickup truck that looked as though its front half had been ground into the pavement by a gargantuan heel. Evidently, the bus and truck had collided head-on; the pickup must have been coming the wrong way on the one-way road. And the bus had somehow caught fire.

Dunn stood for a few minutes, just trying to stay out of the way as a hundred emergency workers dashed among the figures scattered over the ground. He watched a helicopter take off and another land, the thumping of the rotors not quite drowning out the screams of agonized and terrified children. Then a state trooper asked him to go look inside the bus.

Smoke and steam curled from the charred hulk. A firefighter stood guard silently at the back door, with a hollow look in his eyes. Dunn opened the door and climbed into the vehicle. It was still hot. The odor was overwhelming, burned rubber and upholstery and, weighing heavy on it all, the stench of burned hair and flesh. He swept his flashlight around and thought, "This cannot be true. I am having a nightmare." He turned around, got off the bus and shut the door behind him.

But as he stood a few moments, something—the hard road beneath his feet, the glinting contours of the cars, the urgent activity surging on around him—told him that this was real. "I'm gonna have to see what's inside," he said to himself.

He climbed back through the rear door, intending to count the fatalities. Directly in front of him the tops of two skulls flashed in the beam of his light, the bare white bone streaked with crimson: Two bodies were lying face down in the aisle where they fell, one atop the other; no, that was three bodies in a stack, he could just make out the one on the bottom. To the right of them, two bodies were draped over the back of a seat, their flesh seared tight to their ribs.

Every trace of clothing had been consumed by the flames. He couldn't tell if he was looking at males or females. All he saw was burned meat and bone. But he could see that these human beings' last moments of life had been spent desperately trying to get to the rear door; they were piled headlong in the aisle and on the rear seats, stretching out toward him. He counted seventeen or eighteen at the back of the bus. Some, he could tell by their size, had been children.

Dunn went back to his car, lit a cigarette, and got on the car phone to his wife. He told her to call Dr. George Nichols, the state medical examiner.

Nichols was getting ready for bed at his home in Louisville, fifty-five miles away, when he heard from Mrs. Dunn that there were some eighteen dead in a school bus up in Carroll County. He got in his silver VW Jetta and lit out for Carrollton, tuning his radio to a big Louisville station to listen for news. As the white lines flashed by in rhythm to the beat of AM rock and roll (WHAS Classic Hits Weekend!), Nichols discovered with some satisfaction that his little car could do 128 mph. He did not have a police escort, emergency lights, or a siren, but long stretches of the road were straight and empty and he was in a hurry: Decisions had to be made on the proper handling of the scene before it was too late. He'd be living with a crash like this for years, in the courts and in the press, and if the evidence was screwed up at the git-go you could never straighten it out again.

Nichols knew he had his work cut out for him. The forty-one-year-old pathologist had seen his share of catastrophe in eleven years as the commonwealth's chief medical examiner. His first was the Scotia Coal Mine disaster in 1976: twenty-six dead in two explosions. "I was with the second rescue team, which pulled out the bodies of the first rescue team," he'd say, with dramatic effect. His biggest was the famous Memorial Day Weekend, 1977, Beverly Hills Supper Club Fire: 164 dead. There had been others since, and they shared one thing in common: As he explained on the lecture circuit, "In mass fatalities, the usual problem is to decide who is who." As he turned up the volume on the first news bulletins from the crash site, he was hoping that the victims would be visually identifiable. He was hoping the remains would not be strewn along the highway.

By the time Nichols arrived, around half-past midnight, all the injured had been taken to hospitals, including the driver of the pickup truck. Dunn and the state police had secured the scene, deploying yellow barricade tape to keep out the hundreds of onlookers who had walked up from their blocked-in cars to see what they could see. At least the disaster was confined to one enclosed area, Nichols thought, as he parked his car on the median.

A state trooper directed him to Coroner Dunn, who was standing over by the bus. Nichols asked Dunn how bad things were. He said they were terrible. Nichols asked two police officers for their flashlights, stepped up on a red and white plastic cooler and then onto the rear bumper of the bus, and entered through the open back door. He could see partially incinerated, commingled remains, at least eighteen, he thought. As he stood in the aisle of the bus-turned-charnel-house, inhaling the too familiar odor of fire death, he was already taking mental notes: The bodies were three deep in the aisle. And there were many people sprinkled around behind them, primarily to his right. It was pretty clear that everybody had been attempting to flee a fire at the front of the bus. Bang! Something happens. It's dark. They can't see. There's extreme terror. One person falls down and a couple of others fall over him, blocking the aisle. So the rest have to go up and over the seats, into the intense heat near the ceiling. And that means hair and clothing catch fire. When the back door opened, that fed the fire oxygen, allowing it to spread explosively. After that, it was probably all over in two minutes.

Nichols climbed down, ripping his blue jeans on the door as he did so. He sat in Kentucky State Police Lieutenant Ray Herman's car, blinking his eyes, hoping that he would wake up and what he'd seen would go away. In fact, Nichols had once dreamed that a plane had gone down, and when he came to work he called his staff together to begin work on the emergency. None of them had heard of it. He phoned the news media to check, and only then did he realize that it had all been a dream.

Not this time. Nichols huddled with Dunn, and state cops Neil Brittain and Herman, reviewing their options. If they removed the remains all at once, they would never be able to reconstruct in detail precisely what had happened. The devastation was so extreme—it reminded Nichols of a plane crash—that they couldn't even get an exact count of the victims. Yet, if they kept the highway closed and tried to meticulously chart and chronicle the position and condition of each body, the task could take days, and create all kinds of problems in the hot sun. They decided to remove the entire scene, intact; that is, move the bus with the bodies in it.

By now, representatives of the governor's office had arrived, and every resource was made available, as is so often the case after some calamity has occurred and it is too late to do anything to avert it. Dunn requested that the National Guard armory in Carrollton serve as a temporary morgue. Within ten minutes he had word that the facility would be opened.

A Carrollton construction company answered Dunn's call for cranes and a flatbed truck and tarpaulins. After the bus and everything on it was photographed and measured and photographed and charted and photographed again, and with a state policeman videotaping the event for evidentiary purposes, the bus was hoisted aboard the trailer, its grisly cargo shielded from curious onlookers by the tarps. It would be seven hours before they would be counted, but the charred remains of twenty-four youths and three adults lay inside.

Southbound traffic was diverted from the interstate, and, as a new day dawned, the bus, accompanied by police cars and a hearse, began the journey four miles back up the road to Carrollton. Moving delicately, at two miles per hour, the procession barely stirred the fog shrouding the roadway.

The school bus was passing the same landscape it had passed just a little while ago, but in reverse. The kids were traveling over the same road aboard the same bus, but before they were heading south and they were going home, and now they were heading north and they were dead. It was almost like running the film backwards, except the children did not come back to life.

It would occur to their grieving parents over and over again that all they wanted in this world was to run the film backwards. Why should one instant change everything forever? But since they could not do that, the parents of two girls who died would resolve, at the least, to delve back to the very beginning of the story—a story they'd had no idea would be their own—to find out exactly why their children had died, and whether other children might be spared in the future.

What they learned horrified and galvanized them: It was a man in an alcoholic stupor who drove the wrong way down the interstate and struck the bus. But, they would conclude, other men, including Lee Iacocca and Henry Ford II, in the executive suites of Ford Motor Company, and even Richard Nixon, in the White House, had made calm and sober decisions that robbed their children of the chance to walk away from the collision.

It would take a grinding four-year legal battle against the most powerful forces a corporate giant could muster, but these determined parents would uncover the evidence to show that Ford Motor Company had knowingly and willfully chosen to put lives at risk. Their children's lives had been figured into the cost of doing business. And there were plenty of blank lines on the ledger for the next innocents to die, and the next . . .

PART ONE

THE END

"**L**ord, as we make another trip, we ask for your hand of protection on our young people," the Reverend W. Don Tennison prayed aloud, just before the old yellow school bus set out on its last journey. "We ask you to give them safety as they go to and fro. We pray the angels to go with them, watch over them, and protect them."

The rotund Pastor T's scrunched-up eyes and downturned face reflected no more than the usual intensity with which he launched his appeals heavenward. His relatively relaxed grip on the padded metal post by the bus's stairwell bespoke a degree of confidence as he sent off sixty-three youngsters, in the care of four adults, to the Radcliff First Assembly of God's May 14, 1988, Spring Fling at Kings Island, 170 miles away. There had been times when the Lord had shown him tragedy ahead, and Tennison, not one to disregard even a hazily revealed premonition, had avoided disaster by changing course. But he hadn't the slightest intimation that two dozen of the high-spirited kids he'd just hushed for prayer would never return.

And why should he? Since the church bought the eleven-year-old bus for $2,750 at auction from the Meade County School District the previous May, the 1977 Superior B-700 had faithfully hauled Pastor T's flock hither and yon without incident. The road-trip bus they had before, a 1970 model, blew its engine—on the way to Kings Island, in fact—back in 1986. That's why they'd bought this one. According to the maintenance log, the county had installed many new parts, including a new air compressor and brakes, not long before selling the bus; a couple of mechanically adept parishioners pulled the vehicle apart after the purchase just to make sure.

This bus had made it to Kings Island, no problem, in July 1987. Then the whole 1988 school year, every weekday morning it took grammar school kids from the church's Dove Academy out to class in a leased building a mile away, then back to the church for lunch, then out to school, then back to the church—four stop-and-go miles a day. It had been over to Owensboro for a gospel concert; out to Paoli, Indiana, for a ski trip; and thirty-five miles from Radcliff north to Louisville repeatedly, for a youth convention, a Redbirds minor league baseball game, a John Jacobs Power Team martial arts exhibition ("God made you to win!"). In this way, the bus had covered 4,000 miles in the service of the Lord, which, when added to the ground previously traversed in a decade's rounds for the Meade County School Department, pushed the odometer to 113,000.

Brother Wayne Spradlin kept a watchful eye on the bus's maintenance, just as he did the U.S. Army's vehicles; he was a civilian supervisor at a Fort Knox* motor pool. In fact a driver wouldn't turn the key without going through a safety check: lights, horn, fluids, brakes, wipers. Just the Saturday before the trip, Spradlin went over to Jerry Hardesty's farm after the Men's Prayer Breakfast and they put on two new Hercules brand front tires—premium road tires, not retreads. Checked the front end—the tie rods, the kingpin buckings—too. Spradlin believed in always checking the front end whenever you changed tires.

Sure as he was of the bus, Tennison was troubled by the number of kids who were clambering onto it. Just the night before, his youth pastor, Chuck Kytta, had reported a total of thirty-five signed up for the $17 outing. Based on past experience—this was the tenth annual Spring Fling —they figured as many as twenty more would show at 7:30 on Saturday morning. But the church kids' invited guests had turned around and invited their own guests, and now there were sixty-three young people aboard the bus, thirty of them not even affiliated with the First Assembly of God or its L.I.F.E. (Life Is For Everyone) youth group.

Pastor T discussed his concern about overcrowding with Brother Kytta, and with associate pastor John Pearman. (Pearman had agreed to drive to Kings Island, as he had so many times before, although he was awfully busy with his work as district court clerk, and had said it would

---

* Radcliff, a town of about 20,000, owed its existence to Fort Knox, a U.S. Army armor training center, which itself had a population of 20,000—half military personnel and half dependents. The U.S. Bullion Depository, commonly known as Fort Knox, is adjacent to, not part of, the army installation.

be nice if someone else were available to take the wheel.) Some of the kids, meanwhile, were vociferously suggesting that everyone would be a lot more comfortable if they were allowed to drive up in their own cars. But what if they broke down? What if they got lost? The idea struck Tennison as imprudent, and he rejected it out of hand. Nor would it make sense to roll out the church's spare bus, for it was mechanically marginal, unsuited to the rigors of the highway. No, the children would go on this bus or not at all. But he was absolutely firm that everyone must have a seat—no standing, no sitting on laps.

"Okay, kids, bunch it up!" shouted Chuck Kytta (whom the kids, of course, called "Chiquita"). "You've got to bunch up." Kids trying to reach the back seats found it easier to get off the bus, walk back and climb in through the rear emergency door, rather than try to squeeze down the jammed, foot-wide aisle.

It turned out that, packed in three abreast, sixty-three kids and three chaperones could just about fit onto the twenty-two bench seats in eleven rows. Indeed, on a little black metal plaque affixed to the interior of the body above the windshield were the words: "Capacity 66 passengers." Although the plaque didn't say so, that number actually referred to school-children, for whom thirteen inches of hip room was deemed adequate. By standard industry practice, the capacity for adults would have been forty-four—two per seat, not three. Just four of the passengers were age thirteen or younger.

As the kids' departure neared, their parents took pains to ensure their safety, as though this were some perilous expedition, not an adult-chaperoned day trip. "You must sit in the front of the bus," one father commanded his son. Katrina Muller's mother, Mickey, was so worried about her thirteen-year-old going away for the first time without her older brother along that she called her off the bus three times, first to urge her not to go to the bathroom alone, then to remind her not to talk to "perverts," and then to grab one more kiss. Finally, her husband made her stop.

Josh and Aaron Conyers's mother, Rebecca, wouldn't let her sons, or Josh's guests, Joseph Percefull and Jim Slaughter, get on the bus at all, until she inspected it, top to bottom and front to back, even trying out the emergency door. Then after she said they could get on, she got on, too. And when they sat down, she sat down in front of them. "Mom, c'mon, get off the bus," the mortified Josh pleaded. But for the longest time she wouldn't get off. They didn't know if she was coming with them or what.

She was just sitting there, running through a long list of reminders: "Be careful. Make sure you guys stick together. And, Josh, watch Aaron." Finally, to her sons' relief, she said good-bye.

One of the four adults who went along, Janey Padgett, had a chilling feeling that something wasn't right, so much so that she had all she could do not to bolt off the bus, which seemed to her remarkably rickety. Padgett, who'd been invited along by her best friend, Joy Williams, a former co-worker at Fort Knox's Ireland Army Hospital, was not a member of the Assembly of God, but she knew that on this very trip a couple of years before, the group had to be retrieved from the roadside after the bus gave in. And she wasn't too happy about the fire ax and emergency road kit in a metal box sitting loose up by the stairwell. What with her heart condition, Padgett was worrying, "Oh Lord, hot as it is, what if we break down? What if we have an accident and that junk starts flying everywhere?" But she kept her fears to herself, only saying to Joy, "There's too many kids on this bus."

"I'm so sorry I brought you," Joy replied apologetically.

"Why?"

"Because these kids are making so much noise."

Naturally, Joy Williams was preoccupied by the kids' conduct. The First Assembly of God meant a lot to her—she served as its music director —and she hoped its reputation might be enhanced by the comportment of these kids, her own two children among them. Robin, ten, and Kristen, fourteen, had almost misbehaved themselves right out of the trip. At the prior Wednesday night's service, her husband, Lee, had gotten mighty upset with them for talking too much in church. "You're not going on any bus trip to Kings Island!" he'd decreed on the spot, adding to his wife, "And you're not going to talk me out of it." She waited till Thursday night before she did. Lee wanted his girls to be good, but he also wanted them to be happy.

And at this moment, they surely were. The whole rowdy lot were bouncing in their seats, blasting their cassette players, trading goofy remarks. They were at an age when life lives you. Years down the road, when they were much older, maybe a breeze would spring up and the trees rustle and whisper in a certain way, and they could feel for an instant as they felt now: in perfect harmony with a perfect world.

Brother Brent Fischel and Brother Pearman checked the battery clamps and dipstick, and looked over the tires. Finally, the bus roared into motion. It seemed like half the kids were hanging out the windows, waving and shouting. "Good-bye, Pastor T! We'll see you tonight!"

Katrina McNickle, sitting in the first row, later remembered watching as Chuck Kytta, stationed at the front stairwell, set about trying to remove a fire extinguisher from its holder, so that he could read the directions printed on the cylinder. "You never know," he said.

It took him about five minutes to get it out. "We're lucky that we weren't on fire," driver John Pearman joked. "We would have all burned up by now."

CHAPTER

2

From two miles away, the strobe lights atop Kings Island's blue, 330-foot, vaguely Parisian-looking Eiffel Tower blasted a silent siren song at the young adventurers: Blink blink blink. *This place has got the juice, This place has got the power*. Blink blink blink. *You're not in Radcliff anymore.*

Row after row of yellow buses shimmered like steel daffodils on the vast blacktop parking lot: It was spring, and Church Day at the park. As the kids piled off to swell the ranks of Christian youth at play, they inhaled the stirring scent of idling diesels that heralds a Big Event.

Well before they passed through the stucco entrance archways, they could hear low rumbles and high-pitched screams wafting on the breeze. Somewhere out of sight ahead, teenagers were enjoying the terror of the Beast—touted as "the biggest, baddest, longest, best wooden coaster in the world."

Uniformed Kings Island workers with cameras waylaid them on their way in; tiny group portraits set in cone-shaped plastic viewers on key chains could be purchased later as mementos of the day. Then they walked past *six* gushing fountains splashing in a very long pool, more fountains than you'd ever need, a lavish display of—*lavishness.*

Overlapping fragments of Muzak Marseillaise and John Philip Sousa poured from loudspeakers into air laden with an admixture of sun-softened macadam, oily pizza, and molten chocolate. This was high school heaven. Just about everybody in the park looked to be in their mid-teens, except for the old people dragging little children around. All the food was junk food, no chaperone could possibly keep up across the miles of hot asphalt promenades, and you could get totally lost without half trying—especially Shannon Fair, who for all her good sense never did have a sense of direction.

She and Mary Daniels, both fourteen, were among a whole slew of Radcliff Middle School Band members who'd been invited on the trip by trumpeter Jennifer Arnett, who belonged to the Assembly of God. Shannon and Mary were going around the amusement park with Shannon's pal Joseph Percefull, and his friends Jim Slaughter and Josh Conyers. The three guys were friends and the two girls were friends, but the guys didn't know the girls; except Joseph and Shannon were really tight, even though he was a high school freshman and she was in eighth grade. They'd met that March at the Kentucky YMCA's United Nations Assembly, where the best sixth-through-ninth-grade students go for three days and present motions and debate world affairs and jump in the hotel pool up at the Ramada Inn in Louisville. He was an adviser and she a delegate representing the Netherlands. They introduced a proposal to establish a humanitarian aid fund to minimize world hunger. ("Nearly 15–20 million people die each year from hunger or hunger-related causes. Unfortunately the majority are children, the world's future . . .") They'd talked to each other about an hour a day on the telephone ever since.

Josh Conyers was in the Assembly of God, and he had invited Joe and Jim. They were widely considered the three smartest guys in their freshman English class at North Hardin High. Slaughter had moved from Michigan just in time for the school year when his father opened a Little Caesars pizza franchise in Radcliff. At first Jim had thought that Joseph was a jerk and Josh a nerd, but soon all three had become good friends. Josh had turned out to be really funny; he always made everybody laugh, even when he was being serious. And he had style: The whole school year all Josh wore was O.P. T-shirts—Ocean Pacific T-shirts every day—and jeans. He must have had twenty different shirts that said Ocean Pacific with surfers and beach scenes on them. Even in the winter, you never saw him wear anything else.

These five never exactly decided to hang together at Kings Island. In fact Joe had spent much of the four-hour ride up talking across the aisle to Shannon about whether Amy Wheelock, Shannon's cute blond friend, liked him. Shannon assured him that she did, but when the bus unloaded, Amy trotted away with Phillip Morgan—so go figure. (It was probably just as well, because everybody ended up standing in lines all day, where you had to make conversation, and Joe was afraid to talk to Amy, because he liked her.) So Joe just said, "Let's go ride the Beast," and Shannon and Mary said, "Yeah, let's," and Jim and Josh said, "Okay."

The Beast line was the longest any of them had ever been in. They stood there for an hour and forty-five minutes. Exactly. All day Shannon kept track of how long it was taking to get on the rides. She'd look at her Swatch with the Coca-Cola-label face and say, "Oh, it's an hour now. We've been standing here one hour." She wasn't complaining, she was just making note of an amazing fact. Fortunately, Josh had won a miniature football by throwing a ball through a distant ring. So as they stood in line, Jim and Joe would take turns throwing passes to Josh, who'd run patterns through the other park patrons, who were unwittingly playing defensive backs.

Shannon and Mary did not play football. They'd talk about how awesome the ride was going to be and what they should all do next, or recount some incredible thing that someone had done or said at school. But every so often they'd turn away and talk quietly together, and the boys wouldn't know what they were talking about. And then Shannon would look up and toss her cascading auburn hair back and laugh, her green eyes sparkling, and Mary would laugh, too, and the boys wouldn't know what they were laughing at. The boys would think to themselves, "Do I have something hanging from my nose?" but it wouldn't be that. They never could figure out what the girls were laughing at, but that's the way girls were. It came with the territory and you had to accept the whole package.

After all that wait, the ride on the Beast seemed to last about forty-five seconds. The girls screamed and the boys yelled. Afterward Josh said it had really been intense; it took him a minute to get steady on his feet. They went to White Water Canyon next. Well before they could even see the water or the canyon, they saw the sign that said, "One and a half hour wait from this point." The line inched along a path with chain link fencing on each side, like a cattle chute, to prevent people from cutting in. At some places the path was shaded by forest, but mostly it was out in the sun, and they stood packed in, sweltering. The cicadas buzzed in the heat like your mind was ringing in an electric dream.

Finally they were hustled aboard a circular boat that rotated as it slid downstream past hidden spouts that exploded in little geysers, Pop!-*shush,* Pop!-*shush,* Pop!-*shush,* drenching some kids and missing others, by luck. They all got soaked, screaming at the shock of the cold water.

They went from White Water Canyon straight to King Cobra, a roller-coaster you ride standing up. Shannon at one time had been afraid of roller-coasters, but she got over that at the age of seven or eight, when she made herself ride one several times in a row. If Shannon was afraid of anything, she was absolutely determined to conquer the fear, no matter how long it took her.

As they were coming off that ride, Shannon spotted Wayne Cox just hanging around outside. Wayne was going with Christy Pearman at the time. And Shannon would be the first to tell you that she and the oh-so-handsome Wayne had absolutely never been a couple, *thank God,* but she did like to tease that boy. Now she gave Wayne a real hard time about his being afraid to ride King Cobra, even after he explained he'd been on it so many times he was bored with it and was just waiting for Christy to get off.

Then Shannon and her friends went back and rode the Vortex, the Twin Racers, and the Skylab. Everything was thrilling, but you knew it couldn't be dangerous. They wouldn't let it be dangerous. What could go wrong at a place where infants could be diapered at the Pampers Baby Care Center, first-aid was rendered under the sponsorship of Super Rx Drug Stores, and dead batteries in the parking lot were quickly and courteously jump-started under the banner of Firestone Mastercare Service Centers? This was not some garish, slapped-together carnival—origin uncertain, destination unknown—where absolutely anything might happen. This was life in the brand-name lane, where there are no surprises. To stand in a place you have seen advertised on TV, surrounded by the logos of vast, powerful, yet friendly and familiar enterprises, is to feel yourself in the gentle embrace of a loving father who knows and controls everything.

Mostly, Joe sat with Shannon and Jim with Mary. Once in a while the girls would ride together and Joe or Jim would ride with Josh so he wouldn't be sitting alone all the time. But Josh was always willing to ride by himself, which was thoughtful of him, because Joe and Shannon were best friends and Jim liked Mary a little bit.

That a relatively cool guy such as Jim Slaughter should like Mary Daniels would have surprised no one but Mary herself, and until that eighth-grade year, it would have surprised her quite a bit. Mary had considered herself overweight, and she was shy, and she didn't even believe she really deserved her slot as first-chair clarinet in the middle school band. She so greatly admired her big sister, Lisa, that she couldn't help but find herself wanting by comparison. Lisa, two years older, was thin and a great flute player; she had lots of friends *and* was popular. (To have a lot of friends was, of course, nice, but even outcasts had their friends. To be "popular" was something else entirely: No amount of loyalty or affection could give you the attractiveness and self-confidence attributed to, if not necessarily felt by, the *popular* kids in school.)

But then the summer before eighth grade, Mary lost weight, changed her hair from limp and straight to styled and sprayed, and started wearing makeup. Everybody said, "Boy, Mary's changed." A lot of kids, girls especially, changed a lot between seventh and eighth grades, and now they were moving into and decorating their new selves.

On the Ferris wheel it was Mary and Jim and Joe and Shannon. They were in open carts, one right behind and just above or just below the other, and as they went around they'd toss this stuffed animal to each other from cart to cart. And Shannon dropped it. This little red stuffed dog tumbled down and down and down and silently hit the pavement. You could just see it take a tiny bounce, and roll and then lie still. A little red dot.

Finally they went up on the Eiffel Tower. Joseph Percefull was afraid of heights, so he stood pinned up against the wall when they got to the top. He could handle the roller-coasters, because he was strapped in, but up here he couldn't go near the sides without seeing himself falling. "I'm getting over that a little bit," he would say, much later. "I say I have a fear of heights, but I think more than anything I have a fear of death."

❑

Joy Williams's older daughter, Kristen, went off with her friends, so Joy spent the day with her little girl, Robin, and Robin's friend Patty Nunnallee. Janey Padgett kind of "adopted" Patty, so they made a foursome. (Padgett felt guilty all day that she hadn't taken along her own twelve-year-old granddaughter. There they were in Hanna-Barbera Land, and

Brittainy would have had such a good time. And the odd thing about it was, Janey always took Brittainy everywhere. She couldn't imagine why she hadn't thought to take her.)

Joy talked about the good times she and her husband, Lee, had while stationed in Germany, and how they were going to go back and Janey must visit them there. Patty told them all about her parents. She said her mom used hair coloring to hide the gray in her hair, but Patty liked it better gray. And she talked about how wonderful her daddy's barbecue sauce was; he made the best barbecue sauce in the whole world.

❏

Jennifer Scoville bought a Kings Island half-shirt—like the top half of a T-shirt—because she'd gotten sunburned on her shoulders and she wanted to take her tank top off because the straps hurt. She put the half-shirt over her tank top, and she was walking around Kings Island taking the tank top off from underneath, practically *stripping,* Emillie Thompson thought. "I can't believe you're doing this!" Emillie gasped.

Carey Aurentz was with them, too. All three were still wet from the Amazon Falls ride when they sat down on a concrete wall to eat hot dogs at the end of the day. Emillie and Carey were both really bony girls, skinny and long. The three of them sat down and when they got up, they'd left wet marks on the wall. "Well, look at those itty-bitty butt marks," Jennifer said, pointing at those of her friends. "Is mine really that big?"

"You've got a big ole butt, Jennifer," Emillie confirmed sadly. Then they started singing, "Jennifer got a big ole butt, oh yeah! Emillie's got *no* butt, oh yeah!" This was just about an hour before they got on the bus to go home.

CHAPTER

3

A thin stream of kids meandered from the front gate past the Huckleberry Hound parking area and the Bamm Bamm area to the Elroy Jetson section, where the legions of yellow buses awaited. They were due back at the bus at 8:30, but it was practically 9:00 before everybody showed up. While waiting for the stragglers, some of the girls found a rap station on the radio and started dancing in the parking lot, right in front of a bus full of boys. The kids' imaginations waxed as the adults' patience waned: A tale made the rounds that a few of the girls had gotten drunk and nobody knew where they were, so maybe they had left with guys or something. This was not the case.

Chad Witt and Wayne Cox were among the last to come back. Chad had won a big inflated crayon—about as big as he was; he wasn't real big —which he'd given to his girlfriend, April Mills. So naturally Wayne wanted to win one, too. He took his best shot at a horse racing game, trying to roll balls into a hole marked "run," or at least "trot," only to see them fall with maddening regularity into the abyss called "walk" as other players' steeds thundered past. Wayne wasn't winning anything, so he tried and tried again, and time slipped up on them and they were late getting back. They ran into Mr. Pearman just as he headed out to look for them. Later Wayne would think about how the bus might have left a bit earlier were it not for him.

Some of the kids tried to convince John Pearman to let them stay to see the fireworks at the eleven o'clock closing of the park, as they had on past trips, when they wouldn't get home till 3:00 in the morning. But their arguments were unavailing, as Pearman said he wanted them to get home and go to bed, so as not to miss Sunday school. Pearman sat down in the driver's seat. Chuck Kytta stood and offered a prayer thanking God for the good day they'd had and asking for a safe trip home. "May God have his hand on this bus," he said.

"I can't believe I wasted that much money on that stupid horse race game," Wayne Cox was thinking, as they drove off just after 9:00 P.M. It was a warm evening and a couple of people put their windows down. But as the bus hit 55 mph, kids who were wet from the water rides complained that they were cold. So practically all the windows were then closed.

An hour and a quarter later, the bus had passed through the brief orange sodium-vapor blare of Cincinnati and was submerged in darkness, like a ship traversing some far cold planet, or an idea lost in an otherwise occupied mind.

John Pearman decided to pull off at exit 62, Route 127 Glencoe/ Owenton, a secluded country road, where a Sunoco station-store-restaurant stood as civilization's lone outpost. "Restaurant, Diesel, KY Souvenirs, Groceries, KY Lotto," the sign said. Chuck Kytta announced that they were stopping for gas, but they didn't want to stop for long, so people should get off the bus only if they needed to go to the bathroom or wanted to buy a snack.

Just about everybody got off the bus, but Sandra Glover, sitting in the next-to-the-last row, did not. She had a window seat, with only Tammy Darnell beside her. In Glover's opinion, the seat really had no room for a third person, unless your idea of comfort was to have half your body hanging off the edge and your legs sticking out into the aisle. She didn't want to risk losing her spot; then she might have to sit in the front of the bus, which she considered a nerdy thing to do. The front was where the little kids and all the chaperones were; she was seventeen, a junior in high school, practically an adult. (In fact, within three years she'd be married with two kids.)

Glover had gotten her Spring Fling ticket for half price, because she and her sister finished third in a youth group contest held by Kytta. You got points for coming to church, and for bringing your Bible and money for the collection. Such motivational techniques were too square by half for some Christian teenagers, who were, after all, teenagers. Only a few girls bothered to earn a crown in Missionettes, which, Jennifer Scoville would tell you, was "a Wednesday night thing for our girls. You go through a book and you earn badges, and you get on, what do you call it, steps or stairs or a stairway to heaven or somethin'. It's like, 'So what, you're supposed to be closer to God because you got badges? Come on. Give me a break.'" But Sandra Glover was eager to please Kytta. He had saved her life.

It had happened a few months earlier, during the bleak, dark winter. Sandra had gone along on a bus trip to Louisville to see John Jacobs and the Power Team. By way of illuminating the power of faith, the six-foot-four, 320-pound Jacobs and his six hefty colleagues crushed slabs of ice with their foreheads, broke out of steel handcuffs, blew up hot water bottles like party balloons, and lifted burning tree trunks over their heads. Between feats they shared their personal testimonies, promised that everyone could be "a spritual champion," exposed the dangers of alcohol, drugs, and teenage pregnancy, and cautioned against suicide ("not the ulitmate high but the ultimate lie"). The message was lost on Sandra Glover. She didn't go in to see the exhibition, but instead made her way out into the middle of the street, where she stood, waiting to get run over.

Her problems were private and, inside of her, large. They may have had something to do with being a native Hawaiian, and, at seventeen, counting her home addresses as Honolulu, then Fort Knox, then Hawaii, then Fort Knox, then Hawaii, then Germany, then Fort Knox. Her father was a career army sergeant. It seemed to her that all roads led to Radcliff, Kentucky, where she did not feel at home.

Alerted by one of Glover's friends, Chuck Kytta grabbed her from the road. Later that evening, she sat with him back at the church and spoke openly of her pain, which she had never done with anyone before. They cried together and prayed together, and he convinced her that Satan was making her see things as worse than they really were.

❏

The stainless steel gasoline pumps glittered beneath the spotlights in the Sunoco station's plastic-clad canopy. Pearman stood in that rectangle of white light in the black night as though on a stage, where nothing is real and everything means something; except all people did here was maybe wipe their windshield, check the oil, and fill their tanks with gas. Janey Padgett watched as he lifted a self-service hose and thunked the nozzle into the big black tank mounted just behind the front door, directly beneath the first three seats. Pearman pumped $60 worth, the gurgle and whoosh of the flowing fuel rising in pitch to a reedy hiss and then cutting off: Full.

As he walked in to pay, Pearman encountered his fourteen-year-old daughter, Christy, and joshed her about sitting in the back of the bus with Wayne Cox instead of up front near him. "Oh Dad, you know I love you," she said, as he ruffled her long blond hair.

Jennifer Scoville went into the ladies' room to put her sweatpants on, because her shorts were wet and she was chilly. The damp and dirty little room was jammed with giggling girls. "Jennifer, you got a quarter?" one asked.

"What are y'all doing?" Jennifer replied.

"We want one of these." They pointed to a battered white vending machine on the wall beside the sink. "New SuperSex French Ticklers in Assorted Styles and Colors," it said. A picture on the machine, of a young woman with her mouth open and head back, had been largely scraped away.

"Y'all are so bad!" Jennifer squealed. "I'm gonna tell your mom."

"I just want to see what one is," her friend insisted.

"Yeah, yeah, sure you do," Jennifer teased, as though she thought her friend's interest in the device went beyond curiosity. This was just about the funniest thing they'd ever seen, as well as the most disgusting.

❑

After the bus was again loaded up, Chuck Kytta asked the kids in front if anyone would be willing to switch seats with Kashawn Etheredge in the back. Kashawn wasn't feeling well, and the ride in the front of the bus would be smoother. Katrina McNickle volunteered to give up her seat in the right front row and try to squish in beside Katrina Muller back in the eighth row. As the bus departed, she worked her way back, climbing over stuffed animals, people's legs, a giant Crayola crayon, and at least one person lying in the aisle. She sat down in Katrina Muller's aisle seat and Muller moved across the aisle and sat on David Walliser's lap.

McNickle scrunched down with her head back and her knees up on the seat in front of her. Occasionally Amy Constance, sitting beside her, would ask a question about school or something, but soon McNickle was almost asleep.

❑

At around 10:30, just as the bus had been leaving the gas station, Clint Bradley was driving his Dodge Colt south, toward Louisville. He was about twenty miles ahead of the bus on Interstate 71, about five miles north of Carrollton, Kentucky, when he noticed a high-riding black Toyota pickup truck making a U-turn across the grass median from the northbound to the southbound roadway. The truck closed in behind him and tailgated for a while, its headlights blinding in the rear-view mirror; then it pulled past and began tailgating a trailer truck up ahead. The trailer truck would hit its brakes, trying to get the pickup to back off or pass by, but the pickup would just hit its brakes, too. Bradley pulled off the highway at Carrollton, to get some cigarettes and soda and put some space between him and that pickup.

❑

Jennifer Scoville was staring out the window into nothingness, thinking about Conrad Garcia. During the trip up Conrad had assured her, "When we get to Kings Island I'm going to be with you," but when they got to Kings Island, he was nowhere to be found.

Emillie Thompson, who'd been sitting in the next-to-last row, decided to go up front to visit with Billy Nichols, and with her close friend Carey Aurentz, whom Emillie had invited to come along on her church's trip. Emillie climbed past a girl sitting on a cooler, and Emillie's brother, Eric Thompson, who was lying in the aisle, then paused to chat with Jennifer Scoville in the seventh row.

Emillie knew Scoville was upset about Conrad Garcia. "Jennifer, men are trash. Don't worry about him," she said. She spoke soothingly, as a mother to her child: "If he doesn't like you, he's not worth it, because you're a sweet girl. You're a nice, sweet girl. You could probably find someone a lot better."

Jennifer was convinced. "Yeah, you're right, he's a little kid anyway." He was fourteen, she fifteen.

"Well, I'm gonna go up front," Emillie said. "Tootles." And she left to see Billy. Emillie had the biggest crush in the world on Billy Nichols. Billy was really quiet, and kept to himself. Everybody would go through his mother, Maddy, to get to him. Maddy would say to Billy, "That Emillie Thompson is a doll baby." And Billy would say, "Yeah, Mom, she's really nice." He just didn't want to go out. He liked to stand beside his '71 Pontiac and watch people.

(His father, an army sergeant, had gotten the car for $500 and had come up with a way for Billy to pay for it. He said for every A Billy got, he'd credit him $20, and for every B, $10. Billy, who was seventeen, also got a weekly allowance for doing chores around the house. He didn't have an after-school job; his parents didn't want him to work. They wanted him to enjoy life and not have to worry about making a living yet. "You've got plenty of time in life to work after you graduate out of high school," they told him, "so enjoy yourself.")

Emillie Thompson sat down on the aisle in the second row behind the driver, beside the chaperones Joy Williams and Janey Padgett, opposite Billy Nichols and diagonally across from Carey Aurentz. Emillie began playing some sort of game on paper with Billy—it could have been tic-tac-toe, or hangman. Carey turned sideways to talk with them—a casual shift of position that probably saved her life.

Before Emmillie joined them, Williams and Padgett had the seat to themselves and, frankly, had hoped nobody would sit there. Now, crammed in three across, and with all the windows shut to keep the wet kids warm, the two women could hardly breathe. "I'm hot; we've got to open this window," said Williams.

"Hey guys, we're burning up," Padgett said, appealing to the kids around them. She knew that she couldn't open the window herself. You needed two hands to squeeze the white plastic clips at the top corners of the window toward the center, and then you needed a third hand to push the upper window down. Phillip Morgan stood and helped the women open it.

Directly behind them, in the third row, Josh Conyers (at the window), Jim Slaughter, and Joseph Percefull (on the aisle) were amusing themselves by tossing Gummy Bears at people. They'd put them on their palms and, without turning around, flick them over their shoulders. They could hear people behind them demanding, "Hey, who's throwing stuff?" They did their best to act as though they weren't doing anything, but they couldn't help laughing. Joe stopped first, since he was on the aisle, and Mary Daniels was on the aisle opposite him, with Shannon Fair right beside her. The girls were bound to see what he was doing and they would probably think it was very immature. He hunched over and started talking with Mary, the two of them shoulder to shoulder in the aisle.

❑

After buying his cigarettes and soda at the Carrollton interchange, Clint Bradley got back on I-71 south. Shortly after he got back on the highway, he was astonished to see a black pickup truck blow past him in the left lane, going north on the southbound roadway.

Jack Armstrong, a sunburned, crew-cut, jug-eared, fifty-one-year-old farmer from Patriot, Indiana, was driving his '79 Olds Cutlass on I-71 north, his wife, Joan, beside him. They were returning from a day watching horse-pulling contests in Versailles, Kentucky. Jack was an accomplished competitor himself, holder of several records; his two Belgians, Mack and Fred, could pull 17,000 pounds. But today he'd just wanted to relax, and left them home.

The Armstrongs had stopped at a mini-mart in Eminence, Kentucky, where he got a Mountain Dew and she a Diet Pepsi and a Mounds Bar. It was 9:25 Indiana time—10:25 Kentucky time—when they pulled off to get the sodas. Joan was in the habit of looking at the time, because she drove a school bus for Switzerland County. She had to milk the cows before she left in the morning, and then she could never do anything the rest of the day without looking at the clock for quarter-to-three, time to set out again. She enjoyed driving the school kids—sixty of them, kindergarten through high school, on a fifty-four-passenger bus. On occasion, Jack drove as a substitute for her. They did pretty much everything together. Farming. Horse pulling. Bus driving. They'd been married thirty-seven years, since he was eighteen and she, sixteen.

Joan spotted a pickup truck going northbound in the southbound passing lane, and pointed it out to Jack. "Isn't that truck going the wrong way?" she asked.

"Yes, I believe it is," he replied. "There's going to be one hell of a wreck." He followed the pickup at a distance of a hundred yards for about two miles, observing that it was going 50 to 55 mph. Joan kept her eyes on it, noticing that it drove straight as an arrow, never tried to get out of anybody's way; there was never so much as a flicker of the truck's brake lights. The terrified and incredulous drivers encountering the truck flashed their lights and blew their horns but the Toyota never wavered: At a meticulous 55 mph, it kept to the right, that is, to the southbound drivers' left, in their passing lane.

Michael Frazier was driving his wife, daughter, and son-in-law home to Campbellsburg after seeing the nine o'clock showing of *Return to Snowy River,* a scenic PG melodrama, at the Carollton Cinemas. He had pulled his Nissan sedan out to pass a trailer truck on a curvy upgrade when he saw headlights that, he testified later, "didn't look like they were in the right place." Frazier hit his brakes and got back behind the trailer truck seconds before the oncoming vehicle whizzed past "just as though that was his road."

Steve Muessle and Tanja Sowder were heading home from Kings

Island in his red Camaro when the headlights came around a curve at them. Until the last half mile, Muessle thought the lights were on the other side of the road. They weren't. Tanja was amazed at how the truck cruised past "just like we weren't there."

❏

You could hear the murmur of music leaking from Walkman headphones, the aching roar of the engine, the whining tires, the symphony of squeaks and rattles as the bus jounced and jittered homeward. An occasional ripple of rowdiness in the back would build into a wave that crashed over the adults up front: The kids were teasing driver John Pearman's daughter, Christy, and his niece, Cheryl Pearman, about their supposedly kissing Wayne Cox and Jason Booher, respectively. John Pearman flipped the interior lights on for a moment, heightening the merriment. Regarding Christy, Jennifer Scoville was thinking, "Man, when you get home your dad is gonna choke you."

❏

That section of Interstate 71, like the two-lane blacktop that had preceded it and the dirt road that came before that and the deer trail that came before that, follows the meandering course of Mill Creek as it joins the Kentucky River—that is, the path of least resistance to the sea. Following this well-worn route (now traversed by 7,500 vehicles in each direction on an average day), the bus left the broad valley formed where the Kentucky flows into the Ohio River at Carrollton—the junction occasioned the founding of that once-prosperous barge-town two centuries ago—and lumbered up a sweeping left-hand curve into the forested hills, which loomed black against the moonlit sky. That curve, ascending, reversed itself into a bend to the right, which climbed into a switchback to the left. After the briefest of straightaways, a massive hill muscled its way down to the right-hand edge of the road, which threaded its way around it. There a chain-link fence stood against the random rock's fall should rain or frost displace the critical grain of sand. No chance of that tonight: The sky was clear, the wind still, the air sweet with the breath of clover.

The truck's headlights burst from around the curve, and then the truck itself.

CHAPTER 4

"**H**old on!" Pearman shouted, as the oncoming headlights whited out the windshield. (Or was it "Oh no!"? Or "Oh God!"?) He yanked the wheel to the left and hit his brakes.

Jim Slaughter, sitting in the third row, looked up and saw bright lights. There was a crash and he hit the seat in front of him. The front of the bus dropped, and it seemed as though they skidded forever.

Chaperone Janey Padgett, asleep in her second-row window seat, woke up when she flew forward and hit her mouth on the seat back. She heard the ripping rumble of steel scraping the road as the bus slid headlong down the pavement. "Oh dear God, please don't let us turn over!" she prayed. She thought they'd had a blowout. The bus finally came to rest, tilted toward the right front as though kneeling, exhausted. Padgett felt enormous relief: "Thank you, God," she said silently.

Back in the eighth row, Katrina McNickle felt a thud. The bus stood still, and everyone sat in silence for what seemed like a long time. "We must have hit a deer," someone said.

It was only seconds before Padgett saw flames in the stairwell, and felt the heat. "We're in big trouble," she thought.

"Get off the bus! Get off the bus!" John Pearman stood up and shouted. His face was bleeding. Kids toward the back saw those in front silhouetted for a moment against an eerie orange glow; then the flames leapt into view, licking their way to the ceiling. The fire, like a ravenous serpent, caught Chuck Kytta and climbed him. He raised his arms upward in a V, took a couple of slow steps, and fell.

The next thing Padgett knew she was standing in grass, looking up at the bus. The grass felt cold. A small woman, only five foot two, she had squeezed through the nine-by-twenty-four-inch window opening beside her seat. Now flames were shooting out that window.

The bus's right front had been hit head-on by the pickup truck's right front. The front door of the bus had been knocked away and the gas tank behind it pierced; a furious fuel-fed fire had engulfed the front of the bus and was spreading toward the rear. The impact had merely jolted the bus passengers. None of the children suffered so much as a broken bone, and as they rubbed the sleep from their eyes they became fully aware of what was happening to them. The bus filled with smoke and screams.

Conrad Garcia, sitting on Stephanie Howard's lap in the last row, was right beside the rear emergency door, so he got up and tried to lift the red metal handle, but was so scared that he fumbled with it. He resorted to kicking the door, and after a few blows it flew open. Garcia jumped off and ran. Howard tried to follow him, but the exit was already jammed with people all trying to get off at the same time. The last two seats protruded into the doorway from both sides, with only twelve inches between them. Except for the hard-to-open, nine-inch-high upper windows, that one-foot passage was the only way out.

Allen Tennison, the pastor's son, had been asleep in the ninth row; he was awakened by a scream. Everything was pitch black, with an orange glow. All he would remember later was that mixture of black and orange, a color combination seen as though for the first, or last, time. (Who had ever thought those familiar Halloween hues were the colors of smoke and fire?) He jumped up, turned around, and was pushed to the emergency door, where he saw E. J. Obergone fall out in front of him and run away. Tennison ran after him to ask why he was running.

Jamie Hardesty had been lying back with his eyes closed across from Tennison. When he banged his lip on the seat back, he, too, thought maybe they'd hit a deer. But when he looked up, he saw fire, and within ten seconds the bus was filled with thick, black smoke—you could cut it with a knife, he said later. It smelled like burning rubber, and made his eyes water and burned the inside of his nose like ammonia. People were piled on top of one another in the aisle, and by the time he climbed over two seats to the back exit, it was already partly blocked by people who'd fallen down. He could feel the skin on his nose tingling as it started to burn. He climbed over the pile of people and fell to the asphalt. As he got up to run away, he heard people shouting his name. Turning around, he saw the kids wedged in the door pleading for help. So he went back and started pulling them out.

"Tammy! Tammy!" Sandra Glover shouted as she shook her sleeping friend. But Tammy Darnell didn't wake up, so she jumped over her. Glover looked across the aisle to where her sister, Kim, had been sitting, but saw no one, so she headed back the one row to the emergency door. People were pushing on her from behind, but the people in front of her weren't moving. Driven by the heat searing her back, she pushed and fell on top of them, and the people behind her fell on top of her. She was sandwiched in, unable to move.

Seeing that the aisle was blocked, Jess Durrance, who'd been sitting in the ninth row, tried to kick a window out, but it wouldn't budge. He climbed over the seats to the back, where everybody was piled up like cordwood in the doorway. Looking for a way out, he turned around and glanced toward the front. It looked as though somebody were standing in the front of the bus with a flamethrower; the flames were hurtling straight down toward him.

Two or three people got off ahead of Durrance and then there was an opening for him; Hardesty pulled him from the back door. Hardesty could see the fire steadily moving down the bus, approaching the halfway point in not much more than a minute. Some people he didn't know were now helping to pull the kids out and drag them over to the median.

❏

James Carl Lucas had just lain down to sleep—his wife and children and uncle were still up watching a crime show (*Hunter*) on TV. His open bedroom window faced Mill Creek Road, which parallels I-71 at the foot of a steep hill. For a dozen years he'd lived in this little brick ranch house, and for him the rush and roar of the traffic on the highway had long since assumed the soothing nature of distant surf. The crash sat him up in bed —it sounded like a cannon shot—and when he pressed his face against the window screen he saw the blaze. He shouted for his wife, Phyllis, to call the police, and, dressing as he ran, rushed out of the house. He clambered over the waist-high, barbed-wire-topped fence at the base of the embankment and clawed his way 200 feet up the brush-covered hillside to the highway. He looked in the bus's back door but couldn't see very far through the thick dark smoke. A girl fell out, with her hair on fire. He heard screaming inside the bus and, amid all the horrific sounds of agony, a woman crying, "My baby! My baby!"

❏

Joan Armstrong, who with her husband, Jack, had been trailing the pickup truck from the safety of the northbound lanes, saw the impact and the big ball of flame. A southbound car ricocheted off the collision and came slashing across the median right at them. Jack somehow managed to avoid it and wrestle his car to a stop on the grass between the roadways, fifty feet from the bus. Joan at first thought the pickup had hit a tanker truck. Then she saw. "Oh my God," she shouted, "that's a school bus!"

Jack threw the transmission into park, put the flashers on, and ran across to the bus. Vicious orange flames were boiling out of the forward windows. As Joan hurriedly put her shoes on, she saw figures spilling out of the back of the bus and running away down the road. But when she got there moments later, the door was blocked almost up to the ceiling by a pile of children. Her husband was grabbing kids and trying to pull them out, but their wedged-in bodies wouldn't budge.

"What the hell am I gonna do?" he asked his wife.

"We got to get them out," she said.

Jack, for sixteen years a volunteer firefighter, climbed atop the back bumper, and, bracing his knee against the bus, managed to yank the children free, one at a time. As they fell to the pavement, Joan dragged them over to the grass.

❑

Though there were only two rows between Kim Farmer and the back door, it was already jammed with people when she got there. She pushed on the people in front of her but couldn't get out. She sat down on a seat and prayed, "Jesus! Jesus, help me!" Then the smoke got darker and there was nothing left to do. She had pushed and she had prayed. She couldn't even breathe anymore. She drifted off and passed out, as though drowning in a hot black ocean.

It seemed to Katrina McNickle, in the eighth-row aisle seat she got when she gave her front row seat to Kashawn Etheredge, that everyone had just sat there for *minutes* after they hit the deer or whatever; then everybody saw the fire and screamed and stood up. She didn't scream. She felt like a robot. She just stood up and turned around and tried to go, but everybody was already at the door when she got there. Everyone was pushing and shoving. She knew then that she couldn't get out the back door, so she turned to look for another way out. She saw Chuck Kytta on fire, and decided that she did not want to go back toward him, so she turned around and started pushing like everybody else. It seemed to get very quiet, and she could hear the little grunts of people being pushed and squeezed as they tried to get out. Somebody to her right said, urgently, "I'm on fire. Help me." She turned to look but she couldn't see anything, it was dark. But she moved the other way, thinking, "Well, if you're on fire, stay over there." Katrina was in a hurry to get out, but she could wait; she saw the horror of her situation but did not fully feel it. In all her twelve years, she had never experienced anything like this, and it was not believable, so it was reasonable for her to think that she must be dreaming, though she supposed that she was not. Then she was standing at the back door, dizzy and falling, and she was on the ground behind the bus, on one knee, and someone was telling her to get away.

❑

Joseph Percefull had been perched on the edge of his third-row seat, his legs in the aisle, his arms on his knees, talking to Mary Daniels, when they were thrown forward. Jim Slaughter, in the middle seat beside Percefull, bolted past him and grabbed him by the shirt and pulled. Percefull, in turn, grabbed Josh Conyers, in the window seat, by the arm to drag him along. But Slaughter didn't hold on to Percefull for long, and Percefull lost hold of Conyers in a split second.

Percefull didn't see what became of Mary Daniels and Shannon Fair. He didn't even realize that he hadn't seen them, until later. He scrambled over the seats to the back. He never tried the aisle, didn't think about whether it was jammed or not. He was just thinking how hot it was, and that he wanted to get out. He headed for what he could see, and what he could see was Jim Slaughter moving in front of him.

Slaughter couldn't make out anybody, just a mass of screaming, flailing figures. He crawled as fast as he could over the tops of the seats, swearing out loud until it got too hot to breathe. He came to a window that was cracked open an inch or two and stuck his face up to it, trying to breathe the cool air of the outside world, and then went on until he ran into people stacked at the door. "Safety windows!" Slaughter remembered. Kick them and they pop out. He sat on a seat back, with one leg in the seat, and kicked as hard as he could with the other. The window didn't come out, and it wouldn't break. There was no time to try to lower the sash. It kept getting hotter and hotter and hotter.

Slaughter was buffeted by an explosion. He saw a six-inch space at the top of the pileup in the doorway and dove for it. He could feel himself kicking people as he tried to force his way through. Some guy from the other side pulled him, and he dropped to the concrete, losing his shoe. Percefull, too, found a hole at the top of the pile.

Wayne Cox, snuggled up with Christy Pearman in the eighth row, had been dozing when he heard the bus hit something. He slid forward a little bit, but he didn't think it was any big thing. Christy just felt the bus shaking. But then she heard someone shout, "Oh my God, fire!" She saw her father, John, standing in the aisle at the front of the bus. She cried out to him, but didn't get any answer.

Then people started running right over their seat, kicking them in the head. Cox stood and pushed Christy toward the back of the bus. Somehow, he got forced out into the aisle. He found himself lying on top of somebody and underneath a bunch of other people. The air was getting so hot he decided to take a deep breath and then try to breathe as little as possible. As he tried to move forward by sort of swimming in a sea of bodies, his arm hit someone's head and he hoped he hadn't hit him too hard, but all he wanted was to get out.

Somehow, Cox raised himself up a little and the person beneath him slid forward and he crawled along with him. Somebody grabbed Cox's arm and yanked him out. He fell to the concrete, got up and kept running until he was on grass.

Between the kids coming over the seats and the kids jamming the aisle, Christy Pearman was trapped. Someone was screaming, "I want to get out! Please, please let me out!" It seemed like forever before she was able to move. She began crawling over the seat backs, and it was like climbing on frying pans. They were so hot they melted her palms. When she finally made it into the aisle, the back door was clear. Jamie Hardesty and a man wearing glasses reached up and pulled her off the bus.

Katrina Muller, who was sitting on Cox's left, had been thrown to the floor right after she heard somebody say, "Oh my God!" She climbed up and stood in line in the aisle, as she'd been taught at school, but she got nowhere so she started jumping over the seats. She hit her head on the ceiling and was passing out from the smoke and found herself on the floor, which was very hot. She felt like she was in a little circle and the heat was all around her.

She was sure she was going to die, and she knew in her heart that if she died right then, she would go to hell, and spend eternity in flames. But she had been taught and believed that if you are in trouble or need anything, you can pray to God and be helped. She prayed not to go to hell: "Please forgive me for all my sins against You." Muller felt like she was floating when she regained consciousness, outside the bus. She didn't know that the tip of her nose had burned off.

When there were no more kids wedged in the doorway, Hardesty could still hear screaming from inside. He picked up a long piece of metal and rushed up and down the sides of the bus, breaking windows, hoping to provide an escape route for those still trapped.

Jennifer Scoville, in the seventh row, just sat for a moment, thinking, "I don't believe this is happening." Then she felt the heat and realized, "I have to get off this bus." But the aisle was already packed with flailing, screaming kids. "Shut up! You all stop screaming," Scoville thought. "If you don't panic we can all get off." But everybody was screaming and pushing and she thought, "Well, there's no way. They're not going to shut up; the only way for me to get out is to crawl over the seats to the back." As she fled for her life, she thought, "My mom is gonna hear about this and she's gonna freak out."

As Scoville climbed over the seats she saw Ciaran Foran lying in one of them. Scoville nudged her with her foot—"Come on, Ciaran, get up, get up, get up"—but didn't lean down to her for fear of falling between the seats. Ciaran stirred and moaned, and Jennifer kept going. It was hard to keep her eyes open, the smoke was burning them so bad.

When Scoville reached the back, she forced her head through all the people, to breathe. But they were choking her, they were pushing people forward and pulling them back, and someone pushed her head away from where the air was and she just lay down on a seat and shoved her shirt into her mouth and said, "God, please don't let me die."

Then it was like when you're asleep in the morning and you hear the alarm and you think, "I don't want to get up, but I have to." She heard something, and then she thought, "Okay, I'm not dead. I can hear glass breaking. Jennifer, you've got to get up." She tried to move and next thing, somebody grabbed her. She was face down as she was pulled off the bus and she thought, "Oh, please don't drop me on the concrete."

❑

Carey Aurentz had been sitting in the aisle seat of the very first row on the right, inches from the flames shooting through the front doorway. But she had turned around, with her feet in the aisle, to talk with Billy Nichols and Emillie Thompson behind her. On impact Aurentz fell out of her seat and landed in a sitting position, facing the back of the bus. Feeling the heat and seeing the orange glow of the fire, she sprang to her feet and tried to make her way to the emergency exit, but the aisle was already packed and she was trapped. The kids were all pushing and shoving and practically running over the top of one another. And the acrid black smoke was like a rope around her neck.

Aurentz pushed her way to about three or four rows from the back, to the jam-up, where she could go no farther. She collapsed onto a seat. Then she was on a roller-coaster, and she was upside down, and she thought, "Oh God, I'm going to die." But then she thought really hard, "I've got to get off of this roller-coaster," and woke herself up. She climbed over the last, red hot seats and fell out the door onto the pavement. "Somebody help me, please!" she screamed. Jason Booher grabbed her arms and Cheryl Pearman grabbed her legs, and they started carrying her away but Cheryl dropped her because her legs were too hot to hold on to. Finally they dragged her over to the ditch beside the road.

After the doorway was clear, Jack Armstrong climbed into the bus to try to save some more. Ciaran Foran had stood up when she heard everyone screaming fire, but she got kicked back down into the seat. "No one would let me out," she said later. She'd been using a big helium balloon as a pillow; it blew up and stuck to her face. Her hair and shirt were in flames as she struggled toward the door. Armstrong got her in his big-knuckled hands and started to carry her away. He tore her burning blouse off. She got her arms around his neck, and when he tried to lay her down she wouldn't turn him loose. She said she couldn't see. Armstrong hollered for his wife to come get her, and he got on the bus again.

Groping along the floor, he felt another body lying in the aisle. He got hold of it and dragged it out. It appeared to be a little girl. She had big cuts across the knees and at first seemed to be dead. He laid her down behind the bus. He'd felt another body underneath hers, and Armstrong was determined to get it. He crawled in and got part way back before the smoke got to him and he had to get out. Then he climbed in again and got the child. That was the last time he could get in; the smoke was too much. He guessed in practically five minutes there was nothing anybody could do.

Smoke and flames filled the bus, from the ceiling down to the bottoms of the windows. There were kids in there but they weren't coming out. The screams of terror and shrieks of pain were fewer and farther between. Then there were no more words, no more desperate cries of

"Mommy! Mommy!" Just low moans, and then nothing but the cold, monstrous roar of the flames.

On the right side, toward the back, an arm reached out a window, as though groping for a way out. After a moment, the arm fell back inside. The fire blasted from every window now, surging twenty feet into the sky.

CHAPTER

5

"**Y**ou're being silly," Janey Fair's sister Gloria assured her. "If anything happened they would call."

It was unusual for Janey to worry so. Her fourteen-year-old daughter, Shannon, had ridden off on school buses many times before—even spent the night in a Louisville hotel for the statewide Kentucky Youth Assembly and Kentucky United Nations Assembly. As Janey imagined those confabs, her daughter would be walking around going to Pizza Hut at all hours. (In reality the great thrill was having pizza *delivered* while you and your girlfriends stayed up through the night telephoning the boys in their rooms.) Janey always cautioned Shannon to stick with at least two other kids, so that if a man jumped them, one could go for help and two could remain together. "Don't ever go anyplace unless you're in threes," Janey said.

The Kings Island trip seemed to Janey a lot less dangerous than those forays into the city. She had traced the route on a road map and found that the bus would be on interstates all the way—no twisty two-lane blacktops. She did worry a bit about the rides, but had inoculated Shannon with advice: If you go on the roller-coaster or Ferris wheel or anything that goes really high, make sure the shoulder harness is fastened on you, because people have died from being improperly buckled in. And don't get on with anybody who would flip it open.

This wouldn't be the first time Shannon came in late from something. When she took a trip with the middle school band, it might be 1:00 or 2:00 in the morning before they actually rolled in. Kids just run late. You could not predict when they'd get back, except that they'd never be early, or on time. They never did want to come home, naturally.

And this trip, they weren't even expected back at the church till around 11:00. But Janey kept going to the front door to look for the headlights that would signal Shannon's return. Jennifer Arnett's dad was supposed to pick the girls up at the church and drop Shannon off. The headlights would poke a white tunnel through the darkness down which would come the warm, familiar sound of the motor, then the clunk of the car door, a faint " 'Night, thanks," and the aluminum storm door would rattle open and Shannon would sweep in and tell her all about the day.

Silence.

Janey's husband, Lawrence, an army lieutenant colonel at Fort Knox, had driven to Johnson City, Tennessee, to pick up his widowed mother for her semi-annual visit. Gloria and Janey had cleaned house all day in preparation, and now lay down side by side in the double bed upstairs. Janey dozed fitfully till 1:00, when they heard something that Gloria swore was the front door closing.

"That's Shannon coming in, I heard her. Now quit worrying," she said.

"No, she would have come up and told us she's home," Janey insisted.

"I heard her come in and go down those steps to the bedroom," Gloria maintained. "She thinks we're asleep, so just go to sleep."

Janey said okay, just to end the discussion. She didn't go down to look because she knew in her heart that she would find nothing.

❑

The phone rang at about 1:00 A.M. The woman's voice on the other end said there'd been an accident.

"What happened?" Janey asked.

"It's serious," the voice replied. "We need you to come down to the church."

"What *happened?*" Janey repeated.

"It's serious, that's all I can tell you. We don't have any of the details." The woman said she couldn't tie up the phone line, and hastily gave Janey directions. Janey didn't know where the church was, in fact, had never heard of the Radcliff First Assembly of God before Shannon asked to go on the outing.

"I'm going down to the church to see what I can find out and I'll call you later," Janey told Gloria, almost in a whisper. She rushed out and pulled the door shut quietly behind her. She was afraid she would wake Shannon's older brother, Donald, who had a big day ahead of him: He and the rest of the North Hardin High School Band were going to Kings Island, and she didn't want to mess up his day.

Janey drove off in her station wagon. As always, it took forever for the light at the intersection of the two main drags, Lincoln Trail and Dixie Highway, to turn green. She thought about running the red—there were no cars in sight—but she wouldn't do that, didn't believe in it. The way she looked at it, once you treat red lights as optional, you're on the road to anarchy.

She turned left on Dixie and started looking for Montgomery Motors, to make a right there on Vine Street. She passed a Pontiac place and the Taco Bell and the White Castle and saw the Ford place and Embassy Furniture Mart. As she squinted through the night at the signs, she noticed how strangely unchanged they were. The world was spinning crazily out of orbit into the frozen void, and it seemed no one but she even knew it. The terrible secret was growing in her chest, making it hard for her to breathe.

There was Montgomery Motors, a VW dealer. She turned right, then left at the Chevron gas and food mart onto South Wilson Road. She wended her way down the hill on a curving, tree-lined street. The drab little ranch houses set back from the road were dark and silent; she might have been the last person alive on earth. St. Christopher's Catholic Church was empty, the Radcliff Elementary School deserted, every playground cry faded away as though it had never been. *Radcliff Dairi Deli. Radcliff Dairi Deli.* She repeated the landmark as an incantation to call it into being, and finally it materialized on her left. So here she turned right onto Rogersville Road, which snaked through the scrub woods and overgrown pastureland on the edge of town.

Shortly she saw two illuminated plastic signs, one above the other: "Radcliff First Assembly of God" and "Dove Academy." There, down a long driveway, sprawled the church. With its broad, low-slung roof and pointy little steeple, it could have been a Howard Johnson's, but two vertical strips of stained glass flanked three long crosses on its brown brick wall.

Then, to her abiding horror, she saw them, the messengers of doom,
TV satellite trucks, their surgical steel arms extended and diesels roaring:
Bad news travels fast.

There must have been a hundred people, huddling in the parking lot
and in the vestibule and inside the sanctuary. Some of them were holding on to each other and crying. Shannon's friend Amy's mother, Janet
Wheelock, rushed over to Janey and said, "Janey, our babies are missing!
They can't find our babies." She was crying, really crying hard, and Janey
couldn't understand why, because Janet was not a hysterical person. Then
Janey saw on the wall the handwritten lists: One said who was in what
hospital and in what condition. The other had nineteen names of those
who were missing and not accounted for. It included Shannon and her
friends Amy Wheelock and Jennifer Arnett and Cynthia Atherton and Denise Voglund and Kashawn Etheredge and Mary Daniels.

Janey, who was already ailing with bronchitis, at once felt immeasurably ill and staggered through the double doors into the sanctuary to sit
down. There were people up at the front, beneath the twenty-foot cross
hanging behind the pulpit, moaning and wailing and speaking in tongues.
They were pounding the altar and chanting and singing and doing one
thing one minute and one thing the next and then everything at the same
time. It was a sort of prayer with which Janey, a Methodist, was not
familiar, so now her situation was not only horrifying, but strange.

Janey believed in God but she practically worshipped reason. She
figured that Shannon and her friends must all have sat together and
therefore were probably either all dead or all alive. If there were only a
couple of unidentified survivors, then to pray that Shannon was one of
the living was tantamount to praying that her friends were not. Janey just
sat there. She was freezing cold, though it had been a warm night. A man
stood up at the altar and shouted for calm, insisting that there were no
confirmed dead. Nothing, *nothing,* he repeated, had been confirmed. The
way Janey remembered it, he was shouting for people to "sit down and
shut up."

At around 5:00 A.M. Janey walked out to the vestibule and picked up a
phone on the wall. "Keep it short!" a man told her. She called Gloria and
told her to wake up Donald, because it was almost time for him to leave
for the high school band's trip to Kings Island, and Shannon was missing,
and she didn't know whether he ought to go or not but he could use his
own judgment.

Donald stayed with Gloria's four-year-old daughter while Gloria rushed down to the church. It appeared to her that not enough was being done to find anything out, so she went out to an all-night market and phoned a friend who was a Louisville police officer. He made a few calls and called her back on the spot; there were twenty-four to twenty-six dead, and he'd call around to hospitals to try and locate Shannon, he said.

Gloria went back to the church and told Janey that her friend was trying to find Shannon; she didn't mention the twenty-four to twenty-six dead. Janey and Janet Wheelock kept looking for their daughters' friends' mothers but they couldn't find them. They remained a group of two until Mary's mother, Diane Daniels, finally arrived as it was starting to get light out. (No one from the church had called her; she heard of the accident from her older daughter, who'd seen reports on TV when she awakened at a friend's house to go to Kings Island with the high school band.)

Janey remembered Shannon's leaving, twenty-four hours before. Janey and Larry had gone to Fort Knox for a predawn ceremony, at 4:00 A.M. Saturday morning, honoring the 46th Infantry Regiment. Candles were lit in front of trees in a grove planted in memory of the dead. They sat on folding metal chairs. It was chilly and they could smell the cold wet earth as the little flames flickered in the darkness.

Mary Daniels had slept over Friday night with Shannon, and they were still up, trying on clothes, when Janey and Larry had left for Fort Knox. "You girls are not going to be able to get out of bed in the morning, 'cause we're not going to be here to get you up," Janey had warned.

"We know, we know," they said. "We're just trying to get our things together." There were clothes everywhere. The girls tried and tried on everything until they had it just right. Mary must have brought her whole wardrobe over with her. Later it took Janey two or three trips to take it all back.

When Larry and Janey arrived home from the ceremony at around 6:00 A.M., Shannon and Mary were just crossing the lawn, heading for Jennifer Arnett's dad's car. Cynthia Atherton had climbed out of the car to greet the girls, and the three of them were chattering excitedly, their voices crystalline in the cool morning air. Janey told them they looked pretty, and they really did. The early-morning sun was shining on their hair like a blessing. Larry patted Shannon on the back and said, "Y'all have fun today." Janey said, "Have fun." It was just a momentary passing. They didn't kiss good-bye.

A churchwoman was gently touching Janey's wrist. "Maybe God took Shannon to save her from a worse fate later on," she said, her eyes brimming with kindness. Janey recoiled. She wondered if Shannon was dead and the church members all knew it and were lying to the parents who weren't in the Assembly of God.

CHAPTER

6

The sudden, chilling notion that the church people knew her daughter's fate had overtaken Janey Fair like a revelation, but it was not true.

Rev. Tennison, who'd been at the church since the regular 9:00 P.M. men's prayer meeting, had started getting concerned when the bus had not arrived by midnight. "Maybe they got a late start," he told himself. "Maybe they stopped at a McDonald's."

At about 12:10 he got a call from the father of Conrad Garcia, one of the kids on the trip. "Brother Tennison, this is Brother Garcia. I just received a call from my son in Carrollton that our bus has been involved in an accident, hit head-on. They're rushing our kids to six different hospitals. I'm gone," he said, and hung up. He was talking so fast that the name Carrollton didn't register with Tennison.

"Folks, we got a problem," the pastor said to the fellows waiting in his office. "Our bus has been in an accident. I'm trying to find out what happened." He called all the church board members, his wife—and his doctor, in case some of the parents needed help. Then he called the state police. They said, "We don't know anything. We'll call you back."

When anxious parents began calling up to ask where their children were, Vicki Fischel, the Dove Academy preschool teacher who'd volunteered to answer the phone, told them that the kids weren't back yet, period—because the church really didn't know anything else for sure. And they wanted people off the phone, to keep the line clear for calls from hospitals or the police.

Then, around 12:45, Tennison remembered the name Carrollton, and called information for a Carrollton hospital. "This is Pastor Tennison of the Radcliff First Assembly of God," he said. "Some of my children may be at your hospital." He was put on hold. Then a state trooper got on the phone. The first thing he said was, "Reverend, your son is okay. Allen Tennison is standing right here beside me. He's okay."

(Much later, when they had time to reflect, Pastor T and his wife, Martha, came to feel that God had allowed Allen, their only child, to survive so that they would be able to devote their full attention to ministering to the other families. "Someone pushed him out the back door," Sister T said. "I'd rather say he's blessed than lucky. God just blessed us.")

The state trooper asked if Tennison knew how many people were on the bus. Sixty-seven, Tennison said; his youth pastor, Chuck Kytta, had the only passenger list with him. The trooper didn't say anything about the bus burning, or people being killed.

It was around 1:00 A.M. when another trooper called and said it appeared that the bus driver was dead. Starting then, Fischel got on the phone to tell people that there had been an accident and the church didn't have much more information. One of the things she did not know was what had become of her own stepdaughter, Dwailla, who was twelve. Vicki and her husband, Brent, had driven to and from Kings Island in their car, with Brent's son Lee, eleven, and their little boy Sammy, five. But Dwailla wanted to go on the bus with the other kids her own age. "She was fixin' to be a teenager," Vicki explained later. "She wanted to be a teenager."

Fischel made a list of all the kids that she could remember having seen on the trip. She started another list of names of children whose whereabouts were learned from hospitals calling in, and she would post it in the hall each time she revised it. She would look at the list of those she hadn't located and think, "Who's going to be next? Who's going to be off the list and who's going to stay on?" She'd recall later, "It was almost like when I had that pencil in my hand I had the power of life and death." But of course she did not, and she could not save Dwailla, who had died in the flames.

Around 2:30 or 3:00 in the morning, a trooper on the phone told Tennison they now knew there had been at least seventeen fatalities.

"Fatalities? You mean dead?" Tennison gasped. He felt as though he had been stabbed in the heart.

"Oh yes, Pastor, I mean dead."

The minister crumpled into his chair and wept. Then he told the officer again that Chuck Kytta had a list of all the passengers' names in his briefcase.

"Pastor," the policeman said, "hasn't anybody told you that the bus burned? There is no briefcase. There is no bus."

Tennison still did not go out to talk to the families because he was rushing from phone to phone trying to coordinate the gathering of information. And there was another reason: Radcliff Police Detective Roger Runyon, a church member, told him and Vicki Fischel that it was important not to give out any unconfirmed information, because if they said something that proved to be incorrect, they could get sued.

"We would be held liable if we said this happened or that happened or something else happened," Fischel would recall being told, "because they were saying on the phone, 'Unconfirmed, unconfirmed, unconfirmed.' And the policeman was saying you can't say this or that, because when they say unconfirmed that means unconfirmed."

Even in the icy grip of ultimate fear, there is room for awareness of the tort system and the prudence it commands. A couple of times, someone would go to the sanctuary and tell the waiting family members that there was no confirmed information about casualties, and say nothing more, except, "When we find out where your children are, we'll tell you." In any case, the pastor's wife, Sister T, felt that to announce there were at least seventeen dead would just create even more anguish, since they didn't know which ones they were.

By daylight, with John Pearman known dead, Vicki Fischel had written twenty-six names on the list of the missing.

CHAPTER

CHAPTER

7

Joy Williams's husband, First Sergeant Lee Williams, had sat alone at home Saturday night watching Charlton Heston lead the defense of the diplomatic quarter against Chinese fanatics—and prevail against the odds—in *55 Days at Peking*. (Williams loved old movies with John Wayne–type heroes and happy endings.) Expecting his wife and two daughters back sometime after midnight, he turned off the TV at 11:00 and went to sleep.

Awakening around 12:00, he called the church and was told that the bus was not in yet. When he called again later, the woman on the line said there had been an accident. He asked, well, what kind of accident? Because he was concerned, at first—until she said a pickup truck had run into the bus.

Williams owned a pickup himself, and he thought, "Well, my goodness, what kind of damage can a little truck do to a great big school bus?" He pictured the bus pulling out of a gas station, the truck runs into the back of it, something like that. He said okay, he'd come down, because he thought maybe they'd need people to drive up and get the kids.

He had last seen his elder daughter Kristen as she left for school on Friday morning, the thirteenth; she was to spend Friday night at the home of her friend Stephanie Howard, who was also going on the trip. "I love you," Kristen had said, and he had replied, "I love you, too, Krissie."

When he came home Friday afternoon from his middle-management job at Fort Knox's Ireland Army Hospital Friday afternoon, Williams worked in the yard with Joy, getting ready to pave the driveway. (They were always working on something.) Then he took Joy and their ten-year-old, Robin, and Robin's friend Patty Nunnallee out for ice cream.

Friday evening, as they did most nights, he and Joy took a walk around the block. They talked about the house. Ever the big planners, they were hoping to put in a pool. On the walk, they ran into Rev. Tennison and his wife, who had just finished dedicating, or blessing, the Uheys' new house nearby.

Pastor T and Sister T accepted the Williamses' invitation to drop in, and stayed about an hour, talking, laughing, drinking coffee. As always when the pastor came to the house, they closed out with a prayer: Thank you for this good fellowship, Thank you for this home of Christian love, Thank you for friends, Give us a safe trip tomorrow. Sister T said to Joy, "Take care of my son," for Allen Tennison was going to Kings Island, and Joy had agreed to be a chaperone, because Robin had said, "Mom, if you go, I can go." Otherwise the outing was for twelve-year-olds and up.

Patty Nunnallee stayed over with Robin Friday night. (Her father, Jim, had insisted she walk up the front path and ring the doorbell by herself; when she hesitated out of shyness, he scolded her for acting like a baby. He would always regret having done that—and never forget seeing Patty walk away, carrying her little blue overnight bag with the red handle— but he was just trying to help her grow up.) Patty's family did not belong to the First Assembly of God, but she and Robin were good friends at school, and had similar interests. Both, for instance, had entered the local Optimist Club public speaking contest, addressing the prescribed subject, "Destiny: Choice, Not Chance." (Patty placed third in the girls' division at the finals, which had been held just three nights earlier. "I feel destiny is a choice made by you," she said. "If you do not make the right choice, your life will not end the way you want it to.") When Lee and Joy went to bed at 10:00, the two little girls were still up, busily playing a board game, the game of Life.

It was 6:00 A.M. Saturday morning when Robin padded into her parents' bedroom and started looking in the nightstand for batteries. She was taking along a tape of the Christian singer Sandi Patti, and needed them for her Walkman. No one could ever find batteries in that house. Lee got up, took some batteries out of one of Robin's toys, got the Walkman up and running, helped Joy pack a cooler, kissed them good-bye, and said he'd see them later.

It was one of the very few times that Williams's wife and children went anywhere without him, but he'd had his fill of Kings Island in years past, and he'd promised to help a fellow church member put in a new kitchen floor that day. He told Joy she should take along her friend Janey Padgett on the family's fourth ticket.

When he arrived at the church, Williams saw that the county coroner was there, and he saw families gathered, and people calling hospitals, and it didn't take but a moment before fear and panic had seized his heart. He dashed all over the place, in the vestibule looking for news and in the sanctuary praying for help. Three or four times he drove home to check the answering machine.

Someone said most of those killed had been in the front of the bus. He recalled that Joy had said they would ride in the front. But then as he was up at the altar praying it flashed though his mind that when he was working on his friend's floor Saturday afternoon, Pastor T had come by and said something—something about the bus being full and Joy making a remark like, "Maybe I ought to drive my own car."

"Man, maybe Joy did drive the car!" Williams thought. Then he froze, because until he found out different, it could still be true. Finally he got up the courage and walked out of the sanctuary and through the vestibule and he opened the door and ran right into Joy's black Ford LTD gleaming in the parking lot.

At 3:00 A.M. Williams was begging God to spare his wife and two children. As the number of known dead kept rising, he found himself bargaining with God. "If not all three, God," he cried, "just give me two." And then, "God, if not three, if not two, please give me one." He begged for just one.

He was swept, for the first time in years, by memories of Vietnam, where he'd served as a medic. There had been a night when he was lying in a bunker and his unit's other bunker was blown up. "Lord, spare some of them," he'd pleaded, but they all were dead, every one. And here again, he had a feeling deep in his soul that Joy and the girls were gone.

CHAPTER

8

atrina McNickle, having fallen from the rear door, found herself on one knee on the pavement behind the bus. Some man was yelling at her to get away, the bus might blow up. She scrambled down the road to the flickering, pale orange forms of her friends, and set about finding her pal Katrina Muller. As McNickle wandered among the people scattered over the ground, somebody behind her called out her name, weakly, in a hoarse voice she didn't recognize. She turned around and saw a figure sitting with its legs crossed, its elbows on its knees and its hands extended. McNickle didn't recognize the person, who actually didn't look like a person at all. The swollen, black, and blistered face looked more like a monster's.

"Who is it?" McNickle asked. "Who called me?"

"Don't you recognize me?"

"Oh, my God! It's Katrina!" McNickle exclaimed. She sat down next to Muller, but not too close. She didn't want to touch her, because she could see that she was badly burned. Her arms, except for the melted green plastic that had stuck to them from the bus seats, resembled steak that had been pulled from the charcoal after falling through the grill: here a crispy black, there a bloody, raw red.

"Please, find my mother," Muller implored McNickle.

The twelve-year-old McNickle, who was experiencing the preternatural calm of the self beheld as protagonist in a dream, reassured her gravely injured friend. "They're finding your mom," she said.

Muller began complaining that the sun was too bright. She said she wanted some sunglasses. McNickle explained that it was nighttime, and that it must be the headlights that were bothering her. A great many oncoming cars had stopped behind them, and they all had their lights on and they were all shining down on them. But Katrina Muller thought it was the sun, and would not be persuaded otherwise. "The sun's too bright," she kept saying, over and over, as she stared straight ahead, into the lights. "Get me some glasses."

❏

After Jennifer Scoville was pulled half conscious from the rear seat where she'd passed out, somebody dragged her over to the median. Moments later, the bus rocked her with a cannonade of exploding tires. Boom! *Boom!* BOOM! "I *know* I have to be dreaming," she thought. "I fell asleep watching some movie with fire in it, and I'm dreaming."

Scoville noticed that she couldn't feel her hands, which were burned black and were full of glass. "You need to sit down," some passersby were telling her. She sat down beside Katrina Muller. It looked to Scoville as though Muller had been wearing gloves and someone had pulled them partway off: It was her skin, hanging from her fingertips.

At first, everyone was saying, "Everybody made it off. Everybody's here." But then, as people were looking for their brothers or their sisters or their best friends, they realized, hey, everybody's not here, we can't find these people.

Janey Padgett had found herself standing at the bottom of an embankment. "Joy! Joy!" she screamed, calling for her friend Joy Williams. Then she saw the flames pouring out of the window through which she had come just seconds before. A small, short-haired woman, who had materialized from nowhere, took her arm. "Honey, you have to run," she told Padgett politely. "That bus is gonna blow." Dazed, Padgett moved down the road. That's when she heard some kids asking, "Where is Brother Chuck? Where is Brother John?"

Padgett walked around looking for little Patty Nunnallee or Joy Williams or Joy's daughters, Robin and Kristen. "Oh, dear God," she prayed, "if I could just find one of them!" She asked everyone if they had seen them. No one had. Then there was a tremendous explosion, sending a mushroom cloud boiling upward from the bus.* That's when she knew that Joy and Robin and Kristen didn't make it.

Jim Slaughter took Padgett over to the side of the road, and then went

---

* This was probably the differential or transmission bursting. The pressure for an explosion cannot build up in a gasoline tank that has been breached and is fueling a fire.

looking for his friends Joe Percefull and Josh Conyers. He couldn't find them. Then he heard Joe yelling his name. The two of them went almost right up to the burning bus looking for Josh, right up to where you could get burned all over again, just from the heat in the air. Then they saw some figures lying in the grass with people helping them. They thought for sure Josh must be one of them so they went back.

Along the way they encountered Jennifer Scoville. She looked at them and said, "Josh is dead."

"No, we're gonna find him," they insisted.

"He's dead," she said. She just knew that he was, the moment she saw Jim and Joe and no Josh. She just knew, and she was right.

It seemed a long, long while before they heard a siren wailing in the distance, a faint lamentation barely audible beneath the triumphant roar of the flames.

❑

Kentucky State Police Officer Robert Strong was parked near the mile 53 marker on Interstate 71, running radar, when he received a call 1046, "injury accident," on his radio. The dispatcher advised him that there was an accident near mile marker 39, and that one of the vehicles was on fire.

He proceeded to the scene, covering the thirteen miles in seven or eight minutes. Before he could see anything, while he was still a mile or more away, he smelled a peculiar smell, something that he had never smelled before. Then, still a quarter to a half mile away, he saw the flames.

He drove down the median and stopped twenty-five yards from the bus, praying aloud that there was no one still on it. The heat was too intense for him to get close enough to look inside, and the only screams he heard were from the children lying on the ground around him. He radioed for medical units. They were already on the way.

The first arrived two minutes later. Seeing that there was nothing he could do for the school bus passengers, Tommy Webb of the Camp-bellsburg Volunteer Rescue Squad went to the mangled pickup truck that was sitting across the road from the rear right corner of the bus. The little truck's roof had been crushed almost level with the dash, but the person lying across the front seat, with the dashboard pushed back tight against his chest, was still breathing. Webb took the unconscious man's billfold from his pocket to find out his name, so that he could try to talk to him. He found a driver's license with the name Larry Mahoney on it. The license photo showed a bearded young man wearing a Harley-Davidson cap bearing the words "Ride Hard, Die Hard."

When Webb reached down to slip a backboard strap around the victim, his hand hit something cold: He looked and found three cans of Miller Lite, two full and one half-empty.

"I got to wake up," Mahoney muttered, as Webb, now assisted by other ambulance workers, gingerly extricated him from the wreckage. "I got to wake up."

❑

Katrina McNickle had sat down on a guardrail and closed her eyes, partly out of exhaustion, partly because she did not wish to see any more. And there was always the possibility that when she opened her eyes, the whole calamity would have gone away. She was sitting with her eyes closed, trying to think what was going on, when some lady came up, slapped her in the face, and asked her if she was okay. Katrina, who had escaped uninjured except for a banged-up knee, said that she guessed she was. The lady then asked her name, age, and phone number, and wrote it all down on a luggage tag and put it around Katrina's wrist. "Stay here and make sure everybody gets to see me so they get their tags," the lady said.

Here they were standing in the middle of an interstate at night, with their school bus an inferno and God only knew how many of their friends being consumed by the fire. The disorder was complete, and completely beyond repair, but at least grown-ups had come; they would know what to do.

David Walliser walked up to McNickle and said he wanted her to help him because his skin was falling off. He said that it hurt. McNickle could see that the skin on his arm had rolled up and was indeed falling off, just as he said. It looked to her as though somebody had poured acid on his arm. She thought it was nasty-looking. She told him to stay right there. She went and got the luggage tag lady, who told her to bring David over to her so he could lie down. The lady put a blanket down on the ground and David lay down on it and went into shock.

McNickle wandered over and joined a group of kids who were standing with their arms around one another, praying aloud. They thanked God for saving them, begged him to help, asked him to answer. A tall, skinny teenager named Juan Holt was exclaiming, "Praise Jesus! Thank you, Jesus!"

Janey Padgett stood against the guardrail nearby. She was coming to a realization about her unprecedented and seemingly inexplicable decision not to take her granddaughter Brittainy along on this particular trip even though she always took her everywhere. "Thank you, God," she silently prayed. "Now I know, God, why you didn't want me to bring her."

(Such thanksgiving raised certain problems. The trouble with thanking God for anything is that, logically at least, one is crediting him with the ability to control everything. For if God, as Padgett supposed, knew that the crash was coming, and was willing and able to micromanage events so as to keep one child safe, then it would seem he could have kept everybody safe, and chose not to. It was exactly this theological sore point that would cause some parents of the dead to so deeply resent the Tennisons' expressions of gratitude to God for saving their own son, Allen.)

"This is God's fault," survivor Pam Uhey was told at the scene by someone who was carrying this sort of thinking to its conclusion.

"No it's not," Uhey declared, just based on faith.

"Was that the Rapture?" one of the dazed survivors was asking. The Rapture is the physical ascent of both living and resurrected Christians at the Second Coming, to meet Christ and be with him forever—and to escape the Great Tribulation, his judgment on the world.

"Was it?" Sandra Glover wondered. "A lot of us were left behind, then." Later, she decided that maybe it *was* the Rapture, in some sort of way, for the ones who didn't make it off the bus.

CHAPTER 9

Chuck and Janet Kytta's kids, Mandy, eleven, and Charlie, ten, had wanted to go on the bus trip their dad had organized, but they blew their chance. "You guys have really been arguing a lot," Janet scolded, "and your dad doesn't need to worry with you that day. He's got a lot of other kids to look after."

Chuck agreed. "Church Day is every year," he said. "Next year they'll be older; they can go then." So Janet kept the children home.

The night before the trip, Chuck took Mandy and Charlie out for ice cream cones. Later, Janet walked into her son's bedroom and found that she had interrupted a father-son talk. Chuck was saying, "Now you pray about that, son, and it will work out okay." She turned around quietly and left.

Chuck went to bed early, because he had to get up by 6:00 to get down to church and meet the kids. Janet stayed up for a while watching TV, but just before Chuck went to sleep, she opened the bedroom door. Chuck was lying on his back, propped up on a couple of pillows on his side of the bed. On the table beside him were two or three Bibles, two or three other books, his cassette and headphones, and a stack of tapes. Chuck loved to sing; he'd sing at the drop of a hat. He had a whole collection of accompaniment tapes he'd sing along to, as well as music for the choir to learn. Janet could never even walk on his side of the bed, there was always so much stuff there.

"Chuck," she said, "I just thought of a really neat song for you to do with the choir." She hummed it to him. It was a medley, blending two or three songs from the hymnal. "It'll work out great," she said. "It would be really simple for the choir to do, but it would be so pretty. The key changes are fine and everything."

Chuck had a sheet covering his chest but his feet were sticking out, uncovered. He always had to have his feet cold, to sleep, and he just about always slept with his index finger crooked pensively over his lip. He was in that pose now, ready to drift off.

"Write that down," he urged her.

"I won't forget it," she said. (As it turned out, she would.) "Love you, see you tomorrow. I put some sausage biscuits in the refrigerator, so you can just pop 'em in the microwave in the morning and go."

The last thing she did before she went to bed was write on the bathroom mirror, in lipstick, "Set the alarm for 8 for me. Love ya." She'd learned that the best way to make sure Chuck wouldn't miss a message was to put it right in front of his face.

The next morning, Chuck wrote "Love ya, too" on the mirror, and drew a heart. He left without waking her.

It was a beautiful day. Janet, who played with Charlie and Mandy out in the yard, would never forget how beautiful. It was sunny, warm, not too hot, not too cold; it was perfect, and she was thinking, "Chuck is gonna be so sunburnt." He always burned real bad, up on his temples, because he had a receding hairline. She used to tease him that he was losing his hair and he'd say, "No, I'm just breaking ground for a new face."

Janet stayed up late that night, waiting for her husband to come home. She watched TV until 1:00 or 1:30 in the morning, and when he didn't come, she thought, "Well, some kid is late getting picked up; they're sitting, talking, at the church." She didn't worry; she just went to bed.

Everyone, always, goes to bed with the knowledge that the phone may ring in the middle of the night, the hope that it won't, and the belief that if it does, life will never be the same.

About 2:30 that morning, Janet Kytta's phone rang.

"Janet, did you know the bus has been involved in an accident?" the woman's voice said in a gingerly tone. It was Linda Tedescucci, one of Chuck's co-workers and a good friend.

"It has?" Janet replied, her fear on the wing like a pheasant from the brush. "Do you think it was bad? Should I, like, call the church, you think?"

"Yeah, I think you better call the church," Linda said evenly. "Call me back, though."

Janet called the church, and in the background she heard all this noise, all this talking, like there was a huge group of people. "This is Janet

Kytta," she said clearly. "I heard there was a bus accident. Do I need to come down there?"

"This is who?" a voice demanded gruffly.

"Janet Kytta."

"Just a minute." Janet held on for she couldn't tell how long. She might have been picturing the unbelievably warm New Year's Eve afternoon in 1972 when she was fourteen years old and first laid eyes on her husband. Her girlfriend Marisa's cousin was coming down from Ohio with his good friend, a seventeen-year-old guy named Chuck. Marisa lived on the other side of a corn field from Janet, so they agreed to meet in the middle like they always did. Janet put on her best jeans and a sweater and brushed her long dark hair that went all the way to her waist back then. As she walked across the crusty orange soil she could see him, in a red and white striped shirt, sitting in an oak tree, his long legs dangling. When she got there he jumped down and said, "It's really nice to meet you." He had a big Adam's apple that moved when he talked, and he spoke in a musical baritone. She knew at that moment that she loved him.

She wasn't allowed to date till she was sixteen, so for two years they wrote each other letters. Finally, when she was seventeen and he twenty-one, they got married, and went straight to Italy, where he was stationed as a code technician in the air force. They did everything together. They were all there was. They lived in a little village with no electricity or running water; there was no go-home-to-Mom if they got into an argument or a fight. Same thing at the base in Texas, where Mandy was born. And Charlie. Chuck said it was okay to name their son Charles John Kytta III, but they had to call him something other than Chuck, because he absolutely would not subject another person to going through life being called Chuck-Kytta Banana, as he had.

"Yeah, you better come down," the voice on the phone said.

"Oh, okay."

She called back Linda to tell her she was heading to the church, and Linda said, "Janet, you know John's dead."

John Pearman. "John's dead?" Janet repeated mechanically. (She would soon observe that that is precisely what people often do when they're told someone has died. They repeat the words, mechanically.) "What happened?"

"I don't know," Linda said, although she did know something, having seen reports of a bus crash and fire on CNN.

Janet called her mother to come over and watch the sleeping kids.

Then she drove to the church. Along the way she realized that she had the windshield wipers on, and that it wasn't raining. She was so scared, she was crying, and so confused, she'd thought her tears were falling from the sky.

Janet was thinking that John Pearman, who she was now supposed to believe was dead, had been driving the bus; so maybe it was a head-on collision. She could picture exactly where Chuck would have been standing, at the top of the stairwell. She felt in her heart something terrible had happened.

When she walked into the church she saw families huddled together, sobbing. One woman was lying on the floor, screaming. She could hear people in the sanctuary praying very loudly. Then state troopers started coming in. And lists were posted, who was in what hospital. Some members of the church who were in the military started arriving in combat gear, airlifted in from field exercises. More and more reporters arrived. Janet recognized one from Channel 3 in Louisville. She knew him slightly, as he lived in the area, so she approached him. "Were you at the scene of the bus wreck?" she asked.

"Yes."

"Did you see my husband?"

"You're Mrs. Kytta, aren't you?" he said.

She said yes. He just looked at her, then lowered his eyes and walked away. Janet wanted to demand an answer, but she felt sorry for him. "Somebody's going to have to tell me," she thought, "and nobody wants the job."

❑

Janet Kytta spent the rest of the night trying to find out what she suspected she already knew. One by one she called the hospitals in Louisville— Kosair, Audubon, Jewish, Suburban, Humana—begging them to tell her that her husband was there. She stood vigil at the phone on the vestibule wall, waiting for a tiny red light to blink off, signifying a free line. She importuned Vicki Fischel, who was taking all the incoming calls, to hand over the receiver whenever she had a hospital on the line. She drove a mile to use the pay phone at the open-all-night White Castle. She couldn't understand why Chuck wouldn't have been identified, because she knew he had his wallet with him. What she didn't know was that there had been a fire.

As Sunday morning dawned, Chuck Kytta's name remained, with

twenty-five others, on the list of those who had not been found at any hospital, and Janet was more sure than ever that he must be dead. That certainty made the uncertainty finally unbearable, as her hope vanished and with it her strength. Exhausted, she walked into the waiting area outside Pastor Tennison's office and said, "I've got to know something. You've got to tell me something, please." She was called into the pastor's study, and just then two of the boys from the bus, Conrad Garcia and Allen Tennison, the pastor's son, walked in from the parking lot. Only slightly injured, they'd been driven back from the Carrollton hospital by Conrad's father. Janet could not have been more amazed had they been ghosts. "How did they get here?" she wondered. "Where's everybody else? Where's the bus?"

As Janet recalled later, it was then that Pastor T said, motioning to the boys, "Now they're going to tell us what happened, but I want you to know Brother John and Brother Chuck were in the front of the bus, and they didn't come off."

She had thought she was prepared to hear this news, which she had been seeking all night long, but the floor came up and smacked her, and she lay there crying.

"Janet, you gotta stop crying." It was her brother, who had come to the church. But Janet wanted to cry, and she didn't stop. A woman police officer picked her up, set her in a chair and said, "Now you're going to pull yourself together, because you're going to start calling people."

"I don't think I can remember the numbers," Janet sobbed.

"Well, you've got to, because if you don't they're going to see it on TV."

By some miracle, Janet remembered the area code and number for Chuck's parents in Ohio and called there. It was about seven o'clock on Sunday morning. "Dad, sit down," she said, when Chuck's father answered.

"Why?"

"I want you to sit down," she repeated. "Dad, Chuck took a group of the teens to Kings Island, and on the way back they were hit head-on by a truck, and, Dad, Chuck was killed."

"Oh."

"He didn't make it, Dad."

"He didn't?"

"No, Dad, he didn't." That was pretty much the extent of their conversation. She said she'd call back later when she had more information.

Janet's brother took her back to her house. There, her mother asked her, "Are you going to wake the kids up?"

"Mom, they've got, what, maybe an hour, maybe two hours more of sleeping, thinking everything is right in the world," she replied. "And when I go in and tell them, nothing is ever going to be perfect for them again."

Soon she heard them giggling upstairs. They thought the family had overslept for church, and they thought it was really funny. She went up and sat on the bed and told them, and they looked at her as though she had stuck a knife through them. She had never hurt anybody so much in her whole life.

Janet saw Chuck's socks lying on the floor in his study where he had taken them off as he watched TV the night before. She went down to the kitchen, opened the refrigerator and saw the sausage biscuits. She could see that Chuck had eaten two for breakfast that morning. "He was here," she thought.

Later that day Janet would go back to the church, where Chuck's little red Chevy pickup truck stood faithfully in the parking lot. She'd sit in the truck, thinking, "He was just here. He drove this here. How can something like this happen to somebody I love, and I don't even know it? How come at eleven o'clock I didn't feel the same pain? He was just here. *How do people die this quick?*"

CHAPTER

10

"**P**oo-ta *wheet!* Poo-ta *wheet!*"

An unseen bird cheerfully proclaimed some incomprehensible bit of good news, always the same. As the sky grew pale, Janey Fair's hopes faded. Miracles might have lain hidden in the darkness, but the merciless sun exposed an utterly barren, spring-green day.

More and more mothers and fathers, called into the church office to be told their kids were at one hospital or another, quickly and quietly left. For the dwindling number who remained, it was like standing in a group waiting to get picked for the team and everybody else gets picked and you're just standing there, more and more rejected, more and more unworthy, more and more alone.

Janey clung to the notion that Shannon, who was carrying no identification, was hurt and couldn't tell anyone who she was. By dawn, there were twenty-six names on the list of the missing posted on the church bulletin board, and forty listed as known survivors. The unlucky families congregated in the lobby area, afraid to stray too far from the phones lest they miss the call that would save them.

Suddenly, they were summoned into the sanctuary. A husky-voiced woman police officer, barking out her words in an okay-listen-up manner, told them that their loved ones had not been found and that they would have to board vans and go up to Carrollton to assist in their identification. "On the way up there," she ordered, "if you would write down, if you can remember, what your son or daughter was last wearing, anything that's unusual, any jewelry; if you can remember, and you don't have dental records, where their cavities are. Anything at all." The army would helicopter up the dental records of military kids; others should get theirs from their dentists.

A radio reporter present, Mary Jeffries of WHAS, Louisville, got the impression that the vans were bound for a temporary morgue, but the trip's purpose was not entirely clear, least of all to the stunned parents. Perhaps because the announcement was delivered without any telltale words of sorrow, empathy, or solicitude, some, at least, did not grasp its import. They thought they were going to be brought around to area hospitals to look for their kids.

Janey remembered that Shannon had worn her plaid Tretorn tennis sneakers, blue and white plaid shorts, and a navy blue sleeveless sweater (which was made of polyester, and Janey knew that meant it would have burned like lighter fluid). Shannon hadn't taken her wallet; a seasoned traveler, she didn't want anything to weigh her down. She had her money in her pocket, and, no doubt, some money in her sock, so she couldn't lose it all. She probably had a comb. A lot of the girls were taking along their cans of hairspray, but not Shannon, though she knew her elaborate Farrah Fawcett–style hairdo would wilt. "The boys will just have to remember what I look like," she'd said, "because I'm not going to carry all that stuff."

Janey and her sister Gloria climbed onto a van with Mary Daniels's mother, Diane, and her friend Joe Wunderlich; Lee Williams, whose wife, Joy, and their two children, Kristen and Robin, were all missing; and a woman whose daughter had escaped serious injury. She came along to comfort the less fortunate.

After they sat idling with their passengers for the longest time, the four vans finally left at around 9:30 Sunday morning. Janey had never heard of Carrollton, and none of her fellow riders knew where it was, or how long it would take to drive up there.

Riding in a van, Rev. Tennison finally had a moment to reflect. He began to think, "What is going to come from this? How can I comfort all these families? Are people going to start suing me, John [Pearman, the driver], the church?" His mind was racing. "I'm the one that's responsible for this. I'm the one that allowed them to set up this engagement. I'm the one that allowed them to leave the parking lot with this bus to go on this trip. All these families are suffering because of the choice that I made to let these people go." He struggled to keep control of himself as he felt a spirit of fear and helplessness grip his heart. Later, he realized, "The Enemy was attacking me, in my spirit, saying, *They're blaming you.'*"

As families, friends, and townspeople gravitated toward the church, the pastor's wife, Martha, stayed behind to lead a worship service, which she began with the singing of "Amazing Grace."

"I do not have any answers for you this morning," she told the 200 people in the sanctuary. Believers would say this so often and with such conviction that it became an answer: The answer is that we have no answers. This was true enough, and true enough for them. "The best thing we can do is get a hold on God, because God is God and He hasn't changed," Sister Tennison said. "I do not have any answers for you, but we serve a God that does. If we could figure him out, He wouldn't be God."

Meanwhile, even as Janey Fair was riding off, she thought, to search for her daughter, back in Radcliff the Reverend Gene Waggoner of the Stithton Baptist Church was speaking of Shannon at his Sunday-morning service. Recalling that she had chosen to be baptized just the week before, he said, "If she didn't make it, I know where she is." As to the other missing children, he went on, "If they didn't make it, I hope they're saved."

❑

Among the teenage friends and classmates of those lost on the bus, the rumor was already spreading that the severed hands of a certain boy and girl who were a couple had been found, still clasping each other, at the roadside. This imagined relic, at once tender and gory, made poetry of carnage and was a testament to the enduring belief in the enduring power of love. In fact, nothing of the sort survived the flames.

❑

In half an hour the vans had passed Bennie's First Chance Liquors, as they crossed out of dry Hardin County into wet Jefferson County. They traversed the honky-tonk-strewn flatlands below Louisville ("GIRLS GIRLS GIRLS. LIQUOR BY THE DRINK"), and were climbing onto the Gene Snyder Freeway and heading northeast, away from the familiar environs of Fort Knox, into the Kentucky countryside. The very beauty of the rugged hills was an affront to Janey, its immutability belittling the cataclysm that had befallen her. Once, the majesty of the granite cliffs might have stirred her soul. Now she saw clearly that beauty is cruelty and the earth's heart is stone. Only for love did she draw her next breath.

"Well, in a year or two you'll get over this and you can adopt children," the mother of the uninjured child was saying. "There are so many out there who need homes." Janey and the others sat numb to the well-intentioned assault. She was wondering how poor Lee Williams could hold up, with his whole family missing.

Janey retreated inward, to where Shannon was safe and Janey could be with her. "What was it, two weeks ago? Exactly. Today is Sunday." It was on a Sunday that Shannon had asked permission to go on this trip to Kings Island, well, hadn't asked permission, really, more like said she was going and could she please have the money. As if they would ever *not* give her the money.

Shannon came hopping up the stairs to settle her accounts, as she did every Sunday. Her dad was sitting in his La-Z Boy watching TV, and Shannon came in and plunked down on his lap. She always planned out in writing what her expenses were going to be and what her schedule was going to be for an entire month. So it must have been two Sundays before, because it was the beginning of the month. Shannon had a sheet of paper with how many loads of wash she'd done; they always gave her a dollar a load. It wasn't report card time or she'd've been hitting them up for a couple of bucks for each A—a real racket since all she ever got was A's.

Shannon wasn't on an allowance, Janey was ashamed to say. There was no use giving her or her brother an allowance, because they needed so much money, they'd come in with two hands open. And they got what they needed, and what they wanted, too, Janey supposed. Anyway, Shannon said I need this money for this and this money for that and this money to pay for my music lessons. And she had a permission slip from the church and asked for $17 to go on the trip, and $13 for spending money at Kings Island. "Jennifer Arnett invited me, she's a real nice girl, she's invited a lot of members of the band, the whole band's going," Shannon said. "I guess I should have asked you if I could go on the trip, but I didn't think you'd mind me going."

Janey hadn't minded. In fact she was glad that Shannon was going to get to go, because this would be the first weekend in memory that she hadn't had some school requirement, even if it was a fun trip like going to Frankfort or Bowling Green with the band. This was going to be purely fun, it wasn't, "When I get there I'm going to have to perform." So as far as allowing her to go, Janey didn't give it a second thought. She'd be riding in a school bus, for heaven's sake, so Janey knew Shannon would be fine.

But now it was about twelve hours since Shannon had been due home, and the van was pulling off the interstate at an exit called Carrollton. Incongruously, skyscraping signs towered over the tobacco fields at the sleepy interchange: Holiday Inn, Exxon, Kentucky Fried Chicken. The bold standards blazed atop soaring stanchions of steel like battle flags.

To Janey's surprise, the van pulled up to the front door of the Holiday Inn. Packs of reporters hustled toward them, but police held the TV cameras at bay. Being an army person, Janey thought the motel had been designated some sort of command center, and that from there they would be taken to area hospitals. Instead, they were ushered into a drop-ceil-inged, industrial-carpeted function room and told to sit down. On the wall was a framed reproduction of two Victorian-era little girls eating strawberries as their collie looked on. The air was thick with the smell of fried chicken, donated by the Colonel Sanders outlet next door. Janey noticed that the hotel employees would look at her and then turn away.

Janet Kytta sat down beside a Kentucky State Police trooper. "You saw the bus, right?" she asked.

"Yes, I was there all night," he said softly.

"Can't I see it?" she implored him. "Because I know that I'll know my husband."

"Mam," he said, "there's nothing you want to see."

A small group of men huddled at the front of the room. One of them, long-haired and disheveled, was Dr. George Nichols, the state medical examiner, though Janey had no idea who he was. Nichols stood and faced the crowd of family members. Some stared at the floor or the ceiling, avoiding whatever might be in his eyes. Some looked at him with great anger. Some were quietly crying. Some were sobbing uncontrollably.

Nichols, who was crying himself, found it hard to speak. "I want you all to remember your children as they are in the pictures in your wallets and in your hearts," he said. He said they could not view the bodies, because there was no reason to view them, because they had all been burned beyond recognition. All of them. The count of bodies on the bus had not yet been completed, but there was no reason to believe there were any survivors other than those already named.

And that's how Janey Fair found out that her sweet, sweet Shannon would not be coming home.

One man stood up and shouted, "No! We thought we were going around to the hospitals." Another man put his head on his wife's lap and began to cry. Another sank to his knees, weeping.

"I'm not here, this is a dream, this is not reality," Janey thought. Almost immediately, the Red Cross workers began interviewing the families about their now-dead children's clothes, jewelry, personal effects. A woman asked Janey what Shannon had on. Janey said Shannon had worn her Tretorn sneakers, and the woman smiled and said, "All the girls had on Tretorns, didn't they?"

Janey could feel her face move; she could feel the muscles in her cheeks pulling her lips, and she surmised that she must have been smiling back at the woman. "Tretorn is the fad tennis shoe," Janey thought. Or did she say it? "All the girls have them."

After about an hour, Janey and the others climbed back on the van and rode in silence down Interstate 71. A few miles south of Carrollton, she heard the tires roll over a gouge in the road: thud-ud-up, thud-ud-up.

CHAPTER

11

Janey had avoided calling her husband at his mother's house down in Tennessee until about 6:00 A.M. She didn't have any facts to tell him, and she knew he'd want to start the 330-mile drive back from Johnson City right away. She wanted him to have some sleep. She didn't want any more traffic accidents.

She figured that if she waited, she'd soon be able to tell him either that Shannon was dead—that there might be problems with identification had not occurred to her—or that she was being taken care of in a hospital. If Shannon were dead, Janey would take her home to Tennessee, and Larry wouldn't need to come back anyway. If she were hurt, then he could come. She felt that definite news, you can handle better. She didn't want him on the highway in a tumult, not knowing anything. And she couldn't bear him hearing a bunch of names read over a car radio.

But as the darkness bled away, she could wait no longer, and asked her sister Gloria to get to a phone and contact Larry. He and his mother, always early risers, had just gotten up when the phone rang in the dining room. Larry gazed out the window across the lawn at the grove of walnut trees he'd planted as a kid, while Gloria told him there'd been an accident and some injuries and they didn't know how bad it was. Larry said he would leave right then, but Gloria persuaded him to stay there, where he could be reached with any news.

Larry walked across the street to the home of his cousin Fran, who had cable television. He watched CNN for the next forty minutes or so, catching short segments on the crash among reports on Iraqi warplanes bombing Iran's oil pipelines and an inmate uprising at an Oklahoma state prison. According to CNN, it was not known exactly how many had died on the bus. Larry went back to his mother's house and packed. Gloria called back around 7:30, and said it was bad and there had been several killed and Shannon was not accounted for. Larry said okay, he and his mother were heading up now, and he'd stop every hour or so and call the house in Radcliff.

It was a clear, dry, sunny day, and Larry drove the twisting two-lane roads a little over the speed limit. He fiddled with the radio constantly, as the signals echoed and faded in the hills. In the course of the six-hour drive, the news got progressively more gruesome. The reports started using the word "tragedy." They started announcing numbers of dead and seriously injured. It seemed that each news report got more graphic: The flames and the screams were described.

As the news got more grim, Larry thought about the confusion, the panic, the congestion, the magnitude of the fire. He was trying to envision what the accident looked like. He thought about Korea.

Back in 1970, Larry had requested assignment to Vietnam, because he knew service there would be an important punch on his career ticket. But he was an armor officer, and there wasn't a lot of armor over there. He was sent to Korea, where he served in a tank battalion in the 2nd Infantry Division at the Demilitarized Zone.

On the afternoon of February 21, 1970, Larry, then a twenty-three-year-old first lieutenant, a driver, and Sergeant Donald R. Page were heading north on a narrow, winding paved road from Camp Beard toward the village of Pobwon-ni. Fair, a motor officer whose primary responsibility was to keep the tanks in good repair, had been down to battalion headquarters for a meeting, and Page had been scrounging up some parts.

Suddenly, a small bus heading toward them, jammed with children on their way home from school, swerved off the road, hit a tree, and

rolled upside down, settling on its roof. Gasoline streaming from its tank
ignited. Fair and Page rushed over and sprayed the jeep's fire extinguisher, to no avail. As the flames spread, they pulled as many of the
hysterical children as they could out through the windows, then climbed
into the burning bus to get the rest. Two girls had their legs caught
between the bus's crushed roof and the top of the seats, and the unconscious driver was pinned between the roof and steering wheel. Larry
climbed out and enlisted eight or nine passersby to push the bus onto its
side so Page could free these last three. After they got everybody out, they
sat down in a ditch and watched as an explosion hurled the bus a hundred
feet away.

Fair and Page had saved thirty lives, and were awarded the Soldier's
Medal, the army's highest honor for courage in peacetime. When Larry
unpacked the medal on coming home from his year-long duty in Korea,
he and Janey talked about how lucky they were to live in the United
States, where children didn't have to ride such rattletrap buses.

❑

As he drove through Kentucky, Larry thought of the wreck in Korea as a
model from which to extrapolate what his daughter had gone through, a
paradigm by which to take the measure of what her chances were. Reason
left him little hope.

He pulled into the driveway of their Radcliff home just minutes after
Janey had returned from the medical examiner's meeting at the Holiday
Inn. As he got out of his car, Janey came out the front door. Just a day
before they had waved good-bye to Shannon where they stood. They
might still have found her footprints in the grass.

"Shannon's dead and all her friends are dead," Janey said. There was
nothing else to say.

CHAPTER

12

Forty of the passengers had been accounted for: Sixteen were in hospitals with burns and inhalation injuries, including nine in critical condition. The rest had been treated and released. Larry Mahoney, the driver of the pickup truck, was hospitalized with various trauma injuries, none of them life-threatening. The other twenty-seven bus passengers were presumed dead, though they would officially remain "missing" until it could be determined which body was which.

By the time he faced the terrified families at the Holiday Inn, State Medical Examiner George Nichols had already put in a long day. He'd packed up his shiny steel paraphernalia and his cameras and tape recorders and driven to the Carrollton armory by 8:00 A.M. He'd found the charred skeleton of the school bus sitting atop a flatbed trailer in the National Guard's garagelike drill room. The concrete floor had been covered with sheets of plastic. Nichols, state trooper Henry "Sonny" Cease, Jr., forensic odontologist Mark Bernstein, and Nichols's autopsy assistant Barbara Ritter climbed in and saw what they could see without touching anything. Then they got out and looked through the bus's windows from a ladder. Nichols was formulating what he called "a game plan" to preserve the evidence. Cease, the boyish-looking twenty-six-year-old who'd been placed in charge of the State Police investigation, charted the bodies' locations.

Before they could count all the dead, a couple of representatives from Rev. Tennison's church came to the armory to ask whether the families should be brought there. Nichols advised them that visual identification was impossible, and that the families should stay away. After looking through the bus's rear door, the men agreed. Instead Nichols addressed the gathering at the Holiday Inn.

When Nichols returned to the armory, Cease and Bernstein were each counting the bodies; each kept arriving at a total of twenty-six. For about an hour, they went through the bus, trying to find number twenty-seven.

Carroll County Deputy Coroner Steve Meadows, a burly emergency medical technician, assisted in the search for that last body. The hardest thing he had ever done was climb through the bus's back door to get started. The carnage was the worst he'd ever seen, and he'd seen a lot. The gruesome spectacle was made even more horrible by the knowledge that what he was looking at had been a bunch of kids.

Body number 26 was a female bent over on a seat, seventh row on the right side. Meadows was pulling up on her shoulder and Nichols was pushing up on her chest when Meadows cried out, "Goddamn! Look." On the floor he could see the head of a girl sticking out from under the seat in front of her. "There's number 27." Meadows's heart sank. Now there was no hope left.

Nichols, who had not harbored any illusions that anyone not accounted for had survived, felt relieved: A problem had been solved, an uncertainty eliminated. Now he could finally call the ministers remaining at the Holiday Inn to pass the message to the families: There were twenty-seven bodies on the bus. No longer need they cherish any false hope, though some might prefer that to no hope at all.

Nichols's disaster team turned its attention to the task of removing the bodies without damaging them and destroying their evidentiary value. The problem was that the aisle was only twelve inches wide, and the bodies were piled up, blocking it. They thought about cutting away the sides of the bus, but its structural condition, too, had to be preserved as evidence for the criminal and civil trials Nichols knew would be coming. So they decided to cut out the seats, after the bodies in each row were removed, in order to gain access to the next row without damaging the bodies stacked in the aisle.

It was very difficult to move around without disturbing the bodies, much less to extract one body without doing too much damage to another adjacent or below. (Some damage was unavoidable, for the heat had fused some bodies together in a sort of lava flow of blackened flesh.) Bags were placed over the heads to catch any teeth that might fall out, as the teeth would be critical for identification.

"We'd work for fifteen minutes and then sit on the armory floor and cry and have a cup of coffee, and then get on the bus and work some more," Meadows recalled later.

The bodies were assigned numbers in the order in which they were removed, zippered into black vinyl bags and placed on stretchers on the floor along the right side of the bus until the arrival of the refrigerator trucks that had been volunteered by a supermarket chain.

Nichols and two doctors on his staff performed the autopsies. He would climb aboard to remove two or three or four bodies, then do autopsies to get out of the bus for a while. It was five o'clock before all the bodies were off the bus.

The dental identification process was going on all the while. One dentist examined the jaws of the dead and noted their identifying characteristics, including fillings and irregularities in, and spaces between, the teeth. This information was recorded on postmortem odontograms, or dental charts.

Another dentist recorded all available dental information (antemortem data) about the victims on another set of odontograms. Each set of charts was sorted into five groups: a) those with many fillings (total, 4); b) those with adult teeth and few fillings (total, 7); c) those with adult teeth and no fillings (total, 8); d) those with orthodontic appliances (total, 4); and e) those with some baby teeth (total, 4). Then the antemortem dental charts were matched with the postmortem charts.

By 8:30 on Sunday evening, all twenty-seven autopsies had been completed. They could be performed so quickly because, other than the burns, there was no trauma to describe: no broken bones, no internal injuries. Tentative identifications were made, but Joy Williams alone had been positively identified—by exclusion, as the only adult female.

On Monday, two dentists worked ten more hours confirming the matches between the jaws and dental records, using X-rays, photography and plaster-casting where necessary. No errors in the initial matchups were found. The identification process was completed by 6:30 P.M.

In the end, twenty-three bodies were identified through dental records, two through other identifying physical characteristics, and two through the process of elimination and personal effects such as jewelry.

White posterboards had been taped to the right side of bus: Bodies 1 through 27 were listed, and beside them their location in the refrigerator trailers, and their status in the identifying process. As Steve Meadows recorded the information with a black marker on the white board, he was struck by how similar the act was to keeping score at a basketball game.

*#17 Shannon Fair, 14, White Female. Identified by compati-
bility with medical history [appendectomy] and personal effects
[no jewelry]. No identified traumatic injury other than smoke
inhalation and burn. CO saturation 69 percent.*

Shannon Fair's blood had a higher carbon monoxide (CO) level than
that of any other victim, which meant that of all those who perished on
the bus, she had stayed alive the longest.

❑

It was apparent to Nichols that at least some of those who died must have
suffered burns while they were alive, and that Chuck Kytta had died by
burning, but the medical examiner told a press conference on Monday
afternoon that all twenty-seven had died of smoke inhalation. "It's easier
for parents not to think their child was alive and burning," he explained
later. (Not that smoke inhalation isn't horrible in itself: "It's panic, gagging, choking," says Nichols. "It's not, 'I'm going to sleep now.' ")

But whether or not smoke inhalation was *the* cause of death, as he
said then—or the primary cause with burns a contributory cause, as he
said later—Nichols never varied from one conclusion he announced on
the very first day: There were no significant impact injuries, and no one
would have died had there been no fire.

At that same press conference, State Fire Marshal Bill Martin revealed
that a two-to-three-inch gash had been found in the bus's gas tank. Then
Carroll County Commonwealth's Attorney John Ackman, Jr., announced
that he was charging the driver of the pickup truck, factory worker Larry
W. Mahoney, thirty-four, with twenty-seven counts of murder, and that he
would seek the death penalty. Mahoney, whose condition was upgraded
from critical to serious on Sunday, had been placed under arrest in his
Humana Hospital room on Monday afternoon. One sample of Mahoney's
blood taken an hour and a half after the crash had an alcohol concentration of .24 percent, nearly two and one half times the level at which one
is legally drunk in most states, including Kentucky.*

Monday night the National Transportation Safety Board called a press
briefing of its own. NTSB member Joseph Nall pointed out that the bus
was not equipped with a metal cage to protect its gas tank; school buses

---

* By Kentucky law, one is guilty of drunk driving at a blood alcohol concentration (BAC) of 0.10
percent; that is, a concentration of 100 mg of alcohol per 100 ml of blood.

of its type had added the cage to comply with a federal safety standard that went into effect on April 1, 1977. The date of this bus's manufacture was yet to be determined.

Even as the grim work of identifying the bodies was concluding at the Carrollton armory, the Fairs received an odd visit at their home. On Monday evening, Larry and Janey were sitting in their living room with half a dozen friends and relatives when the doorbell rang. Janey opened the door to find Kay Bennett, the wife of prominent local attorney Terry Bennett, and Mike and Sandy Skeeters, the brother and sister-in-law of Bennett's law partner, Don Skeeters. Janey knew Kay and Sandy from the Radcliff Middle School Parent-Teacher Organization. The women hugged Janey, and they all wept.

The visitors brought dishes of food, which they set down with the accumulated offerings of prior callers. Larry and Janey weren't hungry, for grief is such a powerful sensation that it overwhelms all wants except the desire to do what is right. The traditional gift of food was perhaps meant to offer not merely sustenance but a reminder of the duty that one owes to life, which is the duty to live.

In the midst of expressing his sympathy—a sympathy the Fairs count as sincere to this day—Mike Skeeters, without a transitional phrase, launched into some advice about the ongoing business at the makeshift morgue in Carrollton. "You should get a blood gas test done on Shannon," he said in hushed tones, as he huddled in confidential conversation with Janey. He said that there had already been an investigation, and that there were problems with the bus. Toxic fumes were probably given off when the bus seats burned, and the poison gases would show up in this special test that might not ordinarily be done in an autopsy. He said the absence of such testing had caused critical problems after the Beverly Hills Supper Club fire, so the Fairs should request it.

Everyone knew about the supper club fire, a landmark horror in that part of the country. One hundred sixty-four people had died. The massive dining and entertainment complex, located just across the Ohio River from Cincinnati in Southgate, Kentucky, was jammed with 3,500 Memorial Day weekend patrons—including guests at four weddings and a bar mitzvah—when fire broke out in one of its twenty-one dining rooms on Saturday night, May 28, 1977. Most of the dead were among the 1,300 people crammed into the 900-capacity Cabaret Room to hear singer John Davidson. Blinded and gagging in the smoke, they fell down and piled up in the exits, where they were choked and poisoned to death and consumed by the flames. The fire started in defective wiring above a ceiling, and was fed by combustible ceiling tiles. The club had no sprinkler system—none was required by state regulations at the time—even though it had already burned once, seven years earlier, and been rebuilt.

The lack of clear evidence proving exactly which toxic by-products of combustion had caused the fatalities in the supper club fire had enabled the various manufacturers of furnishings and building materials to blame one another for the deaths, while lawsuits dragged on for a decade. So Skeeters's advice about blood gas testing was perfectly sensible. But amassing evidence for litigation was the furthest thing from the Fairs' minds. They still had no proof that Shannon was dead. She had simply left and not come home, and no matter what people said, they weren't quite able to stop believing that their little girl might be wandering in a daze along the roadside somewhere. When they had a chance to talk with each other later that evening, Janey and Larry quickly agreed to let the medical examiner decide what tests needed to be done.

(As it turned out, the medical examiner ordered the victims' blood screened for carbon monoxide, and for cyanide—a by-product of the combustion of polyurethane seat cushions and plastics—but he did not request screening for chlorine gas, produced when vinyl seat covers burn. Chlorine was used in World War I gas attacks. The 2,000 degree temperatures on the bus had turned the victims' blood into a hard, red, bricklike substance that he believed could not be accurately tested for chlorine. Thus it would never be determined with precision how large a role toxic gas from burning vinyl seat covers played as a contributory cause of the deaths.)

Even in their shock and despair, the Fairs clearly understood one thing: The lawyers were up and running.

❑

Cincinnati attorney Stan Chesley's leading role in the supper club litigation, which led to $49 million in settlements, had vaulted him from obscurity to the upper echelon of mass tort lawyers.* By 1988 he had about twenty lawyers—none of whom he'd made partners—working for him in his firm, and he had a demonstrated desire and capacity to be first out of the gate whenever and wherever disaster struck. It would not have been surprising if he contacted or was contacted by local Radcliff attorneys about the importance of the blood tests and the necessity of signing up a client right away, so as to have standing to get access to the evidence while it remained relatively intact. (Chesley later recalled speaking to Skeeters & Bennett "a week or two" after the crash.) In any case, Skeeters & Bennett followed the script, enlisting their first client within twenty-four hours of the accident.

Though it's the plaintiffs' attorneys who are derided as ambulance chasers, in reality they invariably eat the corporate defense lawyers' dust. In the first critical days, most of the victims had no lawyers; Ford had a well-drilled team in place, like a fighter squadron ready to scramble. When Ford engineer Robert Pelkey reported to work in Dearborn on Monday, May 16, he was told not to waste time packing a bag before catching a Northwest Airlines flight to Cincinnati.

As one of the five Heavy Truck Design Analysis engineers whose job was to help Ford's lawyers defend the company in liability suits, Pelkey didn't lack for work; he usually had about forty cases open. Nor was it unusual for him to be dispatched for an on-site investigation. But the speed and scale of this operation was unique. Monday night, Pelkey met at the Carrollton Holiday Inn with his boss, Don Edelen; Tom Boyle

---

* Chesley was a leader in the negotiations that in 1992 produced a $155 million settlement with Pfizer, Inc., on behalf of 53,000 people implanted with possibly faulty heart valves, and in 1994 a $3.7 billion settlement, with Dow-Corning and other companies, of thousands of claims over silicone breast implants.

from public relations; Bill Koeppel from Ford's Automotive Safety Office; Ford's retained accident reconstructionist, John Habberstad; attorney Procter Robison from the Office of General Counsel; and Louisville products liability defense lawyer Bill Grubbs and an associate. They were briefed by investigators from the National Transportation Safety Board, which always invites the manufacturers of an accident vehicle to assist in its inquiry, since they can provide information about the vehicle's construction and materials.* As a responsible corporation concerned with the public safety, and as a likely defendant in multimillion-dollar lawsuits, Ford was understandably eager to lend a hand in determining the cause of the disaster.

Tuesday morning at 9:00 the Ford group joined the NTSB representatives to inspect the bus and pickup truck at the armory. Pelkey said a silent prayer when he realized the bodies were still lying in the refrigerator trailers a few feet from where he stood.

The lawyers and experts working for plaintiffs suing Ford would not get to see the bus, which was soon locked up as evidence in Mahoney's criminal case, until ten months later.

❑

That same Monday night, as he recalls, Pat Butcher paid a visit to Larry Mahoney in his Louisville hospital room. He and Mahoney had grown up just down the road from each other—Larry sometimes worked on Pat's dad's farm. Butcher, who had been saved at the age of seven, had nonetheless gotten "on the fast track," as he put it, after high school, taking a drink now and again. He knew that it could as easily have been he who was in Mahoney's place: banged up, under arrest, and facing the death penalty. But at twenty-eight Butcher had repented and been filled with the Holy Spirit. He went to Bible school, put aside his farming and his feed business, and devoted himself to the harvesting of souls. In no time, the Bible study group Butcher founded had swelled to fifty-eight participants, and he was about to open his own Family Worship Center in a Carrollton strip mall storefront.†

---

* Toyota, maker of Mahoney's pickup truck, also sent a representative. Sheller-Globe—former parent company of the bus body manufacturer, Superior Coach—which had gotten out of the school bus business in 1981, did not.
† Five years later, in 1993, Butcher's Family Worship Center moved into a new, 14,250-square-foot building with seating for 500.

"Larry, your back's against the wall," the flannel-shirt- and jeans-clad pastor said gently, after the police guards let him and Mahoney's sister, Judy, into the hospital room. "There's nowhere else to go. Without God, you're not going to make it through this. Don't you think it's time you gave your heart to the Lord?"

Mahoney, unable to speak with an oxygen mask on his face, nodded.

"I'm a sinner, I need a savior," Butcher said for his friend. "Lord Jesus, will you come into my heart?"

The minister then read from the Book of Romans: "If thou shalt confess with thy mouth the Lord Jesus, and shalt believe in thine heart that God hath raised him from the dead, thou shalt be saved."

As the policemen's stern gaze chilled his back, Butcher again spoke for Mahoney: "I believe Jesus Christ is the Son of God. I believe that he was raised from the dead for my justification. And I confess him now as my Lord. Therefore I am saved! I have received salvation and I am born again. Thank you, Lord!"

A tear ran down Mahoney's cheek, and Butcher hugged him. The pastor felt very, very strange, to find himself in this night with the cops at the door and the streets outside full of headlines about the killer, Mahoney. "I'm not talking to a mass murderer," he thought. "I'm talking to Larry Mahoney." Larry had a temper when he'd drink but was hardworking, soft-hearted, and so shy he couldn't stand up in school and say one word. But as strange as the circumstances were, just that familiar was the miracle before the minister's eyes. He saw Mahoney in that instant enter into a relationship with the Lord and change completely.

"I know God will work through this for good if you stay fast with him," said Butcher as he left.

CHAPTER

14

The families of those still officially listed as missing were summoned to a meeting at 10:00 A.M. on Tuesday at the Radcliff First Assembly of God to be formally notified that their loved ones were dead. The Red Cross set up a cookies, Kool-Aid, and coffee area. Psychologists from Fort Knox and the local psychiatric facility were there, and ambulances were standing by.

The task of speaking the word "dead" was delegated by the state medical examiner to various men of the cloth. Rev. Gene Waggoner of Shannon's church spoke to the Fairs.

It was still going through Larry Fair's head that Shannon was wandering around somewhere off of I-71, but that was just a picture haunting his mind, not an idea to which he gave any credence. "It was notification of something you really knew," he says. "For Reverend Waggoner to say it out loud was akin to giving us permission to say, 'Yes, I know she's gone.' Somebody has to make it official. The important part was it meant the bodies could be released and you could get on with funeral arrangements."

In Carrollton, meanwhile, volunteers from the Kentucky Association of Funeral Directors teamed up with coroner Jim Dunn to embalm all the bodies. At 2:30 Tuesday afternoon, a hearse pulled into the armory; it emerged a few minutes later, and finally one child completed the trip home to Radcliff. Then another hearse came, and another, and another, and another . . . Twenty-seven times over the next three and a half hours a hearse would pull away, at discreet intervals, so as to avoid the passage through Radcliff of a twenty-seven-hearse caravan, a sight deemed too horrible for the community to bear.

Seventeen of the hearses made their way to a two-story, white-shuttered brick house with a blue neon sign reading, "Nelson-Edelen-Bennett Funeral Home." Owen Bennett, Jr. (no relation to the Radcliff attorney), and his wife, Margaret, the proprietors, made a point of not looking at the remains; they left them zipped in their black vinyl pouches. That way, if a family asked what condition the body was in, they would be able to answer truthfully that they did not know.

It was that sort of thoughtfulness that made the Bennetts so good at what they did. What's more, Owen—a short, gray-haired man with a pearly smile—manifestly didn't have a dishonest bone in his body; while Margaret was so warm and domestic she seemed always to have just stepped from the kitchen in mid-pie.

❑

Janey Fair brought to the funeral home the magenta crepe dress that Shannon had worn at her cousin's wedding. It was Shannon's grown-up dress; she looked at least eighteen in it.

"We can't put this on her, you know," Owen Bennett said gently.

"I know. That's why I didn't send over underwear," Janey said. But she left the dress anyway, thinking it would be draped over Shannon's body somehow. Had she known then that what was left of Shannon remained zipped in a body bag, and that the dress would merely be placed in the coffin, Janey would have kept the dress, because it meant a lot to her.

❑

Another visitor at the funeral home was Rosemary Martinez, who lost her only child, Richard Gohn, in the bus wreck. Martinez had long since divorced Richard's father, and did not take her second husband along when she went to select a coffin.

The Bennetts guided her down a steep, carpeted stairway to two windowless, below-ground display rooms. In the first, smaller room, she encountered a picture on the wall of the Statue of Liberty standing tall against the setting sun. From it she might have half-consciously absorbed the suggestion that there are some things larger than we are that last longer than we do and whose light shines on after darkness descends. Or perhaps she was reminded that she was in the United States and that some things still stood. But her attention was quickly, almost violently seized by the caskets.

Caskets lined the walls of the small room, and through the doorway she could see more caskets waiting in the larger room. Martinez had never before beheld caskets on display, and she was stunned by the familiarity of the bright lights and gleaming metal. "This is like an auto showroom," she thought. Neon fixtures hummed faintly overhead; brick-orange industrial carpeting silenced her footsteps. The coffins, radiant under spotlights, unblemished by dust or soil, came in shining bronze, blue- or green- or maroon-tinted steel, copper like a brand-new penny, also rich oak and highly polished cherry. There were twenty-one to choose from, priced from $350 to $6,000.

The least expensive was the first she encountered, a gray, 20-gauge steel, nonprotective model. The top of the line was made of 48-ounce (per square foot) solid bronze, and came with a seventy-five-year warranty against intrusion of "outside elements" (that is, water). The next step down was copper, then stainless steel, then 16-gauge steel, then 18- and finally the 20-gauge steel. (The higher the number, the thinner the steel.) Some of the caskets had pictures, of a bridge or of a stand of birch trees, for example, decorating the corners. Some had a drawing of praying hands on the upholstery lining the upper lid that would close over her son, Richard. The color of the upholstery was most often white, but sometimes champagne (tan) or light blue. (The different upholsteries were not interchangeable between coffins.) On most models, the pall-bearers' handles folded down after use. There were half-couch and full-couch configurations; on the latter, the whole lid, head to foot (instead of the upper half), was lined with fabric designed for open-casket display.

Rosemary Martinez tried to listen to the relative advantages of this one and that one and grapple with her options—should she choose gold- or silver-colored handles?—but she couldn't get past her amazement: *I have to put my child in one of these boxes.*

Finally, she looked at one and thought, "Well, it's Rick. It's Rick. His school colors are silver and blue."

Richard Gohn was a senior at North Hardin High School. He had gone to Kings Island on his senior class trip on Friday, May 13, gotten home at 3:00 A.M., and then gotten up at 6:00 A.M. to go back to the theme park with the Radcliff First Assembly of God Youth Group. "When are you going to get some sleep?" Rosemary had asked him at breakfast that last Saturday morning. "I'll sleep on the way up and I'll sleep on the way back," he had said. He wanted to go. What can you say to a nineteen-year-old? And it was his money. They sat and had breakfast, and he told her about the fun he'd had the day before. Then—he was at an age where he didn't kiss his mother good-bye—he just bounded out the door.

He was to have graduated on May 27. Now he would be buried instead, on May 21. A brand-new gray Plymouth Horizon, wrapped in a giant red ribbon, was still sitting in Rosemary's driveway, a graduation present waiting to surprise Richard when he returned from Kings Island.

That her son would ever graduate from high school had once, long ago, seemed too much for Rosemary to hope for; more recently, it had become a fact on which she could rely. Born with a congenital heart defect, her little boy was at first too frail to play with other children, so he palled around through toddlerhood with Suzie, a little spaniel-terrier mutt she got him.

At the age of five, Richard underwent open heart surgery. (Clutching a popsicle in his hospital bed, he smiles bravely still, in his mother's photo album. A few pages later he is six years old, and sits astride his Big Wheel trike. Rosemary learned from that tricycle that Rick was going to be mechanically inclined. It took two adults all night to put the thing together; he sat on it once, and took it apart in about ten minutes, and she never got it back together again.)

It was later that year, when he was six and a half, that Rick had a catheterization of his heart; a blood clot developed in his leg and went to the brain. He woke up not knowing how to count. You could hear him after that, as he played quietly in the yard, repeating to himself, "Two times three is six . . . ," because he knew he would forget by the next day if he didn't go over it and over it and over it. His learning disabilities proved no match for him, though, and by high school he got a 97 in advanced algebra, the best in the class. He passed his medical checkups with flying colors, too—he had just hit six feet tall, and loved to ski and hike and bicycle—and he was going to go to college.

Rosemary put Rick's graduation cap on top of his casket at the funeral. "I was bound and determined he was going to have that cap," she said.

ROSEMARY MARTINEZ

Rosemary wears her son, Richard's, high school ring on a chain around her neck. The titanium ring, with its blue stone, survived the flames, and was recovered from his hand.

"Rick fought for his life all his life. I just think the world is not going to be as good as it should have been, without him. It's such a tragedy that he had to fight so hard for his life from the time he was a small child, just to even live, and overcome the learning disabilities, the physical disabilities, and then to die in such a senseless tragedy. That is something I will never get over.

"Metal had twisted around him and he'd melded to the seat. That's hard. I know it's just a body that's burned, but it's still my child. It's horrendous. It's a horrendous end for your child. That's a hard thing to accept, that they were trapped and burning and trying to get out. I have nightmares still of my child dying in that bus. And even though I wasn't there, I guess as a mother, you feel your child. At times I will wake up and feel him, that frustration that 'I'm not gonna make it, I'm not gonna get out.' I can almost feel him dying. I guess maybe I do feel him dying.

"I lost my identity in this. I lost my identity as a mother. My husband dropped me off at a supermarket and came back an hour later and I was just standing there. I was so used to Lucky Charms and peanut butter and macaroni-and-cheese. You wouldn't believe the number of times you think of your child in a day, to get him up for school, make sure his clothes are clean; that sense of identity as a mother is totally gone. Yet I want to hang on to it.

"People ask you, 'Do you have children?' It's hard to truthfully say, 'Yes, I have a child, but he's dead.' If it's a complete stranger, I say, 'Yes, he's nineteen,' and leave it at that. Sometimes I pretend he's still alive. I say, 'He's nineteen. He's a student. He's going to go to college.'

"The other two children who were sitting with Rick made it out, and Rick was at the aisle. That's why it makes no sense he didn't get out. A woman said, 'Well, when you get to heaven you can ask him what happened.' It's a common idea, 'You'll know all this when you get to heaven.' And I thought, 'I won't care.' I can just see myself, shaking my finger at Rick, scolding him: 'Why didn't you get out of that bus!' " She laughs at the image. "It won't be important. I won't know and I won't care. I'll just be glad to see him."

CHAPTER

15

*I woke up in the morning to find that you
had risen with the sun.*

—from a poem by Mary Daniels's
good friend Kari Knight

On Thursday, May 19, which had been declared an official day of mourning by Kentucky Governor Wallace Wilkinson, the funerals began. Josh Conyers and Julie Earnest were laid to rest in Radcliff; Chad Witt in Liberty, Kentucky; and Tina Mustain back home in Texas.

There was a triple funeral for Mary Daniels, Denise Voglund, and Amy Wheelock. More than 500 mourners packed St. Christopher's Roman Catholic Church and stood listening in the parking lot, on a hillside overlooking the Radcliff Middle School, where the three girls and thirteen others of the dead had been students just days before.

The Reverend Leo Craycroft sprinkled holy water on the three identical white and rose caskets below the altar. A pall was placed on the coffins in remembrance of the baptismal garments.

Psalm 23 was read: "Yahweh is my Shepherd, I shall not want.... Though I walk through the valley of the shadow of death I shall fear no evil." And then 1 Thessalonians 4: 16–17, in which Paul writes: "For the Lord himself will descend from heaven with a cry of command, with the archangel's call, and with the sound of the trumpet of God. And the dead in Christ will rise first; then we who are alone, who are left, shall be caught up together with them in the clouds to meet the Lord in the air; and so we shall always be with the Lord."

The second Gospel reading was John, Chapter 11, verses 17 to 27, in which Jesus, before raising Lazarus from the dead, says, "I am the resurrection and the life; he who believes in me, though he die, yet shall he live, and whoever lives and believes in me shall never die."

Rev. Craycroft prayed, after the communion rite: "May this sacrifice purify the souls of your servants: Amy, Denise, and Mary, which have departed from this world. Grant that once delivered from their sins, they may receive forgiveness and eternal rest." And in the invocations he prayed: "Father, into your hands we commend our loved ones. . . . Welcome our loved ones to paradise and help us to comfort each other with the assurance of our faith until we all meet in Christ to be with you and with Amy, Denise, and Mary forever."

A piano and flute duet played "Amazing Grace" as the hearses took the three girls to North Hardin Memorial Gardens, close by North Hardin High School's football field, where the three would have marched in the band that fall. After spring ended and summer came and went, on a bright crisp autumn Saturday, standing by their graves, you could hear the cheers, the trumpet charges, the cow bells and snare drums wafting softly on the breeze like intimations of another world, delicate, gentle, and terribly, terribly beautiful.

❑

That same Thursday night more than 5,000 people attended a memorial service at the football field. Governor Wilkinson headed the dignitaries on the dais, and Rev. Tennison of the First Assembly of God read messages of condolence from President and Nancy Reagan and Vice President and Barbara Bush. "Our hearts and prayers go out to each of you," Ronald Reagan's letter read. "May you find consolation in the knowledge that your fellow Americans all across our land share your sorrow."

Then Rev. Waggoner, the minister at the Baptist church Shannon attended, delivered the memorial message. "I would suggest that you do not blame God. God did not cause this," he declared. "There is sin in this world. There is evil in this world and there are those who make terrible choices, wrong choices. And innocent people pay an awful price.

"Life isn't really that complicated," he concluded. "We live a few short years. We die. We stand before God. And we go to heaven or hell." Then he sounded the theme that those without faith find so curious, namely, that things not only are not what they seem; they are precisely the opposite of what they seem:

"Would you try to think of these deaths in particular as not an elimination but an emancipation? Think of the death of these not as a destruction but a deliverance. Think of the death of these not as a losing but as a gaining. Not an ending but a beginnning. Not a going away but an arriving. Not a parting but a meeting.

"Or even next week, when many of us shall return to this very spot:

It will be graduation time for the seniors of North Hardin High School. I submit to you that three adults and twenty-four young people have already graduated.

"Absent from the body; present with the Lord.

"Absent from the body; present with the Lord.

"Absent from the body; present with the Lord.

"God bless."

❑

Larry Mahoney was taken the next day from his Louisville hospital bed to the Carroll County District Court for a 3:00 P.M. arraignment. As was standard operating procedure for felony defendants, Mahoney was transported with wrists cuffed and ankles shackled together, and the chains lent him the aura of a violent desperado.

The authorities were surely more concerned about protecting Mahoney from the public than vice versa. The police car carrying him drove over the sidewalk and up on the courthouse lawn, to shorten his walk to the door. The whole building was carefully checked before his arrival, and those few allowed to enter had to pass through a metal detector. There had been talk around Radcliff of getting guns (if anyone in that army town didn't already have a gun), and of Mahoney not living to face trial. But taming rampant emotions is what the judicial system does best. Even the strongest of feelings are no match for the impervious routine that prevails within the four walls of the courtroom. Lawyers turn passion to procedure as deftly as engineers turn garbage to energy, and the wheels of justice keep turning.

Mahoney's mother, among a handful of friends and relatives permitted in the courtroom, wept as the thirty-four-year-old factory worker, still wearing his hospital ID bracelet, shuffled in with no shoes on, looking frail and dazed. He'd suffered a concussion, a banged-up knee, and a collapsed lung in the wreck, but his blue jeans and polo shirt covered all evidence of injury save a gash on his chin and a piece of gauze on his forearm.

The local prosecutor, Commonwealth's Attorney John Ackman, Jr., had announced Monday that he would charge Mahoney with murder and seek the death penalty. But Ackman, thirty-eight, had suffered a heart attack on Wednesday. (The prosecutor, a father of three, was described by his mother-in-law as "a very sensitive man" who had bottled up his emotions since announcing that he would strive to have Mahoney executed.) So it

was Assistant Commonwealth's Attorney James Monk who ritually informed the court and Mahoney that the defendant was charged with
twenty-seven counts of murder.

Mahoney sat with head bowed and said nothing as the strangers representing him that day—a public defender and a lawyer retained for him
by his auto insurance company—entered not guilty pleas on his behalf.
The judge, as he could in a capital case, denied bail, and on motion of
the prosecutor ordered that Mahoney, who was reportedly exhibiting
deep depression, be held under twenty-four-hour suicide watch at the
Kentucky Correctional Psychiatric Center. The prosecutor wanted Mahoney interviewed and observed in order to head off any claim that he was
incompetent to stand trial.

After the twenty-minute proceeding, which kicked off a criminal case
that would grind on for a year and a half, Mahoney was taken outside,
where a crowd of more than fifty local people had gathered to express
their support for the defendant—a spectacle the families of the dead
would long remember.

"Hang in there brother," one man shouted. "Our prayers are with
you," added Juanita White, who explained to Debbbie Wright of Carrollton's *News-Democrat* that it just wasn't right to charge Mahoney with
murder, because, "He didn't intend to do this." (Here, as sometimes
happens, the snap judgment of the street yielded a fair approximation of
the result that would be reached after eighteen months of heavy lifting by
the state, bench, and bar.)

Ms. White, who said she was a friend of Mahoney, pointed out that he
loved children, which was true, and argued that it was outrageous for the
prosecutor to seek the death penalty, because even a man convicted two
years before in the hatchet slaying of an elderly local couple had not
been sentenced to death.

(In fact, prosecutor Ackman *had* sought capital punishment in the
case of Kevin Fitzgerald, the twenty-two-year-old college student who had
fallen upon Roy and Ruby Bickers one night as they were eating bread
pudding in front of their TV, and killed them with multiple chopping
blows to the head and neck—Mrs. Bickers's right middle and ring fingers
were amputated, perhaps as she tried to stave off the first of nine blows
to her skull. But as the nature of this particular burglary amply demonstrated, the perpetrator was highly agitated, and the jury—informed by
the defense that Fitzgerald, a Carrollton High School honors graduate,
had been adopted and raised by a demanding, perfectionist mother only

to fall under the baleful influence of a cocaine-dealing fraternity brother at school—concluded that he had acted under extreme emotional disturbance. Thus they found him guilty not of murder but of manslaughter. He was sentenced to forty-years-to-life.)

The Kentucky attorney general himself, Fred Cowan, had come to court for Mahoney's arraignment and announced that his office, in the person of Assistant Attorney General Paul Richwalsky, Jr., director of the Special Prosecutions Division, would be handling the case, under the system in place for just such eventualities as the local prosecutor's heart attack. Cowan reaffirmed the goal of having Mahoney executed, saying that the ultimate sanction was justified by "the severity of the numbers."

One might ask why the act of driving drunk and hitting a crowded school bus is any more venal than the act of driving drunk and hitting a lone pedestrian, or for that matter the act of driving drunk and fortuitously not hitting anyone at all. Why should the chance result of an evil act determine one's culpability, rather than the evil of the act itself? (Why is the man who shoots and misses guilty of a lesser offense, attempted murder, than the man who shoots and kills? Their intent is the same. Is it bad acts or good marksmanship that we wish to punish?) Maybe the emphasis on result stems from the idea that, since we cannot look into the heart of the doer, the best way to measure the evil therein is to weigh the deed: The true nature of the act reveals itself—comes out—in the outcome.

At any rate, executing Mahoney seemed like a good idea to Cowan at the time, and the Kentucky legislature had provided that the death penalty could be imposed only when one or more of seven aggravating factors was present. The only one conceivably applicable to Mahoney's case read: "The offender by his act of murder, armed robbery, or kidnapping knowingly created a great risk of death to more than one (1) person in a public place by means of a destructive device, weapon, or other device which would normally be hazardous to the lives of more than one (1) person."

It fell to Paul Richwalsky, who had been apppointed director of the Special Prosecutions Division just a week before, to deal with this issue of the death penalty, and he approached it in the manner that twelve years of lawyering had by now ingrained in him as the way to think: He looked up the law, and he looked up how the law had been applied by courts in the past. To ask whether Larry Mahoney ought to be executed was to ask whether persons similarly situated, in light of all the surrounding circumstances, had been executed before. If they had, then

Larry Mahoney ought to be a candidate for execution. If they had not, then Larry Mahoney ought not to be.

The term "destructive device" was defined elsewhere in Kentucky law as a "bomb, grenade, mine, rocket, missile, or similar device." Though a drunk-driven car could aptly be compared to a ticking bomb, no court had found a motor vehicle to be a "destructive device" as contemplated by the death penalty law. Richwalsky discovered that vehicular homicides had resulted in as many as 200 murder convictions in the history of the United States, but the death penalty had not been imposed for any of them. Indeed, his research did not turn up anyone executed in recent years in any state for killing wantonly, that is, as a consequence of such screw-everybody, I-don't-care behavior as drunk driving. The death penalty cases on the books, which all dealt with intentional murders, did not, as Richwalsky put it, "jeehaw" with, or fit, the case of Larry Mahoney. So Richwalsky decided not to seek a capital murder indictment.

Reaction among the grieving families was mixed. One First Assembly of God member who'd lost his only child took to wearing a T-shirt with a drawing of an electric chair over the caption "Regular or Extra Crispy." But Karen Claybrook, whose son Anthony Marks had been killed, said, "I would never want them to execute Larry Mahoney. That would be letting him off easy. He wouldn't have to remember."

The way Larry Fair looked at it, "The law is the law." If the law then in place had not put Mahoney on notice that he would face the death penalty for a fatal drunk driving crash, then the death penalty would not be appropriate, Fair thought.

Janey Fair had opposed the death penalty before the May 14 crash and continued to oppose it afterward. "I don't believe in it, period," she said. "I just don't believe you should take someone's life."

❑

Richard Gohn was one of eight victims who shared a funeral at the First Assembly of God, on Friday night, May 20. Only when his mother, Rosemary Martinez, saw the eight coffins stretching from one side of the church to the other did it really hit her that so many others had died.

Her son's coffin was on the far right. Chuck Kytta, a veteran, was in the flag-draped casket in the middle. Chuck had worked with Rosemary on one of her Red Cross committees, emergency food and shelter. Anthony Marks was next to Rick; Emillie Thompson was next to him. Rosemary could still remember Emillie trotting down the aisle in church, pigtails flying, when she was smaller. And Dwailla Fischel, Phillip Morgan, Billy Nichols, Crystal Uhey—she knew them all. It was hard, grieving not only for your child, but twenty-six others.

There was time at this funeral for Rev. Tennison to say only a few sentences about each of the eight. When he came to Rick, the pastor, perhaps inspired by the mortarboard Rosemary had placed on his coffin, observed: "Rick has graduated. The perfect graduation."

Here again was that graduation theme, enunciated just the night before, at the memorial service, by Rev. Waggoner. Death is like a graduation. No, in fact death *is* a graduation. In fact it is *the* graduation and all other graduations are like *it*. The mourners found some comfort in the belief that everything earthly was a reflection of something spiritual, everything temporal the shadow of something eternal.

JANET KYTTA

"When I got home from finding out that Chuck had died, I saw his socks lying on the floor in his study where he had taken them off watching TV the night before. And his dirty clothes were in the bedroom, like always. He always had one place he'd put his dirty clothes, and I'd get mad. I'd say, 'Why don't you pick up your mess?' But this time, I was just like, 'Don't move it, don't move it. Chuck put them there, and once people move them, he's never going to put them back again.' Well, they had to move them, family was coming, you can't leave a pile of dirty clothes, I guess, sitting in the bedroom.

"I got a call from the lawyer's office one day, about three months after the wreck. He said, 'We've been sent some of the stuff. Your husband's wallet is here.'

"I thought he meant, like, a *wallet*. I went down there and they handed me this baggy with a black blob in it. I just started crying, because this was more like Chuck's body than anything I'd ever had. And I said, 'What about his wedding ring? Isn't that here somewhere?' And in one little bag marked 'unidentified wedding band' there was this ring and it was blistered, it was black, it looked more like a washer off a faucet or something. And they gave me his watch, a steel Timex watch with a Twistoflex band."

[A visitor pointed out that the hands of the blackened, skeletal watch, melted to the face, read 10:50.]

"Really? That would have been the time of the bus crash: 10:51. Chuck was the first to die.

"And his Bible that the choir had given to him: I thought he had it on the bus that day. Somebody came to me and said, 'Oh, by the way, here's Chuck's Bible.' I said, 'I thought it was on the bus.' Charlie said, 'Don't you remember? Dad lost it Wednesday night before the bus crash.' So it was at church the whole time.

"He had underlined a scripture from Matthew, and it said, 'Fear not him that can destroy the body but rather him that can destroy the soul.' He had it double underlined and highlighted. It was almost like he was saying, 'Don't worry, the body is destroyed totally, but rather fear him that can destroy the soul.' I guess that's all.

"If Chuck came back into our lives today, I'd have to say, 'Chuck, this is what Mandy looks like. She's grown about twelve inches, put on about forty pounds, she's going through high school now. We got a new dog. I changed the bedroom furniture. The house we lived in held too many memories of the crash, so we moved.'

"Your life goes on. And I found the first time the seasons changed—I woke up one day and it was autumn—I realized everything moves ahead. And it just doesn't seem right.

"I thought what Lee Williams said to me in Sunday school was really true. He said, 'You know, if our loved ones had the choice to come back or not, they wouldn't want to come, because where they are is wonderful and beautiful and peaceful. They wouldn't want to come back.' So the other alternative is to let them go. And that's the painful part, to let them go. Because, you see, that meant I ended up without a future. 'Well, let's retire, we'll get a little place down in Florida, we'll do this, we'll do that.' All of a sudden my future was gone. It boggles my mind, because here I thought I had a general scheme of how things were gonna be. It's not gonna be that way.

"It wasn't a final ending; I don't mean that. It wasn't a good-bye. It was just kind of like getting lost, in the middle of a good marriage. When I look back at Janet Kytta on May the 13th, 1988, I don't feel associated at all with that person. There is nothing that has been the same again.

"The horror that lives with me is that I remember sitting down one night, watching some kind of suspense thriller with him and saying, 'Chuck, if you had a choice of the way you were going to die, what would it be?'

"He said, 'I know one thing, I don't want to burn.' He said, 'If I had my choice, I would want to die in my sleep.'

"I know that Chuck never even had time to suffocate, and I realize how horrible it was. He burned to death. I would do anything to spare him that. I don't understand why it had to be that way. I've sat down and thought, 'Well, what could I have done to save him?' I've gone back and thought, 'What if they hadn't stopped for candy and filled up the tank? And what if the kids had taken less time in the bathroom? What if this swerve of the bus had been a little bit different?'

"We've all sat down together and talked about it, and each one of us feels like *there must be a way we could get our loved one out of that bus.* It's hard to realize, it's hard to really accept, that, yes, little kids burned. And my husband burned. And there was nothing we could do to help.

"I have driven on I-71 past the site of the wreck a lot of times. With people you love, you want to share things. If they go into surgery, you want to hold their hand. I turn on my car lights as I pass. There's a choking, dark, terrible feeling. I turn on the lights, just something to say I remember. Twenty-seven people died here on this spot. And it was right here that someone I love lost his life, never made it one step further.

"When we pass, Charlie just gets quiet. Mandy has been able to cry."

CHAPTER

16

Shannon Fair was buried on Saturday, May 21, one week after she had climbed aboard a school bus to go home.

Her remains had been shipped via air freight from Louisville to Tri-City Airport near Johnson City, Tennessee, her parents' hometown. According to standard practice, the casket was covered by a cardboard box, toward one end of which the word "HEAD" was printed in blue letters, with an arrow pointing forward. The marking ensured that the baggage handlers would load the body with the head pointing toward the nose of the plane. It was important that cadavers be oriented in this way, so that when the plane climbed steeply on takeoff, fluids would not run out of the mouth, nose, and ears.

Larry and Janey, and Shannon's big brother, Donald, drove down I-75 to Tennessee, just as they always had with Shannon for summer vacations and Christmas holidays. Donald and Shannon would stay at Janey's sister Patty's home, which served as hostel and clubhouse for an ever changing cast of neighborhood kids, all of whom were "cousins," whether related or not. Aunt Patty called her house "The Land of Do-As-You-Please."

About fifty miles south of Lexington, at the edge of the Daniel Boone National Forest, they passed the exit for Route 25E, where blasting had exposed a layered cross section of sedimentary rock.

Janey remembered how they used to stop to let the kids chip fossils out of the cutaway. Shannon and Donald were great ones for fossil hunting, here or up by Louisville at the Falls of the Ohio River. When she was eight or nine, Shannon wore big wide-rimmed glasses, and as she clambered about in the hot sun they would keep sliding down her freckled nose. She'd have handfuls of rocks and not be able to push her glasses back up, so they'd get way, way down on the end of her nose, and she'd be squinting over them; that was a picture for you.

More recently, in the eighth-grade year that was just then ending, Shannon had discovered and become an enthusiast for Thomas Huxley's essay "On a Piece of Chalk." In that discourse, delivered on a cloudy afternoon in August 1868 to an audience of British workingmen, Huxley explained that "the bit of chalk which every carpenter carries" turns out, under the microscope, to be primarily composed of the skeletons of tiny marine creatures. From that observation, he reasoned that Britain's great chalk cliffs are nothing but the dried mud of an ancient sea. "Thus evidence ... compels you to believe that the earth, from the time of the chalk to the present day, has been the theatre of a series of changes as vast in their amount, as they were slow in their progress ... one species has vanished and another has taken its place; creatures of one type of structure have diminished, those of another have increased, as time has passed on. ... And in the shifting 'without haste, but without rest' of the land and sea, as in the endless variation of the forms assumed by living beings, we have observed nothing but the natural product of the forces originally possessed by the substance of the universe."

(That Shannon spent some of the latter days of her life fascinated by the transience of all things could be seen as ironic, or even portentous. It could be that things are portentous only in retrospect. Or maybe every-thing is full of meaning all the time. That things suddenly seem meaning-ful when followed by death suggests that everything is meaningful, since everything is followed by death; and it suggests, further, that death is the author of meaning.)

The fossils Shannon would most often find preserved in the primor-dial muck were trilobites. All the surface rocks of Kentucky are sedimen-tary, laid down starting half a billion years ago in a warm, clear sea. These two- or three-inch arthropods—ancestors of insects, spiders, lobsters, crabs—scurried about the ocean floors as long as 570 million years ago; and lived, generation after generation, for about 330 million years, until the last of them perished 240 million years ago. To see a creature that had lived and died and then lain hidden and impervious while a thousand years passed, and passed again, three hundred thousand times over, day by day by day; while mountains rose and wore away, and oceans filled and then dried up; while everything that ever happened, happened. To see this creature brought to light in the palm of a little girl's hand, it was like looking at a circle closed, somehow, a destiny fulfilled.

Shannon was outside time now, Janey supposed, or outside the illu-sion of time. She hoped Shannon was in heaven. She hoped she would see her again.

❑

Rev. Gene Waggoner came down from Radcliff to conduct Shannon's funeral service at the Morris-Baker Funeral Home in Johnson City, at 10:00 A.M. on Saturday.

After Scripture, and prayer, and song ("I sing because I'm happy, I sing because I'm free. His eye is on the sparrow, and I know he watches me"), Rev. Waggoner delivered the eulogy.

"Shannon Rae Fair was born on January 31, 1974. She died on May 14, 1988," he began. "The question that would be of most importance would be this one: Was she ready to go? Yes, she was ready to go. She made her profession of faith in our church on March the 6th, 1988. But she had become a Christian prior to making public her profession of faith. She was baptized on Easter Sunday, April the 3rd, 1988. Yes, she was ready to go. She was a believer. She was a Christian. It seems so untimely, yet we must remember that God is in control."

Then, as custom commands, he counted the shards of her shattered life: "Shannon was born at Fort Knox. She attended kindergarten in Germany, first grade at Fort Leavenworth, Kansas. She lived in Radcliff since 1981. She was an eighth-grade student at Radcliff Middle School. She made all A's, except back in the fifth grade she made a B plus. She was a runner-up in the Optimist Club hortatorical contests; she had the lead in class plays. She had superior ratings in the alto sax solo and duet state competition. She was first chair for two years in the Radcliff Middle School band. She was second chair in the A band of the all-district band. She had been accepted into the North Hardin High School marching band..."

Shannon was buried in Johnson City's expansive Monte Vista Burial Park, where, not long before, she had secretly learned to drive on the blacktop roadways that wind across its gently sloping lawns. Janey liked Monte Vista because it was so big that it was as sure as any place could be to remain a cared-for cemetery in perpetuity, unlike the derelict Civil War–era graveyards that you could find in the weeds and brambles outside town; they were even sadder than graveyards needed to be.

It was a beautiful day, this seventh of an uncountable number that would go on without Shannon; her funeral procession passed parents and little children feeding ducks on the sun-dappled pond by the cemetery gate.

Shannon's grave site was in the Garden of the Word, which was just past Baby Land, where the grave markers were heartbreakingly close together. Shannon would be interred near Larry Fair's father's grave. Beside Larry's dad's grave was a space for Larry's mother and for Larry himself, and then there were four lots for Janey, Shannon, Donald, and Donald's wife, who, wherever she was, did not yet know she would be Donald's wife, much less that there was a space for her here. Janey's mother was buried in the next area over, the Garden of Light. Janey had been dismayed to find that Shannon's site, near the edge of the cemetery, was disturbed by the noisy ventilator fan of a florist's greenhouse. Janey would not have gone for that if she'd known. Still, the seventy mourners could hear the oddly comforting cacophany of songbirds resting in the trees.

The casket was a shiny white, with a tinge of pink along the edges. Her father had picked it out because he thought it matched her taste: simple but elegant. A blanket of pink rosebuds was placed on top.

Shannon's Aunt Patty stood at the precipice of the grave, her heels sinking into the cemetery grass. She remembered the time Shannon swept into Patty's living room declaring, "Hey, all you lucky people, I'm here!" Shannon unfurled her coat with a flourish, and broke two china doves.

When they returned to Kentucky from Shannon's funeral Sunday night, Larry and Janey got a phone call from someone who said there was going to be a meeting that Tuesday evening of all the families who had people on the bus.

Within a day or so of burying her daughter Mary, Diane Daniels had received a similar call. Someone said that she should come to a Family Support Group meeting. "I didn't know what that meant," she said later, "but, I guess because of Mary, I went. Like if your child's in school, you go to the PTA. I thought, 'Well, Mary's involved in this, so I'll go.' I wasn't sure for a long time what the purpose was."

All the parents got the call, and a lot of them, including the Fairs, shared Daniels's mystification over the genesis of the Family Support Group—"It just appeared from nowhere," Larry Fair recalled. Some would grow to doubt just what the group's true purpose was. It apparently began simply enough: Dick Booher and Ron Cox, whose sons Jason Booher and Wayne Cox had escaped the bus virtually unscathed, thought it would be a good idea for the families to help one another rather than deal with their crises in isolation. But more than a few parents would later feel that the group had been used to steer them into the maw of a local law firm.

Booher, owner of the local Radio Shack, rose to address that initial meeting in the basement of Stithton Baptist, Radcliff's biggest church. The first thing he asked was, Do we want to have a group? People said yes. And the next thing was, Do we want to have legal questions answered? People said yes again, so Booher's wife went to make a phone call. Then Booher said, Let's elect a president of the group, whereupon he himself was elected president, more or less by acclamation. Then Terry Bennett, Esq., of Skeeters & Bennett, arrived.

Bennett, his voice choked with emotion, read a passage from the Bible, and then said that his firm—which like others in the area had already announced in the local paper that it would handle bus victims' probate and insurance matters for free—would be honored to help the families. But, he declared, he would not sue the Radcliff First Assembly of God or the estate of the bus's driver, John Pearman, nor would he represent anyone who wished to do so. (Bennett's later insistence that he laid down this proviso at the behest of his clients is hard to reconcile with the fact that he mentioned it right at the start, and included it in the retainer agreement people signed to *become* his clients.)*

Larry Fair could see no good reason to release a couple of prospective defendants from liability right from the git-go. He wondered whether Bennett was protecting the church at the expense of the plaintiffs he would be representing—a conflict of interest. But as it turned out, Bennett had not cut a deal with the church. The First Assembly of God's pastor, Rev. Tennison, later recalled being "shocked and happy" to hear Bennett announce his no-sue policy; he and the lawyer had not conferred before the meeting, even though the church, having retained Skeeters & Bennett in the past on some real estate matters, "basically considered this firm our attorneys." (According to legal ethics, past representation of a potential defendant does not alone preclude a firm from representing the plaintiffs, so long as the relationship is disclosed. However, as far as the Fairs could recall, it was not.)

Bennett's insistence on not suing the church could have been just a marketing ploy; he may well have thought that the clients he was wooing were virtually all members of the First Assembly of God. In fact, nearly half the passengers, and thirteen of the twenty-seven dead, had not been members of the church.

---

* "I/We have counseled with the above attorney and it has been agreed that during my/our legal representation as to this incident, no court action will be initiated in my/our behalf against the First Assembly of God Church of Radcliff, Ky., and/or John Pearman," reads a retainer agreement obtained by the author.

Looking back on it, some who became Bennett's clients would recall his entry into their case as though he had parachuted in under cover of darkness; he was just *there* before they knew it. More than a few would speculate that Booher and Tennison must have anticipated some monetary reward for delivering to this particular lawyer a flock of clients, stunned insensible by grief, whose collective cause of action held the promise of a fee worth more than a successful small-town lawyer might reasonably expect to earn in a lifetime. But in fact Booher simply called Bennett because he'd handled a few business matters for him before; and the thoroughly exhausted Tennison, none too sophisticated in the best of times, just went along with the situation as he found it.

No wonder Bennett wept as he stood up and spoke to the families. One can only imagine the emotions that must have been at war within him. He knew many of the people and no doubt keenly felt what this tragedy meant to them, but at the same time how could he not think of what it meant to him? His share could be millions of dollars. *Millions,* a whole honorable career of divorces, fender-benders, bankruptcies, wills, real estate closings, and zoning board appeals, all compressed into one electrifying front-page case and dropped in his lap.

Among the good reasons to choose the firm of Skeeters & Bennett, according to Bennett, was that they were local lawyers who had been around a long time, eighteen years, and they weren't about to try for a quick buck and then strike their tents and move on. Skeeters & Bennett retainer contracts were made available at the next week's meeting (where the families also voted that they did *not* wish to cooperate with Geraldo Rivera, who had inquired about doing a show on the tragedy). But it was at the June 14 meeting that the legal resolution of the bus crash calamity suddenly accelerated.

Al Davidson from the Brotherhood Mutual Insurance Co. of Fort Wayne, Ind., made a presentation. His company represented 12,000 churches, he said, the Radcliff First Assembly of God among them. Brotherhood Mutual printed Galatians 6:2 on each of its policies ("Bear one another's burdens, and so fulfill the law of Christ"). In accordance with this philosophy, Davidson explained, even though the church had not requested underinsured motorist* coverage in its application for insurance, Brotherhood Mutual had voluntarily decided to make available $1 million in such coverage, because "It would be the right thing to do."

This declaration of adherence to principle was greeted not with the

---

* Mahoney had only $75,000 in liability insurance.

hosannas Davidson might have expected, but by murmurs of suspicion. "Nobody pays a million dollars out of the goodness of their heart," Katrina McNickle's father, Kevin, was thinking.)

(As a matter of fact, Davidson later explained to the author of this book, his insurance company had accidentally typed "$1 million" on the underinsured motorist coverage line of the church's policy. (The church *did* have $1 million in liability coverage.) Rather than contest the validity of the underinsured motorist coverage, Davidson decided to go ahead and honor it, knowing that by the terms of the policy each dollar paid out in underinsured motorist (U.M.) coverage reduced by a dollar the available liability, or bodily injury (B.I.), coverage. "That's why I agreed to pay out the U.M., because I knew it would exhaust my B.I.," he explained, as only an insurance man could. If Brotherhood Mutual paid out nothing in underinsured motorist coverage, it could get whacked for a million in liability coverage in the event that someone successfully sued the church for overcrowding the bus. But if the insurance company "voluntarily" paid out the $1 million up front, it could then turn its pockets inside out.)

What's more, Davidson explained to the Family Support Group, Brotherhood would pay out this money on the basis of need, as determined by an independent committee, "without waiting for lawsuits and without resorting to the courts," thus avoiding the expenses and delay of litigation. He noted that, by the way, anyone who sued the church instead of taking his company's offer would probably end up with nothing, for all the insurance funds would quickly be paid out to those who accepted the money now.

Besides the $1 million in underinsured coverage, Davidson added, there would be payments under no-fault insurance of $1,000 per death, and up to $10,000 per injury. That's when the meeting went berserk. *Ten times as much for your kid's injury as for my child's death?!* Among the families there were affluent and poor, military and civilian, Born Again and secular; parents of children who died, parents of children disfigured for life, parents of kids who got out without a scratch. The idea that a group with nothing in common but a collision—which had affected them in vastly differing ways—could long remain united did not survive the moment when money was put on the table. "I have never seen such pandemonium in my life," recalls Rosemary Martinez.

Despite the tumult, the meeting was restored to sufficient order so that Bennett could introduce the first in a series of big-name lawyers who would parade their wares, so that the families could decide which one should handle the lawsuit they fully expected to launch. (Local lawyers ordinarily hand off complex litigation to larger firms with greater resources and expertise, and can get as much as half the fee just for referring the case and doing a little routine work.) It would later become an article of faith for many of the families, particularly members of the First Assembly of God, that the school bus on which their children had been trapped and burned left absolutely nothing to be desired in terms of safety. But much of the activity in the Family Support Group was at first explicitly aimed at launching a punishing lawsuit against the manufacturers of the bus, not only to gain compensation but to send a message to the industry as a whole that it had better build safer buses.

On the night of June 14, a Los Angeles attorney with the colorful name Brown Green introduced himself as a leading champion of asbestos and Pinto-fuel-tank victims. He said his firm, twenty-three lawyers strong, had done some preliminary investigation and concurred with the *Courier-Journal,* which had reported within days of the crash that the church bus had at least three deadly features: The fuel tank was exposed, unprotected, and positioned right beside the main door; the seats were made of highly flammable materials that produced toxic gases as they burned; and there was only one emergency exit.

The manufacturers of the bus were at fault, Green said, because they had every reason to know the dangers their bus posed—papers published by the Society of Automotive Engineers had for decades stressed the importance of shielding fuel tanks from impact. The Superior Division of the Sheller-Globe Corporation had built the body of the bus (rear of the dashboard from the floor up), and Ford Motor Company had built the chassis and engine. Both corporations, he argued, had a "corporate mentality" that could compare the cost of producing safe vehicles against the cost of building unsafe ones and paying damages for deaths and injuries, and decide that it was more profitable to produce unsafe vehicles. The only way to change corporate behavior, he said, was to sock the manufacturers with lawsuits that would reverse the equation, making it uneconomical for them to keep building dangerous vehicles. If you take a settlement rather than sue, he warned, "Ford will require that the settlement be confidential, so it will be buried along with your children and your loved ones." He concluded by reciting the all-but-official mantra of the plaintiffs' bar: "More changes are accomplished by lawsuits than by all the laws passed in Washington."

Brown Green had brought with him from L.A. an automotive safety consultant named Byron Bloch. Bloch, despite a lack of extensive training in automotive safety engineering, had by dint of relentless self-promotion established himself as an expert in the field; that he had reported on auto safety regularly for KABC-TV News in Los Angeles, and occasionally for *20/20,* attested to his stature. Green left Bloch cooling his heels during the support group meeting, perhaps out of concern that an excess of zeal on Bloch's part—he tended to view his crusade for automotive safety in messianic terms—would detract from Green's own comparatively under-stated salesmanship. But it was announced that anyone wishing to explore the grounds for a lawsuit more fully could meet with Bloch the next day. Only two families did: the Fairs and Jim and Karolyn Nunnallee, who'd lost their ten-year-old, Patty.

❑

Janey Fair arranged to meet with Bloch the next morning at the Super 8 Motel in Radcliff to inquire further into the circumstances of her daughter's death. (Larry had returned to work at Fort Knox two days after Shannon's funeral, because he felt staying out served no useful purpose.) Bloch and Janey sat down on the blue sofa in the motel's tiny lobby. She showed him Shannon's school yearbook picture, and her report card, which had arrived in the mail just the day before. Then she asked him to explain to her in detail what was wrong with the bus.

"Do you really want to know?" he asked her, because he had observed over the years that a lot of people would rather believe that a death was fate or predestined or God's will and that there was nothing that could have been done to avert it.

"Yes, I really want to know," she said. Bloch considered Janey Fair courageous for being willing to confront the horrifying prospect that her daughter's death had been needless and avoidable. But Janey would have described herself as *needing* to know everything, more than wanting to; and far from being strong and courageous, she felt as though she were succumbing to an irresistible urge.

❑

Janey Fair had always had a special need to know the truth. In fact, one of her earliest memories was about being lied to.

Janey got thrush when she was eight months old, and spent the next four months in the hospital. Thrush is a fungal infection that's easily handled today with antibiotics, but back in the 1940s, in Johnson City, Tennessee, babies died from it. For the longest time the doctors didn't think Janey would live. They got down to putting IVs in her heels, because all the other veins had collapsed. She'd get better and then relapse and have to go back into the hospital, and this went on well into her toddlerhood.

One time when she was getting out of the hospital, Janey was sitting up on some sort of ledge, on a bench or windowsill, and she was looking down into a boy's bed, a white iron bed. She could still picture it, decades later, though she never really believed that the image came from an actual memory until she described the scene and her mother said, "That was the room." Janey's mother wouldn't tell a lie to save anybody, and never exaggerated anything, and never bragged on her three girls. (Once when Janey was grown, she asked her mother why she never told her kids that they did things well or that they looked nice, and she said, "Well, I was always taught that praise would ruin you, that you wouldn't be a good Christian, that you might grow up to be proud." So if Janey's mother said something was true, it was a fact. She never embellished anything.)

As Janey remembered it, this little boy was crying that *he* wanted to go home, too. He was dying of cancer, but of course Janey didn't know that, and she said, "Why can't he go home?" And the grown-ups who'd come for her said, "His folks don't have a car." And the precocious Janey said, "He could ride with us." And they said, "We're going in opposite directions." She said, "Then call a yellow cab." And they said, "Well, he doesn't have any shoes."

"When they said that, it made no sense to me," she says now. "I thought, 'You don't need shoes to ride in a cab.' And it sounds strange, but I remember thinking at that moment that adults really were not in charge, that they really could not cope with what was going on in the world. And I can remember having my first fear. After that I'd trick adults into lying to me just to see if they would, and I would ask Mama, and she'd say, 'They're just trying to be nice to you.' But I said, 'Mama, people are supposed to tell you the truth; how else can you know what's going on?' I was forever catching grown-ups in lies all the time. I shouldn't say lies. I guess adults always try to cushion things and dissimulate to protect kids, but it didn't make me feel protected; it always frightened me."

(Janey, as a result, tried never to lie to her own children. "I never even told them that there's a Santa Claus. I think that's a terrible thing to tell a child—gives them the idea that God loves well-off kids better than poor kids. I did give Shannon a tooth-fairy pillow when she was losing her first tooth, though. She said, 'Mom, how can you tell me there's a tooth fairy when there's no Santa Claus?' I kidded her, "Hush up. Do you want the money or not?' ")

❏

Janey already knew from the *Courier-Journal* that federal law had required all school buses built starting April 1, 1977, to have at least a minimum level of crash protection for their fuel tanks. And she knew from the newspaper that the church bus, a 1977 model, must have been built sometime before the April 1 deadline, for it lacked a protective cage around the tank. But that was all the fuel system history she knew.

Bloch took some documents out of a bright red three-ring binder and said, "Let me show you what Ford knew and when they knew it." He showed her the National Transportation Safety Board Report on a 1972 accident in Reston, Virginia, involving a Blue Bird school bus built on a Ford chassis. A car ran a stop sign and crashed into the right front side of the school bus at 25 mph. On impact, the bus's gas tank ruptured, detached, and burst into flame. The front door of the bus was rendered inoperable. As it happened, the fire stayed with the gas tank and the car as they careened away from the bus. The car's driver was ejected and severely burned, but the occupants of the school bus escaped serious injury.

The safety board faulted "the vulnerable location of the fuel tank and the absence of crash-protection design features," and concluded:

> *If the impact speed had been slightly less, it is not inconceivable that the school bus fuel tank would still have ruptured, but might not have separated from the bus. Under those conditions, the fire would then have followed the trail of gasoline to the bus, and engulfed the area around the service door.... A large-scale tragedy could easily have followed. Speculation as to such tragic results cannot be brushed aside. The scene was set. It should not be necessary to wait until such a tragedy has in fact occurred to appreciate how closely this event missed becoming such an example, and to remove the elements which brought it to the brink.*
>
> *It seems almost self-evident that, in its present location, and without additional crash protection, the school bus fuel tank represents a real and unnecessary hazard.*

The NTSB urged, in that 1972 report, that school bus fuel tanks be relocated away from the exit doors, and be better shielded. Five years later, Ford was still building buses with the tank unguarded, outside the frame rail, right beside the exit door, and Shannon and twenty-six others had burned to death on one.

Ford had long known how to make safe fuel tanks, Bloch said, and had even advertised their protected location on some vehicles. He showed Janey an advertisement for 1975 Ford pickup trucks trumpeting this safety advantage. "Ford fuel tanks," it read, "are located between the frame rails on most models. They're not hung on the outside frame." But on the Ford school bus chassis, the gas tank *was* hung on the outside of the frame.*

"I know Ford, I know fuel tanks, I know school buses, and in my opinion this did not have to happen," Bloch said. "There did not have to be a fire."

CHAPTER

18

"**Y**ou've got a lot of audacity calling us like this," Larry Fair said, when yet another lawyer phoned him at home to offer his services, one night late in June. "We fully intend to examine all of our options and proceed in what we determine to be a reasonable and prudent manner, and people who invade our privacy and try to take advantage are not likely to be real high on the list."

---

* A rash of fire deaths attributed to fuel tanks hung on the outside of the frame led to widespread demands for the recall of all 1973–87 General Motors pickups with sidesaddle fuel tanks. A jury awarded $100 million to one GM pickup fire victim's family in 1992.

John P. Coale, Esq.—senior partner of Coale, Kananack & Murgatroyd, an internationally renowned law firm (his brochure said) with offices in Los Angeles and Washington, D.C.—felt as though he had been yelled at, though Lieutenant Colonel Fair had in fact lowered his already soft drawl to a steely murmur. Coale did not like being yelled at—it signaled that a negotiation was not going well—but, like all good attorneys, he endeavored never to say or do anything except for a reason, so when he yelled back, it was as the result of a lightning calculation of yelling's likely consequence: Fair was a military man. Southerner. Straight-shooter. After the parade of smooth-talking lawyers that Coale knew had auditioned at the Family Support Group, a little high-volume bluntness with all the indicia of candor would represent a refreshing change. "Hey, wait a minute! *I'm* not the enemy!" he shouted. "You've got the wrong guy here. I may be able to help you, and I may not. But let's talk."

Fair found himself liking Coale at that moment, just as Coale had hoped he would. Fair invited him to come on down and drop by.

Though he had never heard of Coale, Fair had it right when he accused the lawyer of having a lot of audacity. Coale's brazenness had been the subject of controversy throughout his career; in fact, it practically *was* his career. He'd won fame—and the tag "master of disaster"—not so much for the way he handled cases as for the speed and aggressiveness with which he went after them. Ambulances chased *him.*

When his law practice, based in Washington, D.C., had not swelled to meet his expectations by 1976, four years out of the University of Baltimore law school, Coale hit upon the idea of drumming up business by looking over police blotters and then writing letters to drunk-driving defendants suggesting that they retain him. If this rudimentary form of direct marketing did not quite amount to rocket science, it did require what lawyers of that bygone macho era might have called brass balls. For direct solicitation of clients was then against the rules, and Coale immediately found himself in hot water with the bar association, as he knew he would. But the Maryland Court of Appeals, in a precedent-setting decision, ultimately upheld Coale's right to comport himself like the Fuller Brush Man if he chose to. In Coale's view, the bar's traditional impediments to hustling business were never designed to protect bewildered clients from lawyers but to protect old lawyers from new lawyers. "To my knowledge," he notes, "no one has ever died from or been seriously injured by solicitation."

Coale was making a living, but it was not his idea of a life. He'd put together a small firm, handling inglorious personal injury cases—"run-of-the-mill slip-and-fall," as he puts it—"and auto stuff." This was a serviceable practice for an up-and-comer trying to scrap his way to the top. Coale, however, was born at the top. He had to find something else to do, other than just making money. The scion of a prominent old Maryland family—his industrialist grandfather, envelope baron Howard S. Jones, had bought the St. Louis Browns baseball team and made them into the Baltimore Orioles—young John grew up with the run of the dugout. So whatever he did, it had to be big-league. Like many a bright kid born to wealth and privilege, Coale felt a peculiarly vital animosity toward abusers of power and a keen identification with their victims. He loved fighting Big Money as much as he loved having it. For such champions of the disadvantaged, God created a calling, and it is liability law.

Coale's breakthrough came in 1981, when he sued Iran and the Ayatollah Khomeini in federal court for $30 million on behalf of three former American hostages. The suit was ultimately dismissed, but not before Coale had hit the headlines. "That was very exciting and I got a lot of notoriety out of it, and the big cases started to come," he recalls. Two years later, in 1983, Coale sued Blue Cross/Blue Shield of Maine when it refused to pay for fifty-one-year-old Grace Jacques's heart transplant on the grounds that the operation was experimental. The suit led to a change in Blue Cross policy, compensation for Jacques, and an article in *People* magazine for Coale, the first of three *People* stories he would score in the next five years.

Coale was most famous, or infamous, for his activities in Bhopal, India, after a gas leak at a Union Carbide pesticide plant killed more than 2,300 people and badly injured as many as 40,000, in 1984. Coale hired as his assistant the Indian closest at hand, his tailor, and rushed with him to Bhopal, arriving within a week of the disaster. "Melvin Belli had hit the media saying he was going to Bhopal," Coale recalls. "I got there first. Everybody was waiting for the American lawyers. It was like Jesus was coming any day now, the American lawyers were coming. When I got there it was like Palm Sunday. To think that there was improper solicitation [as had been alleged] is absurd. People were signing up at the rate of six to ten thousand a day. These people were frantic to get at Union Carbide. It was a question of how fast retainers could be printed." And also how fast they could be signed by often illiterate claimants, many of them blinded. Coale soon represented the city of Bhopal and 50,000 individual clients—some of whom signed his retainer contracts by thumbprint.

The Indian government eventually took over the plaintiffs' case, leaving the American lawyers with nothing to show for their efforts but their expenses. (India settled for $470 million in 1989, but by 1992 the money still had not been distributed among the 600,000 claimants.) But Coale had put himself at the service of a trio of America's leading disaster attorneys, Wendell Gauthier and John Cummings III, both of New Orleans, and Stan Chesley of Cincinnati. Chesley, Gauthier, and Cummings had worked together on the 1980 MGM-Grand Hotel fire: 86 dead, 1,500 plaintiffs, 119 defendants, a $210 million settlement. Coale puts his and their collective Bhopal losses at $800,000. "These things are high-stakes poker," he says. "You lose, you lose big. You win, you win big."

Bhopal was not a winner for Coale, but it gained him publicity (not all of it good: Former Chief Justice Warren Burger denounced "the shocking spectacle" of "open solicitation by a handful of lawyers who dashed off to India," and observed that "few things have done more serious damage to the standing of the legal profession"); and he had made connections.

When a New Year's Eve fire at the DuPont Plaza Hotel in Puerto Rico took ninety-six lives in 1986, Coale got a call from Gauthier, who was busy settling a Pan Am air crash case in New Orleans. Gauthier invited Coale to go into the hotel case with him, Chesley, and Cummings. Coale threw a few things into an overnight bag, hit the tarmac in San Juan on January 2, had his first suit filed in federal court on January 5, and soon had thirty clients and another *People* story. Just four days after the San Juan fire came the Chase, Maryland, Amtrak-Conrail crash: sixteen dead. August 1987 brought the crash of Northwest Airlines Flight 255 in Detroit: 156 dead. In May of 1988, Coale was still working on the Puerto Rico fire case with Gauthier, and still pulling together the Northwest case. The Chase train crash settlement was wrapping up, "coming down to the short strokes," Coale says, using an inelegant expression widely employed by lawyers. Then Larry Mahoney went for a late-night drive, and the action was in Radcliff, Kentucky.

"When the bus accident happened, every mass disaster attorney was running around," Coale recalls. "Phil Corboy from Chicago was down there. Brown Green. Stan Chesley was sniffing around. It was the All Star Game. I called Wendell [Gauthier]. In Puerto Rico and Bhopal, I went in with Chesley, too. But in Radcliff, I was with Wendell. Wendell and I are close friends. We talked about going in with Chesley, but you don't want to go in with ten lawyers. So everybody was juggling, dancing.

"We'd gotten some intelligence that Skeeters & Bennett didn't like me, so Wendell went down there to talk with them. We thought the case would come in from the top, through Wendell. I was talking to individual plaintiffs. I just called them up after my investigator, Teddy Dickinson, talked to them. I didn't make cold calls. Larry Fair was one of the few who had expressed an interest in talking to someone other than Skeeters & Bennett."

Coale had just merged his law practice in 1986 with that of his child-hood buddy George W. (Skip) Murgatroyd III and Coale's University of Baltimore Law Review chum Michael Kananack, whose offices were in L.A. Coale, operating out of Washington, assumed the role of rainmaker for the firm, and it was he who flew down to Kentucky to pitch the Fairs.

As he drove out of the Louisville airport, Coale passed the sprawling Ford plant where they assembled Bronco IIs—liability lawyers called the sport-utility vehicles "Tumbleweeds" because of their propensity to roll over.* Then came the billboard with the cowboy-hatted, jeans-clad blonde resting her hand lovingly on a blue pickup's fender: "Welcome to Ford Country," it said.

That got Coale's juices flowing. It was always fun going up against a really big defendant. It would be all-out war. And here he was behind the lines in enemy territory!

Forty minutes later, as he drove under the gun of the M-48 tank on display at the roadside ("Fort Knox and Radcliff, Two Communities Grow-ing Together"), the urban-civilian Coale felt as though he had, indeed, crossed some sort of border. After the pawn shops and tattoo parlors, everything about this army-base town was a little too familiar: There was a Kentucky Fried Chicken and a Long John Silver's; a Pizza Hut and a Domino's Pizza; a Burger King and a Wendy's and a White Castle and a McDonald's and an Arby's and a Hardee's. The whole town looked like a thirty-second spot. Every national franchise was there, and nothing much else. It was as though aliens had constructed an "America World" habitat and were stumped when it came to anything local.

In fact there appeared to be, strictly speaking, no locality at all: no courthouse green, no village square, no big old factory-owners' houses, no factories, no Main Street, no sidewalks—no *people,* that you could see. Just cars stopping and going, north and south, east and west, on two food-gas-lodging thoroughfares.

---

* From 1986 to 1990, rear-wheel-drive Bronco II's had a rollover death rate in single-vehicle accidents of 3.78 per 100,000 vehicles, the highest of any sport-utility vehicle and more than triple the 1.11 rate of the Suzuki Samurai.

(That those two intersecting main drags were called Lincoln Trail and Dixie Highway gave the residents no more cause for reflection than the fact that McDonald's grilled on one side of the crossroads while Burger King broiled on the other. Honoring the Great Emancipator and the Confederacy was no problem in Kentucky, which was in more ways than one a Border State, where opposites co-exist rather than contend. Split personality was a theme there: Fundamentalism flourished, the Bible reigned supreme, and bourbon, tobacco, and horse racing were the leading industries—if you didn't count marijuana, which law enforcement authorities ranked as the state's biggest cash crop.*

Coale finally found the Fairs' little white-siding and brickface tract house, where Larry and Janey had been joined by parents of three other girls who had died: Jim and Karolyn Nunnallee; David Voglund, father of Shannon's friend Denise; and Diane Daniels, the mother of Mary.

Though little more than a month had passed since the crash, there were already increasingly insistent rumors circulating that Skeeters & Bennett were about to strike some sort of deal with the school bus manufacturers, Ford and Sheller-Globe. To the Fairs, the notion of settling, putting the tragedy behind them and moving on, was inconceivable. As Larry said, "At this point, you're still going down the hall to wake Shannon up for school in the morning."

As Coale remembered the meeting: "These people were really upset that the case was being settled, that the opportunity to really give value to their children's lives was flitting away. It was going away with Skeeters & Bennett and their deal with Ford. These parents were truly concerned that the kids didn't die in vain, that something would happen—drunk driving, school bus safety—something would come of this. They didn't want to confront that maybe their children just died and that was it."

Janey took him down to Shannon's bedroom, where just about everything was purple: drapes, bedspread, rug, pillows—Shannon loved purple. Janey showed him pictures and report cards. She told him about the one time Shannon got a B and thought it was a terrible catastrophe. She showed him the ribbons Shannon had won in band. Coale felt thoroughly disgusted at the waste of life. He was hardened to these things—death

---

* Revenue from the 1991 marijuana crop was estimated at $1.4 billion, far exceeding the $843 million tobacco crop. Marijuana is cultivated mostly in the hills of eastern Kentucky, where hemp was grown to make rope during World War II. As coal-mining jobs have been lost, marijuana farming has increased.

and dismemberment were his bread and butter, after all. But the way Janey told the story of how she found out Shannon was gone, he could feel it, it was so terrifying: the late-night phone call, then down to the church, something awful has happened and half of them are dead, and all this time getting closer and closer to the worst thing that could happen.

"These good people were just sitting there, trying to make it, trying to do the right thing all the time, trying to raise their kids," Coale thought, "and all of a sudden one night it's over."

Coale listened as the bereft parents described the children they had lost. He learned, for instance, that Patty Nunnallee had always been a thoughtful child. Even as a toddler in day care, she would save some of her lunch to give her mother. "Once I asked her, 'What did you have for lunch today?' " Karolyn recalled. "She said, 'Ravioli. I saved you some,' and she had a pocket full." From the age of three, Patty made her own bed, and at ten, she taught her six-year-old sister, Jeanne, to tie her own shoes and to read. (Patty won a writing contest in school with an essay about her little sister, "Jeanne, Jeanne, the Bouncing Machine.") Patty loved to read: She took a couple of *Nancy Drew* books on the bus trip, along with her Magna-Doodle, which she could share with her friend Robin. "She always thought of others," Karolyn said. "Like at a buffet line, she'd stand back and let everybody else go first." The thought hung in the air that Patty might have done just that in the rush to escape the bus. "She was a good little girl."

Coale knew it would matter in litigation that the kids had shown talent and done well in school and, when asked what they wanted to be when they grew up, had said things like "doctor" or "lawyer." That would put bigger numbers on the board when it came to loss of lifetime earnings. But to the people in that living room the numbers didn't mean a thing; in fact, nothing meant anything, except trying to do something, somehow, for their children.

As he drove back to Louisville late that night, the faces of the people he'd met kept intruding on Coale's calculations about the case. "Janey, she grabs you by the throat and sits you down and says, 'Let me tell you how it was,' " he thought. "Larry's always looking a step or two ahead: 'Now, if this happens, we do this, and if that happens, we do that.' Always looking a step ahead, so he won't have to look back."

CHAPTER 19

The Fairs did not select Coale on the spot. (They did *nothing* on the spot, having imposed on themselves a seventy-two-hour cooling-off period before making any important decisions.) They had seen other lawyers, and continued seeing more, until they had interviewed about thirty. Small firms they rejected for having insufficient resources to carry on a protracted battle against huge corporate adversaries. Big firms often disqualified themselves for conflict of interest, because they had represented Ford in the past. With two giant assembly plants in metropolitan Louisville, Ford played a dominant role in the local economy,* and the Fairs soon decided they would have to hire a lawyer from some distance away in order to have any confidence that he was beyond Ford's influence.

Skeeters and Bennett, of course, were eager to add the Fairs to their client list. Having publicly offered to do all the bus crash victims' estate and insurance work for nothing, Bennett's four-lawyer firm was soon faced with processing the probate and insurance claims of some fifty-nine individuals. Janey Fair, a former legal secretary, volunteered to help out, without pay, starting the week of May 23, right after Shannon's funeral. In the course of her work at Skeeters & Bennett's office, she noticed that one client had signed a retainer on May 15, one day after the bus crash. The alacrity with which the firm had moved impressed her, but not favorably. She wasn't in the office a week before Terry Bennett attempted to get Janey to sign a retainer herself.

---

* According to Ford Motor Company's Governmental Action Program Handbook, in 1992 the two plants had 5,911 employees, with a payroll of $271,789,641, and paid property taxes of $1,627,776. In addition, Ford's purchases from Kentucky suppliers totaled $63,600,000.

Janey balked at the clause specifying that the plaintiff would pay Skeeters & Bennett one third of any settlement or judgment. While one third was a typical fee for a lawyer representing one client, she knew that lawyers representing scores of plaintiffs in a mass disaster normally took a substantially smaller percentage from each.

"Terry, this is not right," she told Bennett. "I don't think it's a Christian thing to do. Plus, you're going to have to hire product liability lawyers, and they'll take a percentage, too."

He said that the one third would cover those lawyers, too.

"Terry, the contract doesn't say that," Janey insisted. "I can't sign it the way it's written."

Bennett, who looked as though his feelings had been hurt by her remark about un-Christian behavior, didn't press her further. And after that week, Janey, whose bronchitis was worsening by the day, stopped working at the law office. It was then, two weeks after the crash, that Larry Fair got a call from Bennett asking him to come down and talk.

"I got off from work and went down and Terry Bennett basically said, 'We've got to get something straight here. You've got to get your wife to sign this contract,'" Larry recalls. "I just sat there and listened to him talk about different things. He was talking to me alone without my spouse there, which was not something rare with this law firm, getting clientele. The possibility of settlement was innuendoed through the talk. Finally I looked at him and said, 'Terry, you've got a bigger problem than getting my wife to sign that contract, because I haven't signed it either.' He was completely aghast. He was under the impression that I had signed it. He was virtually speechless. It pretty much terminated the conversation then and there, and I left. If you want Janey or me to do something real bad, the best way to get us *not* to do it is to demand that we do it. Maybe that's just hardheaded Tennessean, I don't know."*

The Fairs decided in late June to retain John P. Coale. In addition, they retained Ann Oldfather of Louisville as the local counsel who would serve as the out-of-towner's expert on local law and custom, as well as his interpreter at those critical junctures when it was best to talk Kentuckian to the judge or jury.

The Fairs could only hope that Coale was a great litigator, but they could see for themselves that he was unrivaled at capturing the attention

---

* Bennett declined to be interviewed for this book, citing his concern over issues of lawyer-client confidentiality. Skeeters, who granted the author an interview in connection with a 1989 *People* magazine article, denied that the firm pressured clients or prospective clients in any way.

of the press. And press coverage was a key part of their strategy. Larry had approached their situation in a military, analytical way, and in consultation with Janey had settled upon a battle plan. They had identified their objective: Make school buses safer. The means to reach that objective would be a three-pronged attack: 1. Get stricter government regulation. 2. Win a stinging victory in court to deter manufacturers from building unsafe vehicles in the future. 3. Increase public awareness of school bus safety issues, to help push through the regulation and achieve the deterrence.

Publicity was to Coale what air is to other people. How many lawyers had glossy brochures touting their practice? How many had glossy brochures consisting almost entirely of press clippings, illustrated with eleven pictures of themselves? And how many would start those brochures off like this?

> *John P. Coale has been practicing for 16 years and has been involved in some of the most famous, and controversial, cases in modern legal history. When John becomes involved in a case he can bring the scrutiny of the national media to it. John has been interviewed by such newscasters as Tom Brokaw, Peter Jennings, and Dan Rather. He has appeared on "60 Minutes," "ABC Nightline," "The Today Show," and all three national networks' nightly news.* People, Time, Newsweek, The Washington Post, The International Herald Tribune, *and* The New York Times *are just a few of the publications that have profiled John Coale and his work.*

Only the Fairs chose Coale. Jim and Karolyn Nunnallee followed her lawyer-brother's advice and hired a pair of Louisville lawyers, Larry Franklin and Mike Hance, who had whipped Ford before. (The Fairs, too, had been impressed by Franklin and Hance, but they didn't meet the criterion of being from out of town. In fact, their office was then two floors below that of Ford's Louisville lawyers, a proximity that made the Fairs jumpy.) The others who'd met Coale wished the Fairs and Nunnallees well but decided they just didn't have the stomach for years of litigation; they signed on with Skeeters and Bennett, who were thought to be on the verge of a settlement.

The retainer Coale had originally submitted called for no more than a 20-percent fee, since he anticipated representing a number of clients.

When it turned out that Larry and Janey were Coale's only clients, Larry felt uncomfortable accepting the group rate and asked him if it would be all right to *raise* the fee to 30 percent. Coale acquiesced.

❑

Even as the Fairs were getting ready to begin their battle with Ford, Skeeters and Bennett were about to finish theirs. Toward the end of June the Fairs got an urgent phone call from one of that firm's clients. "You've got to get signed up [with Skeeters & Bennett]," he said. "There's a settlement offer in the works, it's great, it can't be better. There's gonna be plenty of money for everybody. If Janey apologizes to Terry [Bennett], I think he'd take you. It'd be worth a try."

The caller sounded nearly hysterical. It was apparent to the Fairs that he was concerned about more than their welfare. They figured that whatever deal Bennett was working, his clients must have believed it was contingent upon his getting substantially all of the potential plaintiffs to accept it. Other, similar, phone calls followed, and each had the effect of hardening the Fairs' resolve not to consort with Skeeters & Bennett.

Other grieving parents were easier to convince. Diane Daniels, who lost her daughter Mary, recalls:

"The third or fourth [Family Support Group] meeting, Mr. Bennett and Don Skeeters were there and talked about litigation. I was surprised. I just listened. I was just not able to comprehend specifics. Then there was the settlement. They talked to us about that. They told you what to do: 'Come to our offices and sign.' " She was content to do just that.

The plaintiffs in fifty-nine of the sixty-seven cases signed with Skeeters & Bennett. Those in six other cases chose other lawyers, but ended up accepting the settlement negotiated by the Radcliff firm. Only the Fairs and the Nunnallees held out.

On Friday, July 1, seven weeks after the crash, Don Skeeters called a press conference to announce that virtually all of the school bus passengers' families had accepted a settlement from the bus manufacturers. The agreement required that all parties keep its terms secret, but Skeeters said it was "reasonable" and would "spare the families the expense and trauma of years of litigation."

According to sources close to the case, $750,000 was paid out for each of the twenty-four children killed, and much more than that for each of the three adults who died; $63,000 was paid to each uninjured or only slightly injured passenger; and payments varying with the severity of the injury to those more severely hurt. In addition, $1,920,000 was entrusted to Skeeters & Bennett as a fund to cover unforeseen future medical expenses of some of the more gravely injured survivors. Finally, as "a lasting monument" to the crash victims, Ford and Sheller-Globe agreed to jointly contribute $500,000 to an as yet undetermined fund to fight drunk driving. (The money ended up going to Mothers Against Drunk Driving.) The total settlement well exceeded $40 million.

The unprecedented swiftness with which potentially crippling mass-disaster litigation had been stifled in the cradle, before a single lawsuit was filed, amounted to a brilliant financial and public relations coup for Ford Motor Company. Ford had initiated settlement talks with Skeeters & Bennett a few weeks after the crash, in early June. (Sheller-Globe went along for the ride.) By successfully concluding the negotiations with the little local law firm, Ford had kept first-class disaster litigation attorneys out of the case. The specter of twenty-five grieving relatives parading to a nationally televised witness stand had been forever dissolved, as had the nightmare of a mega-million-dollar judgment. With any luck, the last, pesky couple of holdouts would ultimately be bought off or ground down, and a trial, with all of its embarrassing discovery and disclosure, could be avoided altogether. Graduate business school students would be studying this exemplary crisis management for as long as MBA degrees were minted. Modest in their moment of triumph, neither corporation sent a spokesman to the press conference.

Ford associate general counsel Jack Martin did tell *The Wall Street Journal* that Ford and Sheller-Globe, which shared the settlement costs equally, both maintained that they were in no way at fault in the accident. They just paid up because they wanted to avoid "years of litigation in which ultimately a local Kentucky jury would be asked to make a decision as to whether any party could have done anything different" to avoid the deaths. That is, they had reason to fear they would lose. By settling, Martin said, everybody would benefit. The companies avoided "millions and millions of dollars" in defense attorneys' fees as well as the risk of a big jury award. The families got assured compensation.

Ford spokesman Robert Waite said that the families' acceptance of the settlement offer "is a testament to the kind of people they are." Presumably, he meant they were good, nonavaricious, nonvengeful people, which could be taken to imply that those who declined to settle were not such good people.

Rev. Tennison, while not passing judgment on anyone who would insist on pressing a suit, nonetheless did see acceptance as a sign of good character: "The families in accepting were saying, 'I'm not greedy. I don't want to go after Ford Motor Company. Nothing can replace my child.'" He had never dreamed the case could be resolved so favorably so fast, so to him the outcome could mean only one thing: "The settlement was, I feel, a miracle from God."

If so, it was an instance of God helping those who helped themselves. Ford dodged a bullet, and Skeeters and Bennett got rich. Ford and Sheller-Globe paid them a fee of $4.6 million, $2.6 million in cash and $2 million in annuity premiums. Wanting to entice as many potential plaintiffs as possible into settling, Ford had negotiated the lawyers' fee down, so that the clients would get more of the money Ford paid out. The fee came to just over 12 percent of the settlement, not the 33 percent the Skeeters & Bennett retainer agreements had specified. And it was paid directly to the lawyers by Ford and Sheller-Globe *in addition to*—not deducted from—the families' settlements.

To Skeeters and Bennett, an advantage of direct payment from Ford and Sheller-Globe may have been that they did not have to get each client to express his satisfaction by endorsing a check made out to both lawyer and client, as would usually be the case. This way, the law firm was likely to get its money faster. Matters were further expedited by the fact that Skeeters or Bennett *signed* at least some settlement agreements on behalf of their clients, using a power of attorney—which helped explain why some of their clients seemed so thoroughly unfamiliar with the settlement they'd accepted.

Asked about allegations that they had pressured some of their clients to settle by saying that everyone would suffer if anyone held out, Don Skeeters replied, "Each and every one of our clients, independently, made a separate decision that did not involve any of the other clients as to whether or not they wanted to accept a settlement."

That's not the way several of his clients remember it.

Gary and Debbie Atherton's thirteen-year-old daughter, Cynthia, had been especially excited to go on the trip because it was the first big social event since she'd had her braces taken off. She sat in the front row, right behind the driver. After losing their little girl, the Athertons had gone in search of some kind of peace in Gulf Shores, Florida. On the morning of their first day away, Terry Bennett called them. "You need to get back here!" he told them. "You need to be here before midnight."

Debbie Atherton was stunned. "My first thought was, 'They found her.' " But Bennett was calling to say Ford had made an offer, and it had to be dealt with immediately. He picked them up that night at the airport, and took them with him as he rushed to a Louisville hospital; the Athertons waited outside while he conferred with the parents of a badly burned survivor there. Then, Bennett drove to Radcliff with Gary Atherton beside him and Debbie Atherton in the back seat.

"As I sat in the back of a car going down I-65, he explained the settlement offer," Debbie recalls. "I thought, 'I'd rather have my child back. I don't know what you're talking about.' He said we all had to be in one hundred percent agreement or no one got anything. And it had to be by midnight. We were given the impression that everyone had pretty much agreed, and we didn't want to screw it up for everybody else. We signed in the driveway of our house. I felt like I was being herded into a corral ready to be branded."

Mickey Muller, whose daughter, Katrina, was severely burned, had a similar experience: "We were called to Skeeters & Bennett and not told why," she remembers. "We were told, 'Here's the settlement. Everyone must sign by midnight tonight or no one gets anything.' We were given about five minutes to choose a payment option while the lawyer went to the bathroom or something."

All the plaintiffs who were probating a child's estate or serving as the guardians of a minor did go before a judge and affirm that they understood the settlements and had entered into them voluntarily. But that may have been just one more procedure that at least some of them were in no shape to comprehend.

"You were in a daze," Rosemary Martinez recalls, trying to explain her condition in the weeks following her son, Rick's, death. "You went where you were told. You did whatever they—whoever—said. You were in such shock. If they called you from the church and said there's going to be a memorial service at such and such a time, you went. If they said there's going to be a funeral at such and such a time, you went. I just did whatever I was told to do."

Martinez still hadn't brought herself to move the shiny new car in the driveway, the surprise graduation gift that awaited Rick's return from Kings Island, when the phone call came from the lawyer, the phone call about the money.

"We were called to the attorneys' office and the papers were put in front of us and we were told we had about ten minutes to decide [whether to take cash or an annuity]. "We were never asked whether we wanted to accept a settlement at all. I just assumed the attorneys made the settlement. I assumed attorneys did this, they made the settlements between themselves, or the judge ruled, or whoever, and you accepted it.

"They told us everyone had to sign or no one got anything. In fact, whoever the attorney was in the room at the time said to me, *'If I have to fly to Pennsylvania today to get your ex-husband to sign this piece of paper, I will.'* It was like, everyone had to sign.

"We [she and second husband Richard Martinez] both work and make good money and we had insurance on Rick. It wasn't like we didn't have any money. But some of the families we knew didn't. They had nothing. And to be told that no one would get anything— I said, 'Well, we can't be the ones that hold out and leave these other people not even able to pay for the funerals.' So we signed. Weeks later, I thought, 'What the heck did I sign?' They didn't explain to me what it was."

Other Skeeters & Bennett clients are consistent in their recollection: They were given about ten minutes to choose a payment option; they were not allowed to take any documents with them or even to take notes; they were told not to discuss the settlement with anyone, including other clients; they were told everyone must settle or no one would get anything.

Ford's lawyers deny that the settlement was contingent upon Skeeters & Bennett's delivering all of their clients. One thing is certain: the more clients settled, the larger would be Skeeters & Bennett's fee.

The death settlements were in the upper range for children killed in Kentucky, though they were dwarfed by those reached in the aftermath of a September 21, 1989, school bus disaster in Alton, Texas. A Valley Coca-Cola Bottling Company truck with poorly maintained brakes ran a stop sign and knocked a school bus packed with eighty-one students, aged twelve to eighteen, into a pit filled with ten feet of water. Nineteen students were trapped inside the Blue Bird bus, which had just one emergency exit, and drowned. Two died later of their injuries. Seventeen families who lost children settled with the bottling company for an average of $4.5 million per child.

CHAPTER

20

Even before Skeeters announced the settlement, John Coale denounced it. He called it "unheard of" and "unconscionable" to settle without investigating whether Ford knew there were defects in the bus and had decided not to correct them, in which case it could be liable for punitive damages. He said the Fairs would take the bus manufacturers to trial even if they had to do it alone.

The day the mass settlement was disclosed, the Nunnallees made a stunning counteroffer to the bus manufacturers: Instead of $750,000, they would take *one dollar* if Ford would agree to recall the 19,200 Ford-built, pre-1977-standard school buses the company estimated were still on the road, and either install a cage around the gas tanks or remount them inside the frame rails. Jim Nunnallee explained, "If someone was ever injured or killed in a similar accident, and we hadn't done everything we could to prevent it from happening again, we couldn't live with our-selves." If a recall was not feasible, the Nunnallees suggested a buy-back or trade-in incentive program.

Ford spokesman Robert Waite replied publicly that Ford had been "actively considering" a voluntary recall ever since the crash, but that it would absolutely not agree to a recall as part of a settlement. An auto company had never before recalled vehicles as part of the judgment or settlement in a liability case, and Ford apparently didn't want to set a precedent.

Waite cautioned that although Ford had considered retrofitting its older buses, the cost of modifications could be almost as much as the value of the buses, some of which then sold for as little as $1,000. He also said Ford was concerned that modifying the old buses might give their owners "a false sense of security," encouraging them to keep buses running that should be retired. You can't "make a twenty-year-old bus brand new," he said. The Louisville lawyer retained by Ford, Bill Grubbs, said that Ford officials wanted to meet directly with the Nunnallees to discuss their proposal.

The Nunnallees met on July 8 with Grubbs and Procter Robison of Ford's corporate law department. Afterward, the Nunnallees's attorney Mike Hance announced that the Ford lawyers had said "something like this would be the right thing to do and they would like to try to do it." Assuming his paraphrase to be accurate, a careful reader will note that the Ford lawyers did not say they would do it; they did not say they would try to do it; they said they would *like* to *try* to do *something like* it. Still, Jim Nunnallee came out of the meeting very pleased. "I trust their sincerity," he said.

The Ford lawyers said the company would take thirty days to evaluate the feasibility of the plan—which was perplexing, since just the day before they'd said Ford had been studying the advisability of a recall ever since the crash in May.

On July 11, the Fairs filed suit in Carroll County Circuit Court. Their complaint against Ford Motor Company and Sheller-Globe Corporation sought punitive damages, alleging that the manufacturers had acted recklessly, willfully, and wantonly—*consciously disregarding* the danger they were creating—when Ford placed an unshielded fuel tank next to the front door of the bus; and when Sheller-Globe built a school bus body with flammable seats, inadequate emergency exits, and a too-narrow aisle. The Fairs said they had never even considered settling, as it would do nothing to promote school bus safety. "There can be no justice for Shannon," Janey said, "but I don't want another mother to have to put her child on a school bus over an unprotected gas tank. I want safety for all children." They would consider dropping the suit if Ford actually came through with the action the Nunnallees were seeking, but they doubted that would happen.

The Nunnallees filed suit the same day to meet a legal deadline, but continued their negotiations with Ford on the recall. On August 27, they returned to Louisville to meet again with Ford's lawyers Grubbs and Robison, thinking at last Ford would be ready to move on their proposal to retrofit the older buses. They were disappointed. Ford's engineers had found that the installation of cages on the old buses could present serious safety risks. To mount the cage two dozen holes had to be drilled in the frame. Besides, the company was now estimating the cost at up to $2,000 per bus, though a Ford spokesman stressed that safety, not cost, would determine Ford's final decision on what to do.

Impatient for action, the Nunnallees made another proposal: If it was impractical to retrofit all the older buses with cages, they would be satisfied if Ford would endow a fund to promote school bus safety, through research, or perhaps by providing free push-out windows and additional emergency doors for buses that needed them. (The *Courier-Journal* editorialized in support of this proposal.) Ford said they would think it over and give the Nunnallees a final answer by the end of September. "We feel like they're dealing with us in good faith," Karolyn Nunnallee said hopefully.

Ford never got back to them, and that fall the Nunnallees gave up and decided to pursue their lawsuit.

CHAPTER

21

The Fairs were not litigious people. They'd never filed a lawsuit before, though they'd had their chances if they were of a mind to. When Shannon was two and a half, in the summer of 1976, she made a mistake. She ran between two parked cars into the street, and was struck by the rear wheel of a Corvette that an off-duty soldier was driving by. Her leg was broken. That she had come through all but unscathed was cause for celebration and thanksgiving in the Fair family. But for a while, thoughts of how close Shannon had come to being killed would drift through their minds like black clouds in a threatening sky. Sometimes it seemed the evil that might have happened was more real than the good that had in fact transpired, so much more gripping is terror than joy.

In such circumstances people commonly expiate their fear by turning it to anger and suing the bastard who drove the car. The Fairs did not. "The guy didn't do anything wrong," was how Larry looked at it; Janey, too. Shannon was just wild, that's all. She even kept climbing the slide in the playground with that little cast on her leg; the doctors had to constantly replaster it.

Now years had passed and the worst had happened, and this time the Fairs believed it *was* someone's fault. Their inclination was to fight. That's what people like them did. They were hardheaded rednecks (self-described), and each had their family stories to instruct them.

Larry was the only child of Hazel and Ray Chase Fair ("Chase" to his close friends, and "R.C." to everybody else). Larry's dad had "run a hard road," as folks say in Tennessee. He had to quit school at fifteen and go to work as a water boy for the construction workers building the Bemberg Rayon factory in Johnson City. Pretty soon he was working in the plant itself; he made first-line supervisor in two years, in charge of ten or twelve workers spooling rayon, but that was as far as he could go, with no education, and after twenty-seven years he gave two weeks' notice and quit.

He told Hazel, "Hon, I bought us a grocery store."

She said, "We'll starve."

And he said, "How can we starve in a grocery store?" (Hazel's face would turn red every time she told that story.)

She quit her job at the plant, too. (Hazel, who did have a high school education, had a position at the same level as her husband, having been promoted during World War II when the men were all gone, and frozen in place thereafter.) They ran a small general store on the outskirts of Johnson City, with one gas pump by the steps; after a dozen years they tried to retire but couldn't make it and opened a little store again. All together they rang up twenty-odd years of fourteen-hour days, six-day weeks, no vacation, until they finally sold the store to Janey's sister Patty and her husband in 1971. R.C. died five years later.

The grocery was of course a total-family enterprise. Larry's mother kept the books and Larry, who started stocking the shelves in third grade, was putting in sixty-hour weeks while he carried a full load at East Tennessee State, getting his degree in elementary education.

Larry learned a couple of things working in the store: 1) He never wanted to work in a store again. 2) His folks were "fanatics about honesty." R.C. would run credit all week and his customers would settle up on payday. The story goes that one Friday morning a man came in and said, "Give me two dollars of gas and I'll pay you this afternoon." The afternoon came and went, but the man did not return. A couple of years later, the same man, now with a reputation as a thug, came in with a friend and bought a 25-cent pack of cigarettes with a $20 bill. Larry's dad laid the bill on the register as he always did, to avoid any disputes about the denomination, and counted out the change: "Twenty-five and seventy-five is one, two, three, four, five; and five is ten, five is fifteen, three is eighteen; *and the two dollars you owe me for gas makes twenty.*"

The man reached over to snatch back his $20 bill only to find that R.C. had a .38 pistol leveled at his nose. "Will you please leave the store," R.C. said firmly.

The man called the cops, and shortly R.C. was arrested for menacing, or some such offense. He pled guilty and was fined $68.

"It cost you $68 to collect that $2," Hazel observed dryly.

"Yes, but the son of a bitch paid me," R.C. replied.

❏

It was at the store that Janey Mullins and Larry Fair discovered each other, though they'd known each other just about all their lives. They grew up as neighbors, three quarters of a mile apart but with only a few houses in between, in the semi-rural, working-class Johnson City section called Pine Grove. Until the third grade, Janey, the second of three daughters of a long-haul trucker and his wife, lived high up on a hill overlooking her family's eleven-acre field of corn and vegetables. Then they moved down into a white clapboard ranch not far from the cemetery.

Both their families could easily walk to the little brick church down the road, Pine Grove Methodist, every Sunday morning and Sunday evening and Wednesday night, and they did.

But Larry was a couple of years younger, and to Janey he was still just some kid who was around, when she graduated Daniel Boone High School and went away to take business courses in St. Petersburg, Florida, where she stayed with an aunt and uncle. But she came back a year later, and went to work as the legal secretary for Robert Mahoney May, Esq., who was the mayor of nearby Jonesborough and also the lawyer for the county and the bank and the railroad. One day in 1966 she stopped at the Fairs' store for help because her car had been making an awful noise since she'd had a tire changed. Larry found a lug nut rolling around inside the hubcap. He yelled at her about how dangerous that was and what a lousy job it was.

Soon after the lug nut episode, Larry teased Janey about how dirty her car was. She was surprised to hear herself say, "Let's wash them," her car and his. He may have said, "How about a movie instead?" Anyway she can't remember washing her car. Maybe they washed his. They never stopped dating after that, and two years later, in the spring of 1968, as he was about to graduate from college, Larry proposed. They were sitting in his car, maybe at a drive-in movie. Janey can remember him, as he popped the question, holding the steering wheel tight with white-knuckled hands, like he was about to drive off a cliff.

They got married that August of 1968 at Pine Grove Park Methodist Church, with the reception downstairs.

❏

While Lawrence Fair was courting Janey Mullins, far away there occurred a disaster that they would one day come to know too well.

On the afternoon of March 7, 1968, near Baker, California, a short-order cook, who had gotten drunk and quit his job, tossed his girlfriend's phonograph records into his car and drove off to see her in Las Vegas, ninety-five miles away. Ten minutes later, he was driving his white 1964 Chevy Impala at 65 mph on the wrong side of a divided highway, Interstate 15, and ran head-on into a Greyhound bus bound for Las Vegas from Los Angeles. A spring from the bus's right-front suspension was rammed backward and pierced the diesel fuel tank mounted just behind the right-front wheel. Diesel fuel sprayed up through the damaged plywood floor into the passenger area, and a fire erupted.

None of the bus passengers had been killed in the collision itself. The National Transportation Safety Board's investigation found that the bus outweighed the car 33,000 to 3,750 pounds. When objects of such disparate mass meet, the heavier acts like a baseball bat, and the lighter like the ball. The bus, which had braked to 25 mph, continued forward at 17 mph after the impact. The instantaneous 8 mph deceleration jolted the bus passengers no more than if the bus had run into a wall at 8 mph. But because of the rapid spread of the fire and the lack of adequate emergency exits, nineteen of the bus's thirty passengers were trapped and died in the conflagration. (The car, which had braked to 53 mph, instantly lost all of its forward velocity and was pushed backward at 17 mph. Its driver was killed instantly.)

Noting that several people, including his boss, co-workers, and roommate, had observed that the cook was too drunk to drive but had done nothing to stop him, the NTSB recommended that the government launch urgent programs to impress upon the public each person's responsibility to prevent others from driving drunk. The safety board also urgently called for federal regulations requiring that bus fuel tanks and emergency escape systems be performance-tested so that future calamities might be avoided.

Nine years would pass before a certain school bus was built, but the suggested fuel tank and escape route regulations would still not be in force.

❑

In wedding Janey Mullins, Larry Fair had married the descendant of a rich and powerful old American family, though that and 50 cents might have gotten him a ride on the subway (had there been a subway in Johnson City, population 40,000). It had been generations since her branch of the family tree had borne financial fruit, but the fact that she and her sisters and cousins grew up in modest circumstances in no way diminished Janey's pride in her progenitors and in the nobility of spirit that had been her sole inheritance. Early on she'd surveyed her prospects and found she had two options in life: She could be poor but honest, or she could just be poor. So she treasured her integrity.

Janey knew who she was, and anyone who tried to take advantage of her would soon find out. As her little sister, Gloria, the brassy one of the three Mullins sisters, lately employed as a prison guard, put it: "I'll tell you one thing. Ford Motor Company picked on the wrong family when they picked on us."

Stories of their forebears' standing up for themselves, and for what was right, had been fed the Mullins girls with their mother's milk. And Gloria had festooned this oral history with little jewels of fact dug out of the library. Thus, when harried by visions of Ford's armies arrayed in full battle dress at the courthouse steps, Janey could trumpet into the field the legions of her ancestry. Leading the charge would be her indomitable forefather Johann von der Heydt, who, it was said, fought in court for half a century to defend his lands and finally prevailed.

Johann, a member of the Huguenot Protestant minority in France, was a prosperous young baron when his father, mother, sister, and fiancée were slaughtered by Catholics in 1705. The twenty-one-year-old fled to Amsterdam, where he married and became a successful banker and merchant; from there, he set sail for the New World.

Now known as Joist Hite, he bought 40,000 acres near what became Winchester, Virginia. When the British colonial governor granted him another 100,000, Hite's toubles began. Much of the land had never been surveyed, and an Englishman, Lord Fairfax, believing he already owned it, filed lawsuits to challenge Hite's title to each new parcel.

The lands in question lay west of the Blue Ridge Mountains in Spotsylvania County, which then extended indefinitely westward. To record and defend his property deeds, Hite wanted a courthouse within a couple of days' ride, preferably one where Lord Fairfax's connections were inferior to his own, and how better to get in on the ground floor at a court than to build it yourself? In 1734, Hite petitioned the governor and carved a new county, Orange County, out of Spotsylvania. Four years later he carved out another county, Frederick, with the county seat at Winchester.

"Joist Hite didn't believe in 'tommy-hawk' rights to land, where ownership was recorded by blazing a tree," Janey Fair explains. "He wanted everything done legal at a courthouse. He spoke German, French, and Dutch but didn't speak English very well; he thought people would try to slick him out of stuff. So he wanted everything recorded. And if he had to build a courthouse to have things recorded, that's what he did." The cause of *Fairfax* v. *Hite* dampened and flared for fifty-six years before being resolved, but in the end—long after the original protagonists had died—the Fairfax claims were defeated.

Hite's son John became a friend of George Washington, of whom the elder Hites didn't approve. ("They thought Washington was a money grubber. Plus they did not like the way he played fast and loose with Sally Fairfax," Janey confides, referring to the already affianced Washington's avowedly unconsummated love for the wife of his friend and neighbor, George William Fairfax, Lord Fairfax's second cousin. "They thought that was scandalous.") Captain John Hite fought and was captured in the Revolutionary War, and was awarded 4,000 more acres for his trouble.

The Hite family grew even faster than its lands, and after 200 years all the descendants could hardly have stood side by side on the estate, had anyone been able to put it back together.

One of John Hite, Jr.'s, score of offspring was Andrew Hite, who was Janey's mother's grandfather. Andrew's wife, Great Granny Hite, was a tiny woman who had to climb onto her mule from a tree stump. A midwife before there were any doctors in Rock Springs, she rode that mule around eastern Tennessee, taking care of the sick and delivering babies. (One of them grew up to be the area's first physician, and she would one day work with him.) Great Granny Hite kept on ministering to the sick into her old age, when her arthritis got so bad she could hardly hold on to the reins. She told the Good Lord, "Lord, You've got to cure this arthritis if I'm to keep helping people." And, the story goes, on a clear, bright sunny day, as she was hanging out the laundry, a bolt of lightning hit her and her arthritis was gone. Great Granny Hite thanked God, got on her mule and rode off to help the next person. She lived ten years after that, and her arthritis never did come back.

Andrew and Great Granny Hite's daughter, Sarah Isabelle (who swore she saw that lightning bolt), would be known to Janey's generation as Granny Angel. A midwife herself, she wed Thomas Angel, who reputedly had just the right temperament to marry into the Hites: As a little boy in North Carolina, the story goes, Grandpa Angel would advertise his family's abolitionist beliefs by standing atop the fence, shouting, "Hooray for Abraham Lincoln!" as the Confederate soldiers marched by.

In 1911, when Grandpa Angel was fifty-six, Grandma Angel bore their ninth child, Frances, who would marry T. R. Mullins. Frances and T.R. had a son who died at birth, and three daughters, Pat, Janey, and Gloria.

T.R. was the tough son of a mountain man. "A lot of people would walk forty miles of bad road to avoid my grandpa," Gloria notes, not without pride. But Grandpa Mullins had his gentler qualities, too. Patty remembers him showing her how to lift a heavy object using a board and rock as lever and fulcrum. "See, you can do anything you want," he said.

"These are the people who lived many years ago," Janey Mullins Fair says, when she introduces you to her ancestors. "We should be so"—she searches for just the right word—"*stalwart.*"

CHAPTER

22

For a couple of months after the calamity, Janey Fair joined a handful of bereaved parents, mothers mostly, for group counseling once a week at Ireland Army Hospital at Fort Knox. (Larry found emotional support in his own way, frequenting the Army Legal Assistance Office, where he'd mine the Martindale-Hubbel attorney directory for lawyers' names, and ask questions about the legal process.) The chaplains doing the counseling seemed always to be asking whether the parents were angry. Janey didn't feel angry. She couldn't feel anything.

The group met at the social services office on the second floor, which was just downstairs from the maternity ward where Shannon had been born fourteen years before. One minute Janey would be thinking, "I can't believe I was ever right here giving birth to her"; and the next minute she'd be thinking, "I can't believe I'm here *now,* for a reason so—opposite." It was as though the past and the present had collided with such violence that both were destroyed, casting Janey adrift.

She could remember—could not help remembering—the day Shannon was born, January 31, 1974. When the labor pains started at five o'clock in the afternoon, Janey began walking around and around their Fort Knox apartment. With her firstborn, Donald, she had heeded the advice of her midwife grandmother and scrubbed the floors during the first hours of labor, but this time her mother was with her and wouldn't abide that harsh prescription. So they walked, for two hours, until her mother declared it was time to go to the hospital—though Janey knew it was too soon. Larry drove them over, and there the three of them walked the halls for two more hours.

At nine o'clock Janey phoned the army obstetrician on call, who was at a dinner party across post, and said, "You're going to need to come in now. I'm ready." Then, at a nurse's insistence, she went and lay down on a bed. The doctor arrived within ten minutes; Janey was watching the clock. She'd learned from delivering her first baby not to give up your eyeglasses. (Somebody's got to time the contractions.)

Larry had stated that he did not desire to be present at the delivery. It wasn't allowed when Donald had been born two years earlier at Fort Polk, Louisiana, and Larry saw no reason to depart from procedure now. He and the doctor were talking about moose hunting in Wyoming when all of a sudden Janey said, "I'm having the baby!" The doctor made Larry push the bed into the delivery room, and quickly told him to lift up Janey's back. The baby shot out across the room and was fielded by the doctor at about 10:00 P.M. She was as chubby as she could be, seven pounds, six ounces, and nineteen inches long, with a full head of hair.

They named her Shannon Rae Fair. Rae was after Larry's father, Ray. And Shannon, Janey had picked from a book of names, because she liked the sound of it.

❑

The year of Shannon's birth would also be the year that Congress passed the Motor Vehicle and School Bus Safety Amendments of 1974. Congressmen John Moss (D-Cal.) and Les Aspin (D-Wisc.) had introduced the legislation in the wake of several highly publicized fatal school bus crashes. The law required the secretary of transportation to propose safety standards for school buses no later than April 27, 1975, including standards for emergency exits and fuel system integrity. After a period for public comment and revision, regulations were to take effect no later than October 27, 1976.

It wouldn't turn out that way. Thanks to the automotive industry's unremitting opposition to safety regulations—and the federal government's waning commitment to regulatory action—the school bus safety standards would be delayed until April 1, 1977. The bus chassis that would carry Shannon Fair and her friends to their deaths would roll off the Ford assembly line nine days earlier, on March 23, 1977.

PART TWO

THE

BEGINNING

CHAPTER
23

School bus standards were already years overdue when Shannon was born. The National Traffic and Motor Vehicle Safety Act of 1966, which created the National Traffic Safety Bureau,* had required the issuance of initial motor vehicle safety standards by January 31, 1967. Seven years later, only two safety standards drafted specifically for school buses—regulating mirrors and window retention—were in effect.

The safety act had been passed in response to steadily mounting carnage on the nation's highways; deaths had reached a then-all-time high of 49,163 deaths in 1965. The medical and scientific community had begun to look at auto accidents as a public health problem. It had long been known that the least effective public health measures are those whose success depends upon a change of behavior by millions of individuals; the most effective steps change the environment in which individuals behave. A modern sewer system and municipal water supply combat cholera more effectively than any amount of public instruction on hygiene. Similarly, a change in the motorists' environment could be expected to reduce the rate of traffic fatalities more effectively than law enforcement and public information campaigns aimed at getting people to drive more carefully. Since changes in the environment outside the vehicle—the road—could never entirely eliminate driver error and crashes, safety engineers had begun to turn their attention to "the second crash," that of the car occupant's body with the interior of the car. Seat belts, energy-absorbing steering columns, padded dashboards, the elimination of sharply protruding instrumentation—these measures, which

* The forerunner of the National Highway Traffic Safety Administration (NHTSA).

would enhance a vehicle's "crashworthiness," held the promise of saving lives by the tens of thousands. But they all cost money, and automobile manufacturers were loath to be the first out with a higher sticker price for features that did not shine in the showroom.

In 1965, Ralph Nader's book *Unsafe at Any Speed* popularized the notion that unsafe cars, not just unsafe drivers, were killing people. At least as important as the book was General Motors' ham-handed response to it. The corporate giant played Goliath to Nader's David: When GM was caught sicking private detectives on the author in an attempt to dig up dirt on him, the public rallied to the cause of regulating Detroit.

In those days, the federal government seemed like just the outfit for the job. This was the era, before the disillusionment wrought by Vietnam, when America was going to be a Great Society. If death on the highway was a public health problem, then like all public problems, including poverty, illiteracy, and racial discrimination, it would be solved by enlightened public action. The 1966 act passed unanimously, 317 to 0 in the House and 76 to 0 in the Senate. Powered by that mandate, the new safety agency set about its task of taming the auto industry with great vigor and optimism, issuing twenty-three regulations in its first year. But the automotive industry had other ideas, and soon the regulatory juggernaut had slowed to a crawl. The School Bus Safety Amendments of 1974 were spurred by consumer groups in response to the inaction of the National Highway Traffic Safety Administration (NHTSA).

❏

On May 9, 1973, around the time Shannon Fair was conceived, the House subcommittee on commerce and finance, responsible for overseeing NHTSA, convened in Room 2226 of the Rayburn House Office Building for hearings on the school bus safety bill. Representative Les Aspin, complaining of "delays and delays and continual delays," declared, "Since the DOT is unwilling to exercise its responsibility under the law, Congress must take the lead and must insist that they promulgate comprehensive school bus safety standards within six months.

"The Department of Transportation maintains that in terms of a cost-benefit analysis, it is worth neither the time nor the effort of the DOT to protect our school children from shoddily constructed school buses," Aspin continued. But, he argued, the statistics masked the actual safety performance of school buses. The big yellow vehicles were generally driven slowly and carefully, and other drivers tended to exercise care near them, so the total number of school bus accidents was

held down (to 47,000 in 1971). But when a school bus accident did occur, Aspin said, it was often far more devastating to the occupants than
it would have been had the school bus been safely designed and constructed.

"School buses are probably the unsafest vehicles on the road," he
concluded, "because when they are involved in accidents, the results are
often catastrophic." And yet, he noted, school buses could be made much
safer quite cheaply. In fact, school bus body manufacturers had told the
committee that strengthening the riveting of the body side panels—which
tended to separate along their flesh-ripping edges in a crash—would
hike the retail price just $300 or $400 above the then average $8,000,
which was less than the cost of a Cadillac. Emergency window exits, which
two school bus manufacturers, Wayne and Ward, *asked* the committee to
require by law, would run $12 each. The trouble was, no manufacturer
on its own could afford to incorporate safety improvements as standard
equipment, because its less safe competitors would then be able to build
and sell their buses more cheaply—and even a small unit-price differential could be decisive in competitive fleet sales that went to the lowest
bidder. School transportation authorities, perpetually strapped for cash,
were disinclined to insist upon, or even accept, improved safety features,
which they were constrained to view as unnecessary luxuries. Safety features offered as extra-cost options, such as additional seat padding or a
second emergency exit door, had found few buyers. Few safety changes
would be made unless they were compulsory for all.

But the agency responsible for mandating such improvements was
missing in action. Acting NHTSA administrator James E. Wilson testified
to the committee that, although 5,000 children were injured annually in
accidents involving school buses, only about ninety were killed, and of
those, two thirds were pedestrians. Of the thirty or so annual passenger
deaths, most resulted from the child being ejected through a window or
through a breach in the bus's body. He said his agency had already issued
a standard, effective September 1973, that would require the strengthening of bus windows; a standard for energy-absorbing seats was in the
pipeline; and NHTSA was working on joint-strength requirements. As for
fuel systems, Wilson testified, "We question whether death and injury
statistics warrant rulemaking at this time concerning fuel systems." So, he
said, it really wouldn't be necessary for Congress to step in with mandated
rules and deadlines, thanks just the same.

Representative John Y. McCollister (R-Neb.), weighing in against new
regulations, pointed out that if the safety features added $1,000 to the

price of each of the 30,000 new buses sold each year, that would amount to an additional $30 million levy on the nation's school districts annually. He could have pointed out that since only about thirty children per year were dying on school buses, even if the standards could save every one of them (which they no doubt could not), that would be an expenditure of $1 million per life—this at a time when a NHTSA study had put the cost to society of a lost life at $200,000.

Of course, there were all kinds of ways to look at costs. Senator Charles Percy (R-Ill.), who came over to the House to testify at the hearings, argued that $1,000 per bus came to $100 per year over the life of the bus, which came to 56 cents per school day, which came to less than ½ cent per pupil per ride. Subcommittee chairman John Moss pointed out that the same legislators who were debating whether it was worthwhile to spend $1,000 per school bus on safety would be voting on a supplemental appropriations bill the very next day to provide roughly $275 million to fund the bombing of Cambodia for seven more weeks, or enough to spend $1,000 on every one of the 275,000 school buses in America. "So this brings into focus a question of values and judgment and priorities. . . . I think the question really is, Can we afford *not* to provide the safety which is technologically feasible at this time?"

On that ninth day of May 1973, when the conflagration in Carroll County was a spark beyond the horizon, Moss questioned the acting NHTSA administrator, James E. Wilson:

Mr. MOSS: In general, a school bus is a pretty raw piece of equipment that has changed little and offers little prospect of minimizing injury should an accident occur?

Mr. WILSON: We concur.

Mr. MOSS: This includes the body, the way it is put together, the basic design, the number of rivets, the size of panels, the frame, the seats: the whole thing just unfolds as something inviting an accident to occur? Is that too harsh?

Mr. WILSON: At least after the accident occurs, the interior of a bus is a rather hostile atmosphere.

Mr. MOSS: That can be readily envisioned prior to the occurrence of the accident?

Mr. WILSON: It certainly can.

Mr. MOSS: Is it not also true that [the NTSB has repeatedly called for changes in school bus standards] whether it be the *placement of the gasoline tanks and the kind of force they might be able to withstand* [emphasis added] or what appear to me to be unusually fragile seats? . . . Would you want to ride in a school bus to the office each morning?

Mr. WILSON: Hardly.

❑

The National Transportation Safety Board,* which investigated not just statistics but actual flesh-and-blood accidents, had tried to slap the federal highway safety regulators at NHTSA out of their cost-benefit trance. "In the school bus field," the NTSB concluded in a 1970 report on inadequate body strength, "the degree of effort for safety has not been traditionally determined by cost/benefit consideration, but by the unique need for protection of the innocent children who ride school buses, and who are almost totally unable to assure their safety by their own actions." They cannot, for instance, choose which make of bus to ride. "The consideration of justice, in the Board's view, should override the question of whether the cost of complete assembly could be demonstrated to be less than the dollar value of the lives saved."

The NTSB had found that inadequately riveted side panels had contributed to the deaths and injuries in two 1968 Alabama school bus accidents.† The rivets holding the side panels onto school buses were far fewer and farther between than those fastening the sides of transit or intercity buses. In fact, school bus riveting did not meet the Society of Automotive Engineers' (SAE) standards. The yellow side panels of a school bus amounted to nothing more than "covering material," fastened just tightly enough to keep out the wind and the weather but contributing virtually nothing to structural strength in a crash. School bus safety activists called the buses tin coffins, cracker boxes, cookie cutters or yellow tin cans.

The NTSB found that the strength of joints on school buses could be tripled or quadrupled just by increasing the number of rivets. Yet, the safety board pointed out, even this moderate expense raised the question

---

* The NTSB is an independent federal agency established by Congress to determine the cause of accidents, evaluate the effectiveness of government agencies involved in transportation safety, and make recommendations. It has no regulatory or enforcement power.

† A subsequent report on a 1972 wreck in Congers, N.Y., came to the same conclusion.

of what benefit would be bought for the cost, because "the doubling or tripling of the number of fasteners needed in a bus of this type is not a necessity for normal operation, but is required only to obtain crash protection for occupants. . . . The question is, are the safety benefits worth the increased cost of assembly which would be necessary?

"It is evident that the number of lives to be saved annually by such structural changes does not exceed 20 to 30 children. . . . It might well be that, in this particular case, it could be shown that the cost of saving lives by fully joining school bus structures might be relatively high per life saved.

"A second question concerning this proposal is what priority it should enjoy as a project of DOT compared to other methods of reducing highway fatalities. The lives potentially savable by stronger school bus structure is less than 0.1 percent of the total national fatality toll. Thus it can correctly be said that among the various safety efforts which might be applied by such agencies as the National Highway Safety Bureau, efforts to establish this particular correction would be of low priority."

But the NTSB went on, "If the priority of school bus structural improvement is low in terms of the total national needs in which DOT and the National Highway Safety Bureau must function, school bus fatality and injury is nevertheless a predominant concern in two areas, the school bus manufacturing industry and school bus operators and users."

The NTSB report writers, back in 1970, had spelled out a point that would be of critical importance in the Carrollton bus crash litigation: School bus safety may properly represent a small part of NHTSA's business, but it's a big part of the school bus business. Maybe NHTSA, trying to allocate its limited resources so as to coerce the most safety for its regulatory dollar, might put school buses near the bottom of the list. But school buses are at the top of the list for a school bus manufacturer; and a school bus manufacturer has the resources to build a bus that is reasonably designed for the safe transport of children. Therefore, a manufacturer called to account for the deaths of children aboard one of its buses is not making sense when it argues, as Ford would, that school buses have such a low fatality rate that they are the "safest vehicles on the road." The relevant question is not how many people die on school buses compared to how many die in cars or trucks. The question is, how many people died in a school bus who need not have died, had the bus been designed and built as well as it reasonably could have been.

The 1973 subcommittee hearings led to the school bus safety amendments, which were signed into law by President Gerald Ford on October 27, 1974, when Shannon Fair was nine months old. The legislation required NHTSA to promulgate minimum safety standards for eight aspects of school bus construction, including joint strength, emergency exits and fuel systems, to go into effect no later than October 27, 1976.

The legislation was a learning experience for NHTSA. In its notice of proposed rulemaking for the joint-strength standard, the regulatory agency stated, "It is obvious from voluminous mail and Congressional interest that society places a much higher value on the safety of its children than a conventional cost-benefit analysis would indicate."

CHAPTER
24

NHTSA issued a Notice of Proposed Rulemaking for Federal Motor Vehicle Standard (FMVSS) 301-75, school bus fuel system integrity, on April 8, 1975. "Although available data indicate that school bus fires have occurred very infrequently, the potential for such fires exists," read the notice, signed by Robert L. Carter, associate administrator of motor vehicle programs. "The danger to which children would be exposed in the event of a crash-caused school bus fire is great and poses a threat to large groups of individuals who normally travel in such vehicles."

The agency proposed that school buses with a maximum gross (loaded) vehicle weight exceeding 10,000 lbs.—that is, typical school buses, as opposed to small vans—manufactured on or after April 1, 1976, would be subject to an amended Federal Motor Vehicle Safety Standard 301. The standard would require that the bus, with its tank nearly full, must be able to sustain a 30 mph impact at any point by a 4,000 lb. contoured moving barrier* without leaking more than one ounce of fuel per minute from anywhere in the fuel system. The goal of such performance standards was to ensure that no one should die from a post-crash fire in an otherwise survivable accident. Comments on the proposal were due by May 15, 1975.

NHTSA's required Environmental Impact Statement noted that manufacturers of vehicles already subject to a fuel system integrity standard ordinarily complied by "relocat[ing] the fuel tank, fuel tank filler pipe and other vulnerable components to a position that provides maximum protection and shielding by adjacent structural components." Application of the standard to school buses was therefore not expected to increase the vehicles' weight or consumption of fuel. "For compliance, manufacturers have a variety of options, ranging from a relatively simple relocation of the fuel system without any weight penalty to a shielding arrangement which could add as much as 200 lbs. of structure steel. This is considered the most adverse configuration, likely to be adopted by very few, if any, school bus manufacturers."

NHTSA and industry minds did not work alike. Rather than relocate the tank, say between the frame rails behind the rear axle, all the chassis manufacturers would choose to meet 301 by means of a cage around the tank. Precisely why they were so averse to moving the tank would turn out to be a critical issue in the Carrollton crash litigation.

Some automotive safety advocates found the regulation too lenient. The Center for Auto Safety, a private, Washington, D.C., based group, urged NHTSA to impose a zero-spillage standard: "Given the youth of school bus occupants and the existence of fewer escape paths than available for other vehicles . . . the need for a no-leakage requirement for school buses is much greater than for other vehicles."

Physicians for Auto Safety also objected: "We do not think the requirements go far enough. The tank should be placed away from crash susceptible areas and away from doors."

Ford's Automotive Safety Office (ASO) formulated the corporation's

---

* A 30 mph impact by a two-ton steel test barrier is roughly equivalent to a 40-to-45 impact by a two-ton vehicle, because a striking vehicle crumples, absorbing energy, whereas the barrier imparts virtually all of its energy to the struck vehicle.

opinion and sent it to NHTSA on June 27, 1975. (The School Bus Manufacturers Institute, representing the bus body companies, while affirming its commitment to "the design and production of 'safe'* school buses" had, with the support of several congressmen and the Motor Vehicle Manufacturers Association, successfully petitioned NHTSA for a six-week extension of the comment period.)

School bus fires were too infrequent to warrant such a stringent standard, in Ford's view. "Ford endorses the intent of the Notice to reduce the possibility of fire occurring in school buses," read the letter signed by John C. Eckhold of the Automotive Safety Office. But "the stringent timing schedule will create an almost insurmountable problem for Ford as a chassis manufacturer."

If a new fuel tank proved necessary to meet the standard, Eckhold's letter went on, Ford's "best estimate" of the time required to develop a new tank would be fifty-eight weeks. (By comparison, Ford had whipped up an entire car, albeit the Pinto, in three years.) And that fifty-eight-week effort could not even begin until Ford was informed of the school bus body builders' plans to meet the standard; and those plans, in turn, could not possibly be developed until final promulgation of the standard. So all in all, Eckhold concluded, "It is evident that the proposed effective date of April 1, 1976, could not be met."

In fact, according to the later testimony of Chief Engineer John Durstine, it actually took Ford's Heavy Truck Operations just twenty-six weeks to design and test the cage, get the parts on hand, and stand ready for mass production of buses conforming to the regulation.

❑

The industry's familiar plea for more lead time had been addressed at the May 1973 subcommittee hearings by William Haddon, Jr., M.D., the National Highway Safety Bureau's first administrator, who had moved on to serve as president of the Insurance Institute for Highway Safety. He was asked by Representative Moss how much time would be needed to get safer automotive fuel systems into production. "I personally think it would be a relatively easy matter, if the managers involved cared to do so," he replied. "There are many problems in the world for which we do not know solutions, but here is a problem that for many decades we have

---

* The trade association apparently could not bring itself to use the word *safe* without fencing it off with quotation marks.

known how to handle. The approaches are well known and straight-forward. For example, the first approach is to build structure around the tank in such a way that impact forces are less likely to reach it with a violence sufficient to cause rupturing, tearing, and dislocation. . . . There need not and should not be automobile designs that place hostile hard-ware, such as sharp bolts and sharp ridges, adjacent to the gas tank. . . . I am not sanguine that we will see these [improvements] without some sort of coercion, because these problems have been known for a long time, and still they are there. I suspect that if the issue were finding out, about this time of year, that a competing vehicle had a supposedly attractive chromium strip on the side of its car, and that it might detract from sales of his own vehicle, the manufacturer might find a way to make a change before production."

❏

Instead of NHTSA's proposed crash test standard, Ford suggested that the Bureau of Motor Carrier Safety regulation already in force for trucks could be applied to school buses, "particularly in view of the fact that school bus fires have occurred very infrequently." The BMCS standard required that the fuel tank be filled with water and dropped so as to land on its corner from a height of thirty feet onto a concrete surface without leaking. Such a test would be enormously cheaper, since it would not involve the destruction of a vehicle; however, it would not reveal whether the tank as actually mounted was surrounded by componentry that could pierce it in a collision.

Eckhold's comments concluded with a few technical suggestions for revision of NHTSA's crash test, in case "at some future time probative evidence indicates a need for the stringent requirements of the Notice." It may seem an abuse of the advantage of hindsight to point out that such "probative evidence indicating a need" for the safety standard arrived with a bang one May night in 1988; but then, what else can the Ford executive's carefully crafted sentence mean but, *Let's wait and see if a lot of children die, and* then *we can impose the stricter safety standard.*

(Ford's apparent inability to recognize a safety defect until the body count is complete could sometimes strain credulity. A 1975 letter from NHTSA administrator James Gregory to Lee Iacocca, then president of Ford, regarding windshield wipers that had been failing in significant numbers, responded to Ford's contention that the wipers did not consti-tute a defect affecting motor vehicle safety:

First, it is irrelevant that windshield wiper linkages and pivot assemblies of similar design are used on many vehicles worldwide. The failure of these components on the affected vehicles in significant numbers in normal operation indicates the existence of a defect with respect to those particular vehicles. Second, Ford's assertion that prudent drivers can adapt to the situation presented by unforewarned failure of windshield wiper linkages and pivot assemblies or that the Government should wait until events prove that an unreasonable risk did exist are also irrelevant.

(Ford was directed to recall 187,000 1971–73 Mercury Capris. Two more years would pass before Ford dropped its opposition and sent out the recall letters in August 1978.)

Ford was not alone in opposing the school bus fuel system integrity standard. International Harvester's comment flatly declared, "It is apparent that the incomplete chassis as manufactured by IH cannot be expected to comply with the proposed barrier test." But on October 8, 1975, NHTSA—citing "the high regard expressed by the public for the safety of its children"—promulgated Safety Standard 301-75, the fuel system integrity rule for school buses, as initially proposed. However, because of the extension of the comment period, the effective date of the standard was postponed from April 1, 1976, to July 15, 1976.

Ford's position on the school bus fuel system integrity standard was consistent with its reaction to any number of other proposed rules going back to Day One of regulation: Henry Ford II declared that the initial safety standards proposed in 1966 were so burdensome that Ford Motor Company would be forced to "close down"—this despite the fact that the first twenty rules for the most part merely codified existing industry practice. (The fuel system integrity standard, for example, required only that passenger car fuel tanks, which were located in the rear, must not leak excessively after a 30 mph *front*-end barrier collision.) Ford Motor Company's Automotive Safety Office, which was set up to deal with regulation, was soon reeling off a string of arguments-in-the-alternative that would become a catechism of anti-regulatory faith: There is insufficient evidence that the proposed standard is necessary; and even if it is necessary, it's too stringent; and even if it isn't too stringent, it can't possibly be met within the allotted time.

The company's comments are characterized throughout by the complete dissociation of safety regulations on the one hand, from safety on the other.

Automotive safety director Will Scott, for example, in requesting various revisions, refinements, and deferrals of the initial 1966 safety standards noted that "The risk of inadvertent non-compliance of a finished vehicle is of enormous concern to us in view of the consequent $1,000 per car penalties, injunctions and plant closings that could be invoked under the Act." Precision in the standards' specifications, he continued, in comments dated New Year's Day, 1967, is important "not only to the manufacturers but to the Secretary [of Commerce] and to the public.

Obviously, the shutting down of a vehicle line could bankrupt a small manufacturer and its dealers. It could cripple a larger manufacturer and injure its employees, stockholders, suppliers and dealers. It could hurt the economy of the nation. The consequences of any such disaster are too grave to permit the neglect or oversight of any significant problem presented by any proposed standard."

All this talk of the crippling, injuring, and disaster that could result from failure to meet safety standards may suggest a subliminal awareness of danger to life and limb, but if so, it never seems to break through to consciousness.

The yawning chasm separating Ford's concern with safety regulations from its concern with safety was apparent in the company's blithe suggestion that school buses should be grouped with special-purpose vehicles, such as the Bronco, subject to *less* stringent safety standards than cars.

Some of the features of the Ford Bronco sport-utility vehicle "make it physically impossible to bring it into compliance with a number of the safety standards that are proposed for passenger cars," Ford maintained in its comments on the initial rules. "The Econoline Club Wagon represents a similar case. This truck was engineered as a lightweight van without compromises for passenger-carrying purposes.... However ... a model with windows has been developed that is merchandised as an Econoline Club Wagon.

"In addition to the two examples cited above, Ford offers a number of truck chassis and incomplete vehicles that are modified by others for special purposes.... Fire engines, rescue units, *school buses,* multi-stop delivery trucks, ambulances, limousines, airport maintenance vehicles, mobile homes and mobile libraries are typical products of modifiers and converters [emphasis added].

"...Ford's initial view is that, at a minimum, the standards applied to trucks could be applied to special-purpose vehicles as well. In no circumstances is it reasonably practicable or appropriate for the industry to apply passenger car standards to such hybrid vehicles, developed from truck chassis, even though they are put to passenger-carrying uses from time to time by customers."

Ford divided its vehicles into three categories: passenger cars, light trucks, and heavy trucks. Ford's B-700 school bus chassis were designed by Ford's Heavy Truck Engineering Group and manufactured at its Kentucky Truck Plant, and evidently Ford executives came to believe that school buses were indeed trucks, *"even though they are put to passenger-*

carrying uses from time to time." And this was the view the federal safety agency adopted, until Congress forced a change in 1974.

❑

An industry that could get school buses treated as trucks would seem to have enjoyed an influence over its regulators that verged on the hypnotic. But NHTSA could never be responsive enough to satisfy the men at the helm of Ford Motor Company. Not content with the anti-regulatory victories they had gained through the legally mandated procedures of comment and petition and court challenge, Ford's chairman and president decided to seek the special treatment they evidently considered their due, and came calling on the president of the United States.

Anyone opening up *The Washington Post* on April 27, 1971, to the little box setting forth President Richard Nixon's public schedule for that day would have read, listed at 11:00 A.M., "Henry Ford II, National Center for Voluntary Action."

Ford had agreed to serve as chairman of the board of the NCVA, a Washington, D.C.–based, private, nonprofit organization that the Nixon administration had launched. Its mission was to promote volunteerism, which it did through public service messages and the compilation of lists of organizations to which people could give their time. Its underlying agenda—like that of the later, George Bush–spawned Points of Light Foundation, with which it ultimately merged—included encouraging the belief that the poor and weak should get off the government's back and look elsewhere for help; but NCVA may also have marginally increased the chances that here and there they might find it.

Chairing its board was the sort of thing that chairmen of the board do, and it would be fair to describe the demands of the job on Henry Ford as not unduly taxing. At any rate, though at 5:30 that afternoon he would be attending a reception for the NCVA board hosted by President and Mrs. Nixon in the State Dining Room, on this particular morning he had wrestled free of the truly needy's claims upon his attention. The schedule released by the White House was false, and it was intended to camouflage the true purpose of the meeting.* Henry Ford was there to plead for the president's help in blocking auto regulations. Volunteerism was never discussed.

---

* A pre-meeting briefing memo for President Nixon from White House aide Peter Flanigan stated, "Press Plan: Announcement only that Mr. Ford is meeting with the President."

From 11:08 to 11:43 A.M., then Ford president Lee Iacocca and Henry Ford met in the Oval Office of the White House with President Nixon and his assistant for domestic affairs, John D. Ehrlichman. The Ford men had requested the audience after their several previous meetings with DOT secretary John Volpe and NHTSA administrator Douglas Toms failed to free the industry of every regulatory burden. Nixon, presciently fixated on the threat of foreign economic competition, especially from Japan, had been wanting to meet with the heads of America's auto makers anyway. His staff had suggested that the meetings be conducted on the Q.T. An April 21 memo from Peter Flanigan to H. R. Haldeman warned of "a serious risk of adverse publicity that the President 'sold out' to the Big Four* if after [a public] meeting we make decisions favorable to the industry." Nixon agreed to meet the auto executives a few at a time. Henry Ford, already an acquaintance of Nixon—he and his wife, Christina, once had dinner in the White House private quarters—got the first crack.

Unbeknownst to his visitors, Nixon, as was his wont, was secretly taping the meeting; the White House tapes were later discovered and transcribed in the course of the Watergate investigation. And the National Archives' official transcript would, years later, play a role in the Fairs' lawsuit.

Iacocca and Ford would be preaching to the choir when they inveighed against the burdens of federal regulation. Already hostile toward those he termed environmental and safety "fanatics," the president had been thinking big geopolitical thoughts that only heightened his suspicion of no-doubt-left-wing social engineering. The personal and the global were never more than a synaptic spark away in Nixon's mind: If seat belt warning buzzers drove him crazy, then it was perfectly clear that their introduction amounted to a thinly veiled attempt to undermine America's competitive position in the world. He believed that by outcompeting America in the auto industry, Japan could soon reduce the United States to number two in wealth and power. The notion that the United States might prevail by building a better car seems not to have entered Nixon's, Ford's, or Iacocca's mind.

❑

Ford and Iacocca were ushered into the Oval Office, where they were no doubt surprised to confront a garish oval rug, which featured a large

* General Motors, Ford, Chrysler, and American Motors.

corn-yellow eagle and circle of stars (the presidential seal) set into a
bright blue background. A California decorator brought in by the Nixons
had ripped out the room's subdued green carpet and replaced it with this
remarkable artifact. Neither Ford nor Iacocca mentioned it. Iacocca sat
down on a sofa; Ehrlichman settled into the sofa opposite him, and Nixon
and Ford took their places in easy chairs beside the fireplace. An oil
portrait of George Washington gazed at them stoically from the wall
above the marble mantelpiece. The tape transcript memorializes the en-
suing discussion:

PRESIDENT: Well, anyway, uh, I want to say first that, uh, on this
subject that I'm glad to have you come in and, uh, talk about it. And
let me introduce it by, by tr-trying to tell you what I know about it
and what I don't know. And then I want to hear directly from you and
you can talk to me in complete confidence, I can assure you. And John
[Ehrlichman] is a lawyer who says nothing.

UNKNOWN: (Laughs)

PRESIDENT: He damn well better not!

UNKNOWN: (Laughs)

PRESIDENT: Uh, but, uh, my views in this field . . . are, are, are frankly,
uh, whether it's the environment or pollution or Naderism or consumerism, are extremely pro-business. . . . [W]e can't have a completely safe society or safe highways or safe cars and pollution-free
and so forth. Or we could have, go back and live like a bunch of
damned animals. Uh, that won't be too good, either. But I also know
that using this issue, and, boy, this is true, it's true in, in the environ-
mentalists and it's true of the consumerism people, they're a group of
people that aren't one really damn bit interested in safety or clean air.
What they're interested in is destroying the system. They're enemies
of the system. So, what I'm trying to say is this: that you can speak to
me in terms that I am for the system.

UNKNOWN: Right.

PRESIDENT: Uh, uh, I, uh, I, I try to fight the demagogues, uh, to the
extent that we can. . . . I mean, you know, the, it's the kick now. . . . Uh,
the safety thing is the kick, 'cause Nader's running around, squealing
around about this and that and the other thing. . . . Now, tell me the

problems you've got with, uh, the industry, with the Department of Transportation, and all these things and let me listen.

FORD: Well, I'd like to say first, Mr. President, that, first, we appreciate your taking the time to see us. . . . We, we, I have, have seen all these people: [Environmental Protection Agency administrator William] Ruckelshaus and Goalby (sp?) [*sic*] and particularly Thomas in the DOT . . .

UNKNOWN: Toms [Douglas Toms of NHTSA].

FORD: . . . so we don't want to have anybody feel that, you know, we're trying to go over anybody's head. . . .

I think the thing that concerns us more than anything else is this total safety problem. And, uh, what we're worried about really, basically, is—this isn't an industry problem—is really the economy of the United States. . . . Now, if the price of cars goes up because emission requirements is gonna be in there . . . safety requirements are in there, bumpers are in there. . . . We think that the prices of cars are going to go up . . . maybe seven or eight hundred dollars in the next four years because of the requirements. . . .

We see the price of a Pinto . . . going something like fifty percent in the next three years. . . . It's the safety requirements, the emission requirements, the bumper requirements. Now, uh, what we're really talking about? We're talking about trying to put some sense into the Trans— to DOT and how they go about doing their business. . . . [T]he *cost-effectiveness* of what they ask us to do has got to be important [emphasis added]. . . . They've got bumper standards . . . they've got, uh, air bag standards. . . . [T]hese things are all going to cost money. If these prices get so high that people stop buying cars . . .

PRESIDENT: Um-hum

FORD: . . . they're gonna buy more foreign cars; you're going to have balance-of-payments problems. . . .

PRESIDENT: Right. I'm convinced. . . .

FORD: Granted, the foreign [unintelligible] have got to do the same thing, but they're doing it at a wage rate that's half [ours].

IACOCCA: [T]his brings up this whole issue of, uh, how important is safety. . . . The Department of Transportation, not willfully but maybe unknowingly, is really getting to us.... It, it just kills me to see it starting with Ford. We are becoming a great, inefficient producer, what they're doing to us.

But now take safety. It's six years old [referring to the 1966 Highway Safety Act].... But now, with all this time passing, they're saying put in an air bag.... I've been in the office of Secretary [of Transportation] Volpe a number of times on this.... I think they have said in the Department of Transportation that we are dedicated to passive restraints [automatic seat belts or air bags]. The citizens of the United States must be protected from their own idiocy, so we will put in a sophisticated device that will blow up on impact and package him in an air bag and save their lives. Well, we agreed that work has to be done in this area. But look where we are: they have, this is law; this is the law of the land, now, for 1974.* ... And we have on our cars today a hundred fifty dollars of, I don't say all gadgetry, 'cause the steering columns, I think, are saving lives, the collapsible column and the like, but the shoulder harnesses, the headrests are complete wastes of money. Every hundred dollars of, uh, those kind of, well, let's call it [unintelligible] that we put on, we have no doubt that it saves lives. Every hundred dollars is a billion dollars a year to get to the safety problem.... And you can see that safety has really killed all of our business....

... And, and, and ya say, "Well, what has this to do with safety?" Well, it has one big thing to do with it. They are gonna put whatever is demanded by law in this country on at a buck fifty an hour, and we're, we just cracked seven dollars an hour.... [W]hat safety is doing to us is gonna make inflation, in my opinion, look like child's play.... Ford ... is gonna price themselves clear out of the market and we're gonna be in trouble.... And the Japs are in the wings ready to eat us up alive. So I'm in a position to be saying to Toms and Volpe, "Would you guys cool it a little bit? You're gonna break us." And they say, "Hold it. People want safety." I say, "Well, they, what do you mean they want safety?" We get letters [unintelligible]. We get about thousands on customer service; you can't get your car fixed. We don't get anything on safety! ... So this is what's really, I think, the, the load that's really breaking our back.

* The traffic safety agency had first proposed in 1969 that passive restraints be mandatory as of January 1972. The regulation on the books as Iacocca spoke required front seat passive restraints as of the 1974 model year.

PRESIDENT: . . . Now what, what presidential authority's involved in, in, uh, uh, only the authority of reviewing what the DOT [Department of Transportation] does? . . .

IACOCCA: . . . I checked this out with our lawyers . . . and they [DOT] could say, uh, "because of further evidence" or "we want continuing discussions," they could suspend it. . . . That we know could be done under the law.

PRESIDENT: The thing we've got, the thing we have to do, let me, uh, let me say, uh, I, I'll, let me take a look at the whole, uh, John, what I can do here. . . . I'd like for you to . . . sit down with [Pete] Peterson. . . . Peterson now is the head of this investment economic policy thing . . . just let him hear exactly . . . how decisions we make may make our industry noncompetitive with the Japs. I can see that, as we have these damn, gadgets, and the [unintelligible] light on the seat belts is enough. . . . I shouldn't prejudge the case, and I will not. And that's what counts. I'll have to look at the situation, and I will on the air bag thing and the rest. And, uh, and, uh, but, but I think this is an element that had, you see, goes beyond DOT because it involves America's competitive position, it involves the health of the economy. . . .

FORD: I think there are many things in DOT, Mr. President . . .

PRESIDENT: Um-hum.

FORD: . . . that could be done if industry . . .

PRESIDENT: Um, like. . . .

FORD: . . . that you could do by, you know, just callin' em' up. I'd just say, "Well, let's get some . . ."

PRESIDENT: Yeah, yeah, yeah.

FORD: ". . . *cost-effectiveness* . . ." [emphasis added].

PRESIDENT: I want to find out, I want to find out what the situation is, is, cost-effectiveness is the word.

FORD: That's right. . . .

PRESIDENT: You see, what it is, too, is that we are, we are now becoming obsessed with the idea that . . .

UNKNOWN: Um-hum.

PRESIDENT: . . . a lot of, what, what it really gets down to is that, uh, [unintelligible], uh, it, it is, uh, [unintelligible] progress, [unintelligible] industrialization, ipso facto, is bad. The great life is to have it like when the Indians were here. You know how the Indians lived? Dirty, filthy, horrible.

 . . . Now John [Ehrlichman] is your contact here . . . let me see the Volpe thing . . . particularly with regard to this, uh, air bag thing.

❑

A few hours after the Ford-Iacocca meeting, Nixon was meeting with aides to discuss school and housing desegregation. But his mind was still on cars. According to Ehrlichman's contemporaneous notes, Nixon said, "On the merits, I'm against both seat belt buzzers and air bags. It's a boondoggle. Tell [Secretary of Transportation] Volpe to delay all of this on his own responsibility. I'll take the heat."

The "I'll take the heat" comment was one of Nixon's verbal ticks, a stock phrase his aides understood to mean its exact opposite. "In other words," Ehrlichman later testified, "the president was telling me to make sure that Volpe stopped it and took responsibility for stopping it, rather than going out and telling the press that the president had told him to stop it." Ehrlichman said he called Volpe's office that afternoon and told Volpe's administrative assistant that the president wanted Volpe "to stop all the regulations."

The next day, April 28, 1971, Volpe produced a memorandum for the president defending the regulation requiring passive restraints in 1974 cars. By the end of ten years, he wrote, when virtually all automobiles on the road would meet the standard, by the most conservative estimate 5,500 deaths and 200,000 disabling injuries would be avoided *each year*. "If the rule were to be indefinitely suspended," the transportation secretary argued, "DOT believes the auto industry would reduce its passive restraint effort to a token or at least much lower level."

(Volpe was proved right. GM had equipped 1,000 1971 Chevrolets with air bags in field trials, and sold 10,000 air bags as $225 to $300 options in its 1974, 1975, and 1976 Oldsmobiles, Buicks, and Cadillacs. It dropped the option in 1977, when it had scheduled a major dashboard styling change that could be accomplished more economically without accommodation for air bags. Ford, except for a pilot program of 830 air bags in 1972 Mercurys, maintained a policy of implacable opposition to air bags.)

The Fairs' lawyers would argue that the Oval Office meeting contributed to the delay of school bus safety standards. And Ehrlichman swore in his *Fair* v. *Ford* deposition that his mandate to delay regulations had extended far beyond air bags. He recalled that he and Peter Flanigan responded to Volpe's memo by going over to DOT and explaining to Volpe that the president really did want him to stop *all* auto safety regulations.* One of Ford's chief Washington lobbyists, R. W. Markley, Jr., had provided Ehrlichman with a big chart showing a lot of different safety rules the company wanted changed, Ehrlichman recalled. Ehrlichman didn't pay much attention to it, he said. When he spoke to Volpe, "I just said the president wants it all stopped."

Support for Ehrlichman's contention can be found in a May 5, 1971, letter from Ford's lobbyist Markley to Ford and Iacocca in which he reports on the outcome of their trip to the Oval Office:

"I met with John Ehrlichman this afternoon as a follow-up to the request for a suggestion for some late inter-governmental interface vis-à-vis the Department of Transportation. . . . He said that the two of you have a most receptive advocate in the President. He said that after you left, the President told him that, without hearing the other side, a number of things must be done immediately."

According to Markley's letter, Ehrlichman "said his *first project* was the air bag," but that, longer-term, the president "is particularly sensitive to foreign competition" and that what must be done is to "set down the long-range policy for the Department [of Transportation] and then make sure it is followed [emphasis added]." Markley said Ehrlichman agreed that the auto industry needed a mechanism in place to "channel our problems" to the White House so that they could be attended to without the necessity of "the publication of an Executive Order with attendant flak from the Naderites." In other words, the Ford lobbyist had been assured by Ehrlichman that the Nixon White House would help the industry quietly subvert the ostensibly open and public rule-making process.

Further evidence that Nixon meant to slow down safety regulations across the board came on May 13, when General Motors chairman Jim Roche had his at-bat in the Oval Office. "We must fight a delaying action," Nixon told him, to stave off legislation by Congress in response to the public's demand for governmental action. "We can't beat something with

---

* Contacted by the author, John Volpe, aged and infirm, was unable to comment. Peter Flanigan acknowledged that the meeting with Volpe must have taken place, but he had no recollection of it.

nothing, so we have programs." Nixon favored a bare minimum of environmental and safety regulation, just enough to keep up appearances.

(Deriding passive restraints as "circus nets," the president added, "I wouldn't drive a car again." In fact, except on a lark once or twice with his friend Bebe Rebozo, Nixon had not taken the wheel of a car since his election in 1968. It was perhaps lamentable that so much power to decide life-and-death matters should reside in a man so far removed from his decisions' consequences.)

Roche suggested his own ideas for deflecting the regulatory heat from the auto industry. Instead of concentrating on the vehicle, a "much broader safety program" could focus on drunk driving, enhanced law enforcement, and compulsory inspection programs. In other words, the government should shift into reverse and return to the pre-NHTSA days when safety programs concentrated on perfecting human behavior rather than vehicles and roads.

A number of NHTSA officials later confirmed to the House Commerce Committee's subcommittee on oversight and investigations that Ehrlichman and Flanigan ordered Volpe to delay the restraint standard. Volpe was described as "return[ing] despondently from sessions with White House officials who rejected his efforts to defend the [standard]."

On September 29, 1971, NHTSA amended its passive restraint standard. The notice, signed by administrator Douglas Toms—who answered to Volpe—said that although the car makers had adequate technology on hand, NHTSA had been persuaded by the industry's petitions that to require the installation of front seat passive restraints on all 1974 model cars would impose an economic hardship on the industry; accordingly, the deadline would be postponed to the 1976 model year.*

---

* A few days after the April 1971 Oval Office meeting, Ford, Chrysler, and American Motors had petitioned the U.S. Court of Appeals to overturn the pending passive restraint regulation, on the ground that regulations requiring the development of new technology were invalid. In December 1972 the appeals court ruled against the manufacturers, but ordered NHTSA to delay passive restraint regulations until a reasonable time after NHTSA could promulgate more exact specifications for a dummy suitable for precisely repeatable crash tests. NHTSA subsequently came up with the refined specifications for the dummy and on March 19, 1974, reissued a proposed passive restraint standard, to be applicable beginning with 1977 cars. Gerald Ford's secretary of transportation, William Coleman, however, withdrew the passive restraint requirement in 1976, before it took effect. His successor under Jimmy Carter, Brock Adams, issued a modifed standard in 1977, calling for the phasing-in of passive restraints beginning with large cars in the 1982 model year; all cars would have to have them by the 1984 model year. Ronald Reagan's Department of Transportation rescinded that rule in 1981, before it took effect. Insurance companies challenged the recision in federal court. Finding the Reagan DOT's action arbitrary and capri-

The Nixon White House had blocked a regulation that NHTSA later estimated could have saved, once air bags were in all cars, 11,000 lives and 170,000 injuries every year.

The author's efforts to afford Richard Nixon the opportunity to confirm, deny, or explain his role in slowing auto safety regulations brought the following response from his assistant Monica Crowley: "Unfortunately, President Nixon's schedule is overcommitted for the foreseeable future and he currently will not be able to accommodate your request. If the status of his schedule changes, we will certainly notify you. The President asked me to relay his best wishes to you and for great success with your book."

CHAPTER

26

Ford and Iacocca's enlistment of Richard Nixon in the auto industry's battle against federal regulation may well have been an accomplishment akin to converting the Pope to Catholicism. ("In this case, he was pretty well preshrunk," Ehrlichman recalled later.) They did direct his hand to a weapon well suited for combatting NHTSA's rules— cost-benefit analysis—but it is impossible to say how much credit the Ford executives deserve for the delays that followed.

---

cious, the Supreme Court in June 1983 ordered NHTSA expeditiously to reinstate the passive restraint standard. In July 1984, NHTSA issued a new rule requiring the phasing-in of passive restraints over the 1987 to 1990 model years. In 1987, NHTSA delayed the passive restraint rule for the front passenger seat, allowing it to have a manual belt if the driver's side had an air bag, through the 1994 model year. In 1991, Congress passed a law requiring dual front air bags in all new passenger cars by the 1998 model year.

The Fairs' lawyers claimed that a flashing neon arrow pointed from the Nixon meeting straight to the lack of a cage on the Carrollton school bus: "In 1967, the federal government proposed the 301 fuel system standard for cars with a possibility that it might be extended to include vehicles and trucks over 10,000 pounds, including school buses," they wrote in a pretrial motion. "However, on April 27, 1971, Henry Ford II and Lee Iacocca met with President Nixon and asked him to delay the implementation of the safety standards in order to protect its [*sic*] profits. . . . In January 1972, the proposed 301 standards were terminated, only eight months after a behind-closed-doors Nixon/Ford/Iacocca meeting to stop all safety standards."

Ford Motor Company's attorneys saw the Nixon-Ford-Iacocca meeting differently. Elegantly distilling the Oval Office conversation to its under-stated essence, Robert F. Redmond, Jr., wrote, "At the April 1971 meeting, the Ford representatives emphasized the need for a more practical na-tional motor vehicle safety program." Moreover, he added, "None of the proposed regulations that were discussed referred to school bus safety in any way whatsoever . . ."

In any case, the Nixon Department of Transportation soon manifested an enthusiasm for cost-benefit analysis that tied up the whole enterprise of safety regulation (including standard-setting for school buses). And this was a result that Ford Motor Company had avidly sought.

The White House's Office of Science and Technology had in that spring of 1971 formed a committee to study the costs and benefits of auto regulation. Its report, "Cumulative Regulatory Effects on the Cost of Automotive Transportation (RECAT)," actually came to the conclusion that automotive safety regulations *saved* money. RECAT found two man-dated safety improvements in particular to be real bargains: The collaps-ible steering column cost the consumer $22, but averted $82.75 worth of deaths and injuries per car over 9.4 years (a car's useful life). And lap belts, which cost $25, averted $64.75 in deaths and injuries, even with only 25 percent of occupants buckling up. The benefits of the lap belts and steering column taken together exceeded one auto manufacturer's estimate of the total cost to the consumer of *all* the federal safety stan-dards per vehicle in 1971, $132. Safety standards were an even better deal if you accepted the Bureau of Labor Statistics per-vehicle cost estimate, $81.50.

"Thus, it can be concluded, with respect to the various early safety standards, that their benefits exceed their cost, and their total effect has been to reduce, rather than to increase, the cost of automobile transportation," RECAT reported.

However, the committee was less sanguine about the economic justification for proposed regulations still in the pipeline, and its overall recommendation could be summarized in two words: Slow down. Regulations' effective dates should provide plenty of lead time and never require a change within a model year, RECAT urged. And, most important, cost-benefit analysis should be conducted *before a rule was even formally proposed.*

In theory, the suggested analysis was really unexceptionable. Comparison of benefit-to-cost margins would permit rational choices between versions of a given regulation, or between various regulations competing for priority, all of which could not be imposed simultaneously because of the less-than-limitless resources any industry could devote to accommodating changes. But in practice, the comparison was subject to limitless manipulation. There are few impediments to the imagination when it comes to estimating the cost of an item not yet built; and it is nearly impossible to demonstrate the benefits of a step not yet taken. Comparing test fleets of vehicles equipped and not equipped with a certain device couldn't reveal small but significant differences in the rate of accident or injury. As one safety advocate put it, "You can always prove that two things aren't different if you have little enough data."

Preproposal cost-benefit analysis could be a recipe for delay, and the Nixon transportation department embraced it. By October 1971, NHTSA had revised the introduction to its guiding document, the Program Plan, to read: "Approval of Rulemaking Plans is based on a careful analysis of safety payoff in terms of lives saved and reduction in injuries and on estimates of cost to the consumer." Before Nixon's spring 1971 tête-à-têtes with Ford, Iacocca, and the other chief executives, the Program Plan introduction had given much less emphasis to cost-benefit calculations: "Standards must be reasonable, appropriate and practicable," it read. "Design and production feasibility as well as economic implications must be considered in setting standards."

On January 18, 1972, Robert L. Carter, NHTSA's acting associate administrator of Motor Vehicle Programs, took his first action in conformance with the new orthodoxy. He suspended rule-making activity on twenty-two motor vehicle safety standards that had been proposed but never issued. One of them, Docket 3-2, an Advance Notice of Proposed Rulemaking issued back in October 1967, had announced that NHTSA was considering extending the applicability of the fuel system integrity standard, which applied only to cars, to include requirements for "multipurpose passenger vehicles, trucks, *buses,* and motorcycles" (emphasis added).

Ford had objected to Docket 3-2, arguing that crash testing of vehicles produced in low volume, such as trucks and bus chassis, would impose "an unreasonable hardship"; it joined other manufacturers in suggesting that, instead, the Bureau of Motor Carrier Safety drop test should be utilized for side-mounted tanks (such as those on school buses). However, the manufacturers' comment continued, "Bureau of Motor Carrier Safety tests for side mounted tanks, including the 30 foot drop test, should not apply to tanks *not exposed to direct impact.* New tests should be developed for the more conventional tanks . . ." (emphasis added). Here was an explicit statement that Ford and other manufacturers *knew* that side-mounted tanks—such as the Carrollton bus's—were exposed to *direct impact,* whereas tanks in "more conventional" locations were not.

Now NHTSA was suspending the rule making that could have mandated a fuel system integrity test for school buses, with the following explanation: "This proposed rule-making action has been terminated at this time since there is insufficient information to indicate that the magnitude of the safety problem is sufficient to warrant any rule-making action at this time. Accordingly, existing resources are being expended on items which are indicated to have a higher safety payoff within practical cost limits."

Cost-benefit analysis soon had NHTSA tied in knots, and any hope that the agency might soon free itself was promptly dashed by the judiciary. In December 1972, the Seventh Circuit Court of Appeals struck down NHTSA's standard for retread tire performance on the ground that the agency's failure to identify costs associated with the proposal and determine that these costs were outweighed by "reasonably predictable benefits" constituted a failure to demonstrate that the rule was "reasonable, practicable and appropriate" as required by the 1966 Motor Vehicle Safety Act. (The court did not explain why manufacturers pleading excessive cost were not required to reveal the actual costs involved; or how NHTSA was supposed to rebut the cost argument, without access to the cost figures.) NHTSA faced a Catch-22: It couldn't put a new standard on the road until it had proven its effect on safety; but it couldn't prove its effect on safety until it had put it on the road.

The politically and judicially imposed burdens on NHTSA slammed the brakes on the rule-making process. Twenty-nine standards were issued in NHTSA's first three years (1967–69); sixteen new standards from 1970–73; zero in 1974 and one in 1975. (Four would be issued in 1976, but three of those—all school bus standards—would be mandated directly by Congress.) NHTSA was bogged down like a brontosaurus in a tar pit.

A House Oversight Committee report attributed the slowdown to the growing complexity of rule-making actions, shrinking public support for regulation, increasing resistance from industry, and political interference in NHTSA rule making by the White House and the Office of Management and Budget:

"Most of the political opposition to . . . important NHTSA actions has come in the form of benefit/cost analyses that are critical of NHTSA actions and in the form of demands that NHTSA itself conduct more extensive benefit/cost studies," the report noted. The industry's cost-benefit strategy was creating "paralysis by analysis," despite the fact that Congress, when it passed the Motor Vehicle Safety Act, had specifically rejected industry-sponsored amendments that would have barred any regulation unless the "costs [were] commensurate with the benefit to be achieved." The express intent of the legislation was that "safety shall be the overriding consideration."

It was in response to the logjam at NHTSA that Representative John Moss drafted and Congress passed the Motor Vehicle and School Bus Safety Amendments of 1974, requiring NHTSA to issue school bus safety standards regardless of whether their costs might exceed the dollar-equivalent value of the lives saved.

The legislation also required that manufacturers who objected to a safety regulation on the basis of cost must reveal to NHTSA just what the additional cost to the manufacturer and consumer would be. Ford Motor Company objected that the costs of the Cost Information Reporting regulation would outweigh the regulation's benefits.

CHAPTER

27

To satisfy the mandate of the 1974 school bus safety amendments, NHTSA in February 1975 proposed an amendment to Federal Motor Vehicle Safety Standard (FMVSS) 217 that would require school buses to have either a single rear emergency door or two side emergency doors, one located in each side of the rear half of the bus. The exits would have to be sufficiently large and accessible that a rectangular object 48 inches high by 24 inches wide and 24 inches deep could pass through. The rule was to become effective April 1, 1976—nearly a year before the Carrollton bus chassis would be built.

The prior FMVSS 217, which had been in effect since September 1973, began with an observation indicative of the caution with which NHTSA habitually proceeded; no fact was too obvious to belabor. NHTSA "has concluded that passenger egress is enhanced when several emergency exits are provided," read the preamble. But that 1973 standard's section on emergency exits read, "Buses other than school buses shall provide unobstructed openings for emergency exit [totaling 67 square inches for each seating position]. . . . The emergency exit requirements do not apply to school buses." After a number of ejection deaths, NHTSA's primary concern was keeping students *in* the bus. Fearful that *too many* exits might lead to more students tumbling out, the agency ended up not requiring any at all.

At least one bus manufacturer thought the belated exit proposal too lenient. In April 1975, Robert B. Kurre, director of engineering at Wayne Corporation, wrote to NHTSA suggesting that school buses ought to meet the same exit requirements as nonschool buses. "The difference in requirements does not make sense," he observed.

The consensus of school bus body manufacturers was just the opposite. In June, Byron Crampton, manager of engineering services for the School Bus Manufacturers Institute, whose six members, including Sheller-Globe, produced 95 percent of all bus bodies in the United States, commented that the requirement of a clear opening at the rear door would eliminate two seating positions yet "does not, in our opinion, appear to help anybody gain better access to the exit except the rearmost four passengers, since the others still have to pass through a presently twelve-inch aisle." He suggested as an alternative that one or more pairs of push-out windows be required.

The Thomas-Built bus company also complained about the loss of two seating spaces for a clear path to the rear emergency door. Sheller-Globe lodged the rather fanciful objection that the exit requirements, in combination with the pending requirements for seat backs that could deflect on impact, could somehow reduce the capacity of a sixty-six-passenger bus to forty-eight. The National School Transportation Association, representing contract operators of school buses, wrote, "There is no reason to have a larger space for exiting when the aisle to the back of the bus is only 12 inches wide and will serve only as a funnel. Only one person can exit the emergency door at a time."

(The manufacturers' and operators' argument—that a clear exit at the back would be useless, given the narrowness of the aisle—anticipated exactly the testimony that Robert L. Carter, NHTSA associate administrator for motor vehicle programs in 1975, stood prepared to deliver as an expert defense witness for Sheller-Globe after the Kentucky disaster. Carter, who for years had been entrusted with the protection of life and limb on the highways, avowed that rear seats blocking all but a 12-inch gap at the center of the only possible exit for sixty-seven people in a burning bus "did not unreasonably obstruct the emergency door opening for evacuation purposes. A wider aisle at the rear of the bus at the emergency door was not necessary, and in the face of panic, the bus occupants would likely jam in the doorway regardless of aisle width. . . .")

Even before he had ceased to regulate and become a consultant and champion of the regulatee, Carter appeared something less than a zealot with regard to school bus standards. In June 1975, he wrote to Senator Robert Griffin (R-Mich.), who had forwarded a letter from Robert Bursian, the transportation supervisor for the Traverse City (Michigan) public schools. Mr. Bursian, "very much concerned and chagrined" by the proposed exit standard, had complained that a rumored requirement for two side emergency doors would greatly reduce the seating capacity of a school bus and increase the cost of pupil transportation. In a letter that suggests NHTSA was a watchdog of the toothless variety, Carter assured the senator that the new standard wouldn't amount to anything. The proposal "permits a single rear emergency door in lieu of two side doors," he wrote. "Most current school buses are equipped with a rear emergency door; thus, our proposed standard would not impose any additional seating penalty in most cases.... Finally, most of these standards have been adapted from the industry itself, and we have adopted, in large measure, *the criteria the industry has proposed*" (emphasis added).

At the same time, Carter's boss, NHTSA administrator James Gregory, was somewhat less convincingly conveying just the opposite message to New Jersey Democratic congressman Dominick V. Daniels, who had passed along a complaint from the Physicians for Auto Safety that the proposed exit regulation didn't go far enough. (The physicians group, noting that fire or immersion requires speedy evacuation, and that doors are often disabled in a crash, called for *four* exit doors *and* two roof hatches.) "The NHTSA is unable to agree that its proposal for emergency exits would only perpetuate the status quo," Gregory wrote. "For example, the notice proposes that each school bus contain either a single rear emergency door, or two side emergency doors, one located in each side of the passenger compartment.... The use of roof hatches is being reviewed ... and they will be thoroughly considered." Gregory claimed that his agency couldn't require more because "the extremely short lead time" mandated by Congress limited the design changes manufacturers could be expected to make.

NHTSA usually knew better than to blame its paymasters in Congress for the lack of progress on school bus safety. The regulatory agency's written submission to its oversight committee in 1976, for instance, pointed the finger at school system budgets:

> Problem: *The traditional school bus has evolved very little since the first all-metal body was attached to a truck frame.... It has proven to be a relatively safe vehicle due to its restricted operational and exposure parameters. Nonetheless the vehicle is structurally inadequate ... and has been a source of fatalities and disfiguring injuries in slight to moderate crashes. Improvements could be made rather easily except for the fact that school bus manufacturers are caught between the expense of these changes and budget-restricted school boards across the country. The problem is then to make meaningful safety improvements or changes without adversely affecting price, size or weight.*

On January 22, 1976, NHTSA finally amended FMVSS 217 to require an at least somewhat accessible emergency exit on school buses. Noting that many comments had been received objecting that the proposal provided for too few emergency doors, NHTSA responded: "The agency does not discourage the inclusion of additional emergency exits in school buses." Under the new rule, the 12-inch-wide aisle, rather than continue all the way to the back, would have to broaden into a 24-inch or wider space at least a foot from the rear door. Most manufacturers would meet the requirement by reducing the breadth of one rear bench to seat two instead of three, or by leaving space behind the rear seats to create a sort of foyer for the exit.

The emergency exit rule, along with the congressionally mandated standards for seating, joint strength, and rollover protection, were to go into effect on October 26, 1976.* The fuel system integrity standard, which had been issued earlier, would go into effect earlier, on July 15, 1976.

The School Bus Manufacturers Institute opposed the schedule for the new standards, insisting that the nine months from issuance to effective date allowed insufficient time for compliance. The exit standard, for example, though it called for minimal changes on most buses, was said to "require retooling and production setup for the left-hand emergency door location." This assertion came despite the fact that at a 1973 hearing SBMI had proudly cited its history of offering safety options, including "emergency pushout windows with positive locks and additional emergency doors in the left side of the bus."

Moreover, SBMI complained, the deadline fell in late October, at the end of the heaviest production period, just after the delivery date of most school bus orders. The standards would have to be dealt with during the peak summer production months, requiring the manufacturers to make "running changes" in midproduction. "The standards are, in effect, being imposed in the middle of the school bus model 'year,' " SBMI said. The body builders wanted the effective date put off from October 1976 to April 1977.

Curiously, when the fuel system integrity standard had earlier been scheduled to go into effect on April 1, 1976, Wayne Corporation had asked for a delay until September 1976, complaining that the April date would fall between normal model changes. If a regulation was set for the

---

* Without changing the effective date, NHTSA subsequently amended FMVSS 217 to drop the two-side-door option and require school buses to have either a rear emergency door, or a rear push-out window (at least 16 inches x 48 inches) and a left side door in the rear half of the bus.

fall, the fall was impossible, it had to be spring. If it was set for the spring, the spring was impossible and it had to be fall. Congressman John Moss, looking back on his many battles for health and safety regulation, recently explained industry's shifting views this way: "It's always tomorrow. They can live with tomorrow. They don't like to live with today."

Since a law passed by Congress, not just a NHTSA administrative regulation, had set the effective date, only Congress could permit an extension. SBMI lobbied the House Commerce Committee's subcommittee on consumer protection and finance to delay the body standards' effective dates until April 1977. The body builders did *not* ask for a further delay of the fuel system integrity standard, which SBMI described to the subcommittee as "primarily of concern to chassis manufacturers."*

The subcommittee, voting in closed, executive session, would go along with an extension of just two months, to January 1, 1977. Not content with a two-month delay, SBMI went to the full Commerce Committee, where Democratic Representative Richardson Preyer, whose North Carolina district was home to the Thomas-Built school bus company, won support for a postponement to April. The fuel system integrity standard, for no particular reason, would be delayed along with the others. The full committee's report to the House recommended passage of H.R. 9291, a bill authorizing $60 million a year for NHTSA, with an amendment postponing the school bus safety standards' effective date to April 1, 1977.

Congressman Bob Eckhardt (D-Texas), Representative Andrew Maguire (D-N.J.), and Representative Henry Waxman (D-Calif.) opposed the delay so strongly that they took the unusual step of having their dissent published separately at the end of the committee report.

"We are very much opposed to the Preyer amendment postponing the implementation of school bus safety standards," Eckhardt wrote. "This amendment will postpone the effective date of the standards from January 1, 1977 to April 1, 1977. This appears to be a short extension, but in reality it is extremely dangerous."

Under the law, he explained, as long as the chassis was built before the regulations came into force on April 1, the body subsequently mounted on it did not have to comply with the regulations either:

---

* SBMI's expression of indifference regarding the fuel system standard would one day prove inconvenient to Ford Motor Company, when the chassis builder tried to blame the body builders for the lack of a cage on the Carrollton bus.

*The impact of this extension is that children will be riding around
in substandard school buses for years to come.*

*. . . [A] noncomplying chassis purchased before April 1, 1977,
may be a foundation for a bus built in December of 1977 or later.
This will result in substandard buses being turned out for months
after the supposed implementation of the safety standards.*

*. . . I wish to be accommodating to industry, but the needs of
the children of the United States for safe transportation are far
more important than accommodating industry.*

Eckhardt urged his colleagues to restore the January 1 deadline, or
failing that, at least to prohibit the use of noncomplying pre-April 1 components in buses whose bodies were completed after April 1.

❑

On Friday afternoon, June 11, 1976, the House, after some inconclusive
consideration of legislation to establish a federal policy on oil and gas
exploration on the outer continental shelf, turned to the routine business
of churning out authorization bills.

Bob Eckhardt rose to offer an amendment, striking April 1, 1977, and
inserting January 1, 1977, as the regulations' effective date. Eckhardt,
who'd been a trial attorney in Texas, spared no tricks of that trade to
capture an audience's attention: The plaid vests and oversized plaid bow
ties he favored were easy to mock but hard to ignore. Though his attire
and country-boy accent suggested a fresh arrival via hay wagon, his fellow
legislators repeatedly voted him one of the ten smartest congressmen.

If, as the School Bus Manufacturers Institute argued, most bus production took place in the summer for delivery in September and October,
then a January 1 effective date would allow the manufacturers to incorporate the safety standards in a new model year, Eckhardt said. The bus
manufacturers were not suddenly being asked to meet standards without
adequate notice, he argued; rather, they were being asked at long last to
rectify hazardous conditions on the vehicles children had to ride.

"These buses, lacking the proper safety equipment and construction,
will continue to carry children, driving along our streets and highways, *a
hazard waiting to become a tragedy,*" he concluded (emphasis added).

The bus industry's chief advocate that day was once again the moderate Southern Democrat Richardson Preyer, a frequent ally of Eckhardt
whom the Texan held in high regard. Preyer, a Princeton and Harvard

Law School educated heir to the Vicks Vaporub fortune, had resigned a federal judgeship to enter politics and had earned a reputation as a gentleman of integrity. He'd opposed the Vietnam War before it was popular to do so, and resigned from the Internal Security (Un-American Activities) Committee, hastening that witch-hunting body's dissolution in 1975. High-minded but not impractical, Preyer found himself consistently in agreement with whichever policies the North Carolina tobacco interests thought sound. And he had no trouble seeing the merit in a position espoused by the Thomas-Built bus company.

In fact, to think twice about a request from a home district industry for a few months' delay of a safety regulation simply was not in the congressional playbook. Even to oppose a committee colleague on such a trivial matter verged on the bizarre: Delay was the universally agreed-upon price of getting safety measures passed at all.

Preyer emphasized that the bus manufacturers had assured him that an extension to April 1 would affect at most 16 percent of 1977 school buses, the portion of annual production that was normally manufactured in the months of January, February, and March—or about 4,000 buses. (As it turned out, Ford Motor Company alone would build 2,900, or 56 percent, of its 1977 school bus chassis in January, February, and March.) "I want to make sure, here, today, that the school bus manufacturers get adequate time to make these new buses the soundest and the safest ever built," he concluded.

Eckhardt's amendment lost, thirty-one to eight, and the House passed H.R. 9291, with Preyer's delaying amendment, by voice vote. As a Texas liberal, Eckhardt was used to losing, often expected to lose, almost seemed to thrive on losing, sometimes, as though defeat confirmed a nobility of purpose that would always elude the merely victorious. But this time he felt truly discouraged, because he knew something terrible would happen.

❑

All that remained was for the Senate to approve the legislation and the president to sign it. Late in the afternoon of June 24, 1976, the Senate passed the Horse Protection Act Amendments of 1976, which strengthened the Department of Agriculture's authority to ban the practice of laming competition walking horses in order to induce a high-stepping gait. It passed the Scrimshaw Art Preservation Act, exempting bones already in artists' possession from the Endangered Species Act's ban on the whale bone trade.

Then Senator Vance Hartke (D-Ind.) introduced H.R. 9291, citing written assurances from SBMI executive director Berkley Sweet that "the extension of the effective date of the school bus safety standards to April 1, 1977 . . . will *not* be used to produce a large portion of the 1977 bus orders according to 'old' standards. Every manufacturer has told me personally that his company will begin to incorporate the required features as soon as possible in the 1977 production run."

(Sheller-Globe, at least, would not incorporate the required features "as soon as possible." Not one of the safety features mandated for April 1 was included in the Carrollton bus body, which Sheller-Globe mounted on the Ford chassis in *July* 1977.)

Democratic Senators Alan Cranston and John Tunney of California, noted that they were shocked and saddened by a recent Yuba City (Calif.) High School bus disaster, in which twenty-seven students and an adult died when their bus's brakes failed and it plunged off the side of an overpass. They successfully offered an amendment requiring the U.S. Department of Transportation to issue a study on how school buses could be made safer.* "Because of the tragedy, we have resolved to take whatever steps we can to reduce the chances for future school bus catastrophes," Cranston said, before joining his colleagues in passing the law delaying safety standards—without debate, by voice vote. Having devoted ten minutes to the motor vehicle safety bill, the Senate continued its forced march through the mountains of authorization bills, amendments, and amendments to amendments it was trying to dispose of before adjourning on July 2 for the Fourth of July Bicentennial break.

By unanimous consent, the House concurred in the Senate school bus amendment on June 29, 1976, and President Ford signed the bill into law on July 8, 1976.

In and of itself, Congress's postponement of safety regulations did not cause the Carrollton bus to be a firetrap. The delay of regulations codifying certain minimum standards of safety left the manufacturers in the same legal (and moral) position they were in before the standards were issued—that is, with a duty to produce vehicles that were suited to their foreseeable use, and that were as safe as their users would reasonably

---

* In January 1977, DOT secretary William Coleman would dutifully forward to the Congress a School Bus Vehicle Safety Report, as required by Cranston and Tunney's amendment. In a dizzying display of self-referential circularity rare even in government studies, Congress's mandate for a study on school bus safety had spurred DOT to report that the best way to make school buses safer was to apply the then-pending school bus safety standards that Congress itself had already both demanded and delayed.

expect them to be. If anything, that duty was heightened by the manufacturers' increased awareness of potential hazards, as a result of the regulatory procedure of announcement and comment in which they had participated. What made the regulatory delay deadly—the Fairs and Nunnallees would argue—was a corporate policy at Ford Motor Company not to add safety equipment until required by law.

CHAPTER

28

On January 13, 1976, M. A. Richards, Ford's Heavy Truck Product Planning manager, issued Heavy Truck Product Letter 76HT77 authorizing all actions necessary to conform to FMVSS 301-75, the school bus fuel system integrity standard, by the then-pending July 15, 1976, effective date.

As a result of the product letter, the Heavy Truck Chassis Design Department came up with a design for a fuel tank guard made of rectangular tubes of quarter-inch-thick steel. The vehicle engineering department put together a preliminary product verification plan—a self-testing program that would enable Ford to certify that the standard had been met. Product Change Request Number 785037 alerted all departments to make such changes as would be necessitated by the addition of a protective fuel tank cage and related components. A Product Change Request (PCR) ensured that a designated change would occur in a controlled manner, all parts arriving simultaneously and compatible with one another. The PCR number maintained correlation in the computerized information files known as the release system. The release system disseminated the PCR information to the Preproduction Control Activity, which would query Purchasing Activity as to how soon the parts could be acquired from the various suppliers. (The cage would be fabricated by Wall Tube & Metal Products Company of Newport, Tennessee.) When apprised of the feasible delivery dates for all the affected parts, Preproduction would establish a common delivery date and inform the Material Control System at the assembly plant.

Ford's innumerable, elaborate systems—which like all by-the-book prescriptions were fitfully adhered to—rose like an impenetrable thicket in the path of anyone attempting to follow the paper trail of decision making. A liberal-arts-educated plaintiffs' attorney, however determined to prove that the corporation did wrong, could not entirely suppress a sense of awe that the corporation did anything at all. How in the world did the nuts from Kenosha fit the bolts from Taiwan, and arrive together to be assembled by an army of workers at a plant in Kentucky, where somebody unfailingly turned the lights on in the morning and off at the end of the day, and everyone got paid? It was incomprehensible. But a lawyer could not let his admiration, much less the sense of his own technological incompetence, unsettle his certainties. Whatever it was these Ford guys did, if they were going to do it at all, they had to do it right or face the consequences.

❑

A steel cage guard was the only means of meeting the fuel system integrity standard that Ford considered. Moving the fuel tank from its mounting on the outside of the frame rail was not contemplated. Significantly, there was never any question at Ford that *something* had to be done to protect the fuel tank in order for it to pass NHTSA's impact test. Ford had never performed a crash test on a school bus *without* a cage, nor had it ever subjected its school bus fuel tanks to a failure modes and effects analysis —the standard engineering practice by which components and systems are stressed to the point of failure so vulnerabilities can be exposed and designed out. But despite their lack of information, Ford's engineers apparently were quite clear on one point: The tank positioned as it had been for years—positioned as it would be on the Carrollton bus—could not sustain a 30 mph impact from a 2-ton barrier without leaking.

Heavy Truck Component Design Engineering executive engineer Robert Kraemer "tasked" his chassis design manager, D. J. Karalash, to design a fuel tank guard. Kraemer never thought that the bus without the cage could meet the standard, yet, he maintained later, he still thought the integrity of the fuel system was sufficient without the cage.

But if the cage enabled the fuel system to withstand an impact test it otherwise could not withstand, didn't that mean that the cage made the bus safer? he would one day be asked. "I can't use the word 'safer,'" Kraemer insisted at his *Fair* v. *Ford* deposition. "It supplemented or enhanced the integrity of the system." Kraemer explained that he had never heard of the Reston crash, where a Ford school bus fuel tank caught fire, but he would have paid no attention to it even if he had. Sound engineering practice, he believed, demanded that one take cognizance only of broad statistical history, so as to design for the most prevalent and probable conditions, not idiosyncratic or unique crashes. He resented the implication that he and his Ford colleagues were not sufficiently concerned with safety: "I would say, to use the word, that 'safety' is one of the highest-priority things we shoot for."*

Karalash, for his part, did once ask someone why the school bus fuel tank was located just where it was, beside the front door. Not that the location looked dangerous to him, he insisted later; he was "just curious." He recalled being told that the right front was the area of the bus least often struck. In fact, Ford had never done any tests or studies to determine the best location for fuel tanks on school buses, nor, so far as any Ford employee could recall, had any thought been given to the advisability of locating the fuel tank by the main exit. That was where most purchasers specified it should be; that's where it had been as long as anyone could remember; and the safety and performance track record had not set off any alarms.

John Durstine, Kraemer's and Karalash's superior, appeared equally disinclined to brood excessively over the genesis of his assigned tasks. Asked at his deposition, "Were you aware, Sir, of the purpose of 301-75 of preventing the deaths caused by the spillage of fuel upon impact?" he replied: "No. I was aware of the design requirements and the specifications of the barrier test. . . . Having read the regulation as an engineer, it said: You must test your vehicles as follows with this barrier at this speed at this angle and here must be the results after you have run this test. Therefore, I was designing vehicles to meet that specific regulation test."

Asked if he thought the cage was a good idea, Durstine replied, "Any federal regulation is meaningful and should be complied with." Beyond

---

* Other, competing-goals designers have to consider include low cost, light weight, durability, style, and ease of manufacturing.

that, Durstine, who held a master's degree in business administration from Harvard Business School as well as an engineering degree from Georgia Tech, had no opinion.

"Did you ever consider the surrounding componentry of your own vehicle as being a source of what could penetrate the fuel tank?"

"No."

Apparently, to the extent that any governmental entity assumed any responsibility for safety, Ford unburdened itself of just that amount of responsibility, in an equal and opposite reaction, so that overall attention to safety could never be increased.

❏

On March 24, 1976, Keith Lewis, the Heavy Truck Vehicle Engineering manager, set out the details of the product verification plan to ensure that B-series chassis would comply with FMVSS 301-75. There were to be two moving barier crash tests, one from the side and one at an angle from the rear. There would be no simulation of a head-on collision.

The Test Operations and Engineering Services Office, Car Engineering Group, completed Crash Test No. 3241 on March 27, 1976. A 4,034 pound barrier was run at 31 mph straight into the side of the bus at the fuel tank. The impact was so severe that the bus's frame rail was bent and the driveshaft knocked about a foot to the left. The 263-pound protective cage was bashed into the side of the fuel tank, deforming it, but there was no leakage. Two weeks later, in Crash Test No. 3255, the impact was at a 45-degree angle from the rear, at the right rear corner of the tank. Again, the tank did not leak, and this time the bus could be driven away.

On the basis of the crash tests, Lewis assessed the school bus fuel system integrity program "no risk," meaning that there was no risk that the chassis would fail to comply with the federal standard. The final engineering sign-off, approving the cage-protected fuel system for production, was signed by nine men after Lewis. By his signature, each man signified that he had reviewed the documentation and agreed with the assessment. Job 1 was now set for July 6, 1976; the first bus chassis to be equipped to meet Standard 301-75 would head down the assembly line on that date. On May 20, 1976, the Kentucky Truck Plant completed a "functional build" of a B-700 bus with a cage. Ford was ready to mass-produce buses with cages to protect the fuel tank.

But on June 23, 1976, Richard T. Evans of Heavy Truck Component Design sent out a Product Change Request directing the assembly plant *not* to install the fuel tank guard unless it was specifically ordered as an option by the purchaser. The PCR explained: "Condition Necessitating Change: Delay of FMVSS 301 Effective Date to 4-1-77." The frame assemblies would still have holes drilled in them to accommodate the cages, but the cages would not be put on. Interestingly, when the PCR was sent, the U.S. Senate had yet to pass the bill delaying 301-75—it would do so the next day, June 24—but apparently no sparrow fell in Washington without Ford's knowledge, and the fate of the bill was considered certain.

A Product Letter signed by chief engineer John Durstine followed, advising the Automotive Assembly Division that Congress had postponed the effective date of FMVSS 301-75 to April 1, 1977. "Because of this postponement, the following actions are required," the letter said. "Revert to carryover hardware where possible until the 4-1-77 effective date of the standards," which meant that, to the extent that irreversible changes had not been made, the plant should go back to making the fuel systems as they were before they'd been modified to meet the safety standard.

While a meticulous paper trail documented the instructions, approvals, and concurrences regarding putting the cage on, no documentation could be found fixing the responsibility for leaving it off (or more precisely, making it optional, which resulted in leaving it off). In fact, an almost complete institutional amnesia seems to have afflicted the corporation and everyone in it on this point. After the Carrollton crash, Ford engineer Keith Lewis helped conduct a genteel ("I didn't want to offend anybody") in-house investigation. "A lot of people asked around," he reported, and "nobody could clearly identify who made the decision."

"[The decision] may have been as a result of meetings with any number of the components in the company," design engineer Kraemer would explain. "You can't define it exactly. If you work for a big company, there are many, many ways that things get done."

Kraemer himself did not participate in the decision to change the cage from standard, he was certain. "Remember, my responsibilities end with completing the design and releasing the information to other people," he said.

Kraemer's boss, John Durstine, was sure only that the decision did not come from his department. "That comes from someplace else," he would swear, after the crash.

"What is that someplace else?" asked John Coale's colleague Phil Allen.

"That someplace else is a management decision."

"Do you know where in the management that decision was made?"

"I don't recall that either. Those are case-by-case things that come up, so there is not any specific way I would say [what] generally accepted practice is, so, therefore, I don't know."

Asked where some written documentation of the decision might be found, Durstine replied, "I don't think such a thing would exist." He said there were "rigorous administrative systems" to implement management decisions once made. But as to the decisions themselves, "After a large discussion, they say, 'We will do this.' Then Product Planning puts the Product Letter out and says, 'Do that.' I don't know of any documented system that will allow you to go behind any of that and find any management decision."

❏

Durstine's boss, Heavy Truck Operations manager Edward Mabley, took responsibility for the decision, more or less. Though he understandably could not recall the details fourteen years after the fact, he knew what would have happened in the ordinary course of business. "I concurred in the consensus, the decision after it was made and recommended to me by groups of people at lower levels," he said. "The sales and marketing manager would have to be part of the consensus; the plant would have to be part of the consensus, so we all consensed [*sic*]. . . . That's as far as it went." Mabley was not required to inform anyone higher in the corporation. "This was clearly within my responsibility to keep my vehicles . . . within the federal standards."

❏

As to *why* the decision was made not to make the tank guard standard equipment, the Product Change Request and Product Letter seemed to state quite clearly that the reason was the government's postponement of the standard. In fact Durstine, when asked in May of 1990, replied, "It is to align the product actions to basically be consistent with the standard." But a few minutes later he had remembered that Ford had been forced to act because the body manufacturers were having trouble mounting their bodies over the cage. "The reason it was delayed," he said, "is some of the body manufacturers could not get their bodies modified. Part of the structure on certain of the bus bodies interfered with the guard rail that was there, so you just physically couldn't put it on the chassis." Mabley, too, vaguely recalled that "the balance of the industry downstream from the chassis was not ready to implement the standard."

In fact, though some of the body builders were having a tough time meeting the deadline for the seating standard or the joint-strength standard, there was no persuasive evidence that any body builder was unable to accommodate the fuel tank guard as of the standard's original July 1976 effective date. Richard Premo, who in 1976 was Sheller-Globe's director of Advance Vehicle Engineering, testified that Superior's bodies, just as they were, without alteration, would have fit a Ford 1977 B-700 school bus chassis—including the Carrollton bus—had it been equipped with a fuel tank guard.

If Sheller-Globe had no problem, then no manufacturer had any problem, since all their bodies were built to the same dimensions, according to Berkley Sweet, who in 1976 (and 1994) directed the School Bus Manufacturers Institute. Sweet never heard of any manufacturer having any problem fitting the body over the cage.*

❑

Mabley, who could see the carcasses of crash-tested Pintos at the test-track junkyard outside his office window, was so busy dealing with safety regulations that he could not attempt to micromanage what was or was not being bolted onto every vehicle. "I would have no business, as a senior engineering executive, of second guessing design detail," he said. "That part was entrusted, you know, to managers who were very competent at lower levels, and my overview really had to be based upon the performance of the entire program to meet objectives on time."

Up to a certain point in the corporation, people did not really know what was going on above them; past that point, people did not know exactly what was going on below them. Detail people did not have the authority to shape policy, and policy people did not have the capacity to grasp detail. In a sense, no one knew what he was doing.

"If we had a standard, we had to meet it," Mabley said. When the standard was delayed, meeting it was delayed.

---

* Ford defense attorney William King was prepared to argue that the Ward bus company had such a problem, citing as evidence the words "cage itself goes out to 42 inches. Simpson— modify gussets" in someone's handwritten notes of a 1976 Kentucky Division of Pupil Transportation meeting with manufacturers' representatives. Simpson represented Ward. Gussets are the cross pieces beneath the bus's floor, some of which would have had to be cut to fit the cage. Robert Pelkey, the engineer working on Ford's defense team, told the author in King's presence that "It's no problem to snip a couple of gussets"; at which point Pelkey would have been struck dead if King's looks could have killed.

CHAPTER

29

On September 8 and 9, 1976, at the Frankfort Holiday Inn, Paul E. Jones, director of the Department of Education's Division of Pupil Transportation, presided over the annual specification revision meeting to prepare Kentucky's orders for school buses. The state would be inviting bids on 674 1977 school buses, including 556 sixty-six-passenger models, four of them for the Meade County school district. As had been the practice in Kentucky for some thirty-five years, the state would purchase the chassis from chassis manufacturers, who would have them delivered to entirely independent body manufacturers, with whom the state had contracted for the bus bodies. The specification revision committee consisted of local school superintendents and directors of pupil transportation and their maintenance mechanics, as well as a representative of the state Division of Purchases and one from the State Police.

At the request of the specification committee, bus manufacturers' representatives attended the meeting. ("This committee needs your technical advice," the invitation read.) The Division of Pupil Transportation did not have a single design engineer of its own. Jones, who had a master's degree in education, relied for engineering expertise on his assistant supervisor, Sam Jackson. Jackson had a master's degree in industrial education—he was trained to teach the basic crafts at trade school. He had been working as a mechanic at an Oldsmobile dealership when his wife pressed him to get a job with retirement benefits, which he found at the Department of Education. Lacking the resources or facilities to study or test equipment, Jackson depended on information from the manufacturers. Four Ford representatives joined those from GMC, International Harvester, Dodge, and Chevrolet at the chassis specification meeting.

The impending fuel system integrity standard was discussed in some detail. Ford's represenatives said that the installation of a cage would not affect the company's ability to meet Kentucky's specification that the center of the fuel fill-pipe cap should be 39.5 inches from the center line of the chassis (plus or minus one half inch). It was noted more than once that the effective date of the standard had been postponed to April 1.

There would be some disagreement later as to whether Ford ever informed the Kentucky committee that the cage guard could be ordered in the meantime as an option. Jones later said that Ford had not. Certainly, the Kentucky committee could have looked at the August 1976 *Ford Truck Data Book*. It listed as optional equipment a frame-mounted, steel, bolted/welded construction fuel tank guard. The wholesale price of the cage, delivered, was projected to be $285; suggested retail would be $385.76. Sam Jackson later acknowledged that he didn't always take the cellophane off the data books when they arrived in the mail, since he would be getting information from manufacturers' representatives at the specification meetings anyway. The Kentucky specification committee was hardly sitting down with a blank piece of paper to design a safe school bus; it couldn't have if it tried. In reality, there was some question as to who was specifying to whom.

(The chairman of the 1988 NTSB inquiry into the Carrollton crash would ask a Ford engineer, "Are you aware that the Ford Motor Company does assist states in preparing specifications, so that your buses will qualify for the specifications that are set forth?")

("For the most part," the Ford man replied, "I think our sales people don't leave anybody untouched if they can.")

Ford would argue that as a contractor, it could not be held responsible for the fuel tank's location and lack of a guard, because Kentucky's specifications required an unguarded fuel tank, located exactly where it was. Ford contended that Kentucky, "a highly sophisticated school bus purchaser," not only ordered its buses without a cage, but insisted on delivery before April 1 to *ensure* that they could come that way; and Jones and Jackson inspected the pilot models (the chassis twice, the bodies at least fifteen times) to make sure they were getting just what they ordered.

The Fairs and Nunnallees, on the other hand, would insist that Kentucky's Division of Pupil Transportation was not capable of developing its own specifications and had not done so, but had merely gone along with specs that had originated with the school bus manufacturers.* Those manufacturers, they contended, should not be allowed to plead that they were just following orders, when they themselves had effectively issued the orders. At a minimum, the plaintiffs argued, even if Ford was justified in following the specs and leaving off the guard, it had a duty to warn Kentucky of the danger of an exposed fuel tank.

Jones and Jackson might have been in a position to clear up how the bus came to be equipped as it was, but by the time they were through defending their own expertise on the one hand, while minimizing their responsibility on the other, what they knew and when they knew it remained as murky as ever. Ford's characterization of Kentucky as a "highly sophisticated purchaser," however, did not fare well in its encounter with reality.

"[Kentucky's] 1977 specifications were essentially the same that was [*sic*] in there before I became the director and before I had the final responsibility for the specifications," Jones recalled. He said he didn't know how those specifications had been arrived at.

Kentucky's standards closely tracked the suggested Minimum Standards for School Buses promulgated at the 1970 National Conference on School Transportation, sponsored by the National Education Association. The NEA standards specified that the fuel tank be on the right side of the chassis frame. That location had been adopted by a consensus of school transportation officials and bus manufacturers at the first National School Bus Standards Conference in 1939, based on the intuitive notion that the side of the bus away from oncoming traffic would be hit least often.† The goal of that first conference was to establish uniform standards that would promote safety, eliminate "unnecessary luxury," and facilitate production "at the lowest possible cost."

---

* They also noted that Patty Nunnallee and Shannon Fair were not the purchasers of the bus, so it was at least debatable whether their claims could be foreclosed by the contractor's defense.

† Actual statistics are meager and contradictory. According to the School Bus Manufacturers Institute, from 1969 to 1971 the rear of the bus was least frequently struck. NHTSA's Fatal Accident Reporting System (FARS) data show that, in those 1975–87 accidents that involved a school-bus-type vehicle and a fatality, the left side of the bus was struck least frequently (12 percent)—slightly less than the right side (14 percent); 30 percent of the fatal accidents were head-on. The NTSB report on the 1972 Reston crash stated, "It has been the experience of Fairfax County [Virginia] that the vast majority of the school bus collisions with vehicles or with fixed objects have occurred on the right sides of the school buses...." But a 1988 review by the Louisville *Courier-Journal* of 5,800 school bus accidents in six states found the forward area of the right side had been hit marginally less often than the corresponding area on the left.

❑

Frank W. Cyr, a professor of school administration at Teachers College, Columbia University, initiated that 1939 conference. Cyr had done pioneering work in the consolidation of small rural schools into central school districts, a process made possible by the advent of the school bus. ("It was the school bus that revolutionized the schools, not the teachers or superintendents," Cyr recalled in 1993, at the age of ninety-three. "The same thing will happen in the next fifty years with TV, computers, and fax machines.")

The Rockefeller Foundation had given Cyr a grant to study school transportation. He found that some rural states had no standards at all, and it was not unusual to find children being hauled to school in hay wagons or cattle trucks. More commonly, the welter of conflicting state standards impeded production efficiency, which drove up the cost of buses while insufficiently guaranteeing their safety. (The red, white, and blue exterior required by some districts may have achieved its intended goal of instilling patriotism, but it did nothing to enhance visibility in rain or fog.) As usual, studying and identifying a problem did not solve it; so Cyr got the National Council of Chief School Officers to sponsor, in April 1939, a week-long conference of school transportation officials and industry representatives at Teachers College, to hammer out a list of uniform recommended standards. He obtained another $5,000 from the Rockefeller Foundation, which was sufficient to provide roundtrip railroad fare (lower berth) to New York City plus a week's room and board in Columbia University dormitories for one representative from each of the forty-eight states.

Cyr knew nothing about engineering and neither, for the most part, did the school officials. "They lacked expertise," he recalls. "They didn't know how to establish standards." For seven days he presided as the conferees sat at forty-eight typewriter tables arranged in a semicircle in the Grace Dodge Room at Teachers College, listening as spokesmen from two dozen manufacturers, including Ford and Superior, proposed standards that would meet the conference objectives of economy and safety. It was at this conference that a high-visibility orange-yellow beat out forty-nine other hues, ranging from bright red to lemon, as the color that the U.S. Department of Transportation would one day designate as National School Bus Glossy Yellow.

Before the conference, when Cyr was conducting his research, he had visited body companies and found ten-to-fifteen-foot-high piles of truck fuel tanks discarded behind the factories. "They'd throw away the tanks that came on the truck chassis," he recalls. "It was cheaper for them to make their own rather than change the body around to fit each tank that came from Detroit." He suggested that the body and chassis manufacturers should agree on a standard tank size and location. At the conference, W. G. Echols of the Mississippi State Department of Education was appointed chairman of a subcommittee to recommend a standard fuel tank location. The location of the tank "directly on the chassis frame on the outside and to the right side" was one of forty-four standards adopted at the 1939 conference.* In most cases, that's where tanks were already located, though they could occasionally be found inside the passenger compartment, under the driver's seat. The fact that the tank would be adjacent to the front door was at that time an unavoidable consequence of putting it on the right. With the short wheelbases on buses of the day, there was no way to move it back without hitting the rear wheel assembly.

The standardization process inspired by Cyr was carried on at a National Conference on School Transportation in 1945, when the fuel tank location was specified more precisely: The distance from the cowl to the front of the tank should be 42 inches minimum, and from the cowl to the center of the filler cap, 57 inches. Subsequent national conferences in 1948, 1951, 1954, 1959, 1964, and 1970 left this location undisturbed, and it was repeated in Kentucky's specifications.

The precision of the specification lent it a scientific aura, and Ford Motor Company would point to its repeated renewal as affirmation of the wisdom of locating the tank just where it was. But though the general idea of putting the tank on the right was to avoid impacts, the precise location at the front door had nothing to do with safety; it had to do only with standardization for production efficiency. Its origin was not prescriptive, but descriptive: When you put the tank on the right side of a typical 1939 school bus, it's 42 inches behind the cowl. That's the way it was found, and that's the way it was left. The point was to ensure that any

* Balancing the goal of safety against the imperative of economy, the conference wrote standards for school buses constructed of bodies mounted onto truck chassis, such as remain prevalent today. It rejected the conclusion that the National Safety Council had reached six years earlier, in 1933: "The bus chassis should be especially built for the transportation of people—that is, it should be a motor coach chassis. This will give the chassis sufficient strength; it will provide for a lower center of gravity making it less liable to tip than a truck; it will provide for greater comfort than a truck; and it will prove equally or more economical in the long run."

manufacturer's body would be able to drop down onto any manufacturer's chassis, and the fuel filler door would match up with the filler pipe. The original national standards had ratified the status quo, not optimized design. As the 1970 NEA Standards themselves stated: "Note: Measurements shown below are for guidance of chassis manufacturers and serve only to prevent need for relocating the original tank." Indeed, the standards' "Guiding Principles," enunciated in 1939 and repeated in every edition since, clearly stated that the purpose of specifiying exact dimensions was "to increase the efficiency of volume production"; and that "the actual designing of school buses is a responsibility of the manufacturers."

❑

On September 30, Jones wrote a memorandum to all school districts urging them to decide on their school bus orders as soon as possible. He explained that, "with the impending federal regulations, the cut-off date for add-on orders will be much earlier." The invitation to bid he sent to manufacturers specified that all chassis had to be delivered to the school bus body plant no later than April 1, 1977.

Jones and Jackson later swore that the April 1 deadline had nothing to do with avoiding the requirement for safety features, but was set simply to ensure that there would be time for the body builders to complete the buses before school started in the fall.

("Certainly you didn't want to have the date of April 1 so that you didn't have to pay more money for a bus that had to comply with FMVSS 301?" the Nunnallees' lawyer Mike Hance asked Jones. "Well, I don't think that got into it," Jones replied.)

On November 19, 1976, a Heavy Truck Product Letter prepared by Robert Pelkey informed Ford's various departments that on April 1, 1977, the law would require compliance with FMVSS 301-75, and therefore, as of that date, the status of the fuel tank guard would be changed from optional to standard. The guard would remain optional in Canada.

Sealed bids on Kentucky's school bus order were opened on November 23. Lester Motors of Central City, Kentucky, a Ford dealer, entered the low bid and was awarded, on December 6, a contract for 620 B-700 chassis to be delivered to Sheller-Globe's Superior Coach Division, which won the bid for bodies, "before April 1, 1977." The price for the Carrollton chassis was $8,565.

In January 1977, Michigan Fleet Equipment Company of Grand Rapids,

Michigan, manufactured the 60-gallon fuel tank that would be installed in the Carrollton bus. The Kentucky Truck Plant began building vehicle number B70EVY28196 on March 14, 1977. A bar code was slapped onto the frame rails to guide them on their journey through the half-mile-long assembly building. Fed by conveyor into a computer-controlled 200-ton press, the rails were pierced with a pattern of holes, including a dozen for the fuel tank guard that would never be mounted.

Later, on the frame-assembly line, the cross members were slid into position, then trapped between the rails and bolted into place. The skeleton thus formed proceeded down the line belly up, so that the heavy componentry could be dropped down on it rather than raised up to it. The suspension brackets and springs were attached, then the axles, then the fuel tank brackets and straps. The frame was turned over, hoisted on an overhead conveyor, robotically painted, baked in an oven, then sent down a slope to the workers on one of the chassis lines.

Viewed from high above, the 2,000 men and women laboring at the assembly plant might have been ants in a hill or pedestrians in a metropolis. Their fragmentary tasks were woven together in a pattern so complex it appeared random or nonsensical, at best a mad choreographer's dance. Yet by virtue of an overarching scheme of which no individual could be fully aware, on the appointed date, March 23, the completed chassis rolled off the line.

The cowl—hood, grille, and fenders—gleamed brilliant yellow; behind it stretched the bare frame, as black as black could be, and beautiful. You could eat off the tires. It was thrilling, this transient moment of perfection, this fleeting instant of grace. Now life would begin.

On March 28, a truck from Dealer Transport Company of Louisville picked up the chassis to haul it to Superior Coach in Lima, Ohio.

The bus was sent out into the world at a time when their experience with the Pinto must have been searing into the minds of Ford executives the importance of fuel system safety. In response to a 1977 NHTSA request for information, Ford said that it knew of thirty-five cases where Pinto rear-end impacts had resulted in fuel leakage or fire. Twenty-nine lawsuits or liability claims had been filed against the company, and big compensatory damage verdicts were starting to come in: $3.3 million in Florida in 1975, $1.2 million in Alabama in 1976.

The Fairs would argue that the Pinto's history should be admitted in their case as evidence tending to prove that Ford was aware of the danger of exposed fuel tanks, and that the company willfully disregarded the danger because of a policy of keeping costs down even at the expense of safety.

Ford had begun designing the Pinto in June of 1967; Lee Iacocca, then a vice president, conceived the project and was its principal proponent. In order to keep the car under 2,000 pounds and its price under $2,000 —Iacocca's two-pronged strategy for capturing a share of the subcompact car market—the chassis' rear section was stripped of its reinforcing steel skeleton. Only nine inches of crush space separated the front face of the fuel tank from the protruding bolts of the differential housing at the center of the rear axle.

Iacocca was battling to attain the presidency of Ford at the time, and had reason to hope that a triumphal introduction of the Pinto would send his stock soaring. For him, the 2,000-pound, $2,000 goal was not simply a corporate strategy but a personal one. The trouble was, when Ford ran rear-impact tests, again and again the Pinto tanks sustained damage and sprang leaks. (In November of 1971, the Insurance Institute for Highway Safety reported that in a moderate-speed *frontal* impact crash test, the Pinto's fuel tank ruptured.) Yet the car was put on the market without remedying the problem.

In his autobiography, Iacocca denies having cut corners "to save a few bucks" on the Pinto or any other vehicle: "Even Joan Claybrook, the tough director of the National Highway Traffic Safety Administration and a Nader protegé, said to me one day: 'It's a shame you can't do something about the Pinto. It's really no worse than any other small car. You don't have an engineering problem as much as you have a legal and public-relations problem,'" he wrote. Given the implausibility of any NHTSA administrator's making such a statement, it's not surprising that Claybrook categorically denies ever having said any such thing.*

It appears that Iacocca, in the spring of 1977, was in fact deeply concerned with issues of safety—his own. He and his allies in the company had fallen out of favor with the chairman of the board, Henry Ford, who, Iacocca wrote, "held the power of life and death over all of us." In April, Iacocca was reduced to third in command and suffered the agony of being put at table number three at company dinners. "Every day I found another part of my body missing," he wrote. When, in 1978, Henry

---

* Attempts to obtain an interview with Iacocca were unavailing. "I'm sorry, but we'll have to decline your request," read the reply from his spokeswoman at Chrysler. The author was unable to determine just why Iacocca could not respond.

Ford finally fired him, Iacocca recalled, William Ford expressed regret over what his brother had done. "Thanks, Bill," Iacocca remembered saying. "But I am dead, and you and he are still alive."

CHAPTER

30

Superior did not finish building vehicle B70EVY28196, the Carrollton bus, until June 28, 1977. But by virtue of its March 23 chassis completion date it was legally a pre–April 1 bus, so the April 1 safety standards were not compulsory and a cheaper bus could be built for the Commonwealth of Kentucky. Superior had continued to build "pre–April 1" buses long after it had begun building buses that *did* conform to the new standards. The absence of safety features on the Carrollton bus had nothing to do with an inability to implement them.

The view of safety features as a burdensome expense (rather than as *safety* features) was so widely shared by manufacturers and purchasers alike that avoiding them could be explicitly and unselfconsciously discussed. For example, D. J. Hardin, sales manager, School and Transportation Buses Division at Sheller-Globe, had dispatched a "Sell-O-Gram" to all Superior school bus dealers in March 1976: "Subject: Price Increase. The price on all the Superior School Buses . . . will be increased on bodies completed on chassis that are built after [the federal standards' effective date]. This body price increase has yet to be determined, but it is a direct result of several Federal Standards . . ."

Regarding the fuel system integrity standard, Hardin wrote: "This standard will require a heavy cage around the fuel tank. It will obviously increase the cost of the school bus chassis and it would be to your customers' advantage to get their chassis built prior to [the effective date]." He wrote in the same vein of the pending requirements for a rear emergency exit not blocked by seats, stronger body construction, and energy-absorbing seat backs, concluding: "It certainly behooves your good customer to buy buses immediately because of the above extra requirements that will increase the cost."

At the same time, as though in a walled-off segment of their minds, the bus builders *knew* what it was they were dealing with. Thus Sheller-Globe's vehicle safety director, Richard Premo, could write to a Superior school bus dealer that, because the fuel tank guard would weigh two or three hundred pounds, it might be advisable to move the fuel tank toward the rear to keep the weight off the front axle; and, he wrote, *"There is also another advantage to the rearward location. It will move the fuel tank away from the entrance door if there should be a fire"* (emphasis added).

Years later, long after the damage was done, Premo was confronted with this letter at his deposition and asked what he had thought would happen if a crash ruptured the fuel tank and rendered the front door inoperative.

"It would be a problem; it sure would be a problem," he replied. "You can't get out the door and you have got a fire; you have got a problem."

"Did Sheller-Globe have a policy not to implement the changes necessary to comply with a federal safety standard until the effective date of that safety standard?"

"I would say most of the time correct, because they were cost increases to the consumer, and things of that nature," Premo said.

Sheller-Globe's executives, like Ford's, insisted that, as helpless pawns of Kentucky's Division of Pupil Transportation, they were just following specifications. Even had this been true, the Fairs and Nunnallees argued, the company would still have had a duty to warn of its product's concealed hazards: extremely flammable, highly toxic seating materials and extremely limited avenues of escape. In fact, however, Sheller-Globe had *not* followed at least one of Kentucky's specifications: "The seat side windows are to be 'Split Sash' type in which the pane of glass and its frame can be kicked out in case of an emergency," providing twenty-two avenues of escape, one on each side of all eleven rows.

Sheller-Globe had not supplied kick-out windows because they had been illegal since September 1, 1973, when FMVSS 217, Bus Window

Retention and Release, went into effect. It required that a minimum of 1,200 pounds of force be applied before a bus window frame would pop out—far more than even the most desperate child could muster. The regulation was aimed at keeping children from being ejected in rollover accidents. (Superior *could* have supplied a two-step, unlatch-and-push window that met the retention requirement and still provided the emergency exit Kentucky desired.) The Kentucky Division of Pupil Transportation nevertheless continued to specify kick-out windows, year after year, and was never told by Superior that it wasn't supplying them.

By measuring the distance between the point where they had been seated and the point where their bodies were found, the Fairs' fire experts, Berkeley professor Brady Williamson and his associate Fred Fisher, were able to demonstrate that—with the exception of Chuck Kytta, who was engulfed in flames—each and every one of the passengers who died had moved far enough to escape safely, had there been the specified window exit for each row of seats. Even those in the first rows on the right whose own windows might have been blocked by fire—including Shannon Fair and Patty Nunnallee—fled a sufficient distance that they could have made it out window exits on the opposite side.

But the rear door was the only emergency exit. As the children rushed in panic down the narrow aisle, they tripped and became entangled. However, the pileup in itself was not a fatal event; they could have disentangled themselves and moved on, had there been time. It took a combination of two factors—lack of exits and rapid fire spread—to cause the deaths, and the school bus had both. If the seats had been padded with neoprene—commonly used, in accordance with federal guidelines, on public transit buses—the fuel-fed flames pouring through the front door opening and up between the buckled floor panels would have caused the upholstery to slowly char, according to Williamson.* Instead, row after row of polyurethane seat cushions, which burn as hot and fast as gasoline itself, rapidly ignited—filling the bus with choking smoke, searing hydrogen cyanide gas, and ferocious flames—killing the children as they struggled to get free.

---

* Neoprene did not serve as well as polyurethane as a cushion against impact injuries. Even so, Brady Williamson suggests, it could have been used in the bottom seat cushions and forward portion of the seat backs, with the more shock-absorbent polyurethane restricted to the rear seat back surface that kids are thrown forward into. Or, a thin layer of neoprene could have been used as a fireblock over an inner core of polyurethane. Since the time the crash bus was built, superior fire-retardant materials have become readily available, if too rarely utilized.

Shannon Fair (above) and Patty Nunnallee were among the twenty-seven who died on the bus, which state troopers floodlit and videotaped at the scene of the crash.

Interior of a 1977 Ford/Superior B-700 school bus. A foot-wide aisle led to the only emergency exit, a back door obstructed by the rear seats.

4

"Ride Hard, Die Hard," read the cap Larry Mahoney wore in his driver's license photo. He escaped serious injury, though his pickup was destroyed.

5

6

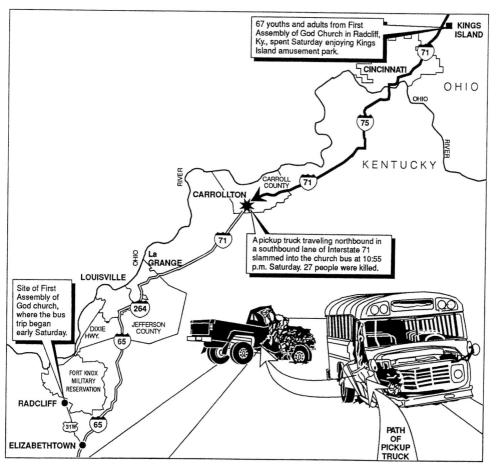

67 youths and adults from First Assembly of God Church in Radcliff, Ky., spent Saturday enjoying Kings Island amusement park.

A pickup truck traveling northbound in a southbound lane of Interstate 71 slammed into the church bus at 10:55 p.m. Saturday. 27 people were killed.

Site of First Assembly of God church, where the bus trip began early Saturday.

KINGS ISLAND

CINCINNATI

OHIO

OHIO

KENTUCKY

CARROLL COUNTY

CARROLLTON

La GRANGE

LOUISVILLE

JEFFERSON COUNTY

DIXIE HWY.

FORT KNOX MILITARY RESERVATION

RADCLIFF

ELIZABETHTOWN

PATH OF PICKUP TRUCK

If the pickup had hit a few inches to the right, it would have been stopped by the bus's frame rail instead of shearing through sheet metal toward the fuel tank.

7

8

With the bodies still on board, the bus was hoisted onto a flatbed and covered with a tarp for transport to a temporary morgue.

This chart shows where 62 of the 67 passengers were at the moment the Radcliff First Assembly of God bus crashed May 14. It reflects the recollection of the 19 survivors who agreed to be interviewed.

Those in white letters on black backgrounds died.

Witnesses were unable to place two survivors, Aaron Conyers and E. J. Obregon, and three who died, Julie Earnest, Dwailla Fischel and Shannon Fair.

STAIRWELL			
	Jennifer Arnett	Patricia Nunnallee	Denise Voglund
Chuck Kytta	Kashawn Etheredge	Robin Williams	Mary Daniels
	Carey Aurentz	Billy Nichols	

DRIVER			
John Pearman	Phillip Morgan	Emillie Thompson	Joseph Percefull
	Amy Wheelock	Joy Williams	Jim Slaughter
	Cynthia Atherton	Janie Padgett	Joshua Conyers

A National Transportation Safety Board investigator compared the leading edge of the bus's leaf spring to the tear in the fuel tank.

SOME FEATURES OF THE BUS
1977 SUPERIOR BUS
WITH FORD CHASSIS

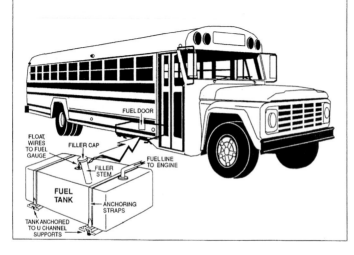

FUEL DOOR

FLOAT, WIRES TO FUEL GAUGE

FILLER CAP

FILLER STEM

FUEL LINE TO ENGINE

FUEL TANK

ANCHORING STRAPS

TANK ANCHORED TO U CHANNEL SUPPORTS

The 60 gallon gasoline tank was mounted outside the frame rail, adjacent to the front door.

10

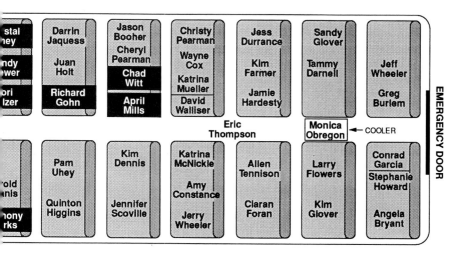

Seating chart:

- stal / ney | Darrin Jaquess / Juan Holt / Richard Gohn | Jason Booher / Cheryl Pearman / Chad Witt / April Mills | Christy Pearman / Wayne Cox / Katrina Mueller / David Walliser | Jess Durrance / Kim Farmer / Jamie Hardesty | Sandy Glover / Tammy Darnell | Jeff Wheeler / Greg Burlem

Eric Thompson

Monica Obregon ← COOLER

EMERGENCY DOOR

- ndy / ewer
- ori / lzer

- old / anis
- ony / rks | Pam Uhey / Quinton Higgins | Kim Dennis / Jennifer Scoville | Katrina McNickle / Amy Constance / Jerry Wheeler | Allen Tennison / Ciaran Foran | Larry Flowers / Kim Glover | Conrad Garcia / Stephanie Howard / Angela Bryant

11

On Father's Day, 1988, the Louisville Courier-Journal *ran this seating chart of those who lived and died. Shannon Fair was actually in the third row, right, center seat, according to Percefull and Slaughter.*

12

Kentucky State Trooper Sonny Cease's *sketch of the victim's locations showed that they died struggling to reach the back door.*

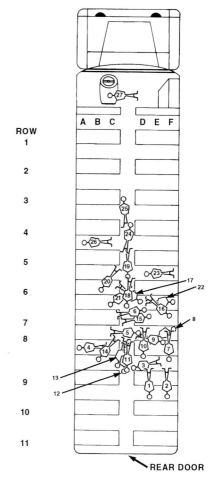

ROW
1
2
3
4
5
6
7
8
9
10
11

A B C   D E F

REAR DOOR

13

Mahoney, testifying at his trial beside photos of the passengers, was responsible for the crash. But the Fairs contended that an Oval Office meeting of (from left) John Ehrlichman, Henry Ford II, President Nixon, and Lee Iacocca planted the seeds of the disaster.

14

15

A few months after the crash, Larry and Janey Fair visited the spot where Shannon died. Jim and Karolyn Nunnallee watched as Jeanne, then six, watered a tree planted in her sister's memory by Patty's Girl Scout troop.

16

A month before her death, Shannon enjoyed a moment with her friend Scotty Higgins in Johnson City, Tennessee.

SHANNON RAE FAIR
JAN. 31 1974 MAY 14. 1988
"MANY DAUGHTERS HAVE DONE VIRTUOUSLY.
BUT THOU EXCELLEST THEM ALL."
PROVERBS 31:29

PART THREE

JUDGMENT

31

Shannon Fair turned fourteen on January 31, 1988, and not a moment too soon. No one was ever entirely comfortable being thirteen. At thirteen, you could not possibly look in the mirror and see someone totally cool; you were obviously a novice teenager, a sort of provisional one. And then there was the imbalanced and graceless nature of the unlucky number itself. But fourteen! For sheer mellifluous numerical pizzazz, those pulsing inner double sevens could not be beat. And though you might be an eighth-grader now, before this year of your life was out, you would be in High School, the Land of the Free.

It was pure passion, turning fourteen. Shannon and her girlfriends celebrated their birthdays at a round of giddy slumber parties where they all acted "crazy." It was good to be crazy, because it loosened the boundaries of possibility. It meant you could be wonderful in ways your parents could not conceive, and it meant you couldn't fail, because there were no standards for people quite like you. But most of all they acted crazy because they *were* crazy, ready to burst with an energy for which there was no decent outlet.

At these parties, a girl would call up a boy whom she liked at that moment—you could go steady for a day—and then surreptitiously pass the phone around to all her friends while the boy (supposedly) thought he was still talking to the first girl. Such small betrayals were an odd way to express tender feelings, but then it was not really the boy who was the object of affection. The girls were in love with love, and in love with one another for being in it together.

Anita Ardisson's party in February got off to a rollicking start when ten girls piled on hands and knees atop one another to make a cheerleaders' pyramid. Shannon, in faded blue jeans and a Radcliff Middle School T-shirt, climbed to the pinnacle. (She and Anita had tried out for the eighth-grade cheerleading squad, but had not made it.) Shannon let out a whoop, her fist raised, as Anita's big brother saved the moment on videotape. There was no shadow looming, no intimation in the air.

Was that pyramid, in that room, in that house, in that moment, on a sort of raft, borne on a river of time toward a bus crash waiting downstream? Would it have been true to say that four of the girls were going to die in three months? Because time is like a river? Or would it have been true to say that they were going to die in three months, because time is like a clock, and the wheels had been cast, assembled, and set in motion: Larry Mahoney had his problems, breweries sold beer, a bus had been manufactured in a certain way, the church was planning a trip, it would be necessary to stop for a certain number of minutes on the way home while kids used the bathroom? Or would it have been true to say that those four girls were not *going to* die in three months; that future was not awaiting them; that future did not exist; that future did not lend poignant meaning to the moment? They were just *alive,* Shannon, and Amy Wheelock, and Kashawn Etheredge, and Cynthia Atherton. Death came later.

At midnight, Shannon and Amy nestled like fawns on the sofa, as the party took a breather to watch the movie comedy *Clue.* Kashawn was the first to fall asleep, and therefore had to have a trick played on her. Her bra was put in the freezer.

After the movie was watched, and the pizza eaten and the board game played, the time came, as it always did, for Truth or Dare. When it was your turn, you could pick anybody out of the group, and she would choose a category: Truth, Dare, Double Dare, Promise to Repeat, or Death. If you chose Truth, you had to answer true or false, like, "Did you kiss so and so?" Dare, the person who picked you would dare you to do something, like call up a boy and tell him you liked him. Double Dare was tougher, like, run barefoot outside in the snow once around the house; Promise to Repeat—you would have to say what you were told to, for instance, "I love so and so," when you really didn't (or did); and Death was a really bad dare, like a triple dare. Then it would be your turn, and you could put someone else on the spot.

Truth was the easiest. The truths were no big deal. Promise to Repeat they didn't do much; they thought it was dumb. They wanted to get to the dares. Anita had to run barefoot in the snow. Christy Pearman had to do a dance with just a towel on. The dares got worse as the night went on, but you'd have to do them, or Shannon would get you. Shannon was big on thinking up punishments if you didn't do the dare. She even suggested flushing heads in the toilet, but everyone did the dares.

Shannon herself was dared to stand at the window with no shirt on, and just at that moment Anita said, "Oh there's Tommy and Michael!"

That would've been the Tommy to whom the "I ❤ Tommy" on Shannon's notebook referred. Tommy Hill wasn't really running around outside Anita's house with Michael Jefferson at that precise moment, but he could have been. He and Michael once phoned Autumn Dempsey at 3:00 in the morning—her stepfather got on the phone! And another time they shined a flashlight and threw pebbles at Christy Pearman's window, and her mother caught them. "My parents don't approve of Tommy Hill," would have gotten a resounding "True" from everyone at Anita's slumber party.

"I was a pretty bad kid in eighth grade," Hill reflected, a few years later. "I'd get in fights; I'd be smart with the teachers; I wouldn't do none of my homework till I had to, to pass. It wasn't no trouble like killing or stabbing people or nothing like that. It was just, like, kid trouble. It was just—*hectic.*"

Why merely date some guy when you could be *saving* one? Shannon had no use for handsome princes out to wake helpless females with their kisses; she saw herself in the opposite sort of story, where it's the power of the woman that changes frog or beast to handsome prince. Reclaiming good bad-boys was shaping up as Shannon's M.O., and in Tommy—a baby-faced, crew-cut blond who played football when his grades allowed —she'd found the leader of the pack. Her friends didn't get the attraction. "He was very loud and obnoxious back then," recalled Autumn Dempsey, who was a middle school honor student and cheerleader. "It was very odd that Shannon was drawn to him. She was quiet around people she didn't know, very reserved. Shannon was very mature. Sometimes it was hard to talk to her because of that. Some things, you never knew if she was going to understand it the way that you did. Sometimes she'd get a look on her face where you knew she thought what you said was dumb."

Tommy and Shannon often talked about why they were together. "We'd say, 'How come we're friends? We're so opposite,'" Tommy remembered. "The friends I hung around with, they thought she was like a rich girl and I shouldn't be going out with her." In a community where one's precise status was often emblazoned on the shoulder, Shannon's father was a lieutenant colonel; Tommy's was a sergeant first class. Her family owned a split-level house; his rented an apartment across from Wal-Mart.

He asked her to help him in science class. "I couldn't comprehend the teacher, but Shannon would explain it so it was easy. She just had a way." He flirted with her. Soon Shannon got Tommy and her friend Cynthia Atherton together, because Shannon wanted to go out with Tommy. That was the prevailing mode of launching some kind of relationship: You hooked up the person you were interested in with your friend. Anyway, "dating" meant you and your friend went places with your boyfriend and his friend. In due course, Shannon and Tommy "went out" for practically a month, but before, during, and after the romance, most of their friendship was on the phone.

Shannon lived on the floor of her bedroom. She chose not to have a bed, just a purple futon cushion. She'd lounge on it with her homework at her left hand and her TV at her right and her lavender Princess phone cradled against her ear. (The walls, couch, chairs, and rug were also shades of purple.) She could talk for two hours to Tommy without breaking a sweat.

"We'd call each other and talk forever," he recalls. "We talked about boy-girl things, football, classes. I think she'd always try to make me jealous about guys. She'd tell me there was this guy that she likes. I was like, *Oh no*. We just talked about everything there was, because it was so easy to talk to each other. One time I called her house and she kept playing over and over a real old song, like '50s or '60s old hard rock. I'd like to get that record though. I wonder what that was."

Shannon stuck up for Tommy. People would tease him about his shoes: He was shuffling around in no-name stuff from Payless or Pic 'n Pay while his classmates cruised in Nikes or Reeboks. "Shannon would talk to me. She'd say, 'It's no big deal. People should like you the way you are.' She gave little speeches: 'Don't let people get to you.' Shannon would keep me in line." She wanted him to become religious, straighten up his ways, get baptized. (He finally would, on May 14, 1989, the first anniversary of the bus crash.)

Sometimes it got on his nerves that she knew all the answers to all the teachers' questions, but what really got to him was when she'd share her fears that she might get a B. "I was like, 'What are you talking about? My parents would give me a party if I got a B.'"

Shannon took a new interest in her hair, in eighth grade. She used to part her long, wavy, auburn hair in the middle and let it hang straight down to her shoulders, the red highlights shining. That was before she discovered hair spray and curlers. "She would always say it was so ugly. And I would say, 'No, it's not. Just keep it the same,' " Hill recalled. "And then she changed it and parted it on the side and she came in to school one day and freaked me out: I thought she was so beautiful."

One spring night Tommy and Shannon and Frank Birch and Kari Knight and Jason Booher went out to the Triple Gold Cinemas to see a voodoo thriller, *The Serpent and the Rainbow.* (Actually, they didn't *go* out; they were taken out. Those who lived too far to walk were driven by their parents and dropped off—a mortifying ritual of public humiliation that notified everyone in line that the kids arriving were only in middle school.) As they sat through the hallucinatory violence of the nightmarish zombie movie ("Don't bury me! I'm not dead!"), Shannon and Kari listened enviously to the gales of laughter coming through the wall from the adjacent theater showing *Good Morning, Vietnam,* which they had wanted to see. But Frank had sold the other guys on *The Serpent and the Rainbow,* so Shannon and Kari had to go. They'd learned that it was more trouble than it was worth, trying to change boys' minds.

Tommy's friend Mike Jefferson, who had sat down behind them, kept poking Tommy. "Kiss her, kiss her," he urged.

"He was always trying to pressure me into doing something," says Hill. "He'd done that to me with Amy Wheelock: I went to go kiss her and Amy went BAM, she just slapped me. And everyone found out about it, somehow."

This time Hill resisted Jefferson's proddings and awaited a more propitious moment. Shannon lived three quarters of a mile from the movie theater, and the group walked her home. Just past McDonald's, where there were vacant fields alongside the road, he and Shannon lagged behind. They turned; he thought fast about what she was thinking that he was thinking, and what she thought of it; she thought about what he was thinking that she was thinking about what he was thinking; dizzied, they took a deep breath and did it. Their teeth bumped, which was not supposed to happen, but they had kissed.

They kissed only that one time. Shannon told him soon after, on the phone, that everything was better before, that they were more comfortable before. He agreed, and they remained friends to the end.

When the 1988 Radcliff Middle School yearbooks were handed out at the school library that spring, Shannon took up most of the last blank page in Tommy's with her inscription:

Tommy,
I can't believe you didn't reserve me a spot [to sign on the cover]. Oh well, I'll live. This has really been a good year for me. I'm glad that you were a part of it. I've made a lot of memories for myself and hopefully some for you too. Maybe one day when you're old and decrepit (← look it up) you'll look back on your yearbook and remember all the good times. Well, you're going to North next year and I'll be with you. I'll be cheering you on out on that football field with the band and you can know that I'm watching and playing for you. I'm not even going to bother wishing you luck, because I know you don't need it. As long as you don't let anybody change you, you'll go far in life. I hope your future holds in it everything you want. I'll always remember you.

Love,
Shannon Fair '92

"I hope I can help them be remembered," Tommy said later, of Shannon, Amy Wheelock, April Mills, and all the others. "It's been forever since I've seen them."

CHAPTER

32

On Easter Sunday, April 3, 1988, Shannon, whose folks were something-less-than-rigorous Methodists, got baptized at Stithton Baptist Church. The way it had started was that Shannon would be sleeping over Saturday night at her neighbor Tanya Blair's house, and Tanya would go to Stithton on Sunday morning, so Shannon would go along. (Tanya and Shannon were blood sisters: When Tanya was nine, and Shannon eight, Tanya got a cut on her finger. Seizing the opportunity, Shannon nicked herself with a razor blade, and they pressed their fingers together.) Eventually, even when she wasn't sleeping over, Shannon would walk down to Tanya's on Sunday morning and catch the yellow school bus the church sent around.

At the time she began going to Stithton, Shannon was crazy about her classmate, the smart, handsome, athletic, and very popular Wayne Cox. "Wayne goes to Stithton," she told her friend Kari Knight. "He went last Sunday!"

"You're so silly, Shannon," Kari teased, "to go to church to see Wayne!"

But if Wayne had ever been a reason, there were others more enduring. Shannon studied the Bible in Sunday school, where she, Stacy Crump, Autumn Dempsey, and Cynthia Atherton comprised a class. (Boys and girls were taught separately.) Shannon was not really well versed in the Bible, but she was learning. She read it every day. There were a lot of things she wanted to know.

"In church, she was told that if you pray and live right, things will work out," says Janey Fair, "but she knew they didn't. And she was told at school that if you study hard, everything will work out. She knew that wasn't true. She had this global confusion about why the world was in the situation it was in."

A month before Easter, Shannon dedicated her life to Jesus, on the last night of a visiting evangelist's revival. Dedicating your life to Jesus was not an unusual thing to do in Radcliff, Kentucky. It wasn't as though lots of Shannon's friends hadn't already done it; Autumn Dempsey, who was thirteen, had dedicated her life three years earlier. But Shannon was really nervous about it. "I'm not going to do this unless you walk up there with me," she told Autumn. So Autumn rededicated her life that night, and Shannon dedicated hers.

Not long after, Stithton's Rev. Waggoner called on Larry and Janey, to consult with them about their daughter's desire to get baptized.

"It's her decision," said Janey.

"She makes almost all her decisions on her own," Larry explained.

During the Easter service, Shannon entered the baptismal font with Rev. Waggoner. "I baptize you in the name of the Father, and the Son, and the Holy Ghost," he said, as he immersed her in the waters as an outward sign to the world that she was dying to sin and rising to walk with the Lord. Rev. Waggoner looked in her face, and thought, "She is so beautiful. I wonder what life holds for her."

❑

For the April school break, Janey and Shannon drove down to Johnson City, Tennessee. Vacation meant a sojourn at Uncle Jim and Aunt Patty's house, where Janey's mother, Frances, was living, as well. (Three years earlier, Frances had awakened from a simple hemmorhoid operation brain-damaged, unable to identify herself or those around her. Ever since, Janey and Patty had taken turns caring for her.) Here and there along the road they glimpsed the purple redbuds' poignant flower, its bloom the more beautiful because so fleeting.

At Patty's, each bang of the screen door heralded another friend or neighbor or relative, blurred and interchangeable categories of fondly connected people, such as Scotty Higgins, Shannon's first love, who lived near Jim and Patty's little convenience store. Exigent circumstances had once commended him to Patty's care for a couple of weeks, and without much to-do he'd stayed off and on for a couple of years. He and Shannon would climb the hill behind Patty's house and sit there for hours, talking about God knows what, they were so different. Shannon was a prep (nice clothes); he was a freak (long hair). She was college bound. He would drop out: The earth was going to be bombed and destroyed, he'd heard, so what was the point of finishing high school? But she understood him better than anybody, as though she could read his thoughts in his beautiful, light blue eyes.

After Pine Grove Methodist's morning service one Sunday that April, Shannon exchanged good wishes at the church door with Clara Fillers, an elderly woman whose husband was in the hospital awaiting a kidney operation. A moment later, Shannon stopped, turned around, and ran back up the ramp. "Don't worry, Mrs. Fillers," she said, patting the woman's back. "Mr. Fillers will be all right; we're all praying for him."

"Maybe God took Shannon because she had fulfilled her destiny, and He wanted her before she was old and worn out like us," Mrs. Fillers, whose husband indeed recovered, told Janey a few years later. "When I think of youth and beauty, I think of Shannon."

❏

In late April 1988, during Teacher Appreciation Week, Shannon wrote a thank-you note to each of her teachers for contributing to her education. All but one were women, and she bought each a potted mum. But for Brian Morrison, her band instructor—she looked at the flowers and said, "He's a bachelor. He wouldn't have that two weeks before it would be dead." She bought him a pen.

At the Radcliff Middle School Spring Arts Festival, Shannon blew the sax in the eighth-grade band concert, and performed in a play. Then she and Amy Wheelock, who would also die in two weeks, read "A Final Farewell" to their teachers:

A Final Farewell

It's been a great year/and we're here to say/Good-bye to you/in a special way!/We've had our laughs/our sorrows, too/It's hard to believe/We're almost through./When we look back/upon this year/the memories/will be quite clear./A final farewell, to you we say/the friendship we've shared/will always stay!

❏

Shannon was thinking about moving on. She knew the world was bigger than Radcliff, and she had every intention of exploring it. In her school essays, she had written approvingly, if humorously, of feminism and the liberation of women, ideas that remained controversial in the heavily fundamentalist military outpost. "A mother is expected in many homes to take the children & mold them into mature adults, while the father brings home the money," she observed. "Now this itself is difficult, but then when you consider the wife part of this deal you have to get into dishes, laundry, & general cleaning, along with doing the grocery shopping. Plus trying to buy clothes for the kids, & that means finding the right size & trying to please the child. These are just the basic jobs. You know that all this must have been difficult or women wouldn't have rebelled by starting organizations like women's lib.

"Women have come a long way, & I'm happy for that. . . . & I'm really glad I'm not somewhere where they sacrifice women to volcanoes."

She had written whimsically of not quite finding her place in Radcliff: "I'm different & I'm proud of it. I like to think of myself as being between the snobby 'in-crowd' & the nerdy 'out-crowd.' If you're part of the in-crowd, then hey, that's great, & if you're part of the out-crowd, well, then, bummer, but don't flaunt it and certainly don't dwell on it."

Behind the jaunty words lurked a real, unsatisfied need for connection. "Because Shannon was so mature, she really didn't have peers," Janey recalls. "She couldn't really fit in completely with kids her own age, and of course she couldn't with adults, so she was ultimately alone. So sometimes she did get lonely. She'd often take naps on Sunday, and I'd go down and take her in my arms and she'd say she felt alone, and I'd explain she was likely to remain so, until maybe she went to college back east, but certainly as long as she remained here. Then she'd say, 'Okay, it's your turn.' And we'd switch and I'd put my head on her shoulder. Of course, I never really told her anything that was bothering me, because I didn't want to put that on her."

For the moment, Shannon longed for mobility itself, without caring too much about destination. She had envisioned her friends and herself in the not too distant future, in her seventh-grade novella, *Sweet Sixteen*: "They went wild, with their cars and everything else that came with being sixteen. This was the time that their parents had been dreading, for a good reason!" In reality, cars bestowed upon Radcliff's teenagers the freedom to hang out in the acres of free parking in front of Rose's Department Store and the Winn-Dixie supermarket. (The strip mall they anchored was called Radcliff Square, a vague reference to the dimly remembered public spaces of another time, when towns had centers.) Or they could cruise the lake—that is, drive back and forth in Freeman Lake Park behind the Coca-Cola bottling plant in nearby Elizabethtown.

Broad lawns surrounded that small pond, beside which were displayed a couple of rough-hewn log cabins that Abraham Lincoln's father, carpenter Thomas Lincoln, had helped to build. (Abraham was born and spent the first seven years of his life in what was now Larue County, just a few miles away.) A hundred and fifty yards north of the cabins, a stone wall surrounded an elm and a maple, at the foot of which were eight crumbling gravestones, including those of "Catherine Hayden, daughter of Jacob and Lettecia, aged 1 year, 11 months, 1841"; "Infant son of Wm. H. Thomas"; "Charles, infant son of Wilson A. and Mary A. Vaughan, January 8, 1878." The grief seemed very much alive, long after the grievers had been forgotten. One stone, illegible, was enfolded by two roots, as though safe in a mother's arms. From time to time, a train whistle moaned softly in the distance.

Alongside the lake ran a road with a U-turn at each end. One complete circuit was a mile. The teenagers would drive back and forth, back and forth, endlessly.

❑

In May 1988, Shannon's long-haired white alley cat, Sir Richard Flokati—who had gotten so fat that she called him Little Buddy Butter Buns, or Bunsy Broadbottom, for short—disappeared. After five days, he finally dragged himself home, ragged and desperately sick; he had been shot through the surface of his abdomen. He was put on an IV at the vet's, and Janey took Shannon up every day after school to hand-feed him turkey that they'd ground up in the food processor. "You all are gonna spoil that cat so if he lives he won't eat regular cat food," the vet warned, but they went right on.

Shannon and Janey were forever adopting stray cats, including the one who was Bunsy's mother. Another, Cindy, whom they'd found in Kansas in 1980, evidently had been abused, because Shannon and Donald never could pet her. Janey told them, "We'll take her, she's our responsibility, but you're just gonna have to leave her alone. This is what happens —animals are just like people—when they're mistreated they're never the same." ("I tried to use Cindy for an object lesson," Janey recalled later. "She never did get friendly. She just stayed here and ate, for eleven years. In fact she outlived Shannon.") One kitten got run over, and when Shannon was nine she gave one away, but only after very closely interviewing the prospective owners to make sure they were suitable. Bunsy was Shannon's favorite; every Sunday afternoon he lay on her lap as she read a book. Bunsy recovered, but the next spring, one year after the bus crash, Bunsy came down with feline leukemia and died. "That was hard," Janey says. "Losing her pets is hard too."

❑

On Wednesday, May 11, 1988, Shannon went with her dad and got a water bed. Donald had prevailed upon his parents to get him one, so Larry asked Shannon if she wanted one, too. "For a couple of days she batted it around—I don't know if I talked her into it, she didn't talk into much— but she finally decided she would like one," Larry recalled later. "So we went down Tuesday to two or three different places. Wednesday we bought it; Thursday we put it together and filled the mattress. So she slept on it two nights."

On Friday, May 13, the day before the bus trip, Shannon showed up at school with a tan. She told Leeann Riley, her eighth-grade social studies teacher, that Estée Lauder was the best artificial tanner; QT turned her orange.

During spring break, Shannon had wanted to go to a tanning salon in Johnson City. "She said, 'I'm going on a trip and I'll get a burn if I don't have a tan,'" Janey recounted later. "She didn't like the freckles on her nose, and they would get more pronounced after a sunburn. I hate to have a disagreement with her: I lectured her that she would get skin cancer or be old before her time. I told her about bottled tan. Our compromise was three sessions in the tanning bed, and then we'd get some Estée Lauder at the PX. The year before, she'd gotten a bad burn, and we spent the whole eighth-grade year bleaching her freckles out with liver-spot remover, plus foundation makeup."

Shannon had been very much a tomboy when she was younger, but the last couple of years her brother, Donald, who was two years older, couldn't help noticing that she was growing up a lot. "I remember walking around the house one time," he recalls. "She was lying down in her swimsuit beside the house. I walked around the corner, and she made me look twice. She went to a band tryout—me and her both played saxophone—my friends were like, 'Dang! Donald, your sister's fine.' And I was like, 'If you touch her, I'm killing you!' I mean, actually, she was just becoming a woman."

CHAPTER

33

Larry Mahoney got off work at 7:00 A.M. on Saturday morning, May 14, 1988, completing his third consecutive twelve-hour overnight shift at the big M & T Chemical plant in Carrollton. A tenth-grade dropout, Mahoney had hired on there as a laborer and advanced to the $11-an-hour position of operator, running machines that measured, mixed, cooked, and dried diverse noxious elements into substances useful for making plastics and paint. He would now have three days off before the next three-night marathon. And so it would continue: three twelve-hour shifts, three days off, switching from night shifts to day shifts every six weeks. Uninterrupted operation best suited the rhythm of the machinery. During each twelve-hour session, Mahoney had three breaks, of twenty minutes, thirty minutes (for dinner), and twenty minutes. There was no union at M & T.

Mahoney drove his black Toyota pickup out Route 227. Right after it passed the I-71 interchange on the edge of town, the two-lane blacktop left behind the contentious jumble of roadside businesses and followed the Kentucky River back up into the hills where everything was pure and quiet and beautiful. Mahoney enjoyed five miles of peace, then hung a hard left and a quick right and jounced over a half mile of crude gravel road through a hollow to the rear, less desirable section of the muddy trailer park that was wistfully named Eagle Creek Camp Ground. He stopped at the run-down, green and white little mobile home he'd rented a few months earlier. He'd had this idea that he and his first ex-wife, Janice, should, nine years after divorcing, move back together and make a real home for their fifteen-year-old son, Tony. This was the home. A bare bulb glowed grimly beside the gray metal door; a rust stain dripped below the knocker. Mahoney, who grew up on a hillside tobacco farm, didn't like this trailer; it was too close to the neighbors, he told Tony. Inside, it was even closer to Janice. In that dreary and confining place, Romeo and Juliet would have been at each other's throats before dawn.

Mahoney caught about five hours' sleep before Tony awakened him sometime around noon. (Janice was already at work at the Interstate Carry-out.) That brought to about fifteen hours the total sleep Mahoney'd had in the past three days, which was considered about average for a guy on the night shift; he'd remained alert enough to work.

Between one and two o'clock, Mahoney showed up at Drifter's Tavern ("Ice, Pool, Cold Beer") on the western edge of Carrollton. He sat alone and nursed two Miller Lites through the next hour, during which time he did not engage the blond, pony-tailed bartender, Jinky Simpson, or anyone else, in conversation. Simpson, who knew him as an occasional customer, later assessed Mahoney as not intoxicated and to all appearances just "his normal self."

Around three o'clock, Mahoney came into Tubby's Tavern, a ramshackle white roadhouse a few miles away on Route 227 at the south side of Carrollton, which was on his way home. ("Tubby's Last Chance Tavern," a sign said, since it was close to the line of dry Owen County, where Mahoney lived; or "Tubby's First Chance Tavern," when you were coming the other way.) The half dozen stools were occupied, so Mahoney stood at the pillar at the end of the bar. He looked just like always—"sober and clean-cut," as the grandmotherly bartender Jean Chandler later recalled; she swore he consumed just one Miller Lite while the red digits of the illuminated Coors clock in front of him slid through an hour. Again, he said nothing, except to ask what was wrong with somebody he overheard the bartender describing as ill. They thought it was cancer, she said.

Mahoney was never much of a talker. He had no interest in sports and there was only so much you could say about the weather, so he'd sit quietly. And because he was good-looking in a delicate, almost feminine way, it was easy for people—especially women—to imagine that he was thinking deep, sensitive thoughts when in fact he might just be half listening to the jukebox and feeling tired.

Of course, it didn't take much to look like a gentle soul against the background of Tubby's. The cinderblock walls, the concrete floor, the green-vinyl-covered chrome stools, everything was as hard as the lives of the sinewy tobacco farmers who partied there. The funny thing was, with their shoulder-length brown hair, half of them looked like Jesus—albeit a ticked-off Jesus, ignored for too long. They worked too hard, toiling in the tobacco fields when they got out of the factories; they had too little money; and they were sure that everybody who had more than they did looked down on them, which was pretty much true. They'd play pool and drink beer till they were whooping insanely to some bar band's country music, and more than rarely a couple of guys would end the evening by fighting the enemy closest at hand, which would invariably be each other, since the higher-ups they so resented would not go near Tubby's Tavern.

It was easy to see that Mahoney was different, whether or not he was. He had a sad quality about him, like the sweet soulful fellas in the country-and-western songs who were always so sorry that they'd made a mess of things again. And so first Janice King and then Betty Davis and then Kim Frederick had fallen in love with him, and now he was all tangled up.

Janice King was one of those smart, good-looking women who make things happen in such a way that their lives are always complicated and full of drama. Mahoney was nineteen when they got married. They promptly had a son, Tony. The divorce came seven years later, in 1979. Mahoney agreed to pay her $30 a week child support, except for when Tony was living with him, which he had been for five years before Janice agreed to give togetherness another shot in the trailer.

Back when they divorced, Mahoney had not gotten over Janice easily. According to a complaint she swore out on him in February 1980, he pounded on her door at the Carrollton Village Apartments and shouted that he had a knife and was of a mind to use it on her *and* her boyfriend. A warrant was issued for his arrest on charges of terroristic threatening and disorderly conduct. He pled guilty to the latter and was fined $50.

A couple of years later, in 1982, Mahoney had married Betty Davis, a teacher's aide. That September their daughter, Shawna, was born with spina bifida, a defective closure of the spinal cord. She was hospitalized five times in the first four months of her life. As a result of his baby's multiple operations, Mahoney, who after a stint as a deck hand on coal barges was doing farm work at the time, soon faced $250,000 in medical bills.

In what Mahoney saw as a related event, he was arrested that December of 1982 in the parking lot of Della Rosa Pizza, after some sort of altercation in which he'd been somehow involved—even if only to break it up, as he maintained. A police officer arrived too late to see the fight but just in time to be the target of Mahoney's foul language. He arrested him for disorderly conduct. (Beer and liquor were on Della Rosa's menu, but Mahoney always maintained he was not drunk, and indeed he was not charged with public drunkenness.) At his arraignment on January 6, 1983, Mahoney presumably did his best to mask his puzzlement and arrange his face into a map of remorse as he listened to the odd disquisition of Carroll District Court Judge William Knapp:

"The only thing I know to say to a police officer is, 'Yes sir, No sir,'" the judge began. "If you don't, it's a whole lot like telling a woman to do something she's not of a mind to do. You're apt to get into a whole lot of difficulty. Police officers bear a remarkable similarity to women. They get all bent out of shape if you don't do what they tell you, when they tell you. You understand that?"

"Yes, sir," Mahoney whispered, improbably.

"Tell me what happened," the judge prompted.

"I really don't know," said Mahoney, who didn't have a lawyer but seemed to grasp well enough that he need not provide any evidence to help the prosecution. Instead he immediately launched into what was either a manipulative bid for sympathy or a sincere attempt to account for his behavior: "I've had a little bad luck, with my baby and stuff. She's getting out of the hospital today. She's done been through surgery five times."

"What for?" asked the judge, who must have been grateful to hear anything of interest.

"She had a hole in her spine when she was born," Mahoney explained as best he could. "She'll be four months old the tenth. They had to put a pump in her head and tubes down into her stomach to pump the fluid off."

"Have they got that all straightened out?"

"No, they've changed it three times—the pump—already. It works awhile and then it quits."

"But what's that got to do with a disorderly conduct at the Della Rosa pizza parlor?" the judge suddenly demanded, dashing whatever hope Mahoney might have had that he was getting over. If the judge couldn't see the connection, there wasn't anyone that could explain it to him, least of all Larry, who'd given up on words a long time ago.

"Well, really it doesn't, I don't guess," he allowed. "I've just been having a hard time."

"What all went on at Della Rosa?"

"I really don't know," Mahoney repeated, less artfully but just as effectively as the most sophisticated white-collar defendant. *You can always say you don't remember.*

"We're about to adjourn for lunch," the judge followed up. "Have you been in court before?"

Mahoney had owned up to a disorderly with his ex-wife a couple of years prior. Judge Knapp noted sternly that anybody can make one mistake, but he took a dim view of repeat offenders. "Have you got insurance to cover your baby's doctor bills?" he asked as he considered the fine. No sense punishing the innocent child along with the guilty father.

Mahoney said he was going to have to drop his insurance. It cost $2,400 a year, and wasn't helping much with the bills that were coming in at the rate of two or three a week. For example, the "gas for putting her out," that is to say, the anesthesiologist's bill, was $1,500 and the insurance paid only $500; he couldn't understand why.

This glancing contact with the judicial system—Mahoney's second—concluded with one of those loud warnings about next time that send an unspoken but unmistakable message about this time: *We really don't give a shit about you or what you do:* "If I see you again on any kind of violent acting-out behavior, disorderly conduct or whatever, it's gonna be jail. Do you understand that?" He did. "The court makes a finding of guilt and imposes a fine of $100 and costs. Pay your fine today and be on your way. I hope your baby gets better. I hope it works out for you. It seems to me to be *lunchtime!*"

❑

In 1984, crushed by Shawna's medical bills, Mahoney declared bankruptcy. That was also the year he was stopped for failing to dim his headlights and for weaving; he blew a .16 on the Breathalyzer and was arrested for driving under the influence. His friend Dennis Mefford posted the $350 bail. Mahoney pled guilty to DUI and was fined $140 and required to attend nine hours of Alcohol Driver Education, which he did.

He and Betty got a divorce in 1987, a rather amicable one as divorces go. They remained united in their devotion to their brave little girl, who was confined to a wheelchair. Every week Mahoney visited Shawna and faithfully paid the $40 in child support that Betty had requested, except —she had specified this exception—he didn't have to pay if he'd been laid off.

It was around that time that Mahoney met Kim Frederick. The tall and graceful Frederick was unbowed by her years of labor as "an opener" in the stockroom of a clothing store. Had her circumstances differed she might have served well as a princess, cutting ribbons instead of cardboard, so regal was her bearing. She was the lone and manifestly loving parent of a bright and well-mannered little boy, but somehow she found her way to Tubby's one evening, where she spied that quiet man, Larry Mahoney. It turned out she liked the outdoors, same as he did, and soon they were fishing together, talking, having a couple of beers. She told the police in all good faith that Mahoney was not a heavy drinker, that he never downed more than six or eight beers in a day.

Mahoney had at last found still waters in Kim Frederick's port, but unaccustomed to tranquillity he'd heeded the call to reestablish hearth and home with Janice King for the sake of their son. With scarcely a word of explanation to Kim he'd broken off with her in January 1988 and moved in with Janice. By March, he was being treated for a duodenal ulcer, a condition that, he and his defenders said later, caused him to cut down on his drinking. (A reduction in drinking, in turn, could have reduced his tolerance for alcohol.)

The trailer he shared with Janice was getting smaller every day. He'd applied for a loan to finance bigger digs, and just now, in May 1988, the bank had turned him down flat, pointing to his all-too-recent 1984 bankruptcy. Mahoney thought this rejection unfair in the extreme. As a point of personal honor, he had voluntarily continued to pay off a $10,000 home improvement loan a little at a time over the past four years, though the obligation had been discharged by the bankruptcy. Come to find out, his honor, his honesty, and his effort meant nothing.

This Saturday, May 14, something had to give. From Tubby's Mahoney stopped by his parents' house to pick up his mail. His mother would swear later that he did not seem intoxicated at the time. Of course, God put mothers on earth to stick up for their children, and Mahoney's devout and devoted mother loved him beyond all reason, insisting to this day that the fault for what happened must rest anywhere but with her son. Still, few could doubt Mahoney when he testified that he would not have set foot in his mother's house if he were drunk.

Around 5:00 or 5:30 that afternoon, Mahoney turned up in Burlington, an hour's drive from Carrollton, at the pharmacy/carry-out liquor store where Kim Frederick worked a second job. She did smell alcohol on his breath, but he didn't seem drunk as he confided that he was confused and needed to talk to her. She had told him when he left her that she would always be there if he needed her, and she agreed now to meet him at 10:00 P.M. at a Burlington bar. (Janey Fair would later note that for a man who didn't drink much, Mahoney spent a lot of time in bars, with friends who did the same.) Frederick offered him her house keys and an invitation to crash at her place in the meantime, but Mahoney, fatefully, declined. He drove back home.

At 7:30 Mahoney arrived at the neat white ranch house of Dennis Mefford, a friend and fellow M & T Chemical worker with whom Larry often went coon hunting. Mefford was busy installing a Sony tape player in his Ford pickup truck. (This was just the latest consumer good acquired by Mefford. Mahoney could only wonder at his friend's life-management skills. Mefford's family was intact, his house was spacious, and anytime he wanted to buy something it seemed like all he had to do was go down to the bank and ask for the money.) Mahoney had a six-pack of beer with him when he arrived at Mefford's; he pulled one off for himself and gave one to Dennis. Over the next hour Mahoney may have had another as they shared a pizza.

Then he headed down the road toward his home, but he encountered Taylor Fox on the way and went over to his house, where a bunch of guys were helping Fox outfit an old blue school bus as a motor home. Fox, a part-time tree trimmer, did all kinds of odd jobs and frequently made trips to Florida. In fact, he was leaving the next day, and in this bus he could journey in comfort, with room to spare for such cargo as fortune might provide.

Mahoney had a beer in his hand as he was driving, when he met Fox, and he proceeded to drink a couple more at Fox's house. Fox got the keys for Mahoney's pick-up, either to shut down the country music twanging infernally out of the Toyota's sound system; or to keep Mahoney off the road, or both. The usually taciturn Larry was joking and laughing now, a sure sign to those who knew him that he had a buzz on, at least. So when he asked Fox if he'd drive him up to see Kim later, Fox said he would, because otherwise he thought Mahoney might be stopped for drunk driving and go to jail. By 10:00, Mahoney had consumed some straight vodka and a quantity of Pepsi that, whether he knew it or not, had been fortified with vodka. He said he was too tired to go to Burlington after all, and asked for his keys so he could drive home. That drive was two-tenths of a mile straight down a scarcely traveled paved road to a right turn into the trailer park. You could drive it in a coma, and the chance of encountering a cop was near absolute zero. So Fox handed over the keys. He then watched Mahoney's taillights go straight past the turn and disappear into the distance. In a moment, Mahoney would bear left onto Route 227, toward Carrollton and the I-71 interchange.

Exactly what Mahoney did for the next hour could not be determined.

Because three cans of beer were found still cold in the wreckage of his truck, it was apparent that he had bought beer. Not surprisingly, a canvas of every outlet in the area failed to produce any vendor who was willing to admit he had sold it.

Mahoney got on I-71 north, in the direction of Burlington and Kim Frederick. Perhaps he changed his mind, because four miles north of Carrollton, he cut across the grass median and headed south. He may have pulled into the abandoned truck-weighing station ten miles south of Carrollton, perhaps to relieve himself; he'd had a lot to drink.

The weigh station, five miles south of the accident site, occupied a dark siding parallel to the highway, very much like a rest area. The entrance and exit lacked directional signs. Mahoney may have become confused, reversed himself and reentered the highway in the wrong direction.

At that point, the north- and southbound lanes of I-71 were widely divided by a sixty-foot grass median. Each two-lane, one-way gray macadam roadway, with its dashed white line down the middle, looked remarkably like the two-lane, two-way roadway of Route 227, the road that led from I-71 to Mahoney's home. Maybe Mahoney lost track of where he was and believed he was on Route 227. He kept carefully to the right of the center line. He did not speed. He did not weave. It was as though he were playing a video game, guiding a dot of phosphor on an electron screen: Follow the line. Keep to the right. All the way home.

He made it 1,717 feet north of mile marker 40.

CHAPTER

34

"**I** don't think we really decided *to sue* Ford," Larry Fair recalls. "What evolved was, *we refused to let Ford settle* with us at their discretion—them come down and say, 'Here is the money we're going to pay you for your child's death, and we're just gonna kindly forget about it and let bygones be bygones.'"

The Fairs were willing to consider a settlement based on a commitment by the manufacturers to improve the safety of their buses, but Ford and Sheller-Globe expressed no interest in such a deal, so Larry and Janey dug in for a fight.

Janey, a couple of weeks after burying Shannon, tried to immerse herself in research on buses and drunk driving and grief. But she couldn't read. Her mind would wander off the page before she reached the end of a sentence. "I have no trouble understanding Larry Mahoney," she kept thinking. "It's God I can't understand."

She couldn't eat. She couldn't sleep. She was in one world and everybody else was in another, though they could hear her and see her. She supposed she looked perfectly normal to everybody else, but she knew that she was not. She felt as though she were in a faraway country, far from home, and she could never get back.

Then she woke up one morning in a rage at God. A terrible, uncontrollable rage that horrified her. Yet as she was buffeted by that storm of emotion she felt connected again, to something, and knew that she would not end up in an insane asylum after all.

Now she was able to read, and books were recommended to her, books about people riven by death who had somehow found comfort or meaning—which are pretty much the same thing. Most of the books she found less than completely honest—a little too brave, a little too hopeful. If a single detail seemed false, the whole thing was shaky, and you couldn't lean on it. Then she came across the British theologian C. S. Lewis's book *A Grief Observed,* which spoke to her. The author had found love late in life and had been married just five years when his wife —whom he calls H.—died a slow and agonizing death from cancer. "There is a sort of invisible blanket between me and the world," he wrote on the first page. "I find it hard to take in what anyone says." Here was a person who had felt what she felt; that was a start.

Lewis went on to describe the lack of comfort in comforting words. "It is hard to have patience with people who say 'There is no death' or 'Death doesn't matter.' ... You might as well say that birth doesn't matter. I look up at the night sky. Is anything more certain than that in all those vast times and spaces, if I were allowed to search them, I should nowhere find her face, her voice, her touch? She died. She is dead." And the anger at God, he had felt that, too. "They tell me H. is happy now, they tell me she is at peace. What makes them so sure of this? ... 'Because she is in God's hands.' But if so, she was in God's hands all the time, and I have seen what they did to her here."

Through prayerful concentration, introspection, and the passage of time, Lewis arrived at the realization that "If there is a good God, then these tortures are necessary"; and everywhere he encountered a sense that his beloved was still "momentously real." Finally, as he tried to conceive of the inconceivable—union with God and reunion with his beloved—there came to him the solution: "We shall see that there never was any problem ... some shattering and disarming simplicity is the real answer."

Janey did not wake up one morning in a distinct new stage of grief called recovery. But after a while her rage at God would come and go, and she grew less horrifed by it when she realized that the rage itself was an offering to God, because it bespoke a belief in Him.

She did choose to believe, but she found it difficult, for instance, to imagine what heaven could be. If heaven were to be as she envisioned it, everything would be in a pristine condition; it wouldn't be in a state of transition. Then would Shannon be forever fourteen? Would she grow up? Would it be unfair for her not to develop and experience life, since she was denied it here? How about people who were babies? Would everyone be the same age? If everyone would be the same age, obviously heaven would be much different from what she would envision as heavenly because for her kittens and puppies and babies were things that make life most pleasurable. Her concept of beauty embraced rosebuds as well as full-blown roses; but a full-blown rose was in the process of dying. There were a lot of fundamental questions that she stayed up late at night thinking about. And she didn't come to any answers; nor did she expect to, since she knew that her knowledge was only of earthly things.

CHAPTER
35

The first formal, public attempt to determine the facts of the bus crash came in August 1988, when the National Transportation Safety Board convened a hearing in the Grand Ball Room of Louisville's Hurstbourne Lane Holiday Inn.* (There was nothing grand about the windowless, floral-carpeted function room—though it did have mirrored ceiling tiles—and it was infrequently the site of a ball. The NTSB hearings had been immediately preceded by a baby beauty pageant—Baby Mister and Miss U.S.A.—and would be followed by a Shriners charity dinner to benefit Kosair Hospital.)

After attending every minute of the two and a half days of testimony, the Fairs came away with the impression that the inquiry had relied rather too heavily on information provided by people associated with Ford, and perhaps not coincidentally had failed to explore fully the role of the

---

* The public hearing is actually the next to the last act in the NTSB's fact-finding process. Before the hearing, the board's technical experts have examined the vehicles and scene, interviewed witnesses and studied documentary evidence. The hearing represents a final opportunity to gather information before the board reaches its conclusions and publishes a report.

school bus's design in the disaster, or the danger school buses might continue to pose.

In truth, the NTSB was concerned that the hearings might promote an excessive fear of school buses that could prompt parents to abandon them in favor of private cars, which on the whole would be more hazardous. (Cars had a fatality rate per vehicle mile nearly four times that of school buses.) NTSB technical panelist Byrd Raby had called Ford's heavy truck design analyst Robert Pelkey a month before the hearing to confide that, according to Pelkey's notes, "He [Raby] must address the safety of the current bus fleet tho this will be done lightly. Wants to support public confidence in buses." Raby asked Pelkey to provide such confidence-inspiring information as he might have.

❏

NTSB Chairman Jim Burnett, a former Clinton, Arkansas, traffic court judge who had been known for his tough treatment of drunk drivers, opened the hearings promptly at 9:00 A.M. on Tuesday, August 2, by reading an account of an accident: "A vehicle driven by a man under the influence of alcohol, going the wrong way on an interstate, collided with a bus," he began. "A fire erupted, gutting the bus and killing many of the passengers." He described the crash in some detail, and observed that "We [the NTSB] were very interested in a number of aspects of the accident. What was the performance of the driver under the influence of alcohol? How effective was the design of the bus, including the location of the fuel tank?" Then came the surprise ending: "The Safety Board investigated this accident in 1968, not 1988. The collision occurred on Interstate 15 near Baker, California. . . .'

Burnett turned to the matter at hand: "The accident we are reviewing at this hearing [is] very similar in many of its respects. . . ." He never mentioned Baker, California, again, never explained why he had brought it up, leaving his audience to ponder its significance: Were dark forces obstructing needed safety changes? Were humans by nature resistant to learning from experience? Was the NTSB, charged by Congress with recommending safety measures but with no authority to draft or impose them, in business principally to defuse public passion through the bureaucratic method of studying problems to death? Whatever his intended message, the chairman's opening was certainly not calculated to enliven the hopes of those in attendance that here, at last, was the beginning of action to make things right.

Burnett explained that the goal of the hearing was not to fix blame but to assemble a complete factual record, on the basis of which the safety board would determine the probable cause of the accident and suggest safety measures to avoid such accidents in the future. (There may be a fine line between determining the cause of and fixing the blame for an accident, but as a matter of law, the NTSB's findings cannot be introduced in civil litigation to prove fault.) He listed six issues the hearing would address; and though he took pains to note that no inferences should be drawn from the order in which he named them, the Fairs could not help but notice that the first five pertained to various aspects of the drunk driving problem; school bus safety concerns were lumped together at the end as issue number six.

After two witnesses described the collision and conflagration, Larry Mahoney's friend Phil Downey was called to describe Mahoney's drinking. He said that Larry in general drank only Miller Lite beer; Downey might have seen him take a drink of whiskey once or twice in the dozen years he'd known him. On the evening of May 14, when Mahoney arrived at Taylor Fox's house around 9:00 P.M., "I could tell he had a few beers, but I wouldn't have thought he was drunk." He was just laughing and joking a little more than usual, Downey recalled. "When he's sober, he's really quiet. He's really an exceptionally quiet person, actually."

Well, what *is* really drunk? a board member asked.

"Somebody who's real drunk, he's usually staggering a little bit, or weaving a little," Downey explained.

Another Mahoney friend present that night testified to the same effect: "He wasn't that drunk," said Taylor Fox, who at one point had pocketed Mahoney's keys.

Asked by a member of the board to define the difference between "not that drunk" and "drunk," Fox replied, "I can drink seven or eight beers and I'm not drunk. I don't stagger. I can drink twelve, thirteen maybe, then I'm drunk, you know, falling around and stuff. I mean, that's the difference between drunk and just drinking. . . . I would say, knowing Larry, and I know him pretty well, he might have had seven or eight beers [over the prior six or seven hours] when I first saw him. . . . Larry could handle it real well."

Fox admitted that he himself probably could not drive as well after seven or eight beers as he could sober, but that he had often done so, because he would have to get home and he believed he could drive well enough to make it. In admitting this, he was admitting no more than what

countless people have done at some point in their lives, including the
author of this book.

❏

The next witness, UCLA psychology professor Herbert Moskowitz, tried
to dispell some of Fox's and Downey's misapprehensions about drunkenness in general and Mahoney's drinking in particular.

First of all, Moskowitz said, based on Mahoney's blood alcohol concentration (BAC), measured by one lab at .26 an hour and a half after the
collision,* he must have consumed not seven or eight beers since 2:00
P.M., as Fox had estimated, but, rather, eighteen or nineteen; except if he
indeed was drinking Miller Lite, with light beer's lower alcohol content,
it would have to have been about twenty-four cans.

The fact that Mahoney was able to drive at all with such a high blood
alcohol concentration made it extremely unlikely that he was indeed the
occasional social drinker that his friends had described, according to
Moskowitz. "I suspect that 90 percent of moderate social drinkers who
attempted to achieve this [level of BAC] would become violently ill," he
said. In one study he conducted, half of heavy drinkers threw up before
they reached .15. "So you've got to be a fairly heavy, consistent drinker to
get anywhere close to this level without throwing up." Moscowitz concluded that based on his tolerance for alcohol and his social history (one
DUI and two disorderly conduct arrests), Mahoney was very probably a
problem drinker.

And one problem with problem drinkers, the psychologist explained,
is that they don't know when they are drunk, and don't know when
their drinking buddies are drunk, either. Fox and Downey had equated
drunkenness with staggering and falling down, and had concluded that
Mahoney could drive because he wasn't exhibiting those symptoms. But
Moscowitz explained that alcohol impairs driving performance in significant ways unrelated to physical coordination.

Alcohol impairs your ability to pay attention—to gather and process
information—he said. "You can't survey as many things in your mind as
you normally would . . . and driving is a task which requires dividing
attention among a variety of aspects. You have to keep the vehicle in both
its lane position and heading, which is the tracking aspect; and you have

---

* One lab measured one sample of Mahoney's blood at .26. Another lab measured another
sample, taken at the same time, at .24. From these two starting points, various experts extrapo-
lated various BAC levels for Mahoney at the time of the crash—none below .21.

to at the same time survey the environment for potential dangers, such as other vehicles, pedestrians, traffic lights, and so forth.

"People under the influence of alcohol find it increasingly difficult to monitor all the aspects, and they tend to concentrate on car control aspects, and they're less and less sensitive to their environment." Mahoney, for example, apparently concentrating on the road-tracking aspects of the driving task, drove his truck straight as an arrow and within the speed limit, but "he was insensitive to the fact that he was going the wrong way."

Moskowitz added that the influence of alcohol on Mahoney would have been exacerbated by three other factors related to his having just completed three twelve-hour night shifts at the chemical plant: He was fatigued; he was sleep-deprived; and he had just shifted his waking hours from night back to day, which produces a sort of "waking sleep" state.

Besides having trouble processing information, people under the influence of alcohol also suffer from impaired perception, Moskowitz said. Because the brain is working more slowly, you have to look longer to become aware of seeing something, and sometimes you fail to see it at all. This perceptual impairment plays a far greater roll in drunk driving accidents than the psychomotor ("staggering") impairment that Fox and Downey and, perhaps, most people consider the defining symptom of drunkenness, Moscowitz explained. "The majority of alcohol-related accidents occur with an individual going straight ahead, and the only problem is there's something in the way."

Thus, Moscowitz said, someone who has had two to four drinks at a cocktail party and has reached a BAC of .05 to .10 is severely impaired for driving, even though he can drive a straight line. But such a driver may well be unaware of his impairment: "You can see yourself stumbling, but you can't see that you don't see something that's there. So it's not available to your self-consciousness, and it's not really available to anybody else's perception. Someone would have to know you very well to detect the small changes in your social behavior or in the way you walk at those levels."

❑

The next several witnesses, who took up the rest of the day, all dealt with the question of what to do about drunk drivers such as Larry Mahoney.

Dr. Harvey Siegel, a medical sociologist and substance abuse expert, characterized Mahoney as a binge drinker: "Mr. Mahoney's use pattern emphasized episodic loss of control." The alcohol driver education classes that Mahoney had to attend as a result of his DUI conviction in 1984 probably did him little good, Siegel said. Such classes convey some basic information about the effects of alcohol, and conclude with an anonymous self-evaluation, such as the Michigan Alcoholism Screening Test (MAST), to help problem drinkers identify themselves so they can seek help, but there is no attempt to identify or track those problem drinkers.

CHAPTER

36

The second day of the NTSB hearings continued with yet another witness testifying about drunk driving, Dr. James L. Nichols, chief of the Alcohol Programs Division at NHTSA.

Half of drivers involved in fatal crashes have had something to drink, said Nichols. Two out of five drivers involved in fatal crashes are legally drunk. Three quarters of those legally drunk drivers involved in fatal crashes had never been convicted of drunk driving.

From 9:00 P.M. to 3:00 A.M. on Friday and Saturday nights, an estimated five percent of drivers on the road are legally drunk, he said, but on a given weekend night, no more than one in 500 of them are apprehended.

Alcohol-related traffic deaths had declined 15 percent since 1980, Nichols said, and much of that progress was likely attributable to general deterrence, anti-drunk-driving measures that affect all drivers, not just the drunk drivers who get caught. (Specific deterrence affects the latter.) General deterrence includes increased police activity—such as the apparently most effective anti-drunk-driving tactic, publicized roadside sobriety checkpoints with the threat of immediate license suspension for anyone failing or refusing a Breathalyzer test. Such a program tends to dissuade broad segments of the population from getting behind the wheel after drinking, without their ever having any contact with police or the courts. "So if you ever want to have a major impact on the problem, you have to find some way to deter ... all of the drivers that are out there," Nichols said.

❏

After more than a day of testimony, school bus safety had yet to be addressed. The premise of the proceedings seemed to be that drunk driving was *the* cause of the twenty-seven deaths. This assumption troubled the Fairs, who figured that a similarly designed school bus could have crashed into a bridge abutment with the same deadly result; or that a drunk driver could have crashed into a differently designed school bus with a very different result.

When the subject of school bus safety was finally raised, it seemed to Larry and Janey that the intent was to dismiss the problem, rather than try to solve it. "In the context of the occupants' risk of fatalities, school buses are very safe," declared William Boehly, a nineteen-year NHTSA veteran who was then director of NHTSA's National Center for Statistics Analysis.

Boehly testified that in the prior year, 1987, 150 individuals were killed in crashes involving school buses.* Of those 150 who died, 14 were killed while riding in the bus—which was just about average. Over a ten-year period (1977–86), about one in 10 school bus crash fatalities was aboard the bus; 3 in 10 were on foot (often in connection with getting on or off the bus); and 6 in 10 were occupants of other vehicles involved in a crash with a school bus.

Of those 14 occupant-fatalities, 10 were children, that is, eighteen years old or younger. By comparison, 4,437 children died in passenger cars.

School bus vehicle occupant fatalities associated with fire, Boehly said,

* NHTSA's Fatal Accident Reporting System (FARS) relies on forms filled out by police departments. The FARS "school bus-related accident" category is based on vehicle function, not vehicle type: Accidents involving vans used to transport students to or from school or school-related activities are counted; accidents involving school buses owned and operated by church groups, camps and so forth are not. The National Safety Council defines its "school bus accident" category in a similar way. Therefore, the Carrollton "church bus" accident does not show up in most school bus accident statistics.

were rarer still. In the same ten-year period, NHTSA knew of only nine. All occurred in one 1984 Montana crash, when a fuel tanker truck jack-knifed and hit a bus head-on. Even then, it was believed, all of the children were killed when the bus roof collapsed and crushed them, before they were burned.

Boehly was then asked if he knew how many nonfatal school bus fires there had been. "No, we don't," he said. The National Accident Sampling System (NASS) provided information regarding a small sample of accidents, about 200 school bus accidents per year. None in the sample had ever included a fire. "I think you can say quantitatively you don't know, but you know it's . . . a very, very, very rare problem." Of course, Boehly added, referring to the disaster at hand, "This is one of these things that happens with rare events, is that they do pop up occasionally; and this obviously is one that did happen."

CHAPTER

37

After a twenty-minute break, during which the Fairs mulled over the fact that school bus fires were "a very rare problem," the hearings reconvened at 10:30 A.M. The next witness, Ralph J. Hitchcock, a gray-haired twenty-one-year NHTSA veteran, had since 1982 held the post of director of the Office of Vehicle Safety Standards.

"Do you have any additional experience in this area?" he was asked.

"Prior to coming to the National Highway Traffic Safety Administration, I worked for the Ford Motor Company in the areas of vehicle design," said Hitchcock.

The Ford Motor Company. How nice, thought Janey. She already knew that the only accident reconstructionist to testify at the hearing would be John Habberstad, who happened to be retained by Ford as an expert to help defend the company against her lawsuit; she wondered if the NTSB was running a Ford reunion.

The panel turned to the question of why so many passengers had been unable to escape the fire. There was no flammability standard written specifically for school buses—not in 1977 when the bus was built, not in 1988 when the bus burned like a canister of napalm (and not in 1994, as this account is being written). The federal motor vehicle safety standard for flammability, FMVSS 302, which went into effect in 1972, regulates the burn-rate of materials in a vehicle's passenger compartment. Applicable to private autos, school buses, and trucks alike, it requires that a flame ignited by a bunsen burner must travel across a horizontal sample of, for example, seating material at no more than four inches a minute. A rolled-up newspaper could pass that test. In real life, flames have the chance to leap up vertical surfaces, not just creep across horizontal ones. A couple of crumpled sheets of paper set afire on a bus seat pose a tougher burn test than that of Standard 302. A flaming fuel tank is tougher still.

Dr. Merritt Birky of the NTSB technical panel asked Hitchcock if the FMVSS 302 test revealed anything about how material would burn if it were oriented vertically, like a seat back. "I think it's probably not entirely the best test to measure vertical flammabiliity, if that's a concern," Hitchcock conceded.

(Since 1984, the federal government's Urban Mass Transportation Administration has recommended that upholstery on subways and streetcars be subjected to a vertical test similar to that employed by the Federal Aviation Administration for passenger aircraft: A bunsen burner is applied to the vertically oriented fabric, then removed. The flaming fabric must self-extinguish within ten seconds, and the flame must not progress more than six inches.)

"Does [the horizontal flame test] have any relationship to a large ignition source [such as a fuel fire] on an area like a full-scale seat?" Hitchcock was asked.

"I guess I don't know the answer to that," he replied. He explained that the advantage of horizontal tests is their ease of measurement, objectivity, and repeatability, which make the standard easier to define and enforce. Then, too, he went on, NHTSA didn't want to go overboard with a highly stringent flammability rule, because sometimes chemicals added to impede flaming actually increase the amount of smoke and/or the amount of toxic gases released, so by trying too singlemindedly to solve one problem you can create others. As it was, there were manufacturers arguing that a fifteen-inch-per-minute burn rate, instead of four inches per minute, would be just fine. "[W]e try to arrive at something that's reasonable and practical and meets the need for safety," he said. "That's our statutory criteria."

"[I]t was my belief until May 13th [sic] of this year, perhaps, or, you know, until even, perhaps, after the investigation started," Hitchcock continued, haltingly, "that the—although the bus seats did burn—and the seats in all vehicles burn, and materials in vehicles burn—they did provide an adequate time for the occupants to get out of the vehicle; and that was our concern."

If the concern was to allow adequate time for evacuation, Chairman Burnett demanded, why was there no evacuation-time regulation?

NHTSA did not require manufacturers to determine how long it took a load of schoolchildren to evacuate a particular bus; nor how long it might take for fire or smoke to create a lethal environment in that bus. The manufacturers were not required to find out how many passengers could safely ride on a bus with one exit; or, conversely, how many exits there ought to be on a bus with a certain number of passengers. Regardless of whether a school bus's seating capacity was thirty-six or forty-eight or sixty-six or seventy-two, the aisle width remained 12 inches, and the total number of emergency doors remained one, unless the purchaser specified otherwise. The federal standard requiring exits proportional to passenger capacity exempted prison buses and school buses.

Burnett read aloud a recommendation the NTSB had made *in 1968:* "[N]o new types of buses [should] go into service which have not been tested to ensure that all occupants can escape rapidly. . . ." Passenger aircraft, he pointed out, must pass a test in which evacuation is timed, with some exits blocked off.

Hitchcock noted that such tests would be routinely subverted by the bus manufacturers. (Motor vehicle manufacturers for the most part certify themselves as passing federal safety standards, though NHTSA occasionally runs its own tests as a check.*) "In the typical test . . . you might have

---

* In one notable instance where NHTSA followed up on self-certification by conducting its own crash tests, the agency discovered in 1992 that all 185,000 Navistar International school buses built since September 1, 1978—about half the school buses in the country—would have to be recalled and modified in order to pass the FMVSS 301-75 fuel system integrity standard. It turned out that on impact, the Navistar cage was pushed into the fuel tank and caused a leak.

all the exits available or you have people which are trained, high-skilled people that have practiced a lot getting out of the buses," he explained. "So regulating escape time is not something that we seriously considered for a federal standard. . . . It's not an objective compliance test, I guess we felt, because, again, you get sixty-six athletic, trained people, you can probably get them out of a bus in fifteen seconds; but, you know, the normal people wouldn't be able to do that." Hitchcock had revealed in passing that regulators must take as a given the irresponsibility of the manufacturers they are regulating.

Yet Hitchcock as much as said that those same manufacturers had practically written their own regulations: "I think [the standards] were based historically on the—what had evolved in terms of what *the industry had decided was*—and the customers had decided was a good set of requirements. . . ." (emphasis added). He added, "Really up until this crash, we had no reason to question the adequacy of the bus exits."

Larry Fair clenched his teeth. *No reason to question the adequacy of exits?* When one of only two exits was right beside the fuel tank, so that an impact puncturing the fuel tank was bound to disable the door?

(In fact, NHTSA had plenty of reasons to question the adequacy of exits: Since 1969 the NTSB had recommended *five times* that buses, including school buses, should be required to have more exits. One of those five came in response to an accident that had occurred near Rustburg, Va., on March 8, 1977—just two weeks before Ford built the Carrollton bus chassis. A tractor-trailer had rear-ended a school bus that had stopped on the highway to pick up a child. Three of the thirty-two children on the bus died, one of them when he was ejected from a window and crushed when the bus rolled over on him. Rescuers had a desperate struggle to reach the injured children, because the overturned bus was lying on the right-side entrance door, and the rear emergency door, battered in the collision, could not be opened. The left (up) side of the bus was too high above the right (down) side for anyone aboard to reach and open the windows. The windshield had to be pried out and the injured removed through the opening.

"Had there been a fire involving the bus, the bus occupants probably would not have survived or would have sustained more serious injuries because of the inability of rescuers to gain immediate access to the interior of the bus," the NTSB Rustburg accident report concluded. "These circumstances demonstrate the inadequacy of the FMVSS No. 217 provisions for emergency exits on schoolbuses.")

"We had some close calls," Hitchcock continued, "but people were always able to get out.... [U]p until May 13th of this year we have been patting ourselves on the back saying what a good job we did." Now, after the Carrollton crash, NHTSA would review all of its standards for school buses, Hitchcock said. But, hastening to put the problem of bus safety "in perspective," he suggested that the review would find little room for improvement: "We don't design our requirements to prevent one-of-a-kind accidents, you know." As the Ford defense attorneys later would, Hitchcock spoke of the crash as though it involved some vastly improbable event—as though the bus had been struck by a meteorite, not simply by an oncoming vehicle. "I think the fortunate thing about school buses is that they are so safe," he concluded.

CHAPTER
38

That afternoon, John Habberstad took the stand to explain the precise dynamics of the collision. He identified himself as a self-employed consulting engineer, neglecting to mention that he had been retained by Ford Motor Company to help defend it against the lawsuits filed by the Fairs and Nunnallees. Ford had paid him to go to Kentucky to examine the accident scene and vehicles; Ford had paid him to reach an opinion and write a report. Ford had asked the NTSB to let him testify at the hearing.

According to Habberstad, after the pick-up truck collided right front to right front with the bus, the front end of the bus's right leaf spring broke free and started gouging the pavement thirty feet after impact, then twisted out of the pavement and became "a free-flying projectile" that spun completely around and pierced the front face of the tank.

"How do you think this particular fuel tank performed in this accident?" asked panelist Raby.

"Considering the severity of the accident, to me, well," Habbberstad replied. "It lived through the actual impact. It wasn't until some fifty feet on down the road that basically a free-flying projectile generated the hole in the tank." (The phrase "free-flying projectile" conjured up visions of a stray bullet, as opposed to a component of the bus.)

"In your opinion," asked Raby, "after reviewing this accident, do you have any thought to any possible safety recommendations that might help in the future in this type of accident?"

Habberstad's response gave the Fairs a preview of what would be Ford's defense in their lawsuit. "Mr. Raby, as far as the fuel system, when I consider the severity of this accident—we have an accident here where we have closing speeds of approximately 110 miles an hour; the very, very unique nature of this accident, where we don't get liberation of fuel or loss of fuel tank integrity until some fifty feet down the road—I couldn't honestly make any recommendations, myself, as far as the fuel system's integrity [is concerned]," Habberstad replied. No manufacturer could be faulted for failing to design a fuel system to withstand a unique, and therefore unforeseeable, accident.

Asked by Raby whether a cage around the tank might have prevented penetration by the spring, Habberstad first asserted that the cage was not designed to stop flying projectiles. Then, conceding that a cage would have at least partially covered the tank* thus reducing the chance of its being pierced, he nonetheless insisted that "if the spring would have struck the tank in the same place as it actually struck the tank, the guard would not have made a difference because the guard did not cover that area."

It simply was not true that the guard did not cover that area. The NTSB in its final report stated, "A Ford fuel tank guard would have covered the area punctured on the accident fuel tank." However, the NTSB report did note that the spring might have gone on and hit the tank anyway.

Technical panelist Birky questioned Habberstad's characterization of the crash as unique. If Habberstad had, as he'd said, investigated 2,000

---

* Of the front of the tank, 116.3 square inches (53.2 percent of the surface) would be covered by the guard, and 102.3 square inches would remain uncovered.

accidents in his career; and if, as Habberstad conceded, no two of them were alike, then wouldn't it be fair to say that all accidents are unique? Well, yes, Habberstad said. Then, asked Birky, was Habberstad really trying to say that an accident such as this could not have been anticipated?

"This particular accident with something breaking free like this, I would not know how to anticipate this one. I can anticipate a lot of them, but I couldn't this one," Habberstad replied.

Well, Birky pressed him, would it be possible to anticipate in a general way that you could have an accident with a school bus in which a fire involving the fuel tank took place?

Yes, Habberstad allowed as how he supposed you could.

"So, in light of that," asked Birky patiently, "what type of recommendations or solutions are there for reducing the possibility of a fire as a result of an accident?"

Birky's question set forth the whole purpose for which everyone there had ostensibly come. The NTSB was charged with investigating accidents and making recommendations to prevent or ameliorate similar accidents in the future. Habberstad was supposedly there to help out. But he answered the question as though it had been posed by a prosecutor and he was the defendant: He mustn't give an inch. "Again, I have to say that based on this single accident, which is my only experience with anything such as school bus fire in all of my work," he said, "I personally could not make a recommendation for something that needs to be done beyond the current state of the art."

"In your analysis of this accident," asked Birky, putting it another way, "did you find any instance of a defect in the vehicle that would have contributed to the severity of this particular accident—that is, a fire developing—or the sequence of events that led to such an event?"

"I always have a little trouble with the word 'defect,'" Habberstad began, "but if, basically, the question is, could something have—was there a problem with the basic bus? No, I didn't find anything that I felt caused or contributed to it other than the severity of the accident and the unique nature of it."

Larry Fair wondered whether Habberstad had noticed that a 60 gallon gasoline tank had been mounted right beside the main exit door of a bus designed to carry sixty-six schoolchildren.

CHAPTER

39

At 9:00 A.M. on Thursday morning, August 4, Robert H. Munson, Ford's elegantly tailored director of the Automotive Safety Office, left his chair as the motor company's representative, walked to the front of the room, turned 180 degrees, adjusted his aviator glasses, and became a sworn witness in the NTSB's effort to learn the true causes of the Carrollton tragedy. Though Munson might have been voted least likely source of useful information, the Fairs found his testimony enlightening insofar as it suggested the depth of Ford's commitment to safety.

For starters, Munson, an engineer whose thirty-two-year trek up the Ford organization chart had culminated two and a half years earlier with his appointment as ASO director, acknowledged that he had no formal training in safety engineering. Such training would be a likely prerequisite, if the job was to maximize the safety of the product; so Munson's lack of safety training was one more indication that maximizing product safety was not, in fact, what Ford expected its director of automotive safety to do.* Another indication was that Munson—faced with a cataclysmic accident in which twenty-seven people died horribly aboard a Ford vehicle—evidently had not studied the facts of the disaster nor given it a great deal of thought. He would distinguish himself among all the witnesses as the most slipshod and ill-informed.

Munson began by testifying that a school board in Kentucky ordered the bus. Later he admitted that he did not know who ordered the bus; he

---

* In fact, the ASO's task was to orchestrate the company's response to safety *regulations*. As longtime ASO director John C. Eckhold once described the office, "Its primary function is to face off with the federal government and its regulatory agencies."

just assumed it was a school board because it was a school bus. (In fact, the Kentucky Division of Pupil Transportation ordered it.) But of one thing Munson was certain: Whoever ordered the bus specifically requested that the fuel tank guard be deleted. He testified that starting in October 1976, the guard was a "delete option." That is, it came as standard equipment unless the purchaser specified that he did not want it. In fact, the opposite was true: Ford's school buses came without a cage unless the purchaser ordered that one be added.

Asked what percentage of the school buses Ford sold before April 1, 1977, were ordered *with* the cage guard, Munson said he did not know. The answer was *zero* which, the Fairs would later argue, suggested that Ford had not warned purchasers about the danger the guard was intended to redress.

Chairman Burnett was intrigued by this putative delete option system: "Was the process such that the person placing the order had to consciously reject the safety—"

"Well, he would have to consciously reject the installation of the guard on the chassis," Munson interrupted. One does not use the word "safety" in front of Ford's automotive safety director, Munson made clear. "When you delete an option that is standard equipment," he continued, confusingly, "you delete it because you understand full well what you are doing when you place the order."

"Is that fact reflected in the records you have?" Burnett asked.

"Yes," replied Munson. This was a curious answer. If Munson knew the truth—that the records in fact showed that the cage had *not* been standard equipment and had *not* been deleted by Kentucky's order— he would have known that he was testifying falsely and that the falsehood would be rapidly uncovered. It seems likely, then, that Munson had not carefully reviewed the records. In that case, he was not lying about what the records said, but he was misrepresenting the state of his own knowledge. He might more forthrightly have given his choice of such answers as "I don't know," "I'm not sure," or even the Witness's Friend, "I don't recall." Perhaps he just made an honest mistake, but his subsequent testimony revealed that Munson consistently erred in the direction of minimizing Ford's responsibility.

He was asked whether—now that the cage was required by law on school buses—Ford continued to furnish any school bus chassis "for people-transporting uses" with the cage deleted.

"Absolutely no, that I am aware of," Munson swore.

"Mr. Munson, when the United States government places an order for a school bus type vehicle to be used for their purposes, do they request that the cage be deleted?" Chairman Burnett prodded, helpfully. (The U.S. military was still ordering such buses without fuel tank guards for personnel transport.)

Munson was nothing if not flexible. "I am sure there are some vehicles that are purchased by the government and also by states for people-carrying purposes that may or may not have the cage. For instance, transporting prisoners, they may or may not have the cage. That delete option is available for military buses." He might have added that Ford produced school buses for the Canadian market without fuel tank guards, unless they were ordered as an option.

Asked if Ford had been aware of any other accidents in which similar fuel tanks were punctured, Munson replied, "We have never in the history of providing chassis for buses—and as you know, these chassis are pretty much the same since the 1940s—seen an accident as catastrophic as the Carrollton unit. . . . So we had no reason to believe that the location was anything except a safe location."

But what about the 1972 Reston, Virginia, accident, in which the fuel tank was knocked off a Ford school bus by a car going just 25 mph? Now Munson, who moments before had said, "These chassis are pretty much the same since the 1940s," went into high gear: "The 1972 chassis is a lot different from the chassis that we build today. I don't have any knowledge of how the 1972 chassis was engineered, and I have not compared that chassis with today's chassis." *They are the same. They are different. I don't know.*

Munson also said, in answer to a question by the representative of the Commonwealth of Kentucky, that he didn't know whether Ford had done anything to inform purchasers about the fuel tank guard. "So you are not really sure whether Kentucky was even aware of the gas guard at that time?"

"No, I am not," Munson replied. Thus, a few minutes after saying Kentucky had to purposely order the guard deleted, Munson was saying that he didn't know whether Kentucky had been informed that a guard was available. The inconsistency was so obvious that Munson had clearly left the realm of accuracy and inaccuracy behind and wandered into the unmapped terrain of Say-Anything Land.

He didn't forget, though, to express "on behalf of Ford Motor Company the deep sympathy that all of us feel for the victims of this tragic crash." That sympathy, however sincere, had not apparently run so deep as to inspire him to study the crash or its causes.

❏

Keith Lewis, who had by now become Ford's executive engineer of heavy truck component design, followed Munson and set the record straight: When the fuel integrity standard was postponed, Ford had made the cage optional: "It was available, but [the customer] would have to specify that he wanted it."

Asked if the accident raised the possibility of safety improvements, Lewis readily acknowledged the obvious: "Location of the fuel tank is certainly a consideration that should be looked at." He said Ford was studying alternative locations, including between the frame rails, aft of the rear axle; on the left side of the vehicle; or on the right side but moved back farther away from the entrance door. "We think the location where it is has a proven safety record," he said. But the Carrollton crash "has thrown open the mind. . . . There are other locations on a vehicle. Given the fact that the conditions here set up the potential for—or could have contributed to the situation that occurred, we just want to look at is there a better location for function, for design and structure, and for just fundamental safety."

Lewis's words were about the closest thing the Fairs would ever hear to an acknowledgment by Ford of any possible responsibility for "the situation that occurred."

The NTSB hearings adjourned.

❏

The NTSB published its findings and recommendations in March 1989. The board concluded that the bus's right front leaf spring had probably pierced the fuel tank, but regardless of what pierced it, the vulnerable fuel tank, flammable and toxic seating materials, and inadequate emergency exits had all contributed to the loss of life.

The NTSB recommended that tougher flammability standards be adopted; that FMVSS 217 be revised to mandate more exits; and that FMVSS 301 be revised to require school bus fuel tanks to be moved or better protected.

CHAPTER

40

The children had died a year ago to the day, or so the calendar said. To Janey, time had ceased its orderly progression. There was no sense of distance between May 14, 1988, and May 14, 1989. The crash seemed as though it had happened yesterday. But then, getting from that May to this had also been an almost unendurable slog.

Eight months had passed since the Fairs had filed their lawsuit against Ford and Sheller-Globe, and the lawyers for both sides were still in the early stages of their discovery dance. Written interrogatories had been exchanged. Asked what they expected to recover from the suit, the Fairs had replied, "One hundred fifty-nine million dollars." They'd arrived at that fanciful figure by taking Ford's profit for the year of the crash, $5.3 billion, and multiplying it by—why not?—3 percent. Three percent of a year's earnings didn't seem like too stiff a penalty for wrongdoing that cost twenty-seven people their lives.

It had been March before the Fairs and their lawyers and experts had gotten permission to inspect the burned-out hulk of the bus, which was being tightly guarded as evidence in the criminal case against Mahoney. (Ford's experts—accompanied by Ford's lawyers—had seen it two days after the crash, at the invitation of the NTSB.) Kentucky State Police trooper Sonny Cease had opened the padlocked door to the windowless, cinderblock garage in Carrollton where the bus stood entombed in absolute darkness. After the Fair and Nunnallee team had set up some lights, they could see that the inside of the bus had been burned to bare metal, seared orange and black like an incinerator wall. The heat had buckled the bus's roof and floor panels. In the aisle lay lumps of molten glass, and ashes that might once have been anything. The bus smelled like the bottom of a barbecue grill left out in the rain, a burned, damp, greasy smell. There was a place toward the front where the floor matting had not been burned away, and it could only have been because bodies were piled there, insulating the rubber from the flames. Here and there the exterior of the bus seemed to have been coated by silver paint flowing down the side panels, but the metallic cascades were actually the residue of the aluminum window sashes. The fire had melted them to liquid everywhere except at the right rear, where children's bodies, stretched across the seat backs and pressed against the windows, had formed a shield.

A short distance away, hidden, at first, in the darkness, lay a bullet-shaped hunk of steel that might have been some sort of spent bomb, but upon closer inspection proved to be a black Toyota pickup truck. The front bumper and the roof were squashed against the dashboard on the right; only behind the steering wheel was there a little envelope of space, where Larry Mahoney had been cradled. No wonder prosecutor Paul Richwalsky had termed Mahoney's survival "a miracle."

❏

May 14, 1989, was Mother's Day. Radcliff was putting on a first-year memorial service so the bereaved wouldn't have to endure the anniversary alone. The Fairs, their lawyer John P. Coale, and Karolyn and Jim Nunnallee were sitting at the Best Western Gold Vault Inn, in a motel room the Fairs had rented as a media center to get the word out about school bus safety to all the press that would be in town. The Nunnallees were in from Cannon Air Force Base in New Mexico, where Jim had been posted since November. ("It's very hard to have the movers pack up Patty's bedroom," Karolyn had said that fall, "because we'll never ever set up Patty's room again.")

Janey and Larry had sat in the room for eight hours on Saturday, but only reporters from Channel 32 and a couple of local radio stations had come. On Sunday, by noon, there had been no reporters at all. If they had been throwing a party, it would have been a bust; but it was much worse than that.

Larry sat on the edge of the king-size bed, pulling on one of the 50-cent Dutch Masters panatelas that he consumed as though they were necessary to keep him alive. The pungent smoke bonded with the chlorine from the motel's indoor swimming pool and hung in the air like a headache. (Not long ago, Shannon had made the Fairs' basement-level den her bedroom, and let her old upstairs bedroom become her dad's den, partly to escape cigar updrafts through the floor vents—though she was too kind to say so and claimed she just needed more space.)

On the foot of the bed six three-ring binders lay side by side, neatly matched with fleur-de-lis patterns on the covers, cream, rose, light green, and gray. One of the binders contained the NTSB's Carrollton bus crash report; the rest were filled with Janey's newspaper clippings about the crash and drunk driving.

"Drunk driving is a real big issue down here," Larry remarked. "It can overwhelm the bus safety issue unless someone speaks out."

"Drunk driving is safe for the politicians to jump on," Coale agreed.

"Ford succeeded in diverting the families' attention from bus safety to drunk driving," Larry continued. "It's tunnel vision, and Ford tunneled the vision. That took away our support. I think if we had fifty-seven people out here who wanted fuel tanks relocated and pop-out windows put in on all school buses in the future, we could have it done next week."

Larry shoved a videotape into one of the two video players he'd wired to two TVs—a fail-safe system in case of malfunction. (An armor officer, Lieutenant Colonel Fair was not one to hope for the best; he prepared for the worst with redundant systems and contingency plans.) A pale and streaky copy of Dan Rather introduced an August 1988 *CBS Evening News* report about Ford Econoline van and ambulance fires. After at least forty reported fires and an investigation by NHTSA, Ford had "voluntarily" recalled 16,000 ambulances and 188,000 heavy vans in 1987. The fuel in those vehicles, which were frequently used as airport shuttles, had a tendency to boil in the tank and spurt out of the filler pipe. In August 1988, Ford had just recalled 15,000 ambulances again, this time for coolant leaks that had been linked to twenty fires thus far that year. The fire chief of Madison, Wisconsin, complained that a Ford ambulance had caught fire (and set fire to a hospital) after being recalled three times.

A Ford spokesman appeared on screen, insisting that none of the post-recall fires, or for that matter any of the fires associated with leaky coolant hoses, were Ford's fault. "They're all individual circumstances, all of which we think are explainable by other factors" such as improper maintenance, he said.

"It reminds me of a pro wrestler caught pulling hair, the way he shakes his head in total denial," Larry observed. "They'll use any excuse, denial, anything, and meanwhile, they keep on burning people."

Larry put on a report from *Our Times,* a TV magazine show in Boston.

The immaculate young hosts of the program promised a story about gourmet chocolate and two segments on the Red Sox, "but first: School Bus Fires." (The Fairs were past offense at such juxtapositions. They'd long since learned that the most profound events never stand alone. The contextual details keep on coming: A movie magazine finds its way to the table by the deathbed; the nurses' laughter echoes down the hall.)

Our Times had retained fire experts from Worcester (Massachusetts) Polytechnic Institute to conduct a standard flammability test, known as the Boston Bag Test, on a 1978 school bus, which met the Federal Motor Vehicle Safety Standard for flammability. The bus's engine was removed and its fuel tank filled with water, so that the fire would be fed only by the interior materials of the passenger compartment. A brown paper grocery bag containing four crumpled newspaper pages was placed on its side on a seat cushion, in contact with the seat back, four rows from the rear. The bag and papers were ignited with a cigarette lighter. A camera on board showed the orange flames lazily licking the seat back suddenly quicken and grow as the green vinyl seat cover caught fire. One minute into the test, the air temperature near the ceiling in the aisle at the rear of the bus had reached 284 degrees Fahrenheit. Thirty seconds later, the flame had eaten through the vinyl cover, the polyurethane foam was ablaze, and the bus was filled with thickening smoke. The narrator noted that in the best of circumstances—an evacuation drill with no panic, no injuries, in broad daylight, with both doors available—it would take at least this long, one and a half minutes, to evacuate a fully occupied standard-sized school bus.

In less than three minutes, dense, ink-black smoke had completely occupied the space from the ceiling down to the top of the seat backs, and the temperature above the aisle was more than 400 degrees—all of this from just one seat on fire. The narrator described the searing smoke as "a thick toxic soup," and noted that if one exit were blocked [as it had been on the Kentucky bus], kids would at that point still be trying to get out.

Four minutes into the test, the temperature had reached 1,400 degrees and the fire was leaping from seat to seat. "No one could survive," the narrator noted. Janey Fair and Karolyn Nunnallee turned their backs to the horror and became absorbed in putting on their makeup. But Jim Nunnallee and Larry Fair fixed their eyes on the roaring inferno. Even the window glass was burning now, and a giant black pillar of smoke surged to the heavens. This was an image of the fire that had killed and consumed their little girls, and the men were determined to stare it in the face, as though being brave could do some good.

"The point being," Larry said, "in the Carrollton bus, it wasn't just one seat burning that started the others; because of the gasoline flames coming through the gap in the floorboards, it was several seats, and that geometrically increases the fire."

Janey was holding a curling iron in her hair and trying to find a safety pin at the same time, but her search was limited by the length of the electrical cord. "If Shannon were here, she'd know just where all the safety pins are," she said gaily.

"Oh yes," agreed Janey's sister Gloria, who'd just arrived. "Shannon is well orchestrated."

A reporter and photographer from the Radcliff paper dropped by. The four parents stood shoulder to shoulder for a picture. "Who can suck in their gut the most?" Janey asked with a laugh. They all smiled for the camera. Janey was wearing green pumps, a green dress, and a green jacket. "Green is the color of hope," she said. It was also the color of her eyes. She looked pale and many years older than she had a year and a day ago.

❑

The first-anniversary observances began with the dedication of a monument to the memory of the victims. A midafternoon sun was burning through the haze as the Fairs and Nunnallees joined the other families at the edge of a field beside the bleak, flat cemetery called North Hardin Memorial Gardens. They sat on folding chairs facing two wedges of stone covered by sheets. Warm, wet grass scented the air; it smelled like spring.

Boy Scouts in carefully pressed blue jeans and khaki shirts with red epaulettes handed out mimeographed programs, which listed the Reverend Gene Waggoner as the leader of the opening prayer. "We pray that those who come here in the days ahead will resolve not to drink and drive and maybe even now never to take a drink," he intoned. "Today we've come together *not to think about unsafe buses,* but about unsafe beverages." Waggoner had been Shannon's minister. He'd baptized her by immersion; now he was baptizing her parents by fire.

His was the opening shot of a barrage that would go on all afternoon. The Fairs had known they were being criticized for taking the position that there had been something wrong with the church's bus, though the criticism was seldom made to their faces. It was widely believed that they had sued the Radcliff First Assembly of God, when in fact they had not, though a case could have been made that overcrowding by the church was one cause of the disaster.* The prevailing opinion in Radcliff seemed to be that blaming Ford for selling a dangerous bus was the same as blaming the church for buying it; and that laying an ounce of responsibility anywhere other than on Larry Mahoney amounted to making excuses for him. Then, too, the Fairs' and Nunnallees' refusal to join the mass settlement was seen by some as an implicit criticism of those who had settled. Blaming the church, supporting Larry Mahoney, knocking everybody else—the Fairs had been tried and convicted of all three offenses in the minds of many of their neighbors, but they'd thought they would enjoy a truce at the ceremony commemorating the children. They were wrong.

Kentucky's commissioner of transportation, Milo D. Bryant, spoke next. A habitué of the state capitol in Frankfort, ninety minutes away, he'd not been inoculated with the local orthodoxy and spoke of improving school bus safety as though it were a self-evidently desirable goal. Governor Wallace Wilkinson's Task Force on School Bus Safety, of which Bryant was chairman, had come up with seventeen recommendations, including the installation of a left-side emergency door and push-out windows, the removal of rear seats that block the back exit, and the relocation of the fuel tank to a less exposed area. The governor was also seeking stiffer drunk driving penalties. "These kids did not die in vain," Bryant promised. "Because of the tragedy a year ago, every child who rides a bus today is safer."

As a hymn was sung, four young survivors of the crash rose and took their places by the shrouded stones, ready to pull off the coverings. In the center stood Harold Dennis, his disfigured face held high. Beside him stood Carey Aurentz, a cute teenager with no right foot—the flames got it. Katrina Muller stood on the left; her face was a work in progress, with red and white stripes on her jaw. And on the right stood Aaron Conyers, the remnants of one burned ear protruding from the therapeutic elastic mask that tightly covered his whole head.

As he waited for the cue to unveil the monument, Aaron no doubt was thinking of his big brother, Josh. Josh Conyers had sat in the bus's

---

* The Nunnallees did sue the church, on the advice of their attorney Larry Franklin. He believed it was important, as a trial tactic, to haul all possible defendants in front of the jury so it wouldn't seem as though he were trying to hide the fault of one in order to exaggerate the fault of another.

third row, and died. Aaron had sat in the fifth row, and lived, though with burns covering 25 percent of his body there had been times he wished he hadn't. Two days after the accident, Aaron lay in a hospital bed with his eyes swollen shut, a respirator tube down his throat, and skin harvested from cadavers dressing his raw flesh. His left arm was suspended above him with a steel rod through it. But he could communicate on paper, and he wrote, "Is Josh dead?" His father and mother had never lied to him. They never even told him there was a Santa Claus, because it wasn't true; the family observed Christmas by having a birthday cake with candles for Baby Jesus. So when Aaron asked, "Is Josh dead?" his father said, "Yeah."

Now Aaron stood not far from his brother's grave, and his own. At the back edge of North Hardin Memorial Gardens was a pink granite tombstone with the name Conyers in the middle. On the left it read, "Joshua M., July 12, 1973–May 14, 1988," and on the right, "Aaron C., Mar. 12, 1975," with a space waiting for the date of death. (Between the two names was carved a pair of hands dunking a ball through a basketball net, because Josh and Aaron were forever doing everything together, and they played basketball, always.) That had people talking: A thirteen-year-old with a cemetery plot and tombstone—wasn't right. But Aaron had been so close to his brother it was a comfort to him to know he would one day be close again.

Meanwhile, Aaron had to live through his life, and he had to do it behind burned skin. Now the closest thing to him, his constant companion, was pain. He could be with Josh only in memories, prayers, and dreams. Aaron did dream about his dead brother a lot: He'd see Josh falling off a cliff, and he wouldn't be able to help him.

The songs of praise over, Aaron and the others pulled the sheets off the two black marble wedges. On the left one, under a dove and the words "DECEASED, GONE TO REST, GOD KNOWS BEST" were twenty-seven names. On the right one was a cocktail glass and a car key in a circle with a slash across it, and forty names under the words "SURVIVED, SPARED FOR A SEASON, GOD KNOWS THE REASON."

"Shannon would have liked the monument," Janey's sister Gloria whispered, "because it's simple. She didn't like ornate things. She had good taste."*

---

* The idea that there should be a monument originated with Roy Keith, Jr., whose gravestone company designed and donated the marble wedges. ("In a sense the tragedy created a windfall for us, and it doesn't make you feel very good, to get a windfall from something like that," he

❑

An awards ceremony followed inside the North Hardin High School gymnasium, home of the Trojans, whose basketball achievements ("17th District Champions 1986–87") were celebrated by blue and white banners hanging down from the steel girders supporting the ceiling. Big white letters on the blue stage curtain at the front of the gym spelled out YOU WERE THERE. But before plaques expressing the community's thanks to everyone who had helped in the crisis could be handed out, there had to be a speech, and that was delivered by a Texas-based evangelist by the name of Dave Roever. The Fairs had never heard of Roever, an old acquaintance of the Radcliff First Assembly's Rev. Tennison. Roever had called Tennison to offer his support as soon as he heard of the calamity; and it wasn't long before Roever had come out with an anti-drunk-driving video, which was available by mail order for $30 (plus $1 shipping).

"My friends," Roever began, "it was not a defective bus running down the wrong side of the interstate, it was a drunk driver—and that's what's got to stop!" The audience clapped its approval, but Larry Fair, who as a Family Support Group steering committeeman was seated on stage, conspicuously did not. His always pink complexion darkened a shade or two.

"I've just finished a video," Roever continued, "called *One More for the Road*. It doesn't deal with defective buses. It deals with drunk drivers." Karolyn Nunnallee had fashioned a badge reading "Sober Drivers—Safe Buses," but for some reason that two-point plan comprised one point too many for Roever.

He decried the fact that demonstrators took to the streets to protest the war in Vietnam, where 58,000 Americans died, but those demonstrators were nowhere to be found when it came to protesting drunk driving, which killed that many people every couple of years. "They were hypocrites then and they're hypocrites now," he shouted, "or they'd stand up and say enough is enough!"

This us-versus-them passage was a standard in Roever's stump speech,

---

said. "So we thought about what we could do.") North Hardin Memorial Gardens donated the plot. Later, there was talk among the victims' families of erecting an eighteen-foot bronze statue between the stones, but the $20,000 needed was nowhere to be found. Instead, an eight-foot granite obelisk was purchased, primarily with a contribution from the Louisville *Courier-Journal,* in 1991.

delivered at other times and places in even more fervid terms. "People in this country rioted in the streets, burned the American flag, and urinated on it, and had the audacity to call our loyal GIs baby killers," he shouted at a Dallas rally. "But the drunk driver kills 50,000 Americans every twenty-four months, and they don't burn his car and urinate on him and call him baby killer."

It was in Vietnam that a phosphorous grenade exploded prematurely in Roever's hand, leaving his face permanently contorted by burns—his mouth pulled to one side, his blind right eye blood-red at the edges, his deaf right ear made of plastic. Such disfigurement would have defeated many people and sent them into hiding. But Roever, a minister's son who'd been saved at sixteen, lived in the power and the victory of Jesus and heeded a calling to evangelism. His frightful war wounds became what, in a different line of work, might have been called his schtick. After cranking up a crowd of fundamentalists to a roaring, foot-stomping, whistling celebration of their superiority and victimization—their shared sense of being at once picked and picked on—he would mesmerize them into rapturous silence with the fantastic story of his own redemptive suffering:

When the grenade exploded as he was about to hurl it from his navy riverine patrol boat, he'd recall, "I looked down and laying right in front of me was half my face. It had peeled right down to the bone and it was laying right there. Then it burst into flames, and a gentle breeze turned the ashes into a whirlwind, and it blew across the deck and was gone. Then I noticed that my chest was gone, and I knew I wasn't dead because I could see my heart beating. . . . I jumped off the boat into the water and I continued to burn. . . . I came up out of the water, the first words I said, and I quote verbatim, I yelled at the top of my voice, I said, 'God, I still believe in you!' "

Now Roever and three associates crisscrossed the nation speaking to public school assemblies, reaching, by his estimate, 500,000 students a year. He counted 270 stations carrying his weekly TV show, *Dave Roever Presents.* All of this took money, of course. "My human nature wishes there were no need for money to operate the ministry," he wrote in one solicitation, "but God ordained it to be so." Roever's direct mail appeals offered unending ways of giving. You could join the Dave Roever Support Team: "In joining the Support Team, I promise to pray daily for the ministry. I also pledge to send financial help of at least $25.00 a month." Or you could sign up for a long-distance telephone service that would automatically donate 5 percent of the cost of each call to the Roever Evangelistic Association, of which Dave Roever was CEO. He raised money in all kinds of ways, yet there was never enough, he always needed more, to keep the heat on the devil, to keep the "spiritual-warfare training camps" running, to get new equipment this year for the new TV studio acquired last year. "I have never asked people who support us to increase their financial help," he wrote once. "I will, however, present the need and ask you to be obedient to God if He tells you to increase your giving. . . . Your Servant in Christ, Dave Roever." In 1991, the Roever Evangelistic Association took in $2,078,302.

Now Roever had turned his missionary zeal against the heretics who would suggest that school bus safety could be improved. "The *only* good thing that can come out of this accident is getting drunk drivers off the road," he declared, to a standing ovation. Coale and the Fairs stayed in their seats.

Tokens of appreciation were handed out to the people who had selflessly responded to Radcliff's need—all the various volunteer fire departments and rescue squads and policemen who'd rushed to the crash, and the businesses that had raised or donated money in its aftermath.

Terry Bennett accepted the plaque awarded to the law firm of Skeeters & Bennett.

❑

As the assemblage, with the survivors of the dead in the lead, filed out of the gym into the May air, the grandfather of one of the dead girls strode up to Larry Fair, took his hand, and said, "We appreciate what you're doing, and please don't let up."

On the adjacent football field stood a row of yellow-ribboned wreaths, twenty-seven of them. After the high school band concluded a funeral dirge, bird songs cut through the silence as though giving voice to the souls of the children. Army chaplain Jerry Weaver led an opening prayer. Though he stood on a platform in front of the seated families, they heard his voice coming from speakers in the middle and far distance behind them, twice. "Dear Lord, Lord, we pray that one day we may experience joy again, again."

A message from Washington, D.C., was read: "Every drunk or drugged driving death is a national tragedy. Barbara and I want to extend special good wishes on this Mother's Day. We are with you not just today, but every day.—George Bush, President of the United States." (This was before Bush suspended federal rule making, in 1992, delaying safety regulations at NHTSA.)

Kentucky's governor, Wallace Wilkinson, delivered a speech of unusual simplicity and power: "If we can't find a reason, if we can't change reality, what can we do? We share. We remember. We carry on. If there were a way we could protect our children from every danger, we should surely do it. . . ."

The West Hardin Concert Choir sang, "To everything there is a season . . ." its dulcet tones punctuated by the distant *whump! whump! whump!* of tank guns on Fort Knox's firing range. Then, as Rev. Tennison read each victim's name, the surviving family walked to a wreath, placed a yellow rose on it, and stood there. It was almost unbearable to behold, grief upon grief, the sheer quantity of it, as the line of the bereaved gradually stretched the breadth of the football field. The late-afternoon sun slanting across the field etched the misery in their downcast faces.

Finally, the bereft were reminded that the dead "are very much wonderfully alive right now," and that someday, everyone would be reunited. "As ghastly as this tragedy is, God can bring some good out of it," the sermon concluded. "The Bible doesn't say God is the cause of everything, but the *master* of everything." In Genesis 50:20, Joseph tells his brothers, who had sold him into slavery, "As for you, you meant evil against me; but God meant it for good, to bring it about that many people should be kept alive, as they are today." And the Apostle Paul wrote (Romans 8:28): "We know that in everything God works for good. . . ."

With that, the first-year memorial service ended. Seven TV crews reeled up their cables. There would be no second-year memorial service; these things couldn't go on forever. The mothers and fathers and spouses would henceforth do their remembering on their own.

As the Fairs headed for their car, a reporter asked them if they were going to keep on fighting the bus manufacturers. "This is just the first-year anniversary," Janey said. "We're in it for the long haul now."

CHAPTER
41

$\mathbf{A}$s the first-year memorial service had made clear, Larry and Janey Fair were battling not only Sheller-Globe and the Ford Motor Company, but public opinion in their hometown. The latter was the hard part. "I know half the people in this town," Janey told a friend. "It's really hard to be the only one, like a voice echoing in the wilderness."

Temperance was an article of faith in the Assemblies of God; drinking was an evil that served the devil's purposes,* and drunk driving was an extreme evil that had to be extirpated. The Fairs understood all that, but were at a loss to comprehend why opposition to drunk driving should breed implacable hostility toward anyone who favored improvements in bus safety.

That hostility was on display again in a four-part series on Dave Roever's TV show, available on video as *Our Precious Loss* ($40 for the two-cassette set, plus $3 shipping). "The bus was proven to be absolutely functional. There was nothing wrong with the bus," Roever declared, *after* the NTSB had issued its report blaming the fuel tank, seating materials, and lack of exits for contributing to the deaths.

"The secretary of transportation for the state of Kentucky spoke at the dedication of that memorial," Roever continued, "and for five minutes he hammered away on bus safety. Do you hear me? Read my lips: bus safety! *Bus safety* is not the problem here. . . . The fact of the matter is the *whole* problem, the entire problem with the slaughter on May the 14th, 1988, was not a defective bus on the wrong side of the interstate. It was a defective drunk on the wrong side of the interstate."

---

* "The Devil is using alcohol to maim and destroy thousands of American teenagers today," said the ad for Dave Roever's tape, "One More for the Road."

The curious thing about Roever's conviction that bus safety had reached an unimprovable state of grace was that he clearly expected all good people to share it, as though it were axiomatic, an article of faith. His position was not susceptible to debate. To his mind, any call for bus safety, however evidently sincere or seemingly reasonable, was outrageous on its face. In fact, the more reasonable a bus safety advocate's statement seemed, the more pernicious it actually was. A Roever believer started from the conclusion that buses were perfectly safe, and used that revealed truth as a template to measure any statements at variance with it. This argument by revelation was quite different from the secular world's notion of rational debate, and Janey and Larry found themselves the objects of irrebuttable criticism.

"How do you refute the need for bus safety, and why?" Larry mused after the memorial service. "The NTSB identified three problems. You don't recommend something be fixed if there's nothing wrong."

Janey had become active in Mothers Against Drunk Driving (MADD) —she'd been elected president of the Hardin County chapter that spring —but she saw limits to what could be accomplished in fighting drunk driving in general or punishing Larry Mahoney in particular. "There's no justice for Shannon and those kids. No matter what is done to Mahoney, it won't be enough. That's not callousness. It's trying to think clearly. It's trying to live in the real world," she said. "It's very, very difficult to change human behavior, like drunk driving. It's very easy to make an engineering change. And one key change affects every bus coming down the line."

Larry recalled that the whole Family Support Group, composed of the victims' families, had vowed to improve school bus safety—and was engaged in selecting a law firm to sue the manufacturers at the moment when Ford and Sheller-Globe descended, cash in hand. "It's amazing how $40 million fixed all the buses without a bolt being turned," he observed. Now drunk driving was suddenly the only concern. "What if the guy hadn't been drunk? What if he had a heart attack?" Fair asked. "We want Shannon's death not to have been in vain. We want to generate change."

CHAPTER

42

Skip Murgatroyd, John Coale's partner, had eagerly anticipated the Friday, August 11, 1989, hearing on his motion to compel Ford
to answer interrogatories and produce documents. (Coale, unparalleled
at signing up clients, frequently left the court appearances to his partners.) In the year since the Fairs had filed suit, Ford had rejected as
irrelevant every discovery request for material that dealt with any vehicle
other than a B-700 series school bus chassis, frustrating Murgatroyd's
efforts to explore Ford's corporate policies.

Ford would be liable for *compensatory* damages if the plaintiffs could
prove the bus chassis was unreasonably dangerous. But if a few isolated
engineers in Ford's Heavy Truck Engineering Group, acting alone, had
made the decision to leave the fuel tank unguarded, it was unlikely the
corporation would be hit with *punitive* damages for *knowingly* putting a
dangerous vehicle on the road. It would be hard to find evidence that
those *particular* truck engineers *knew* the chassis design was defective
and built it anyway. And even if the plaintiffs could come up with such
evidence, the corporation as an entity might not be deemed to have
knowingly done what a few of its employees did; the corporation might
even have had a policy in place to guard against such acts. What the
plaintiffs needed to prove was that Ford Motor Company's managers and
employees had done similar things time and time again, *in accord with*
corporate policy and practice—so that the corporate entity itself was
guilty of knowing, willful misconduct.

The Fairs' attorneys, therefore, were trying to broaden the scope of
the evidence. By their lights, if Ford had crimped and stinted on fuel
system safety in, say, Pinto cars, that was evidence of a pattern and practice

of producing unsafe vehicles. If the Pinto's vulnerable fuel tank had ruptured, both in preproduction crash tests and on the road, that was a lesson
the whole corporation must have learned. If the whole corporation had
notice of the danger of exposed fuel tanks, to put one more on the road
was worse than negligence; it was knowing, conscious, willful disregard
for people's safety—which could justify punitive damages. Similarly, Murgatroyd would argue, Ford's history of relentless opposition to safety
standards—whether pursued through proper procedures or through a
secret attempt to derail regulations at the Oval Office—demonstrated that
reckless disregard for safety was nothing less than corporate policy.

Ford's defense attorneys, conversely, argued that the issues in the
lawsuit were narrow and specific, relating solely to this vehicle and this
accident—basically, whether Ford should have built the bus differently
and whether its failure to do so had caused the deaths of Shannon and
Patty. The defense argued that records of Ford's car and light-truck fuel-
system crash tests, for instance, should not be admitted into evidence,
because they did not involve 110 mph frontal impacts and "do not involve
the variables involved in this collision, like the drunk driver, Mahoney."

The defense attorneys described a Balkanized corporation in which
the people and policies involved in designing small cars had little to do
with big cars; those building big cars had nothing to do with light trucks;
and those building heavy trucks and bus chassis operated in a different
universe altogether. Trucks and cars were as different as mushrooms and
toasters, the defense attorneys argued, and so knowledge about one was
totally inapplicable to the other. And anyway, the car and truck organization charts converged only at positions so near the top of the company
that the lofty executives there knew practically nothing about the actual
design of either. Therefore, Ford as truck-builder could not be presumed
to be aware of any useful safety-engineering lessons learned by Ford the
auto-builder. For instance, if Ford, automaker, had seen Pinto fuel tanks
fail, that did not mean that Ford, truck-maker, had gained any knowledge
about the danger that exposed fuel tanks could pose on trucks and buses.
As for the Oval Office meeting, if the Ford lawyers could wall the case
into one narrow production principality, then the political chats of its
corporate chieftains would fall far off the map.

❑

The wind was at Murgatroyd's back as he glided into court, serene in the
knowledge that the law was on his side. Kentucky's rules of civil proce-

dure mandated very broad discovery, even of information that would not itself be admissible at trial. He had so much precedent, chapter and verse, right on point—*Kentucky cases,* Your Honor—that he was positive Judge Charles Satterwhite would give him at least half of the six orders he was seeking. Some of them, there was no issue, just bright-letter law: *Give it up, Ford, rules are rules.* There was no way he wasn't going to come out of today better than he went in. All the scouting reports on Satterwhite agreed he was an intelligent and independent young judge who knew the law and wouldn't be bullied by a mega-corporation that happened to be one of Kentucky's biggest employers. Satterwhite was one of the reasons they'd decided to sue in the county court rather than go up to federal court—an option that just last month had expired forever.

Murgatroyd, his colleague Phil Allen, the Fairs, and their local counsel Ann Oldfather strode into a small, windowless courtroom in the stately nineteenth-century Carroll County Courthouse on the green at the center of town. There the Fairs encountered for the first time the other side's big gun. Ford's local counsel, Louisville attorney Bill Grubbs, introduced them to William Haven King, Jr., of Richmond, Virginia's, McGuire, Woods, Battle & Boothe, one of the five firms in the nation most utilized by Ford. One of 146 partners in the then-296-lawyer firm, where fees ranged up to $250 an hour, King defended Ford in major fuel system cases throughout the country.

Tall and broad-shouldered, King strode into court with the confidence of an athlete, which he was, or had been. As a quarterback, he had set six Ivy League records while leading the 1962 Dartmouth football team to an undefeated season. An All-Ivy, All-East, and third-team All-America selection, King, who also captained the lacrosse team, had been a sixth-round draft choice of the New York Jets. ("You wasted a pick," he told Jets coach Weeb Ewbank. "I don't want to play pro ball. I want to be a lawyer.") A superb rollout passer, King hadn't hesitated to carry the ball himself, especially near the goal line; he scored thirteen touchdowns his senior year. A sports star with brains (and money—his Dartmouth-grad father was then president of the Virginia Bar Association), King was "tapped" for and elected president of the most prestigious senior society. His rep on campus proved enduring; three decades later Dartmouth alumni would elect him to the board of trustees.

Bald and thick-figured now, King was far from the golden boy of that long-ago New Hampshire autumn. But from the first intimidating shake of his large hand, he projected strength as well as confidence, and this could affect the balance of the forces arrayed in the courtroom. The adversary system sublimates trial by combat. If the advocates no longer come to blows, still every argument stands for a fight, and conflict lurks behind conflict resolution. On the Fairs' side, Murgatroyd, boyish-looking at forty-one, was small but quick: he thought fast, talked fast, walked fast, his heart maybe beating like a sparrow's. Opposing him up to now had been Grubbs. At fifty, Grubbs appeared the very model of the corporate lawyer—staid, dignified, and proper, with the somewhat worn WASP look of a men's club sofa. His gestures were tentative and delicate, and one could imagine a much younger Grubbs carrying a briefcase in high school, his shoulders hunched against the taunts of tougher boys who thought it funny to drop the S from his name. (One would be imagining wrong, since Grubbs had captained his high school swim team and even now was a much-feared tennis player.) Now here came King, who could probably beat up anyone in the room, and though that was not going to happen, the fact that it *could* happen was real, and conceivably inhibiting to an opponent. (Though not to an opponent who was a woman: King could not land an imaginary punch on the willowy Oldfather; perhaps that's why he seemed to grow more and more annoyed by her as the case progressed.)

Procter Robison, one of the nearly 300 attorneys in Ford Motor Company's Office of the General Counsel, had also come for the day, to observe. Robison's presence signaled that Ford management was taking an interest in this case, a development that the Fairs found encouraging; better to be crushed than ignored.

Everyone sat down and waited for Judge Satterwhite to arrive. Into the room tottered an elderly gentleman whom Murgatroyd had never seen before, the honorable George Williamson, a retired judge from nearby La Grange. "All right, gentlemen," he began, after exchanging greetings with the lawyers, one of whom was a woman. "I need a program, because this has been rather rushed up, because I got the first wind of this the day before yesterday from the court administrator asking if I would come over. And I really didn't know exactly what was before me." This Mr. Williamson had glanced at the file—he said—but the motion set for argument that day, as well as the meticulously researched and arduously written briefs for and against it, had escaped his notice. All he knew was that he'd been asked to come over and handle this matter. "I said, well, let me come on over since everybody is set to be here today. Maybe I can get started and I will see where I can go, and as I said, I need a program. So, I think I can get myself programmed in; I think I am pretty well programmed already."

"Just a question, Your Honor," asked Grubbs offhandedly. "Have you been asked to take over this case, or just to sit today?"

"No, I have been asked if I would take over this case and I told them, yes," Williamson answered, sounding quite sure of himself for the first time. "I first debated, and said, 'Well, it is not too far away, from here to La Grange, so I don't mind it.'"

Was the courtroom suddenly bathed in a weird orange light, the air eerily still, as though a violent thunderstorm were about to strike? Or did it just seem that way to Murgatroyd?

"Is there any problem?" Williamson asked. "And if there is, why we can stop and you can come back and we can get another judge. There are plenty of them around." He meant did anyone see any conflicts of interest, any appearances of partiality because of past dealings with Williamson's law firm, that sort of thing; not problems like, *This isn't fair; you are ruining my life.* So Murgatroyd said nothing.

"I only raised the question, Your Honor, because we haven't seen the order," Grubbs said soothingly. "It came as a surprise."

What had happened was, Judge Satterwhite had removed himself from the civil case because he was simultaneously presiding over the criminal proceeding against Larry Mahoney. He felt that he would not be able to wall off the evidence he heard in the one matter and ensure it had no influence on his judgment in the other. So a retired judge had been called upon to pinch hit. But no one had breathed a word of this to the litigants assembled that day.

"I have been retired six years, and I have served as a special judge when they can twist my arm long enough to get back into it," Williamson explained. "I am physically able to perform, much better than I was six years ago."

His performance problems had in fact caused a minor sensation a half dozen years earlier, when he left the bench—literally. Williamson, then sixty-three, was presiding over a routine auto accident personal-injury trial in Henry Circuit Court on January 25, 1983. As the plaintiff's lawyer questioned a state trooper, the defense attorney objected. Williamson called the attorneys into his chambers to thrash out the legal argument. As he listened, the thought occurred to him, "I've seen this picture before. There's other things I need to do." Without ruling on the objection, he declared a mistrial and told the attorneys he was resigning.

A former state representative, Williamson had faithfully discharged his duties as circuit judge for Oldham, Trimble, and Henry counties since his appointment in 1970 to replace a judge who had died. In fact, just three days before his sudden abdication, Williamson had bought new snow tires to ensure the completion of his three-county rounds. But, as he explained to a reporter at the time, "I suddenly realized, 'George, you can't possibly, by yourself, at your age and with your lack of energy, carry out your full responsibilities until your term expires.' I thought, *You can't even handle a simple case with seasoned attorneys without losing your judicial temperament' "* (emphasis added). Williamson was afraid that before he reached retirement, which was then a year away, the work would kill him, as he suspected it had killed the man he replaced. The next day he drove to Frankfort to deliver a letter of resignation to the chief justice of the Supreme Court, explaining that he was retiring because of "the multiplicity of the workload." But he felt much better now, and was willing to handle this Ford case, whatever it might be.

❏

After a brief break, for lunch and to give the judge a chance to skim the lengthy briefs, the argument over discovery was joined. King began by letting the judge know that Ford had been more than reasonable. "We have produced two boxes, a stack this high," he said, holding his palm at least three feet above the floor.

"Your Honor, maybe there is some misunderstanding here, and I don't mean to interrupt," Oldfather interjected. "Mr. King said that they produced boxes *this high?* All we got was one manila file folder."

"I wasn't there when you picked up the files, but my recollection is there are at least two, not including photographs," Grubbs suggested hopefully.

"There was just one, Bill," insisted Oldfather.

"You are arguing about something that doesn't really make any—all this is going to be taken up," said King, affecting the tone of a patient parent defusing a childish spat—a nice bit of courtroom thespianism, since he was the one who had hit first.

❏

Ford's recalcitrance in discovery was consistent with what plaintiffs' attorneys, and, on occasion, the courts, have seen as a pattern of obstruction and delay by the auto maker as a defendant in product liability litigation.

The company's apparent policy of nondisclosure had actually been spelled out once in an intracompany presentation by an engineer from the Design Analysis Activity—an office established to provide technical expertise to Ford's defense attorneys. It was 1973, and the corporation was facing mounting lawsuits, particularly in regard to fuel system fires. Design Analysis was trying to enlist Ford's automotive engineers in the defense effort, and lesson number one was that loose lips sink ships. "Engineering information obtained by the plaintiff prior to litigation proceedings can give him a decided advantage in the development of his case," the Design Analysis man explained. "Since engineering information leaks have been experienced, information should be distributed only to selected personnel on a 'need to know' basis and carefully secured by the recipients. . . . In spite of careful security precautions, the plaintiff may determine the existence and identification of engineering records during the pre-trial discovery process . . ." The apparent goal was for everyone at Ford to do his part to prevent plaintiffs from being able to precisely identify documents. If documents were not precisely identified in a discovery request, then Ford could act as though they did not exist.

By the late 1980s, the record of Ford's attempts to keep information secret had itself become part of the evidence that plaintiffs' attorneys used against the company. Yet old habits die hard, and it seemed to Murgatroyd and his colleagues that Ford was at it again, and they would have to rely on the judge to order the defense to turn over what the plaintiffs were entitled to by law.

❑

Murgatroyd's colleague Phil Allen laid out the six categories of material the Fairs were asking the judge to order Ford to disclose.

First: prior claims and lawsuits relating to Ford school bus chassis. Previous cases might identify a defect in Ford's bus chassis, and perhaps establish that Ford knew of the defect, but chose to disregard it.

Second: documents relating to the development and testing of Ford fuel systems, including those of cars such as the Pinto. To prove that the bus's fuel system was defective, that is, unreasonably dangerous, the Fairs had to prove that there were feasible alternative designs available to Ford.

Third: briefings relating to the meeting at which Lee Iacocca and Henry Ford sought President Nixon's help in getting regulators off their back. Such documents might provide evidence of a corporate policy of deliberate disregard for safety.

Fourth: records that might document an alleged company policy of hiding the results of safety tests that Ford products had failed.

Fifth: communications pertaining to the July 1988 mass settlement with the bus-crash families.

Sixth: the names of persons who had provided information in response to the plaintiffs' interrogatories.

King sounded offended by the *unfairness* of requests that could drag into evidence various unfortunate episodes, including the incendiary history of the Pinto. "What the plaintiffs are trying to do is open this up to things that have no rational relationship to the product at issue in this case, which is a specific school bus," he complained. If they were allowed to demand material about other vehicles, he said, "everything would be able to come in, whether it involved fuel engines for space ships, for locomotives, for tanks; for anything else if it had some relationship to a fuel system. . . . You have got to look at what the product is. That's the standard."

"I think everybody agrees that is the standard, gentlemen," the judge concurred, vaguely. Of course, the reason law books are so fat is because *nobody* agrees what general terms such as "rationally related to the product" mean when applied to a particular set of facts.

Murgatroyd responded: "Ford says that there is car engineering; there is light truck engineering and heavy truck engineering and never the twain shall meet. . . . We contend that there is corporate policy, that corporate policy filters its way down into all of the various subdivisions of Ford." School buses comprised less than 1 percent of Ford's product line. The only way to examine what Ford knew about fuel systems and what Ford did about fuel systems, Murgatroyd insisted, was to look at these other vehicles. To restrict the inquiry to the B-700 chassis would be to allow no inquiry at all.

King wheeled out the bus-is-a-truck argument. The product at issue, he said, was "a B-700 series bus chassis. It is a heavy truck. . . . The design considerations, all of the engineering considerations that have to go into the making of a heavy dump truck, for example, or a chassis such as this, require an entirely different set of factors, engineering and design and use and so on, that separates that from a passenger car. . . . [I]t is involved in hauling heavy interstate commerce materials, and it has to meet certain standards because of its weight, its size, its bulk, and the use to which it is put. It is easy to sort of confuse the internal parts of a school bus—because it is a vehicle, it moves along the road, and it carries people in it

—with a car or a light truck. Because if you think about it, it is easy to confuse the fact that it may have a fuel system. But that's not the way the fuel system is designed, and that's not the way the vehicle is designed, and that's not the use for it as well."

If King could get the judge to think of the bus always as a heavy truck, he might not only keep out troublesome evidence; he might cause the judge to half forget what that evidence was *about*. As he hypnotically repeated "heavy truck," King seemed to fall under the spell of his own denial. He'd describe the purpose of a school bus as "hauling interstate commerce materials." He'd insist that "carry[ing] people . . . is not the use for it."

❑

"All right, gentlemen," said Williamson when the lawyers were finished. "On the category of prior claim: The defendant has limited the answers . . . to this Ford, this particular type of truck chassis. I will rule that the answers are sufficient."

Regarding the second category, information regarding Ford's development of fuel systems, "I will not require them to answer it any further."

Regarding the request for documents pertaining to Ford's alleged concealing of test results, the judge looked to King for guidance: "I think you all stated that you had no record of any?"

"That's correct, Your Honor," said King. (In fact, Ford had said they had no such records *regarding 1970–78 B-700 series bus chassis.*)

"They have answered it," said the judge. "So, that's their answer. If you all can prove otherwise, that's their problem."

Regarding the plaintiffs' request to see agreements between Ford and the other defendants, the judge turned to the Ford lawyers and said, tentatively, "I have got a problem with it, I think, on confidentiality of the individual attorneys and their clients, have I not?"

Grubbs told the judge that the judge did, indeed, have that problem, and Williamson ruled accordingly.

Next came the demand for the names of people who had furnished Ford's answers to the plaintiffs' interrogatories. This was the point the plaintiffs couldn't lose, because Kentucky Rule of Civil Procedure 26.02 explicitly provided: "Parties may obtain discovery regarding . . . the identity and location of persons having knowledge of any discoverable matter." And indeed, Williamson seemed to come down on the Fairs' side: "I understood you all to say you had furnished those names to them," he said to the Ford lawyers. "If you haven't, furnish them to them."

"Just to make sure I understand that," King offered helpfully, "the individual who supplied the answers is Mr. Pelkey [the Ford engineer assisting the defense attorneys]; he is the one who had to go throughout the company to gather information from others. Is it Your Honor's ruling that they can depose Mr. Pelkey, and then if he identifies others, then they would be able to depose them?"

"I would think, I don't think I have any right to stop them," replied a somewhat befuddled Williamson.

"I just wanted to make sure I understood," said King innocently.

To the Fairs it seemed that what had started out as a hearing had devolved into a routine, with Williamson playing Charlie McCarthy to King's Edgar Bergen. They couldn't figure out how the judge was able to speak without King's moving his lips.

"They are not required to name to us the people who gave Mr. Pelkey information?" gasped Phil Allen.

"Not as far as I am concerned, no," replied Williamson, sounding more sure of himself. "You have got Mr. Pelkey, so you would have reliable information and not secondary information from somebody in Ford Motor Company scattered all over the United States." Here was a novel analysis: The man who had gathered the information was the most reliable; those who had supplied it were secondary sources.

All that remained was the request for Ford memoranda regarding the Nixon-Ford-Iacocca meeting.

"This is irrelevant to the subject matter in this case because it has nothing to do with heavy trucks," King prompted. "All we know is that that meeting in the White House occurred some six years before any amendment became effective or anything occurred with regard to the fuel systems on heavy trucks and school buses. And that's the reason we think it is absolutely immaterial."

But the delay is the whole point! Oldfather might have shouted in frustration. Instead, she spoke with controlled intensity. "Your Honor," she said, fixing her light-gray eyes on his, "it is our position that Ford *actively engaged in the delay* of the promulgation of those safety standards."

"Didn't everybody?" replied Williamson blankly.

It was too late for appeals to reason. The advocates had advocated; the judge had judged. Now it was time for him to pronounce his final ruling. His mind was clearly already on his peroration, a sort of rhetorical striptease that must be taught in judge school, so universal is its performance from the bench. This is the speech during which judges suggest first that they are ruling one way, then hint that they are ruling the other, all the while showing off the keen legal analysis, tempered by folksy wisdom, that has enabled them to reach a result at once intellectually unassailable and intuitively just.

"Well," Williamson began, "we got into, you get into a situation with the rules of discovery, gentlemen, they are very broad, they are very all-inclusive, and it drops it right back in the lap of the court to try to determine what is going to be within the realm of, not a—the court coined the phrase for lack of something better to say—I guess people understand fish. So, they have used the word 'fishing expedition.' I think it is constantly being used by judges, by the courts and attorneys and everybody else. A fishing expedition. And, of course, they are fishing. You are seeking valid, competent evidence. And so I think your interrogatories that have been answered are sufficient to this point."

Larry and Janey Fair were stunned. He was turning them down on every motion. Every one. They could not believe that their case, stemming from an infamous disaster, with implications for the entire automotive industry and millions of schoolchildren, was being tried in front of a crotchety and distracted man. There was something grotesquely dispro-portionate between the conflict and the means set aside for resolving it. The commonwealth had given them the back of its hand. It was as though, on trial for their lives, they had been ushered into a hearing officer's cubicle at the Parking Violations Bureau.

"So," the judge went on, "I will confine it to the trucks during this period of time and will not require 1970 [sic] conversation between Ia-cocca and the President of the United States and all of the parties to be made a part of this lawsuit, which would become a matter of record for whatever it is worth, because I know it would not be a matter of evidence in the lawsuit as such, as proving the case. I will let it go at that, gentle-men."

❑

Skip Murgatroyd's life may well have passed before his eyes, so nearly terminal were the circumstances in which he now found himself.

The son and grandson of doctors, as a young man he'd inherited a sum of money that, though small, far exceeded his immediate needs and insulated him from the exigencies that can constrain a fellow to give up a thousand potential lives in exchange for a single real one.

Having abandoned college, he went to New York to be an actor in

1971, but his career never got past the taxi-driving stage, and after a year of fruitless auditions he resumed the casual labors of a hippie dropout. Finally, exhausted after a decade of unflagging vigilance against the snares and delusions of middle-class life, he was overtaken by twin certainties: He knew he wanted to do something that interested him, and he knew he wanted to make money. Just then he serendipitously ran into his old prep school girlfriend, Tracy, who was headed to the West Coast, so he joined her—on the coast immediately, in matrimony soon after. Then he took a vocational aptitude test at Los Angeles City College and it came out: lawyer. He tore through college at UCLA, picked up a law degree at Southwestern University Law School, Class of '83, and at the age of thirty-five assumed the role of attorney—without entirely shedding his counter-cultural past. (How many lawyers opposed the death penalty, as Murgatroyd did, on the ground that it just hastened the offender's return to the street, through reincarnation?) By natural inclination, Murgatroyd went into personal-injury work. There followed the merger with his boyhood chum John Coale, and a flock of aviation cases: Arrow Air in Gander, Newfoundland; Northwest Airlines in Detroit, Delta in Dallas, United in Sioux City. People-packed aluminum tubes—their wings iced, their cables sheared, their pilots erring—plummeted from the sky; and the law practice took off.

Now he and his family lived in a two-bedroom white ranch house in the Los Angeles suburb of Tarzana (named for Tarzan, of the movies), up and over the Santa Monica Mountains in the broiling foothills of the San Fernando Valley, where the Bermuda grass remained miraculously green though it was as dry as straw. It was an upper-middle-class 'burb, nothing grand. But on a weekend morning he could slide open the glass doors of his Florida room, slip into a little backyard pool, and float beneath pink oleander blossoms and an azure sky.

Those tranquil moments came at a price. Murgatroyd spent twelve hours most weekdays sealed inside the gleaming black Max Factor Building on Wilshire Boulevard in L.A. He always told his wife he'd be home by 7:30, and he meant it, but when the time came his will was overborne by the goads and seductions of his profession: Surely in that next file folder lurked the fact that could deliver victory or condemn him—and the clients depending on him—to defeat. So he'd work on, his back to the tinted window through which you could see palm trees writhing in the stifling haze and, on good days, dimly, the Pacific Ocean. The white bookshelves reaching from floor to ceiling, the desktop, the floor, even the windowsill strewn with framed photos of Tracy and the two kids were perpetually piled high with paper, giving the office the look of a college dorm room in the middle of final exams. He had consigned himself to a life of endless tests, and always there loomed the specter of failure, and now this.

CHAPTER

43

It was the task of the judicial system to take the horror on Interstate 71 and reduce it to cases that could be duly processed and disposed of. As usual, the primary agent of this transformation was a generous dose of time. One Christmas had come and gone, and another was approaching—merchants' banners proclaiming "JOY! JOY! JOY!" lined the street outside the Carroll County Courthouse—before the six-week trial of *The Commonwealth of Kentucky* v. *Larry Wayne Mahoney* ground toward its inevitably unsatisfying conclusion in December 1989.

Perfect justice was never among the possible outcomes. "There's no balancing the books," Janey Fair observed, as the jury deliberated. "He can't go to prison for twenty-seven lifetimes." But Mahoney, who was out on $270,000 bail—his family and neighbors had pledged their homes as collateral—did face the real possibility of being put behind bars for most of the rest of his life, since he faced twenty-seven counts of murder.

The jury, however, could consider lesser degrees of homicide, the least grave of which was reckless homicide, for which the sentencing range was one to five years. Under Kentucky law, Mahoney would be guilty of reckless homicide if the jury found that he had unintentionally caused the deaths and he 1) grossly deviated from reasonable conduct, and 2) created a substantial and unjustifiable risk of killing someone, but failed to perceive that he was creating that risk. He would be guilty of the more serious offense of manslaughter in the second degree (five to ten years) if he 3) was *aware* of the risk he was creating and *consciously disregarded* it. The three elements—grossly unreasonable conduct, substantial unjustifiable risk, and conscious disregard—together constituted "wantonness." (It was no defense to a charge of wanton conduct that he was too intoxicated to be aware of the risk, unless his intoxication came about involuntarily.) If the prosecution proved a fourth element, namely that the wanton conduct was engaged in "under circumstances manifesting extreme indifference to human life," Mahoney would be guilty of murder (twenty years to life).

A juror who listened very closely to the judge's instructions might have noticed that a reckless homicide was transformed into a second-degree manslaughter solely by the presence of conscious disregard, but that conscious disregard did not actually have to *be* present if the defendant was drunk; and that a manslaughterer who was already reckless enough to endanger people's lives became a murderer only if he exhibited "extreme indifference" to human life. Since laymen are unaccustomed to making such evanescent distinctions, as a practical matter the six men and six women of the jury would simply have to decide unanimously whether Mahoney had acted badly, very badly, or *extremely* badly—which was, no doubt, what the law was trying to say.

State-appointed defense attorneys William L. Summers and Russell Baldani, and volunteer lawyer Jack Hildebrand, had conceded that Mahoney was drunk at the wheel that night in May. But they insisted that he had taken pains not to drive drunk, though he had stopped at a couple of bars to brood over his daughter's illness and his financial woes. Mahoney, who claimed his ulcer had put him completely off alcohol for two months before May 14, admitted that between 1:00 P.M. and 9:00 P.M. he'd had several beers—witnesses testified to seven. But even the prosecution's alcohol expert acknowledged that if Mahoney really had spread seven beers over eight hours, that rate of consumption would have left him sober at 9 P.M., with a blood alcohol concentration (BAC) of no more than about .04—well below the legal limit of .10. But based on blood samples taken at the hospital an hour and a half after the crash, the prosecution argued that his BAC at the time of the 10:55 P.M. wreck must have been at least .21.

Mahoney's defense centered on what had happened while he hung out at his friend Taylor Fox's house between 9:00 P.M. and 10:00 P.M. Mahoney, supported by several witnesses, testified that he drank there only after his pal Fox agreed to drive him up to Burlington to meet Mahoney's old girlfriend Kim Frederick. Otherwise, Mahoney swore, "I would never have drank. This is the God's honest truth." He said the last thing he remembered was drinking some clear liquid that made him gasp —it could have been vodka or moonshine—as well as some Pepsi that may have been spiked. (By all accounts, Mahoney was strictly a beer drinker, unfamiliar with the wiles of whiskey. Indeed, the emphasis his witnesses accorded this particular virtue fostered the impression that, in Mahoney's set, the fact that a beer contained as much alcohol as a shot of the hard stuff was not fully appreciated.) The next thing he knew, he was in a hospital bed.

Witnesses said Mahoney asked Fox for his keys back and promised to drive the quarter-mile straight home. Fox gave him the keys, but Mahoney didn't drive home. Somehow he ended up on I-71. "I really am sorry," said Mahoney, his voice quavering as he addressed the victims' families from the witness stand. "I know it's not going to make you feel any different toward me . . . but that's all I know to say."

According to this defense, Mahoney, far from acting wantonly, had prudently sought and found a designated driver, Fox. Even if Mahoney then voluntarily got drunk, he did so secure in the knowledge that he would not be driving. But, his lawyer Hildebrand argued, Mahoney had gotten drunk *involuntarily,* when he drank spiked Pepsi. By the time Fox reneged on his designated driver commitment and handed him the keys —according to this version of events—Mahoney was too intoxicated to be aware of the risk he would be creating by driving off. Finally, Hildebrand suggested, no matter what Mahoney did, no one would have died if Ford Motor Company and Sheller-Globe Corp. had not built a bus that was an inferno waiting to happen.

Prosecutor Paul Richwalsky pointed out that Mahoney had been drinking and driving, sometimes simultaneously, for eight hours or so *before* he supposedly made Fox his designated driver; and that, in any case, Fox left something to be desired as a designated driver since he himself had been drinking; and that Mahoney had not been slipped some vodka but had *asked* for it. (The testimony was contradictory on this point.) In a closing brilliant for its common touch, Richwalsky torpedoed the argument that any safety defects in the bus could relieve Mahoney of responsibility for the carnage. "The bus would still be on the highway" if Mahoney had not chosen to drink and drive, he said. "What if a motorcycle got in his way and he hit it? What if it was the poorest family in Carroll County, and the poorest family in Carroll County had a twenty-year-old car that was held together by bailing wire? Could he come in and say, 'Hey, it's not my fault, they were poor people; if they had a brand-new Cadillac, or a Mercedes, or the safest car in the world, they wouldn't have been killed'? That's the argument.

"You take your victims as you find them. He's responsible. He set it all in motion."

Richwalsky veered momentarily into the imponderable: "The victims that cannot speak for themselves today, they didn't have a trial. They didn't have a fair judge presiding over them. They weren't even charged with a crime. But they got the death sentence. For what? For being on their way home? For spending the day at an amusement park?" Then he returned to earth for his answer: "They were murdered. This defendant killed those twenty-seven people just as sure as if he'd had a gun."

As he had thoughout the trial, Mahoney sat with his hands in his lap, staring down at a point on the table in front of him as though hoping to find a tiny crack to crawl into.

"I know he regrets it, and I know if he had it to do over again he would do something different," Richwalsky concluded. "And I know he didn't mean it—and that's got nothing to do with this case. The apologies and the I'm sorries, it's too late. Now, it's time to pay."

❏

As it happened, the jury had two benchmarks with which to take the measure of Mahoney's offense. Just three weeks after the bus wreck, Mahoney's distant cousin, Makayla Mahoney—a cheerful, bright-eyed four-year-old girl—had been killed by a drunk truck driver who jumped the curb and crushed her as she walked on a Carrollton sidewalk on a Saturday afternoon. Jeffrey Gill, twenty-eight, who had no prior drunk driving convictions, had a BAC of .28 and joined Larry Mahoney as the first killer drunk drivers to be indicted for murder in the history of Carroll County. Judge Satterwhite, who was now presiding over Mahoney's trial, had accepted Gill's plea of guilty to reckless homicide and ultimately sentenced him to five years probation.

On the other end of the spectrum jurors could find the case of Sam Chowning, a veritable poster boy for extreme indifference to human life.

Early on a Friday evening in July 1989, Chowning, twenty-four, who by his own account had consumed at least twenty beers and nine joints of marijuana over the course of the day, was driving a stolen pickup at 80 mph down a Carroll County road when he crossed the centerline and plowed over the top of an oncoming Honda Accord, decapitating a minister and his wife and killing their sixteen-year-old daughter. The family had been on their way to church.

The arresting officers had asked Chowning, "Did you know you'd had too many beers to drive?"

If one can believe the police report, Chowning, whose license had been suspended as a result of two prior drunk driving convictions, replied, "Hell, yes. But did I give a shit? No."

"Did you consider you might hit another vehicle?"

"I never considered it," Chowning said, "but it happened."

Chowning pled guilty to three counts of murder. Just a few weeks before Mahoney's trial got under way, Satterwhite sentenced Chowning to sixty years, with no parole possible for twenty-seven.

After deliberating eleven hours, the jury convicted Mahoney of second-degree manslaughter, effectively deciding that his actions were worse than Gill's but not as bad as Chowning's. In the end—after all the legal wrangling, the seventeen days of heartwrenching and often grotesquely graphic testimony by 124 witnesses, the nearly two hundred exhibits—it may have been Mahoney's evident anguish that led the jury to tender him a degree of mercy. Three times, while listening to witnesses' accounts of terror amid the flames, he had broken down and wept. The jurors may have agreed with defense attorney Summers that Mahoney would be paying forever, in prison or out. They recommended a sentence of sixteen years,* which under Kentucky law could not be increased by the judge. Mahoney could be considered for parole after eight.

---

* Mahoney was given concurrent ten-year sentences (the maximum) on each of twenty-seven counts of second-degree manslaughter; concurrent sixteen-year sentences on each of twelve counts of first-degree assault (for which the maximum was twenty years) on the seriously injured survivors; and concurrent five-year sentences on each of twenty-seven counts of wanton endangerment, regarding the occupants of cars he barely missed and bus passengers who escaped serious injury. All the sentences were to run concurrently with one another.

CHAPTER

44

It was a devastating outcome for the families of the dead. They had hoped that a murder conviction would signal once and for all that drinking on purpose and killing by accident was as inexcusable as killing on purpose. "To send the message we need to send, he has to be convicted of murder and get the life sentence," Janey Fair had said.

In fact, the notion that the prospect of a murder conviction would deter drunk drivers didn't bear close scrutiny. A drunk driver often doesn't know that he's drunk and certainly doesn't expect to get into an accident. Looking at all the possible consequences of getting behind the wheel, what intoxicated person would say to himself, "I don't mind being arrested, I don't mind losing my license, I don't mind damaging my car, I don't mind getting hurt or killed, I don't mind maybe killing someone else, I don't mind getting convicted of manslaughter, but I would hate to be convicted of murder, so I won't drive"? The marginal deterrence of a possible murder conviction, after all the other potential consequences, would be nil. But the families might have hoped that a conviction on the top count would reinforce the general message that drunk driving is an abhorrent *crime.* And they may also have wanted a murder conviction not for deterrence but for *justice,* which is a good reason.

The Radcliff families could not see how Mahoney's punishment fit the crime. "It's always 'Poor Larry Mahoney, he's got to live with this,'" observed Bill Nichols, whose only child, Billy, seventeen, died in the crash. "But Mahoney can see his family. They can visit him in prison. If I want to spend Christmas with my child, I've got to go to the cemetery and kneel down by a headstone."

Said Lee Williams: "I personally in my heart want to see Larry Mahoney go to prison for the rest of his natural life, never to be paroled. He shed innocent blood. My ten-year-old daughter was lying there asleep when she was killed on that highway. My fourteen-year-old daughter was killed on that highway. My wife was thirty-four. Larry Mahoney took away their youth and he should give up his youth. He took away my wife's life and he should give up his life."

Yet Williams sometimes felt as though prison were beside the point, and that the most sublime punishment would be simply to cause Mahoney to really know what he had done. "Does he know the pain he caused?" Williams wanted to know. "I once said I'd be for dropping the charges if Mahoney would spend three days with me packing up baby blankets and teddy bears and stuffed animals and baseball card collections. I think he should have to personally 'know' each victim." It was maddening to see the killer of one's family fight to stay out of prison, when imprisonment ought to have been a matter of complete indifference to him, his guilt flaying him with such torments that the additional discomfort of being locked up could not even be felt. He should have been begging for the lash in the hope that it might ease the unremitting agony of that guilt, if only by the blessed substitution of some other pain. Forgive him, for he knew not what he had done? That damnable ignorance was the greatest offense. Better first to make him know. The searing knowledge would be so purifying that no forgiveness would be necessary.

Alas, the Larry Mahoney slumped at the defense table had seemed so totally inadequate a vessel for such titanic remorse that at a glance many of the grieving ceased to much care what happened to him one way or another, except as an example to deter others.

❑

If Mahoney had sat with Lee Williams packing up the belongings of the family that he had reduced to ashes, he would have learned that Lee met Joy in high school speech class in Poplar Bluff, Missouri. She was in the ninth grade, he in the eleventh. When he graduated in 1969, he got drafted, but enlisted before induction upon a recruiting officer's assurance (false) that by joining up he could avoid Vietnam. (He chose training as a corpsman, envisioning himself in a crisp white uniform walking the shiny corridors of a clean, dry hospital.) Then he asked Joy to marry him, which she did. (Her parents were against it, but gave their permission with the proviso that she promise to finish high school.) They started their life together in San Francisco, where he worked at a military hospital until he was shipped out to Vietnam to serve as a combat medic.

Kristen was born in 1974, Robin four years later. Had Mahoney been folding up Kristen's security blanket, the one with a pattern of multicolored squares that Joy had saved as a wall hanging, Williams might have told him that of the two girls she had been more like her dad. Kristen could be a little impatient; she sometimes had trouble admitting she was wrong; her feelings were easily hurt; and when she was mad she would pout. She loved the piano, and played clarinet in school band. She loved to write; she'd make up stories about picture postcards. Those teddy bears that Mahoney should lay out carefully in a carton were hers. She collected them, and had an army bear, a doctor bear, and a bear with each New Year on it, up to 1988. (The little dresses on some of the bears had been worn by the girls when they were babies. Joy had thought of putting them on the teddy bears, as a way of saving them.) Kristen slept with her door shut for privacy. She wanted to go to the University of Missouri and be a solo pianist and marry a rich guy.

The little blue and white blanket with chickens on it was Robin's. As she lay in bed, she used to count the chickens until she would fall asleep. Robin was more like her mom—patient, forgiving, loving, caring. She loved her stuffed rabbits, Pinky and Long Legs. Robin slept with her door open and a glass of milk and a cookie on the table beside the bed. She wanted to go to Duke and be a veterinarian and a lawyer.

"My girls wanted to be something," Williams said. "And they both loved God very much."

❑

It was Lee Williams's love of God that got him through his ordeal. He had always thought that serving God was his first priority; his family was second, and worrying about himself and his job came third. "If God was happy with me, and my family was happy, then I'd be happy," he reasoned, and so he had been. Then his wife and daughters were consumed in the flames. His mother had died of cancer six months earlier; his father had passed away five years before that, and Lee had no aunts or uncles or siblings, save an estranged half-brother. Lee Williams was a family man, and now he had no family, so what was he?

He picked out three caskets and buried his girls a hundred yards from where they had so recently stood, burying his mother. He buried them facing east so they could look for the Second Coming. He didn't know what to do next. He would come home from work at seven o'clock at night, change out of his uniform, get in his car and drive fifty miles, have a cup of coffee in a restaurant, and drive back again, just to kill time.

Thoughts starting with "If only" streamed at him like the white lines on the road. If only he'd accepted assignment to Fort Benjamin Harrison, in Indiana, instead of Fort Knox. If only he'd stuck by his guns and not allowed Kristen and Robin to go on the trip because they'd been noisy in church. If only he'd gone with them.

He'd pull into the driveway at 1:00 or 2:00 in the morning and sleep in his car until 4:30, when he'd go in just long enough to shower, put on his uniform and go to work. He could not bear to be in that house, where death was at home and he was a stranger.

For seven months he was stuck in his misery, like a grounded ship waiting for the hour when the tide would rise. Then in the darkest days of December, he had his epiphany. "I told the Lord, 'I'm not going through '89 like I did '88. But if I could have any New Year's wish, could I just talk to Joy for one minute?' And I was looking at her picture. 'If I could just see her for a minute, I want to tell her I love her. I want to tell her I miss her.' And I didn't hear no voices, but it just came to me in my heart. He said, 'If I would let you see Joy for a minute, Joy wouldn't want you to say that you love her; she knows you love her. Joy wouldn't want you to say that you miss her; she knows that you miss her. She knows that. Joy would tell you this: Serve Me and put your life back together.' "

❑

Seven months later, on July 8, 1989, Pastor Tennison presided at the wedding of Lee Williams and Dottie Pearman, widow of John Pearman, who had died driving the bus. Dottie had known Lee's wife well. They used to sing together at funerals and weddings. But Lee and Dottie had known each other only to say hello.

They built themselves a big brick house with three gabled windows, high up on a hillside on the edge of town. Building the house—he did some of the work himself—felt like a healing to Lee. But it felt like a sharp stick in the eye to some people. They'd been sorry for him, expended their feelings on him, and now here he was with a new wife and a new house and several million dollars in settlement money between them. Lee and Dot's critics were really no worse off than they had been before, but they felt suddenly impoverished. You could feel good about feeling bad for people, and even be glad when they got back on their feet, but it was really annoying to see them hop up and sprint past you.

Then, too, the community had dug deep and given generously to aid the bus victims, raising money the hard way, a little at a time: a car wash here, a bake sale there, collection jars by every cash register for miles. Boosted by a $10,000 gift from the Kings Island amusement park, the We Care Fund surpassed $100,000 within two weeks of the crash. Then $40 million rained down from the skies above Radcliff, and not a drop landed on anybody except the victims and their families, some of whom quickly bought fancy new cars. The meek had inherited and the last were now first. What a rip-off.

"There are people who are jealous of me and Dot for putting our lives back together," says Williams. "They feel Dot should have just been an old widow lady living over there with her three kids. And Lee should have been the guy who just about lost it and moved on back to Missouri. That's what they wanted; that's what they didn't get."

Dottie told him, speaking of her life with her first husband, "John was Chapter One. I can look at Chapter One, but I can't live in it. Now we have to live in Chapter Two."

❑

On January 1, 1990, Williams retired after two decades in the army to devote himself to spreading the word of what God had done for him. He crisscrosses the country, speaking almost every week, mostly at Assemblies of God churches and retreats. He calls his speech "From Pain to Promise."

"Most churches have a morning and night service on Sunday," Williams says. "In the morning I give a short testimony of who I am and what happened to me. I'll set up pictures of Joy and Kristen and Robin, because I want them to meet the family I lost. And that usually has a pretty good impact. And this is hard to do—I still find it hard to look at their pictures —I say, 'This is how I knew my family May 13, 1988,' and then turn 'em around and there's a picture of their stones: 'This is how I know 'em today. This is what I get to see.'

"I say, 'Many of you are wondering how can a guy who's just lost his mother and doesn't have a father lose a wife and two little girls, everything he ever had or wanted, how can he lose that and still survive? But God made me a promise that one day I would be happy again.' I tell 'em, 'If you come back tonight, I will give you living proof of how God restored me to complete happiness, not partial, not 50 or 80 percent but complete happiness.' "

As he tells you all this, Williams fixes his pale blue eyes on yours with a peculiar intensity, making you feel so thoroughly observed that it is all but impossible to observe him. It is a technique of control, perfected in his many years as a sergeant shaping up his troops. It does leave you feeling, though, after talking with him, that you have been in a struggle. No doubt it's his struggle, to believe and be believed, and he has to win it every hour of every day.

"When they come back for the second session, I tell them about what God's done for me in my life—given me a new family. Then I set out the pictures of my new family as I talk about them, and people get excited. All I do is use that as a positive motivating thing. Like back in the old days, when you saw a movie and something bad happened, what happened? The movie always had a good ending. People like good endings."

They do. A happy ending is so important that people demand it in a movie, expect it in books (including this one), and cleave to it as a central tenet of their religions.

"I get up and I tell this story over and over, and I'll be thinking, 'God, this is getting old to me, in a way,' " Williams says. "But buddy, every time I do this men come up to the altar and say, 'I am not the husband and father I need to be.' God uses this story to stir up a man's heart, to treat his family a little better. We take our families for granted. I try to get it across that your family is a gift from God.

"Death can rob you at any time. There's no guarantee you're gonna get home today, and there's no guarantee when you get home there'll be anything waiting for you there. Only a fool would promise you that. I don't care how good of a Christian you are. I don't care how good of a person you are. Death is real. And we're all gonna experience it one day.

"That bus wreck changed me. I'm not the Lee Williams I was. A new person. New job, new career, new life, wife, children, dreams, visions." Williams, who as a teenager gave his life to the Lord in 1968, was saved spiritually five or six times in Vietnam, and rededicated his life in 1977, had in a sense been born again, again.

"My ministry has helped my inner healing tremendously. I have begun to feel much better about myself. I still have bad days about this. I don't have all hunky-dory days. I miss my family terribly, but yet I'm smart enough to realize they're not coming back."

In fact, Williams reminds the bereaved that their loved ones wouldn't come back to them even if they could. "Nobody leaves heaven to come back to this place," he says. "Personal opinion: I don't blame 'em. I believe in heaven. I believe it's a place where there's no pain, no suffering, no misery. I believe as a Christian that's my final goal. Some people say they don't believe in heaven. I can't afford not to. Heaven's real. Hell's real. And one hundred years from now, I choose to be in heaven. I chose through my religious beliefs that there is a God, He has a son called Jesus, I've accepted him as my savior, and I'm going home. And I can tell you, for something that a lot of people say isn't real, He's pulled me through an awful lot of things."

CHAPTER

45

Peace eluded Janey Fair and meaning deserted her. She had tried group discussions with parents who'd lost children on the bus, but no one could find anything to say so the group disbanded after three or four meetings. A counselor from the National Organization for Victims Assistance had suggested keeping a journal, but Janey found her days painful enough without reliving them each evening, so she put aside her notebook. Her only therapy was work. She threw herself into working for tougher drunk driving laws, and researching school bus safety for the court case.

Upstairs at the Fairs' house, one of the three small bedrooms was the lawsuit room, and another the Hardin County MADD office. In the MADD room, boards laid across bricks sagged under the booklets and flyers that the organization had accumulated in its eight-year history. In the other work room, legal papers covered most of the red shag rug and packed the white book cases, which Larry had built and had to haul up through the window. ("I told him they wouldn't fit up the stairs," Janey always said, "but he wouldn't believe me.") An address book lay open on the seat of a dusty exercise bike. Both rooms had long since been rendered uninhabitable, as the Fairs' lives were inexorably taken over by their causes. "I'll tell you," Janey remarked ruefully at the time, "piles of papers, they don't keep you good company."

As president of Hardin County MADD, Janey spent hours on the phone vainly trying to get somebody besides the half dozen regulars to come to some church vestry for one of the bimonthly meetings for which, as often as not, she would cook the food and after which she would clean up. (By and large, members of the Radcliff First Assembly of God, despite their insistence that drunk driving was the sole cause of the bus tragedy, did not attend; and Janey had to wonder whether their absence was attributable to her presence.) She mobilized letter-writing campaigns in support of drunk driving laws that did not pass. She stood in supermarket parking lots in December handing out red ribbons that people would forget to tie to their cars as a reminder not to drive drunk. She was available at all hours to counsel the victims of those who did.

Janey and Larry appeared on national television six times to talk about the need for safer school buses. Their media-master lawyer Coale, of course, was instrumental in getting them wired into the talk show circuit; but they themselves were so zealous in their cause that they were beginning to achieve the weirdness that TV craves. In the fall of 1989, after an extensive search, their friend Todd Hendricks finally located a pre–April 1, 1977, Ford-Superior school bus for sale in Indiana. They bought it, for $1,250, and Larry drove it home for use as an exemplar bus for research; for starters, they took out some of the seats and shipped them to their fire expert for flammability tests.

(Until then, every old bus they found would be mysteriously bought before they could bid for it. Larry at first suspected that Ford Motor Company operatives were always one step ahead of them, but he learned that the buses were being bought for export to Mexico and Central America, where rickety U.S. buses routinely ply the narrow, twisting roads until their engines, or brakes, finally give out.)

"When I mentioned [to *Hard Copy*] that we had bought a school bus, they couldn't pass it up; they had to come see us," Larry recalled later. "Lunatics at large," Janey suggested, was how TV producers saw them, and how she sometimes saw herself. She knew she was nearing the edge when she checked her son, Donald, into the hospital for an emergency appendix operation and dashed off to the WHAS studios in Louisville to appear on *Hard Copy* via satellite to discuss the Alton, Texas, school bus disaster.

CHAPTER

46

The sleek dark slab that was the First National Bank Tower soared thirty-eight stories above the Ohio River, dominating Louisville's skyline. Its sealed, tinted windows typified the architecture of arrogance, of unresponsive and unaccountable power: You can't see us, but we can see you. Larry and Janey Fair had been summoned here to be deposed by Ford's lawyers at the offices of Woodward, Hobson & Fulton on this ninth day of April 1990. ("Ryan White, 1971–1990," read the headline on the *Courier-Journal* in the box by the curb. "Teenager Humanized AIDS for the Nation.")

The swift elevator ride to the twenty-fifth floor only exacerbated the sinking feeling in Janey's stomach. If there's anything worse than fear of the unknown, it's fear of the known, and her nine years as a legal secretary had left her with a pretty good idea of what was coming. The defense attorneys had a right to explore her knowledge of facts pertinent to the defendants' liability, so they would ask a lot of questions aimed at denigrating her daughter's talents and prospects in order to knock down the dollar value of her life. Beyond that, there would no doubt be unpleasantness for unpleasantness' sake, to take the fight out of the Fairs and awaken them to the attractions of settling cheaply and going away.

Ford's lawyers did not disappoint. Bill Grubbs, whose office this was, did not welcome the Fairs, introduce them to anyone, or in any way observe what they had thought were the dictates of hospitality. To make them comfortable was not his goal. They were ushered into a conference room and directed to the side of the long table with their backs to the picture window. While her questioners enjoyed the soothing panorama of the blue Ohio, Janey Fair would face nothing but attorneys in blindingly white, starched shirts, no fewer than eight of them arrayed across

from her: four for Ford, two for Sheller-Globe, and one each for Larry
Mahoney and the Radcliff First Assembly of God. That three of her own
and one for the Nunnallees flanked Janey was a comfort, but at the same
time raised the total to twelve, which was more lawyers than ought to be
in any small room at one time and just wrecked all sense of harmony and
proportion.

What am I doing here? Janey wondered for an instant, as the lawyers
wrangled at length about such preliminary matters as whether Ford had
been obstructing discovery. What did all this have to do with Shannon,
the sound of her laughter, the smell of her hair?

"Why don't we see if we can do something about it as gentlemen,"
Bill King was saying to the Nunnallees' lawyer, Mike Hance. No doubt
King simply meant they ought to resolve a dispute honorably among
themselves, without Hance's threatened recourse to a court order; but
King's baritone Virginia drawl gave the word "gentlemen" a resonance it
could never have in Hance's nasal Kentucky twang. Hance's dad was a
maintenance man and tobacco farmer who would show up at court in
overalls and muddy work boots to beam with pride at his lawyer son.
King's father, the Virginia bar association president whose tasseled footsteps King followed into McGuire, Woods, Battle & Boothe, was the scion
of a distinguished family that by now had a substantial equity interest in
everything that was, just as it was. And King was committed to defending
that interest against the roughshod brigands of the plantiffs' bar. (Grubbs,
on the other hand, would have been just as happy representing plaintiffs,
and harbored a still vital, if extremely well concealed, democratic impulse
that led him to do some work on behalf of Louisville's poor.) Hance
sometimes felt a gut hostility for folks like King and Grubbs; he thought
they thought they were better than other people. For his part, King
couldn't be bothered with personal animosity toward anyone in the
room, all of whom were flying below his radar. Yet there was an anger in
King so near the surface it flickered in his eyes, and the courtly Southern
Gentleman could turn menacing in a heartbeat. It was as though he could
tap into a brimming reservoir of resentment, constantly replenished by
underground streams. (Maybe for all his accomplishment he felt he
would never be the man his father was. But then who is?)

King at last turned his attention to Janey Fair. For an hour he took her
through an account of her residence, education, and work history, a task
rendered complex by the nature of an army wife's life: thirteen different
homes in two decades, twenty-six years between the diploma from Daniel

Boone High School and the B.A. in psychology from the University of Louisville. After this arduous but not overly discomfiting inquiry, he probed the more personal and potentially embarrassing area of medical history: "Have you ever had any operations in your life?" was followed by the even more sweeping "Have you ever been under the care of a physician for any illness?"

"You mean other than the common cold?" Murgatroyd asked sarcastically.

"Yeah, other than the common cold," replied King, undeterred.

Janey explained that since all of her medical treatment had been dispensed at military hospitals, she saw a different doctor every time and didn't know their names, in fact couldn't swear they were actually doctors.

"Have you ever been, prior to the death of your daughter, to a psychologist or psychiatrist? Have you ever been to see one since the death of your daughter?" The answers were no and no.

Such questions were at least arguably relevant in case the Fairs pointed to medical or nervous conditions as evidence of the depth of suffering caused them by the loss of their daughter. But, fortified by a lunch break, King pressed on into areas whose relevance to the case was difficult to discern. Had Janey written to any government agency concerning the accident, drunk driving issues, or school bus safety? Where did she attend church now?

There was much more King needed to know: How had she heard about the accident? A phone call at 1:00 A.M.? Was she in bed at that point? Was her husband at home with her? What happened over the next eight hours? Before giving permission for Shannon to go on the trip, had Janey checked the means of transportation? Had she taken any action to check on the maintenance history or the safety record of this particular bus? King made her describe the agonizing hours of uncertainty in the middle of the night at the church, the climactic revelation by the medical examiner that all of the "missing" children were dead, the Red Cross interview seeking descriptive information to help identify her child's incinerated body, everything up through Shannon's funeral, at which point Janey finally gasped and faltered.

"Ms. Fair, I know these questions are hard for you," King said sensitively. "I'm really sorry they are."

In a pig's eye, Janey thought.

"Did you ever have any discussions with Shannon about what it was that she intended to do in terms of an adult occupation?" King asked.

Shannon's goal was to work in the criminal justice system, Janey recalled, but she was also interested in psychology, "although she realized as an eighth-grader that she would, you know, probably change her mind."

"It's fair to say," said King, "isn't it, Ms. Fair, that we don't know what she would have ended up doing?"

"Objection!" snapped Murgatroyd. "Jesus Christ."

Janey understood that this line of questioning was intended to cast doubt on whether Shannon had really said she wanted to be a lawyer, and thus knock down the damages for her lost lifetime earnings. "She wanted to go to law school and then go into politics," Janey replied. "Children that age are still at the stage when they say, 'I want to change the world. I want the world to be better than what I found it,' and that's the stage she was at."

King plowed the same ground when it was Larry Fair's turn, but did it in a single hour, since he'd spent three and a half on Janey and it was late afternoon. Recounting his army career, Fair had reached his first tour in Korea, 1969–70, when King asked, "Why did you not go to Vietnam?"

"Objection! Irrelevant. Don't answer the question," said Murgatroyd.

"You going to instruct him not to answer?" responded King.

"Of course I'm going to instruct him not to answer," replied Murgatroyd. "Quit asking such jackass questions." Such blunt talk was unusual between attorneys speaking on the record, but Murgatroyd had by now concluded that King was impervious to more reasonable discourse. King, who viewed such intemperate remarks as unprofessional, replied to them only in measured tones, or, as in this case, appeared to ignore them altogether. When King got really angry, he would lick his lower lip, and that was all.

He forged ahead, taking care to ask Larry, in even more excruciating detail than he had Janey, about all the things they had not done that some truly caring parent might have done, and that might somehow have saved their daughter:

"Did you make any inquiry concerning the means of transportation to and from the Kings Island outing?"

"Did you have any idea who was going to chaperone the trip?"

"Did you know who was going to drive the bus?"

"Did you know anything about the particular individual's driving record or the maintenance record of the bus or anything else about it at all?"

No. No. No. No. No.

❑

"Maybe they're trying to harass us and scare us from taking the stand at the trial," said Janey as she, Larry, Murgatroyd, and a visitor sat at dinner.

"Absolutely they're trying to harass you, there's no doubt in my mind," Murgatroyd agreed. "The only purpose of these questions is to see how much they can abuse you and how much they can get away with. They're trying to make you think you're not supposed to get on TV, not supposed to let other people know there's a danger."

"Well, I hope they don't think I wouldn't go back at 'em again tomorrow," Janey replied. "I'd go back at 'em again today. Just throw some water on my face and maybe have some coffee."

At last the conversation turned, if only for a moment, to pleasant things. Janey showed off a photo of her first grandchild, her boy, Donald's, strapping son, Stefan, already twenty pounds at twenty months.

"Babies are the most wonderful things in the world," said the visitor.

"I wish I'd had half a dozen of 'em," Janey said quietly.

CHAPTER

47

Though neither side knew it at the time, the real significance of the Fairs' depositions would be that they had occasioned two phone calls by the lawyers to Judge Williamson at his house. In many respects, Williamson was imperturbable: At an earlier hearing Murgatroyd had gone way out on a limb by hinting that the judge ought to withdraw, because his complete unfamiliarity with the law as it had evolved since his retirement might prove a hindrance to the fair adjudication of the case. Murgatroyd had agonized over this risky gambit, fearing that it would fail to move the jurist except to anger. He needn't have worried, as Williamson's serenity was entirely undisturbed by mere suggestions of incompetence. Phone calls home, however, were something else again.

Williamson had with increasing vehemence expressed the desire not to be disturbed at his residence, but there was nowhere else to disturb him; he had no office. When the lawyers could not agree on matters that had to be resolved at once, they saw no alternative but to seek a ruling from the judge, each side hoping that Williamson would blame the other for the intrusion on his quietude. As it turned out, he didn't care who was causing him problems; he just wanted them to stop. A month after the Fair depositions, explaining that the case had turned out to be a lot more work than he'd anticipated, he quit.

Williamson was replaced, in May 1990, by Judge William R. Dunn, who had retired three years earlier from the Kentucky Court of Appeals, the state's second highest court. Dunn affected an unassuming, country-boy persona. ("I've been a police judge, a circuit judge, an appellate judge, just about every kind of judge you can be," he liked to say. "Been a judge for thirty years. Yet when somebody says, 'Hey, Judge,' I still look around to see who the hell they're talking to.") But in fact he'd grown up street-wise as one of a struggling insurance salesman's eight children in Newport, Kentucky, which but for a river would be the underside of Cincinnati. (Newport's putatively robust gambling and prostitution industries had once earned it local renown as the Sin City of the South.) Dunn, who attended Catholic schools there, finished first in the class of 1950 at Chase College of Law, which he attended on the GI Bill. Eight years later he accepted an appointment to replace a deceased police court judge at least in part out of a Jesuit-bred sense of duty. "Someone had to do it," he said.

Dunn had found his calling. On the one hand, he really never could quite get over the fact that little old Bill had ascended to the judiciary: He instructed his family to address him as "Your Elegant Worship"; he signed notes to his wife, "Best Personal Regards, Judge William R. Dunn"; and when he was elevated to the Court of Appeals (whose offices lacked private restrooms), he self-mockingly complained so loud and long about "having to urinate with the common people" that the clerks gave him a bedpan, which he displayed ever after in his chambers. But on the other hand, Dunn felt that he was, and should be, all powerful in his courtroom, because he *knew the law*. And he did believe, as he confided to his family more than once, that he was "the smartest son of a bitch in the state."

His family was inclined to agree, making allowances for the professorial absentmindedness that caused him, for instance, to lock his keys in the car with the engine running at least fifty times, leave his false teeth behind in restaurants almost that often, and on one memorable occasion, do both. He was forever misplacing such things as his wallet and checkbook; after—and only after—he had looked everywhere without success, he would offer a prayer for assistance to St. Anthony, and then find the missing item. Though famous for his fluent profanity, Dunn was deeply religious, carrying novena books, doing the rosary, and attending church almost every day. He had a soft and sentimental side—he had been known to cry while watching *Lassie* with his sons—but it remained well hidden, especially when he was angry, which was often.

Judge Dunn was intent on moving the bus case to trial by August 1991, and would countenance no delays. "Everything I've seen so far about discovery doesn't amount to diddly-squat," he scolded both sides at an October 1990 pretrial hearing. (Ford, which had insisted a year earlier that it had already turned over all discoverable documents, had by then coughed up an additional 20,000 pages.) "I'm for trial by ambulance. Rush up and do it." When the plaintiffs sought what he took to be unreasonable quantities of Ford computer files, he observed, "This isn't a fishing expedition; it's a fishing industry."

A consciously colorful character, Dunn kept himself amused with an endless stream of anecdotes and homely observations. (He maintained a file cabinet full of jokes, indexed, cross-referenced, and rated.) Usually, he would hear the case from the bench and tell jokes in the hall, but sometimes he'd hear argument in the hall and tell jokes from the bench. (For his more off-color stories, like the one about the two dogs and the dumbwaiter, he'd huddle in a corner with the men only.)

Dunn had served in the army as a first lieutenant in Europe in World War II. (He always said he'd found his wife, Laverne Jobert, in the Folies Bergère—"She was the one on the left." But in fact he'd spotted her— the daughter of a Netherlands Plaza bellhop—in Sam's ice cream parlor, in Covington, Kentucky).

At the courthouse water fountain during a break in the October 1990 pretrial hearing, Dunn explained to Lieutenant Colonel Fair why the military life had not suited him:

"I worked for an officer who, I could ask him should I move a chair from here to there, and he'd talk to me for half an hour, and when he was done, I still wouldn't know what he wanted me to do," Dunn said. "So then I would move the chair, and he'd yell at me, 'Don't you ever do that again! I should court-martial you!' And I'd say, 'You stupid son of a bitch, why don't you court-martial me! Anything to get away from you.' He finished 190th in a class of 100 at West Point. Used to play tackle on their fooball team, and if the other team had a good player, his job was to injure him."

"That's one thing I like about the army," Fair replied earnestly. "You get to work with so many different types of people."

Back in court, the lawyers stood holding their little leather appointment books in their palms like missals, reciting in turn the weeks and months they each would be unavailable for trial because of previously scheduled matters. Grubbs mentioned a medical malpractice suit in which his firm was defending Humana, the Louisville-based hospital corporation that had been the subject of some nasty publicity about price gouging. "You folks are *never* going to heaven," Dunn joked. "You better join some religion that doesn't believe in heaven, 'cause you're never going."

Grubbs smiled wanly. It wasn't easy, never being on the side of the angels. Yes, someone had to defend giant corporations against the little guy. You couldn't have every claimant who waltzed into court walk out with whatever award sympathy could command. Without defense attorneys, every business would be bankrupt, no one would have a job, we'd all starve. But it took something out of a man, battling widow after widow, orphan after orphan.

The trial could not be scheduled before the end of March, because the Gulf War had prompted the air force to station Jim Nunnallee in Egypt at least until then. But the Nunnallees' lawyers were booked after that: Hance had a trial set for April, involving a lady paralyzed from the waist down and a brain-damaged little boy. Sheller-Globe's lawyer Mark Arnzen had a May trial representing another client in a case involving brain-damaged babies. The consolidated cases of *Fair* v. *Ford* and *Nunnallee* v. *Ford* were set down for August 5, 1991.

CHAPTER
48

The August 1991 trial date did not hold. At the monthly pretrial hearing in April, Judge Dunn, sounding disgusted with everybody, declared that it would be physically impossible for him to resolve by August all the discovery disputes that were being heaped upon the table. "I'm happy to come out of retirement to hear the case," he said, "but I'm not going to kill myself to do it."

Ford and Sheller-Globe had lately revealed their intention to present a slew of expert witnesses, all of whom the plaintiffs would of course want to depose before trial. The consequent delay was inestimable; Dunn did not even bother to set a new trial date. The Fairs concluded that their adversaries had succeeded at controlling the pace of the battle. "It's inevitable," Janey observed. "We're the invading force. It's their territory: They're in charge of all of the people; they're in charge of all of the documents. It's not like we can just go in there and drop a bomb."

"Well, I would hope we could do something that would be a significant emotional event for them," Larry replied. "We know they out-dollar us. We know they out-man us. But we have to do something offensive, to cause them to be reactive instead of proactive."

If only they could seize the initiative! But there was nothing to do but dig in. For three years now the Fairs had been encamped at the gates of Ford, unable to advance, unwilling to retreat. Their lives were hostage to their own cause. Larry, after twenty-one and a half years in the service, had retired from the military the previous September. The lawsuit was now his sole occupation. Janey thought she'd like to get a job, knew she wanted to do more for her ailing mother in Tennessee. But they were nailed to Carrollton, Kentucky. Nothing could happen for them until they had seen this thing through. A lawsuit is not a duel; it is a siege.

❏

Sometimes the Fairs felt as though they really were in foreign territory, even in their own hometown. That spring, two years after the bus crash, the Radcliff First Assembly of God, which had been using its spare bus, a pre-1977 model, bought itself a new bus for transporting its children: *another* pre-1977, gasoline-fueled model. An incredulous journalist asked Dennis Atchley, the church's new pastor (the Tennisons had taken up the life of traveling evangelists), how his congregation could possibly put its kids on a bus with an obstructed rear exit and no push-out windows,* after all that had happened. He replied that there was nothing wrong with this bus, or the one that had burned. "The bus did not kill those children, and it's our intention to tell the media and everyone else, 'It was not the bus, it was a drunk driver.' " His church, Atchley declared, was not going to be "brow-beaten" into buying a newer bus than it could afford, was not going to be "dictated to," and was not going to "spend the rest of our days in Radcliff apologizing."

His defiant tone notwithstanding, the minister insisted that the choice of bus was based on price and was not intended as a statement. But a post-'77 would have cost only a few hundred dollars more; push-out windows could have been added for about $125 apiece; and a rear seat could have been cleared from the emergency exit for nothing. And his congregants had received more than $20 million in settlement money.

The church's failure to take seemingly obvious steps to ensure bus safety perplexed the Fairs. Rather than take it as a personal rebuke, Janey ascribed the bus purchase to a fatalistic mindset. "In East Tennessee, where I come from, people are so poor that there's a lot of their life they can't control," she observed. "The basic feeling is that things happen from outside forces. The devil brings tragedy into your life and God helps heal it or helps you bear it if it isn't healed. I was away from home a long time before I realized there were parts of my life I could control. But at the Radcliff First Assembly of God, not all the people are poor and it's a mystery to me why they don't try to control things." She shook her head. "It makes me feel like a real outsider a lot of times."

❏

---

* The newly acquired bus, Atchley said, did have a fuel-tank guard, added by the church from which the Radcliff First Assembly had bought it.

That May, Judge Dunn cracked Ford's fortifications. The plaintiffs had asked for all documents pertaining to all of the monthly meetings of Ford's North American Automotive Operations safety subcommittee from 1969 through 1978, in order to search for material manifesting indifference to safety. Ford's lawyers had turned over documents from a scant three meetings. King argued that the request was far too broad. "To allow them to rummage through Ford documents is beyond the bounds of discovery," he said. "If they will tell us what they want, as officers of the court we will get it."

"This is that mystery inside of an enigma that I'm too stupid to understand," Dunn observed wryly, fingering his hearing aid. "If you want to discover something, you're supposed to tell the other side what it is. Then why would you have to discover it? I can't get that through my thick head. I guess the vestal virgins used to worry about stuff like that, too." He ruled that Ford would have to turn over *all* of the minutes of *all* of the safety subcommittee meetings to *him;* then he, not Ford's lawyers, would decide what was relevant to the plaintiffs' case, and pass that portion along to the Fairs' and Nunnallees' lawyers.

Dunn's decisions on various other matters were similarly expeditious. He often pointed out that he had no interest in dragging the case along. As a retired judge, he was getting paid $39 a day. "I could do better at McDonald's," he noted, "and certainly more efficiently than the crew we got at the one up here." He was even emboldened to set a new day for trial. A January date was out, he said, since preparing for it would ruin the holiday season for everyone. He made it February 10, 1992.

❑

The Fairs, in the meantime, though the most assertive of litigants, continued to find themselves in the role of specimens to be examined, albeit by their own side. Their lawsuit sought compensatory damages, which by law comprised three elements: Shannon's loss of lifetime earnings; Shannon's conscious pain and suffering; and their own loss of their daughter's company and affection ("loss of consortium"). The proof of these damages required evidence, and the amassing of evidence required poking and prodding and minute examination that was not to be inhibited by an undue regard for the family's privacy.

They had already met with an economist, who conjured a figure for Shannon's lost lifetime earnings. Shannon's educational testing records placed her in the Very High range, one IQ point away from the Superior range. Her IQ, straight A grades, extracurricular achievements, and her parents' recollection that she had talked about becoming an attorney supported a projection of earnings at the chief executive officer level, which one survey pegged at an average $107,421.57 a year. By adding 20 percent for the value of fringe benefits and multiplying by forty-three years of working life, the economist came up with $5,542,953 in lost earnings. (The interest income that could be reliably generated by receiving all the earnings in one lump, up front, is balanced by the fact that there are no increases built into the future years' salary to account for inflation. Since historically Treasury Bill interest scarcely exceeds inflation, ignoring them both is roughly equivalent to accounting for them both.)

Among the aggressive assumptions in this model were that Shannon would be employed *all the time* and would be paid at the same rate as a male. By statute, *gross* earnings were compensable, with no deduction for personal consumption or expenses or taxes.

Now, Larry and Janey were subjected to the probings of a Louisville psychologist, Larry Raskin, whose expert opinion their lawyers would present to prove the dimensions of the grief that the loss of their daughter's affection had caused them.* After a preliminary interview, Raskin gave them a series of personality tests to fill out at home, including the Beck Hopelessness Scale, Depression Inventory, and Anxiety Inventory, which he would review before interviewing them further.

Larry and Janey cleared a space among the papers piled on their kitchen table and each went to work. They did the Millon Clinical Multiaxial Inventory II:

"Complete the following sentences as rapidly as you can. Write the first thought that comes to your mind.

"The best thing I ever did . . . *was have my children,"* Janey wrote.

"The hardest thing I ever did . . . *was bury my daughter."*

Larry also wrote "bury my daughter." So did Karolyn and Jim Nunnallee.

They filled out the BDI Multiple Choice:

1. I do not feel sad.
   I feel sad.
   I am sad all the time and I can't snap out of it.
   I am so sad or unhappy that I can't stand it.

---

* Raskin would also support the economist's predictions of Shannon's earnings. He tested Larry's and Janey's IQs, since the parents' IQ scores, particularly the mother's, he said, are good predictors of a child's ultimate station in life.

Finally, there was the Minnesota Multiphasic Personality Inventory II, which consisted of 567 true-false questions. Between the first, "I like mechanics magazines," and the last, "Most married couples don't show much affection for each other," were questions trivial and cosmic, transparent and opaque, straightforward and ambiguous. Some of them gave Janey pause.

"10. I am about as able to work as I ever was" (False) and "11. There seems to be a lump in my throat much of the time" (False—the knot in her stomach remained but the lump in the throat had dissipated) she found right to the point. But "108. I just don't have the strength to fight back anymore" she couldn't answer in a syllable.

"322. I am afraid of using a knife or anything very sharp or pointed."

"546. My thoughts these days turn more and more to death and a life hereafter."

"548. I've been so angry at times that I've hurt someone in a physical fight."

"The last time I had a physical fight with anyone was with one of my sisters thirty years ago," Janey said, "but the way it's asked, the truthful answer would be yes. That's why I don't like test questions like that."

"Don't sell him too short," Larry said of the psychologist. "This is just a starting point from which he'll delve in."

"I don't even care about this and us," Janey replied. "What I'm saying is, if you were a teenager locked up in a mental ward and whether you got out or not depended on the test, it's much more scary. For us, I don't think it's gonna matter a hill of beans what we say on there, unless Ford steals it and says, 'See, we told you they were sociopaths.' "

"I took a different approach to it," said Larry. "I went through that whole thing in thirty-five or forty minutes. I just marked it without putting a lot of thought into it."

Janey dealt with her pain by pondering, generalizing, and empathizing her way to the conclusion that other people were worse off than she was. (Not long after the bus crash she'd read several books on the Holocaust "to put things in perspective.") Larry handled his grief by thinking pragmatically, refusing to expend his energy on any but the most useful thoughts.

In the follow-up interview, Raskin told Larry that his self-control was really a strategy for denying his depression and anger.

"Somebody has to be strong in this family," Larry replied, "and I'm trying to be that person."

"You are covering up your feelings," the psychologist said.

Silently, and just for a moment, Lieutenant Colonel Fair began to cry.
"Colonel, you need to deal with this."
"I'll take care of it," Larry said.

CHAPTER

49

That fall, as the trial date neared, Murgatroyd more and
more vividly imagined that the Nunnallees would settle and drop out of
the case, leaving him to square off against Ford's team all by himself. He
and Coale had ended their partnership a year earlier. Coale, in whose
mind lawyers were cowboys who stood alone at High Noon, had found
Murgatroyd's office overpopulated and under-exciting. For his part, Murgatroyd found it hard to match Coale's enthusiasm for headlines about
Coale. Since they had been lifelong friends, the break-up was naturally
bitter and wrenching, like a divorce. Murgatroyd was left with custody of
the Fair case, and Ann Oldfather was promoted to the lead speaking role
in the courtroom. In time it became apparent that Oldfather was likely to
be giving birth just as the Fair trial got under way, and Murgatroyd's
remaining law partners were slated for a trial of the United Airlines Sioux
City crash case at that very time. Prudently, four months before the trial,
Murgatroyd invited Mark Robinson, Jr., to join him. This was a major
move, akin to a ball club's signing an All-Star for the stretch drive.

An obscure, thirty-two-year-old Orange County, California, lawyer in
1978 when he and his co-counsel, Arthur Hews, stunned Ford with a
$127.8 million verdict (later reduced to $6.3 million) in a Pinto case,
Grimshaw v. *Ford Motor Company,* Robinson had since earned a place in

the pantheon of automotive products-liability lawyers. By his own count he'd litigated or consulted on more than one hundred cases against Ford alone, most of them involving fuel system defects. ("I won all my Ford cases—some I thought were losers so I settled for a couple of hundred thousand," he says. "Very few of the cases actually went to trial. Ford doesn't like to try cases against me.") By the time Murgatroyd brought him aboard, Robinson had several times rung up judgments surpassing the $6.3 million *Grimshaw* award, including verdicts of $9 million against Nissan and $9.2 million against GM. (In 1993, he would win a $15 million verdict against Hyundai on behalf of a nine-year-old boy rendered blind, brain damaged, and hemiplegic when, following a collision, the two-point front shoulder belt choked off the oxygen to his brain.) The Fairs, Oldfather, and Murgatroyd all agreed to reduce their percentage of any recovery in order to leave a share for Robinson.

Robinson excelled at hanging Ford with its own documents, which he had discovered by the thousands in the course of his litigation. Using them he would attempt to prove, as he wrote in a *Fair* brief, that "Ford's balancing of lives and limbs against corporate profits evinces a disposition of malicious indifference to safety by placing profits ahead of all else."

Robinson had hit upon this formula in his seminal triumph on behalf of Richard Grimshaw, a thirteen-year-old burned over 90 percent of his body when the fuel tank of the Pinto in which he was riding was punctured in a rear-end collision. (The Pinto had stalled on a freeway—its carburetor float was defective—and when it was hit from behind, its gas tank was rammed into the exposed bolts on the differential housing at the center of the rear axle.) The critical piece of evidence that led the jury to award Grimshaw $125 million in punitive damages (reduced by the judge to $3.5 million) was Ford's 1971 Fuel System Integrity Program Financial Review.

NHTSA had proposed a regulation requiring cars to endure a 30 mph rear impact without fuel leakage. Ford engineers had identified various means by which the standard could be met, including the insertion of fabric-reinforced rubber pads between the gas tank and the differential, at a cost of $7 per car. The company had planned to phase in measures to meet the standard on a few models at a time, starting with the 1974 model year. But then, in the course of its financial review, the Product Development Group concluded that there was only a slim chance that the proposed regulation would be in force before the 1976 model year. By leaving the protective parts off until 1976, the company could save $76 million. However, there was a downside risk: if the regulation actually did go into effect in 1974, the manufacturer's hurry-up design cost would be $18 per car, instead of $7. Balancing the likely savings against the unlikely cost, the financial review concluded, "It does not appear that significant risk exists in delaying incorporation of the 30 mph requirement until a final [regulation] is issued." Ford's decision: Space would be provided for the parts, but "actual hardware will not be added until required by law."

A California appellate court had upheld the admission of these Ford fuel system documents in the *Grimshaw* case as evidence of malice justifying punitive damages. "Through the results of the crash tests Ford knew that the fuel tank and rear structure would expose consumers to serious injury or death in a 20 to 30 mph collision. There was evidence that Ford could have corrected the hazardous design defects at minimal cost but decided to defer correction of the shortcomings by engaging in a cost-benefit analysis balancing human lives and limbs against corporate profits. . . . The conduct of Ford's management was reprehensible in the extreme. It exhibited a conscious and callous disregard of public safety in order to maximize corporate profits."

Ironically, even as it excoriated Ford for "engaging in a cost-benefit analysis," the court itself was doing exactly that, noting that "Ford could have corrected the hazardous design defects *at minimal cost . . .*" (emphasis added). In truth, the very concept of negligence—the very concept of right and wrong—rests on a cost-benefit analysis: We compare the cost and difficulty of guarding against some harm, on the one hand, to the likelihood and seriousness of the harm to be averted, on the other. If a manufacturer can save ten million lives for a dollar, it had better do it. If it can save one life for ten million dollars, it need not. (And probably should not: more lives could be saved by putting the money to use in other ways.) If Ford knew it could prevent school buses from burning by building them out of solid platinum, no one would take the company to task for failing to do so. It's not the fact that a company calculates costs and benefits that offends common decency; it's what it counts as costs, what it counts as benefits, and how it weighs one against the other. It would be Robinson's task to convince Judge Dunn that Ford Motor Company decided to oppose safety regulations in the same manner in which you decide to take your hand off a hot stove; and then, having taken its position, set about marshaling evidence to support it.

In addition to the Fuel System Financial Review, Robinson would seek to introduce as evidence in the Fair case a document known among plaintiffs' attorneys as the Let 'Em Burn Letter.

On September 19, 1973—the day Larry Fair, his pregnant wife, and their two-year-old boy first arrived at Fort Knox—J. C. Eckhold, director of Ford's Automotive Safety Office, petitioned NHTSA to drop a proposed fuel system standard that would have required passenger cars and light trucks to pass a static roll-over test: Turned on their side or upside down they could not leak more than one ounce of fuel per minute. To meet the rollover standard, Eckhold said, a new valve would have to be installed at a cost to the consumer of $11.00 per vehicle. According to the calculations in an appended report by Ford statisticians Ernest Grush and Carol Saunby, with industry-wide annual sales of 11 million cars and 1.5 million light trucks, that would come to a total *cost* to the consumer of $137 million. They calculated that at most the new valve could prevent 180 fire deaths, 180 nonfatal burn injuries, and 2,100 instances of fire damage to vehicles, per year. Given a cost to society of $200,000 per highway death, $67,000 per serious injury, and $700 per damaged vehicle, the losses averted by the standard—that is, its total *benefit*—would be $49.5 million. The standard's cost, the Grush-Saunby report concluded, "has been calculated to be almost three times the expected benefit." Therefore, Eckhold argued, the standard should be discarded.

Ford moved to exclude the Grush-Saunby report from evidence at the Fair trial on the ground that it was not only irrelevant—there was nothing in it about school buses—but unfair. It wasn't Ford that, as Robinson liked to say, had "put a monetary value on human life," but NHTSA itself. NHTSA had come up with the $200,000 figure (actually, $200,725) in "The Societal Costs of Motor Vehicle Accidents" (1972).*

"It is anticipated that the plantiffs will also argue that Ford's profit motive was the overriding concern in using NHTSA's dollar figures in the Grush-Saunby report and in the petition," King argued. "But *nothing in these documents relates at all to Ford's profit, or even its ability to make a profit*" (emphasis in original). The Ford lawyer was right: There wasn't one word in the Grush-Saunby report about Ford's cash flow. Yet for a decade plaintiffs' attorneys had been brandishing the document as though it were the proverbial smoking gun.

---

* In a more recent NHTSA study, the cost to society of a traffic fatality in 1990 was calculated to be $702,000 (*The Economic Cost of Motor Vehicle Crashes,* September 1992, Report No. DOT HS 807 876).

Grush-Saunby's notoriety had begun with an article entitled "Pinto Madness," by Mark Dowie, in the Sept./Oct. 1977 issue of *Mother Jones* magazine, which asserted that at least five hundred and as many as nine hundred otherwise not critically injured people had burned to death in Pintos. It said of the valve discussed in the Grush-Saunby memo, "This minor change would have prevented gas tanks from breaking so easily. . . ."

In fact, according to an NHTSA investigation, the total number of fatalities attributable to Pinto fires resulting from rear impacts between 1971 and 1977 was more like twenty-seven (the same number killed in the Carrollton school bus crash). And the Grush-Saunby study was not about Pinto fuel tanks, or fuel tanks at all. It was about a proposed rollover standard that could be met by the addition of a carburetor valve (which of course could have no effect whatever on fuel-tank ruptures).

The Dowie article won *Mother Jones* a National Magazine Award for investigative journalism.

That a prestigious prize should be awarded for an article that confused the front of a car with the back and had its figures off by a factor of twenty could only have heightened Ford executives' sense of grievance, that nagging feeling of oppression at the hands of the weak that typically afflicts the powerful. Thanks to the Dowie article, it was widely thought that the Grush-Saunby report weighed the cost *to Ford* of paying *liability settlements* against the cost to Ford of making Pintos safe, and that the report concluded that it would be cheaper to leave the cars unsafe and pay the settlements. In fact, the Grush-Saunby memo dealt not with Pintos or even Fords but *all* automakers' vehicles, and it toted up societal costs, not automakers' liability costs.

(To be inaccurately accused in the particulars especially rankles when the larger point is true. No one could seriously think for a moment that Ford opposed a regulation because of its cost to society. It was not Ford Motor Company's job to mind society's balance sheet, but its own. And Ford *did* reach the judgment that it would be cheaper to pay off liability costs than to make the Pinto safer, or the B-700 school bus chassis safer. No document has yet come to light that proves this assertion. But some truths are self-evident. One knows that Ford *decided* to produce a vehicle at a certain level of safety and pay the liability costs, because Ford *did* produce that vehicle in that way. Ford executives could make any vehicle safer and have to charge more for it and lose market share; or they could make it less safe, sell it for less, get more market share, and pay the liability costs. They did what they did, and they do what they choose to do.)

Grush and Saunby had actually apologized in their report for the apparent coldness of their calculations. "To compare the benefits of eliminating the consequences of these rollover fires with the requisite costs," they wrote, "the benefits and costs must be expressed in terms of some common measure. The measure typically chosen is dollars; this requires, then, converting the casualty losses to this metric."

(Given the need to reduce safety efforts and lives saved to the same "metric," it's unfortunate but not surprising that analysts invariably choose dollars. What else is there? They could use time, years of labor expended on a safety device, years of life preserved by it,* but that would be incalculably harder to figure, and would come to the same thing in the end. For time is money, as they say, and money is time, the one ultimately scarce and infinitely desirable commodity. Gold is only a symbol, but time is the source, of value. So much per hour for a worker building a bus, $750,000 for the life of a child killed on it; $12 million for one year of Lee Iacocca's labor [Chrysler Corporation, 1992]—the conversions and equivalences go back and forth, routinely. And yet, when money goes into a moral calculus, how often does the wrong result come out? The means obscures the end, hiding the fact that there is a moral decision being made at all.)

In fact (though no lawyer in the bus-crash case ever pointed this out) the NHTSA societal costs study's authors took pains to state, not once, not twice, but six times in the text, that they were *not* proposing a mathematical formula for regulatory decisions. "Decisions to save lives and prevent injuries are not and should not be based solely on factors that can be quantified in economic terms," they warned. "We are not arguing that it is unwise to spend more than the amounts calculated. These estimates more nearly represent minimal amounts that society could spend to reduce motor vehicle accidents and yet not be worse off economically." That is, since it costs society $200,000 when someone dies in a car crash, society can spend $200,000 to avert a traffic death and be even; it isn't out one dollar yet. "We have provided an estimate of some of the quantifiable losses in societal welfare resulting from a fatality and can only hope that this estimate is not construed as some type of basis for determining the 'optimal' (or even worse, the 'maximum') amount of expenditure to be allocated to saving lives," they wrote.

NHTSA's societal costs study was just a tool. A screwdriver is a tool.

---

* The Nunnallees' lawyer Larry Franklin calculated from actuarial tables that 1,643 years of human life had been lost in the bus crash.

You can use a screwdriver to drive a screw, which is its intended purpose, or you can use it to stab someone to death. Ford Motor Company, Robinson would argue, was not putting the societal costs study to its intended use.

Robinson had no comparable documents regarding the school bus itself. The Product Change Request deferring the cage as standard equipment until it was required by law said nothing about money to be saved by that action. Nor could Robinson explain exactly how Ford expected to increase its profits by making the cage an option instead of standard equipment. The B-700 chassis was no Pinto, intended to conquer a whole market segment if only it could be built cheaply enough. There were no fortunes to be made here, no grand ambitions to be satisfied. If the cage was delayed to keep down the cost of the school bus chassis, it was done less out of avarice than out of habit. Robinson hoped to get his armamentarium of shocking documents into evidence to prove that this habit stemmed from a venal policy of reckless disregard for safety.

CHAPTER

50

Carroll County
Monday, February 10, 1992

The prospect in all directions was brown and gray and black. Cloudy skies glowered down at skeletal forests and withered fields. The barren pastures' endless emptiness was interrupted only by the occasional black Angus foraging in the mud. The absence of beauty was everywhere, yet everyone had faith that spring would come.

Inside the olive drab corrugated metal Carroll Circuit Court annex, about thirty spectators—reporters, mostly—occupied brown vinyl banquet chairs at the back of the tan-carpeted, windowless room. The court was short on civic iconography, or detailing of any kind, for that matter —there were no moldings where the wallboard met the dropped ceiling. There was the American flag, the blue Kentucky flag, a Kentucky seal ("United We Stand, Divided We Fall"), and beneath that, a large red plaque with white letters; "No Smoking" it said. The law was left to its own devices here, with nary a granite step, soaring pillar, or heroic mural to invoke its majesty.

Four Ford lawyers conferred at a long table on the left: Grubbs and his young associate David Schaefer; King and his partner Grace den Hartog, who bore an endearing resemblance to Popeye's inamorata, Olive Oyle. The Fairs and Nunnallees and their lawyers sat at a table on the right. Between them, the lawyer provided for Larry Mahoney by his auto insurance company, Gary Sergent—the only one wearing brown shoes, rather than black—had a little table of his own. (Mahoney was unable to attend due to his incarceration.) At 10:12 A.M., the bailiff called the court to order. "God Bless the United States of America, the Commonwealth of Kentucky, and this court," he said.

"I'm Bill Dunn," said the judge, who'd gotten a perfectly flat-topped brush-cut for the occasion. "Sheller-Globe and the plaintiffs have amicably resolved their differences in this matter," he stated matter-of-factly. The plaintiffs and the bus body builder had settled! "We're here to consider Carroll Circuit Court Case Number 88 C.I. 101, Janey L. Fair versus Ford Motor Company and Mr. Mahoney; and Case Number 88 C.I. 099, James B. Nunnallee versus Ford Motor Company and Mr. Mahoney."

Sheller-Globe and the plaintiffs had reached an agreement just three days earlier, calling for a payment of $1.3 million to the Fairs and the same to the Nunnallees in settlement of all claims. This figure was three and a half times as much as Sheller-Globe had paid for the death of each child to the families who'd settled without suing back in 1988.

Sheller-Globe had not liked its prospects at trial. The plaintiffs had landed a couple of heavy blows in the preliminary sparring: They'd dug up documents showing that Kentucky's specifications had called for kick-out windows, which Sheller-Globe had not provided. And the Fairs' fire expert had demonstrated that all the victims except Chuck Kytta had moved far enough to escape through pop-out windows, if the bus had had them. Then, too, Sheller-Globe lacked Ford's motivation to defend its product, because Sheller-Globe was no longer in the school bus business.

For the same reason, the Fairs and Nunnallees lacked a motive to fight Sheller-Globe to a verdict. "We didn't just fold our tents and slink away," Janey maintained. They couldn't bludgeon the company into making safer buses, because it didn't make buses anymore. And just as Sheller-Globe saw weaknesses in its case, they found weaknesses in their own. The Kentucky State Police accident reconstructionist, Sonny Cease, had disagreed with their fire expert; Cease maintained that Shannon and Patty, seated near the front, could not have outrun the flames no matter what exits Sheller-Globe had provided.

Certain imponderables had also come into play, such as the personal styles of the attorneys. "We've had cordial relations with Sheller-Globe's lawyers, the church's lawyer, Larry Mahoney's lawyer, all except Ford's lawyers," said Jim Nunnallee, explaining why he felt ready to make peace with Sheller-Globe but not Ford. "I've made a conscious effort not to build a grudge against Ford Motor Company, but those two guys King and Grubbs are continuously acting like jerks." His wife, Karolyn, deeply resentful of Grubbs for never having expressed sympathy for their loss, made clear just how painful her experience with the Ford lawyer had been. "I wouldn't spit on Grubbs if he were on fire," she said. (Grubbs is certain that he conveyed his regrets at the very outset, and suggests that the Nunnallees may have been too upset to hear him.) The Fairs also gave the other defendants' attorneys a higher grade for sensitivity than Ford's.

The Fairs found that the seven-figure settlement carried very little emotional weight. "We celebrated by starting the trial," Larry observed dryly. The Nunnallees, too, called the settlement "anticlimactic," and were surprised to find that signing the agreement felt just like signing any other document. The great significance to them all was that it seemed to bode well for their battle against Ford, which they had always considered their main target—because they believed it had done wrong willfully, and because it was still cranking out school bus chassis with fuel tanks by the front door.

"I was talking with Jim Nunnallee the other night," Larry Fair said as the trial began, "and he was saying he'd rather get $3 million and a public verdict against Ford than $5 million in a settlement from them, and we feel kind of the same way."

❑

Conspicuously absent from the courtroom was a jury. Judge Dunn himself would decide whether Ford was at fault, and if so, how much the damages should be. The plaintiffs had originally demanded a jury trial, as either side had a right to do. But Dunn had on several occasions fussed that the case was so complicated that a jury would not be able to understand it.

Ordinarily, someone suing a giant corporation wants a jury of laymen, who are thought to be more easily swayed than a judge by sympathy for the injured and hostility to big business. But the Fairs were leery of a jury here. A lot of folks in Carrollton felt that the bus crash had unfairly tarred their town's name. ("The media called it the Carrollton bus crash when it had nothing to do with Carrollton," said the cashier at Webster's Drug, whose views were typical. "It happened in Carroll County, yes, but it was way down the road." Indeed, if the wreck had been a mile farther south it would have been in Oldham County; and Larry Mahoney was from Owen County.) The jurors might blame the Fairs for reinvigorating all the bad publicity.

Many locals also felt that the crash and its victims should be left to rest. In the experience of hardscrabble Kentucky farmers, a lot of people lose a child; most don't get compensated, and, for certain, the money won't bring the child back. Jurors with some connection to Larry Mahoney —hard to avoid since they had to be picked from a county where he worked and socialized and whose entire population numbered 9,500— might resent the plaintiffs for trying to capitalize on what some viewed as his innocent, though tragic, mistake. ("He was just in the wrong place at the wrong time," said Deputy Coroner Steve Meadows, who helped remove the bodies from the bus.) And then there might be those susceptible to Ford's argument that everyone would have gotten home safe were it not for the drunk driver, period. Finally, if there was no jury, there would be no jury instructions, whose technicalities often provided the loser with issues for appeal.

Murgatroyd had advised that a jury's emotions could lead them to an extremely high figure, but their poor folks' notion of what constitutes a large sum could produce an extremely low figure. The judge could be expected to come down somewhere in between. At a pretrial conference a year earlier, Dunn had told the plaintiffs that if they could prove everything they were alleging, he estimated a jury might award $3.5 to $5.5 million dollars to each family. If the judge were deciding the case, he would set the award as he saw fit—not replicate what he figured a jury would do—but it seemed reasonable to assume that these figures would be in the ballpark.

(Of course, Murgatroyd had no way of knowing the full extent of this particular judge's reverence for the value of a dollar: Dunn, to avoid what he considered unconscionable prices, always took his own hot dogs and buns to Cincinnati Bengals games, where he had them heated up by sympathetic workers at a concession stand.)

The Fairs and Nunnallees quickly agreed to a nonjury trial, provided that Judge Dunn, and not some unforeseen replacement, presided. Sheller-Globe promptly signed on as well. Larry Mahoney agonized for a while but finally decided to waive his right to a jury and take his chances with the judge.

Ford's lawyers hesitated. They were used to being the ones who wanted a judge trial, to avoid the passions of the masses. The plaintiffs were supposed to demand a jury; but here the plaintiffs had gone with a judge. Did that mean that Ford should demand a jury? The idea was just too strange. In the end, Ford, too, agreed to the judge trial.

❑

At 10:21 A.M., Larry Franklin stood up to deliver his opening statement for the Nunnallees. "David," he said to an assistant, "unveil this." In the middle of the room, the young man untied the sheet covering the fuel tank of the Carrollton bus.

"While he's doing that," said Judge Dunn with a smile, "I'm going to reveal my keen interest in this by putting in my second hearing aid." He placed a device in his right ear to match the one in his left.

Franklin had placed the fuel tank into a fuel-tank guard from a post–April 1, 1977, Ford bus. The tank was not a model or a mock-up or an example from the same production run. This rust-orange hulk was *the* fuel tank that had leaked the gasoline that killed the children—that had echoed to the drumbeat of the flames and resounded with the cries of the dying. Perpetrator and witness, it had been there, it had done it. The effect could scarcely have been more chilling if the Grim Reaper himself had clattered in and taken a bow. The instrumentality of death rested in the center of the courtroom. "I will outlast you all," it seemed to say. "My silence will outlast your voices. My iron will be iron when your flesh is dust."

Franklin pointed out that the vertical bar in the center of the front end of the cage rose directly in front of the gash in the fuel tank. "I'm not saying it was a good cage that would prevent all ruptures," he said. "But it would have prevented this one."

Referring to a time line depicted on posterboards, Franklin recounted what he said was Ford Motor Company's history of ignoring warnings that could have avoided this tragedy. He began in 1939, when the school bus industry had agreed on the fuel tank's location based on the premise that, in Franklin's words, "if we all get together and make these buses the same way, we can all save money." (The word "money," as it would be used throughout the trial by the plaintiffs' attorneys, meant something vile— filthy lucre, the root of all evil—a concern for which identified a party as motivated purely by a lust for material things, which is to say, the pleasures of the flesh. Any money that could have been spent on school buses but was not, one was meant to imagine, went straight into the pockets of the rich, who would spend it on ever larger yachts to the exclusion of all else. The notion of money as a scarce resource that had to be allocated between competing needs—so much for school buses, so much for schoolteachers—did not exist in the world Franklin described. He wanted to keep it simple.)

"Nineteen fifty-eight: twenty-six children are trapped and drowned when their school bus, with just two exit doors, plunges into Kentucky's Big Sandy River. Nineteen sixty-seven: UCLA crashes two school buses head-on and demonstrates the likelihood of fire and the need for more exits. Nineteen sixty-eight: nineteen are killed in Baker, California, when a drunk driver runs head on into a bus and its suspension ruptures the fuel tank. April 1971: Henry Ford II and Lee Iacocca meet with Richard Nixon. April 1972: the Reston crash. Nineteen seventy-five: NHTSA runs an Impala into the side of a school bus and it burns to the ground. July 1976: Ford's Kentucky Truck Plant has guards ready for mounting. March 23, 1977: Ford manufactures this chassis. April 1, 1977: the federal fuel system integrity regulation goes into effect. June 28, 1977: the body is put on this chassis."

Franklin dwelled on the Reston Report, with its prescient warning ("The scene was set. It should not be necessary to wait until such a tragedy occurs . . .") about the location and vulnerability of the fuel tank on a Ford school bus chassis. "The only thing Reston didn't tell us was the date, time, and place it was going to happen and the names of the children," he said. "We are going to prove that this accident was foreseeable and survivable. If the guard had been installed, there would have been no deaths. The school bus was extraordinarily dangerous and should not have been sold without the guard." Ford, he said, was completely indifferent to the safety of the children who would ride its buses. Though it manufactured 30 to 40 percent of the country's school bus chassis, it had never crash-tested a bus until federal regulations compelled it to.

As for Ford's assertion that its bus conformed to all federal regulations, Franklin pointed out that federal regulations did not constitute a complete set of instructions for building a bus. In fact, as Ford itself stressed, at the moment this bus was built *there was no federal regulation in force regarding the fuel tank* at all; so Ford was on its own, responsible for building a safe bus. (As Mike Hance put it to a reporter in the hall, Ford's defense that it had violated no federal regulation "is like saying the only reason you don't murder people is because it's against the law.")

Franklin was no thespian. A military man—he graduated from Annapolis in 1959, served on an attack submarine in the Pacific, and now held the rank of two-star admiral in the Navy Reserves—he was a rhetorician from the Dwight Eisenhower mold. He fumbled, hesitated, repeated himself, misspoke. But somewhere in the thicket of words lurked a formidable intelligence. (He had cruised through the University of Louisville's four-year night law school course in three years. "The toughest thing about law school," he liked to say, "is finding a place to park.") Where other lawyers might pierce to the heart of a matter, Franklin broadsided it; he was all over the place, but when the smoke cleared, he'd hit everything.

"The proximate cause of the deaths is the fire," not the impact with Mahoney's pickup, he concluded. "Some of them were burned alive."

> # CHAPTER
> # 51

Though their allegations were identical, and the facts to be proven virtually the same, the Fairs and the Nunnallees each had their own legal team. The attorneys cooperated to some extent, but they could not agree on everything, least of all on who was the best lawyer in the room. Accordingly, after a ten-minute recess, Mark Robinson rose to make a second opening statement, for the Fairs.

When Robinson had first walked into Dunn's courtroom at a hearing a few months earlier, the judge had greeted him with well-bridled enthusiasm. The tall, lean, and tan Californian might be some kind of star out on the Coast, but this was not Hollywood, Dunn let him know; this was Kentucky, where men with callused hands practiced the law. Dunn promptly hit Robinson with an order to hand over to Ford's lawyers copies of all the Ford documents in his possession. He handed over 20,000 pages. Now Ford would know once and for all what he knew.

❏

"On July 15, 1976, Ford had the capability of installing the cage," Robinson began. "Yet on March 23, 1977, the cage was still lying on the Ford plant floor. The Carrollton school bus chassis had everything ready: holes drilled, fuel tank moved back. A Ford school bus chassis built April 1 had the cage. So, this case is about eight days."

Or nine days. Whatever. Robinson was a man on a mission, and no detail would stand in his way. A onetime Stanford wide receiver, he cut a commanding figure in the courtroom; with his chiseled cheekbones, cleft chin, and black-and-silver hair, he looked a great deal like the network news anchor Dan Rather, right down to the mad glint in his green eyes. Yet he delivered his argument in an offhand, conversational tone, rarely glancing at his notes. His was a style calculated to win the confidence of a jury, which, to his dismay, in this case did not exist. (The decision to waive a jury trial was made before he came aboard.)

Why had Ford waited eight and a half months, from July 15, 1976, when it had the cages ready, until April 1, 1977, before putting the cages on? Robinson asked. He answered, this was not an isolated delay but one instance in a pattern of delays of safety equipment by Ford. "They were rountinely putting profits above safety."

He showed a videotape of a Pinto crash test, with fluid splashing out of its unguarded tank on impact. "In seven or eight years, Ford ran hundreds of these crash tests, testing perimeter tanks," to get ready to meet the federal fuel system integrity standard for cars. "You'd think with a school bus carrying sixty-six people, you'd think they'd make that the most protected. Instead, they made it the orphan child of the product line."

Ford knew the importance of shielding fuel tanks, Robinson said. Its corporate design guide for car and pickup truck fuel tanks prescribed locations exclusively inside the frame rails, and its 1974 pickup truck advertisements bragged, "The gas tank is mounted in a protected location inside the frame rails." And, he said, Ford knew that the school bus's unshielded tank could not withstand a side impact: The company hadn't bothered to crash-test a bus to see if it could meet the federal standard without a cage.

Robinson met Ford's toughest defense head-on, that the chassis had been manufactured to meet Kentucky's specifications, and the unguarded location of the fuel tank was open and obvious to all. He argued that although the location was clearly visible, the defectiveness of the design was not, not to a layman. "Up to April 1, 1977, not one bus was ordered with a cage in the United States. If the defect was open and obvious, someone would have ordered one." He ignored an alternative explanation, that there was no defect at all.

Judge Dunn then set a precedent by declaring a luncheon recess of only *thirty minutes,* signaling the seriousness of his intention to whip this case to a conclusion with all deliberate speed. To the general astonishment of all parties, he in fact took the bench again a half hour later.

❑

Bill King was cut from starchier cloth than Robinson, and knew better than to try the conversational style; he stood at the lectern and read every word of his opening argument. "The tragic loss of life in this accident affected all of us," he began, in a gentlemanly drawl redolent of mint juleps on the plantation veranda. "Never before or since has there been a school bus crash of this magnitude." Impressively, King in his second sentence had already made his main point—that the crash was unique, therefore unforeseeable, therefore Ford could not be blamed for failing to design for it—and he'd done it under the guise of lamenting how horrible the accident was.

"The children would be here today were it not for the conduct of Larry Mahoney," he continued. "The school bus incorporated a safe design, the result of forty years' experience." King proceeded crisply and clearly, with an economy of language that left few soft spots in his argument: The disaster was Larry Mahoney's fault. It was not the school bus's fault. The plaintiffs were trying to shift attention away from the school bus itself and make a case of guilt by association. "This is not a case about a Pinto, nor is it a case about a pickup truck," King declared. "It is a case about a school bus and a school bus only." Of course, wishing did not make this so. The judge, not King, would decide what the case was about, and decide whether the plaintiffs' encylcopedic history of Ford malfeasance was admissible in evidence. (The rulings on admissibility of the predecessor judge, Williamson, had gone out the door when he quit.)

Had there been jurors, this question of admissibility would have been critical, for jurors hear only what the judge lets in. But this was a bench trial, and Dunn, as the judge, had to first hear everything in order to decide whether to admit it. His decision to exclude something would be truly effective only if he could successfully order himself not to think about it when reaching his verdict. ("I will listen without judicial retention unless it's admissible," he promised at one point.)

If King could get Dunn to disregard Ford's arguably malodorous history in the automotive safety field and focus exclusively on the bus, then he might win if he could do what defense attorneys always have to do: convince the fact-finder not to use hindsight. Obviously, the fuel tank design had been disastrous in *this* accident. For *this* impact, it would have been better to put the tank anywhere else, even on the bus's roof. But the bus couldn't be designed for one accident, or all accidents. It had to be designed for the most likely sort of accidents. And so it had been, King would insist. "By May of 1988," he said, "250 million schoolchildren had ridden more than 36 billion miles, and never had there been a death or injury by burning of a school-bus occupant from a fuel-tank fire." Except for three teenagers who died in the flames after stealing and crashing a school bus in 1932, this statement was true, so far as anyone knew. And it was a good point. Could a design be deemed defective, that is, unreasonably dangerous, with a track record such as this? Possibly, if its avoidance of disaster could be attributed to dumb luck—that is, to factors other than the design itself, such as the extra caution that motorists exercise in the vicinity of school buses. To eliminate the just-lucky possibility, King recounted his version of the illustrious history of school bus fuel tank design.

The location of the tank outside the chassis rail at the right-front side of the bus, he said, had been selected at the first National Standards Conference in 1939, "where it was determined to be the best and safest location." (What a marvelous tool is the English language! To *determine* can mean to *discover* from facts or evidence; but it can also mean simply to *decide*. It was absolutely true that the 1939 conference decided that the right-front side seemed like the best and safest location; but to say the conference discovered by any empirical or experimental means that it was the best location was absolutely false. King must have known that he could accurately use the word "determine" to mean one thing and have a good shot at having it understood to mean the other.) The prescribed location, King went on, had remained the same through seven subsequent national standards conferences by the time of the Carrollton bus's manufacture. The 1945 conference had gone so far as to specify the location to the inch. (King was under no obligation to point out that the Minimum Standards explicitly disclaimed any purpose for the detailed fuel tank location specifications other than "to increase the efficiency of volume production." The 1970 conference—the last before the Carrollton bus was built—had reaffirmed the location and recommended the use of an ICC tank*—"the standard tank of the heavy truck industry," King pointed out—which the Carrollton bus had.

Judge Dunn interjected a question. "Did this ICC standard include any test for penetration?"

"No, there wasn't," King conceded.

---

* So called because the standards for it were originally set by the Interstate Commerce Commission (ICC). Actually, by 1970, the standards were set forth in Section 393.65 of Motor Carrier Safety Regulations issued by the Bureau of Motor Carrier Safety of the Department of Transportation, but the tanks were still commonly referred to as ICC tanks.

The judge's questions, of which there would be many, served as the tea leaves by which all parties tried to read his mind. Since the Carrollton conflagration had been caused by the penetration of the fuel tank, the Fairs found in this query a heartening inclination on Dunn's part to look past everything that was theoretically right about the fuel tank, and focus on what actually went wrong.

King, attacking the notion that Ford knew or should have known the tank presented a danger, proceeded to pooh-pooh the relevance of the 1968 Baker, California, bus fire that killed nineteen passengers (it was a Greyhound, not a school bus), as well as the 1972 Reston school bus crash (the fuel tank that was crushed and knocked off was not as strong as the Carrollton bus's). Ford did not go ahead and make the tank guard standard, he said, "because not all the body manufacturers were ready to accommodate the guard." What's more, he argued, if Congress believed that unguarded fuel tanks presented a danger, they wouldn't have delayed the regulation. "Ford made the responsible manufacturer's decision," King said. It made the cage available as an option, listed in its brochures and spec sheets. International Harvester, by contrast, made it an option but did not publish its availability. General Motors did not make it available at all.

King concluded with the observation that when the cages were installed, their cost, plus a profit margin, would be added to the price of the bus. Thus, he said, Ford had nothing to gain from delaying the guards' installation.

King having explained that there was nothing wrong with the fuel tank, Grubbs, continuing Ford's opening, argued that if there *was* something wrong with the tank, it was someone else's fault. Kentucky was "a sophisticated purchaser" that chose to order a tank without a guard, and specified its exact location outside the frame rail. The tank, moreover, was actually *protected* by that location, Grubbs claimed, because the right-front leaf spring couldn't pierce the fuel tank without first passing through the sheet metal of the bus's stepwell. According to Ford's accident reconstruction, in this case, only because of the extreme force and unforeseeable nature of the collision, the bus's bottom step had pierced the tank.*

---

* Ford's reconstructionist, Habberstad, had testified at the NTSB hearing that the leaf spring had broken clean off the bus and spun around and pierced the tank; when he later saw the orientation of the spring in a picture of the bus at the scene, he'd decided that it couldn't have punched the hole. Then, after Ford's test crash, he decided the inboard rear corner of the bottom step had done it.

"The Toyota hit just outboard of the bus's frame rail," Grubbs said. "Six inches either way and we wouldn't be here today, Your Honor. That's how freakish this accident was." Janey Fair closed her eyes and nodded.

Grubbs dimmed the lights and showed a videotape of a 1991 test crash conducted for the defense by Failure Analysis Corporation at its Arizona proving ground. A black Toyota pickup, just like Mahoney's, and a yellow school bus, just like the church's (but with no gasoline in its tank), were towed by cables in a slot in the roadway into a head-on collision at a closing speed of 110 mph. Larry and Janey Fair and Jim and Karolyn Nunnallee watched as the crash that killed their little girls was reenacted in meticulous detail. Even in the video's extreme slow motion, it all happened quickly. The truck, coming from the right, and the bus, coming from the left, collided head-on in eerie silence (there was no soundtrack). The truck, its windshield exploding, sliced through the school bus to a point just behind the bus's front door; then, its momentum spent, the truck came to a halt while the bus ran right over it. The yellow sheet metal of the bus body folded inward along the bottom. The truck was seemingly atomized, disintegrating into a cloud of dust and flying fragments. Larry Fair's face turned red; he put his head in his hands.

The test bus's fuel tank had been pierced not by a component of Ford's chassis, as the plaintiffs claimed had happened at Carrollton, but by the bus's front stair, which had been built not by Ford but by Sheller-Globe, Grubbs declared triumphantly. Suddenly he became aware of a heavy stillness in the room and remembered what the pictures were about. "I get a little carried away with the intellectual proof," he apologized. "But regardless, the cause is one thing: a drunk driver. The plaintiffs say they [Shannon and Patty] survived the impact. That misses the point. The fuel tank was breached because components were driven into it by Larry Mahoney. The legal proximate cause, in fact the sole and superseding cause of this entire event, is the negligence of Larry Mahoney."

❑

Finally, Gary Sergent, representing Larry Mahoney, took the floor "just to suggest some ideas." Compared to Ford's defense attorneys, who were being paid a king's ransom per hour and hoped to continue with such work in the future; or the plaintiffs' lawyers, who could hit the jackpot with a big verdict and had desperate people depending on them, Sergent, thirty-eight, had very little stake in the outcome of the litigation. The insurance company that had retained him had already paid in to the court the $75,000 limit of Mahoney's policy, and Mahoney, being penniless, had nothing to defend but his reputation, which at that juncture was pretty much beyond further damage. Sergent, therefore, could view the proceedings with the clarity of relative detachment, his one overriding interest (besides representing his client) being to bring the matter to a close, so that he could get up one day and do something—anything—else. This was a longing shared by Judge Dunn, and for that reason, plus the fact that Sergent had a knack for getting right to the point, the judge seemed to pay particularly close attention whenever he spoke. And he spoke like another lawyer for the plaintiffs, with whom he shared the goal of maximizing Ford's share of the liability.

"Let's talk about forthrightness and culpability," Sergent began. "Larry Mahoney has admitted his culpability." But Ford, he said, had not. Ford kept insisting that school bus transportation officials and the Commonwealth of Kentucky were responsible for the design of the school bus. "Ford Motor Company occupies a superior position to all the government and other entities it keeps pointing the finger at. The organizations that frame specifications on buses look to Ford for guidance, not the other way around." That said, Sergent made a point about the oft-mentioned Reston school bus crash that *had not been made before*. In the Reston crash, he recalled, the metal straps that held the fuel tank on to the chassis had snapped and the tank had been knocked completely clear of the bus, sparing its passengers from the fire. After studying the accident, Ford had strengthened the straps, making the tank more likely to stay with the bus; that is, Ford had responded to the near-disaster by making the tank in some respects *more dangerous*.

"The date of this accident is actually March 1977," Sergent concluded, "when Ford made the decision to put this vehicle in the stream of commerce. My client's actions were the *last* link [in the causal chain]. But for [Ford's] previously neglected duty, the accident would not have occurred. The court should make a finding for the plaintiffs against Ford Motor Company."

CHAPTER
52

The Fairs and Nunnallees had spent nearly four years looking ahead to the trial that would represent their best chance to wring some meaning from the deaths of their daughters. Now, on Day Two, they would each take the stand, if only briefly, to prove an uncontested but essential element of the case: that they really did once have living daughters, who had climbed aboard that school bus and been killed on it. The defendants, of course, would have been more than happy to stipulate to the fact, avoid the flash of raw reality, and continue the proceeding undisturbed in the realm of pure reason where a school bus was, is, and ever shall be a heavy truck. But the parents chose not to accommodate them. Rather, they would have their moment of truth.

Karolyn Nunnallee arrived at court Tuesday morning somewhat agitated. The previous evening, she'd prevailed upon her lawyers to take her to view the remains of the bus for the first time. "Those guys are gonna pay!" she vowed. "If they could just *see*. Not the lawyers—the top guys at Ford. They should be brought out there to look."

(If those responsible for her daughter's death could be made not just to look but to *see,* then, surely, they would strike their own eyes out. Here again was that curious notion, that men who do evil must not really know what they do.)

Skip Murgatroyd was still fired up by Grubbs's opening statement, which he seemed to believe strayed so far from the evidence as to cross even the expansive bounds of lawyerly argument. "Grubbs told about ten lies," Murgatroyd declared. "For one, he said that Ford delayed making the tank guard standard because the body manufacturers weren't ready.

But we have an internal Ford document that says, 'Delay the cage because the regulation has been delayed.'* *We're gonna take them apart!"*

"God Bless the United States of America, the Commonwealth of Kentucky, and this court," intoned the bailiff.

Promptly at 9:15, James B. Nunnallee took the stand. Now a lieutenant colonel, he testified that he had been a bombardier/navigator on F-111s for about ten years when he was assigned to Fort Knox in 1986 as the commander of a small air force unit that advised the army on air-power issues; his wife and two daughters accompanied him to the post. Nunnallee identified two documents bearing red tabs marking them as plaintiffs' exhibits. (Defense exhibits had blue tabs.) Plaintiffs' Exhibit 1 was the the birth certificate of Patricia Susan Nunnallee, born at 8:41 P.M., March 29, 1978, at the U.S. Air Force hospital in Bitburg, Germany; and Plaintiffs' Exhibit 2, certificate of death, Patricia Susan Nunnallee, age at last birthday: ten; time of death: 10:55 P.M., May 14, 1988. Cause of death: smoke inhalation. He repeatedly clenched his fists as he fought back tears and read the documents in his soft Southern drawl. At the plaintiffs' table, Karolyn cried quietly into her handkerchief.

The trial would consist of two distinct phases, the first deciding liability, and if necessary a second assessing damages. In this first, the only question was whether Ford was at fault, not how much damage it had done, so Nunnallee was not asked to describe his daughter's abilities or his love and affection for her.

Karolyn followed. "We had discussions about her going on the trip. I originally said no, because I thought they were going in a family car." She choked up and got the next sentence out with difficulty. "When she said it was on a bus, we said yes. I thought she'd be safer on a bus, so we let her go."

(Patty had never been on a trip without her mother or father before. The Kings Island outing was a milestone—she was growing up—and as such had occasioned some soul searching on Karolyn's part: She must try to keep her child safe, but she must not try to keep her a child. "What could be safer? They'll be on a big bus," Karolyn had thought. "After all, you've got to let them go some time.")

Janey and Larry Fair each took their five-minute turn. "Yes, I allowed

---

* In point of fact, Grubbs was perfectly properly telling the truth about what *his* evidence would show. Ford executives had stated under oath that, as they recalled, the delay had something to do with problems at the body factories.

her to go," Janey responded in a loud, clear voice to Grubbs's question. "I checked the route. There were no mountainous roads. I felt she would be fine."

After crash survivor Jim Slaughter briefly described the horror ("I looked back once. You could see silhouettes moving in the smoke and fire, yelling and screaming."), Franklin called Kentucky State Trooper Henry Cease, Jr., to the stand. Into the room strode a blue-eyed, square-jawed, criminally handsome young man, his patent leather ankle boots, gold buttons, and black-handled automatic gleaming. Not since Sergeant Preston of the Yukon had a law officer so clearly embodied the seemingly contradictory societal ideals of incredible coolness and straight-arrow rectitude. Sonny Cease (as everyone called him) had conducted the Commonwealth of Kentucky's official accident investigation and reconstruction, logging about 2,000 hours of work on the case. Cease was twenty-six years old and had not quite three years' experience as a cop at the time of the crash, and only seven months' as an accident reconstructionist, but unlike all the high-priced experts who would testify, he had not been retained or paid by either side, so his opinion would enjoy a presumption of objectivity.

Cease testified that he had been resting at home, tired and sunburned after a day of waterskiing, when his phone rang at 11:39 P.M. on Saturday, May 14, 1988. The dispatcher told him there had been a "bad crash" and he should "get 10-8 [get to work] ASAP." He rapidly drove thirty-two miles to the scene, arriving at 12:05. Sergeant Jim Sharon, standing at the bus, said he had about eighteen or twenty passengers missing.

"Where are they?" Cease asked.

"Look inside the bus," Sharon said.

Cease looked.

For the next few minutes, Cease sat inside his cruiser, "because, frankly, I didn't know what to do." Then he grabbed his clipboard, tape measure, and spray paint and began taking measurements, which he would continue to do for most of the next five hours. "Trooper Strong, who had been the first officer there, was very upset, so I had him hold the end of the tape," he recalled. Cease climbed aboard and took photos while the bus was still smoldering and dripping with water and fluids.

Cease described how it took seven hours to remove the melted-together remains. On his diagram of the location of the bodies, he numbered them in the sequence in which they were removed. (Janey Fair left the room at this point.) Number 17, Shannon Fair, was recovered from a pile of bodies on the floor between seats 6 and 7 to the right of the aisle.

She had made it a little more than three rows back before she fell down or was knocked down. Number 24, Patty Nunnallee, was lying full length, alone, in the center aisle just behind row 4, with her head toward the front of the bus. She had been sitting at the right window in row 2.

Franklin got ready to ask Cease to identify a stack of eight by ten glossy color prints of the human remains on the bus. Grubbs fervently objected. "This evidence is inflammatory and prejudicial," he insisted. Judge Dunn, noting that the photos helped prove the intensity of the fire, the width of the aisle, and other relevant matters, admitted them.

❏

After lunch, Cease identified each of his many photos of the accident scene, specifying, in some cases (though not Shannon's or Patty's), which body number corresponded to which horrifying charred husk. The Fairs and Nunnallees left the room for the duration of this exercise, which took most of the rest of the day. (Larry Fair, in fact, had already looked at the pictures, to satisfy his need to know everything that could be known.)

Later that afternoon, the Fairs and Nunnallees and their legal teams repaired to a cluttered storage area in the courthouse annex basement, which had been set aside as the plaintiffs' office. As three paralegals kept a fax machine and photocopier humming, the lawyers and clients huddled on a bench and bridge chairs in one corner. A yellow box of over-the-counter drugs, designed for point-of-sale display, sat atop a bookcase: "Pain Relief Center," it read.

A big brown wasp, its long legs dangling, buzzed around, making it hard to concentrate on anything else. "Don't kill it," Janey said to Larry, as he rolled up a newspaper. He swatted it dead against the wall. "I don't kill spiders or anything," Janey said quietly.

Mahoney's lawyer, Sergent, appeared. Respected by both sides and belonging to neither, he was conducting a sort of shuttle diplomacy aimed at facilitating a settlement, and had come to toss out some numbers. Sheller-Globe had settled for $1.3 million to each of the two plaintiffs. If one hypothesized that the judge would ultimately rule that the fault for the deaths was 25 percent Sheller-Globe's, 50 percent Ford's, and 25 percent Larry Mahoney's, then that $1.3 million would represent 25 percent of the whole liability. Therefore, the whole liability would be $5.2 million for each plaintiff. Ford's apportionment would be half that: $2.6 million per plaintiff. That was one way to arrive at a number to settle at.

In Sergent's opinion, Dunn would find Ford liable. He would peg the total compensatory damages due to each plaintiff at $1 million, and say Ford's share was half that: $500,000. In addition, he would assess punitive damages of $3 to $6 million, so the total per plaintiff would be $3.5 to $6.5 million. Five million dollars, the midpoint between these figures, ought to make a satisfactory settlement, Sergent suggested.

The Fairs and Nunnallees had already won, he urged them to realize, because Lou Banciu, a Ford in-house lawyer, had flown in and offered Mike Hance a settlement of $3 million each to the Fairs and the Nunnallees, *eight times* the $375,000 that had been Ford's half of the payment for each child's death made to those who had settled without suing. According to Sergent, Hance had replied that Ford would have to come up with more than $5 million. Banciu had said, "Well, how about four million?" to which Hance had replied, "Four million is not more than five million." Ford, which had then withdrawn its $3 million offer, was still willing to talk, but Banciu had cautioned that they would *never* agree to $5 million.

"I've had two Ford cases in eighteen months settle at more than six million," Robinson interjected, but he conceded that those had been for survivors with burn injuries, which often come in higher than deaths.*

The last item on the meeting's agenda was what to do about Byron Bloch, the automotive safety consultant the Fairs had put on their legal team back in 1988. (Ever the enterpriser, Bloch had gotten himself hired by the Nunnallees as well.) Bloch had insisted from the outset that he would not testify but only consult. As the attorneys brought in experts who had serious credentials and who were ready to testify, Bloch's role had been reduced to a vestigial one. Now suddenly, like an inflamed appendix, he could no longer be ignored: Despite Judge Dunn's repeated warnings that no pictures were to be taken in the courtroom, Bloch on Monday had squeezed off a flash shot of the time-line exhibit of which he was so proud. Dunn, like many judges, *hated* to be disobeyed in his courtroom. He had said nothing at the time, savoring his anger and letting it ripen to its full judicial majesty. Then, this next day, rather than deign to speak to the malefactor, he had summoned Skip Murgatroyd to the bench and told him, in a tone devoid of any irony, that he had "a good mind to lock that fella up."

---

* The medical expenses—not to mention the pain—associated with burns can be almost limitless. For example, within five-and-a-half years of the bus crash, one survivor, Ciaran Foran, had undergone forty-nine operations.

Murgatroyd had decided—and no one save Bloch disagreed—that Bloch had to get out of town and stay out. He had made Judge Dunn angry; he was on the Fairs' team; therefore Judge Dunn might hold his bad act against the Fairs. All other things being equal, in a close case . . .

No, the Fairs thought. Surely after all the briefs and arguments and evidence, the judge couldn't decide the case one way or another because of one snapshot in the courtroom, could he? *Could he?*

CHAPTER
53

On the third day, Sonny Cease gave his reconstruction of the accident: The bus driver hit his brakes and steered to the left in an evasive action an instant before impact. The right front of Mahoney's Toyota pickup overlapped the right front of the school bus by a couple of feet, not quite enough to hit the frame rail, which would have stopped the pickup cold.

"So if the bus driver had not steered to the left, the pickup might have hit the frame instead of just bumper and sheet metal," Judge Dunn pointed out.

The front door was knocked off the bus and the front steps were left dangling. "In my opinion, the steps could not have struck the gas tank," Cease said. Rather, the Toyota knocked the bus's right-front leaf spring's rear hanger bracket into the tank, piercing it. Cease had no opinion as to whether a cage guard would have prevented the puncture.

❑

Paul Richwalsky, the assistant attorney general who had prosecuted Larry Mahoney, was not so reticent when asked whether a better-designed bus could have prevented the tragedy. "The type of vehicle that the victims were traveling in was immaterial and irrelevant," he told a couple of Louisville TV news reporters at the Fair trial. "We believe that Larry Mahoney was the sole causation of this tragedy."

Larry and Janey felt betrayed. At Richwalsky's request, they had kept their thoughts about the bus manufacturers' culpability to themselves until after the Mahoney trial, lest they help Mahoney's lawyers shift the blame from their client. Now the shoe was on the other foot, and here was Richwalsky apparently grabbing some airtime to shout Ford's innocence from the rooftops.

(Asked about it later, Richwalsky cast the incident in a different light. "I went up there to watch Sonny [Cease] testify," he said. "I was cornered by a media person, and I'm not gonna lie. I can't change my position. From Day One we've said it was immaterial what kind of vehicle those victims were riding in: You take your victims as you find them.* This was not a situation where a minor mishap was [turned into a disaster] because of a defect. You're talking about a 110 mph collision. The vehicle the victims were in is immaterial to Mahoney's culpability. And the Fair case was being tried by a judge; there was no jury. My comment wasn't going to undermine their civil case.")

When the TV reporter asked him a question about the Fair case, Richwalsky had given an answer about the Mahoney trial: A defective bus would not relieve Mahoney from responsibility for the disaster he set in motion. But that point of criminal law had no bearing on the civil suit's issues of whether Ford's bus was inadequately designed, and whether that design defect had contributed to the deaths of Shannon and Patty. *Richwalsky* knew what he was talking about, but for his TV audience, the confusion was complete. The notion that Mahoney could be found guilty in one trial and Ford held liable in another was too complex by half. "Ironically, now that Larry Mahoney is behind bars, it is the families of two

---

* Richwalsky was alluding to what is known as "the thin skull doctrine." In *Dulieu* v. *White & Sons,* a 1901 British civil case, the court held that the wrongdoer was responsible for all the damage caused by his bad act, even though the extent of the damage had been unforeseeably increased by the hidden vulnerability of the victim: "If a man is negligently run over or otherwise negligently injured in his body, it is no answer to the sufferer's claim for damages that he would have suffered less injury, or no injury at all, if he had not had an unusually thin skull or an unusually weak heart."

of the crash victims who are trying to prove that Ford Motor Company, not Mahoney, was responsible for the deaths of twenty-seven people aboard this charred church bus," reported Mark Hebert of WHAS-TV 11. The Fairs could only hope that Judge Dunn was as insulated from public opinion as Richwalsky said.

❑

Public opinion, in any case, soon moved on to other things. By the second week, the trial was playing to empty seats. The "Keep Out" sign Judge Dunn had caused to be placed on the door—*A trial is not a circus,* he always said—surely did nothing to boost attendance. But the good people of Carrollton had been studiously uninterested from the outset, and now the press had decamped en masse. Not a single beat reporter remained. It was hard to believe that a calamity of such dimensions could so swiftly slip beneath the waves. Here was a local story with national implications for the automotive industry and for millions of schoolchildren, and it was being fought out in near-complete privacy. To Larry Fair, the discrepancy between the importance of the case and the coverage it was receiving didn't add up, and he could only conclude that Ford had "shut down" the media coverage.

A Louisville TV reporter had confided to Fair that he'd wanted to cover the case one day but had been dispatched by his assignment editor to shoot a piece on the scandalous resurgence of cockfighting in eastern Kentucky. Fair hypothesized a well-placed phone call from Ford, one of Louisville's largest corporate citizens. Ford's influence was indeed ubiquitous: Every morning one station's weather forecast was scrolled over a picture of a school bus with a blue oval Ford insignia. But though such a call might well have been effective, it was almost certainly unnecessary. Lawsuits and cockfights have many things in common, but a marvelous suitability for Eyewitness News is not one of them.

❑

Larry Franklin's accident reconstruction expert, Herb Hill, took up most of the second week. Hill, a sonorous-voiced, rotund North Carolinian with a Ph.D. in mechanical engineering, attacked the defense's oft-repeated claim that the collision, at a combined speed of 110 mph, was so severe that *no* vehicle's fuel system could be expected to withstand it. (In fact, as Hill had pointed out when he was deposed, the little Toyota pickup's fuel system had come through the crash intact.) Hill explained that *for the bus,* the crash was "a minor collision," equivalent to running head-on into a wall at 15 mph, or being dropped on its nose from a height of seven and a half feet. Indeed, one of the surviving kids, Conrad Garcia, had already testified that he'd thought the impact was just a tire blowing out.

Hill had run a computer simulation of the crash, using a program called EDSMAC (Engineering Dynamics Simulation Model of Auto Crashes). According to his calculations, at the instant of impact, the bus was heading south at 52 mph; the Toyota was heading north at 55 mph. One tenth of a second after impact, both the bus and Toyota were heading south at 37 mph. The collision slowed the bus by just 15 mph, while the Toyota had a 92 mph loss (from 55 mph northbound to 37 mph in the opposite direction).

Far from colliding with the bus's fuel tank at a combined speed of 110 mph, the Toyota, by the time its front end had reached the tank area, was moving in the same direction as the bus, Hill said.

"Excuse me," Judge Dunn interjected at this critical point. "I don't want to break your train of thought, but do you do some teaching?"

"Yes, I do," Hill replied cautiously.

"So, you might be called *Professor Hill,* à la *The Music Man?*" Dunn remarked, looking very pleased with himself. How many judges could make that leap from highway holocaust to Broadway musical?

The fuel tank, Hill continued, after everyone shared a chuckle, was pierced when the front end of the leaf spring jammed into the pavement and the bus, continuing forward at a post-impact speed of 37 mph, impaled itself on the spring's rear hanger bracket.

Grubbs, in the course of a numbing cross-examination that would go on for days, harped on every difference he could find between Hill's reconstruction and Cease's, hoping to cast doubt on both and clear the stage for his own expert. Hill said the bus had been going 52 mph. Cease said it was traveling at 55 mph. Cease said the rear of the spring hit the tank, and then the front of the spring gouged the road. Hill said the front of the spring gouged the road, and then the rear of the spring hit the tank. Hill had the truck being pushed southward at 25 mph when its front end reached the fuel tank; Cease had the truck still moving northward at 15 mph. "That's a 40 mph difference!" exclaimed Grubbs, as though he had caught Hill with silverware under his shirt. (Never mind that Ford's own reconstruction expert agreed with Hill about the truck's velocity.)

"I can defend myself," Hill sighed during a recess. "I can't defend Sonny."

Mark Robinson, who had warned against putting on two experts to testify on the same issue, muttered, "I didn't hire Hill. I knew they'd use him to impeach Sonny. Their [Franklin and Hance's] thinking is, 'We hired him, we paid him, let's use him.' "

Of course, Franklin didn't explain his thinking quite that way. Given that Cease and Hill basically agreed, Franklin had insisted, Hill with his Ph.D. would lend more weight to Cease; and Cease, whom the judge liked, would cleanse Hill of his paid-expert taint. "Each helps the other," he said.

❏

As the cross-examination continued, Hill held his ground to the last ditch. He explained again and again that he and Cease agreed that the leaf spring hanger bracket had punctured the tank. Their differences were only about the precise sequence of events within a one-tenth-of-a-second period, and were of no consequence.

"So you both say the same thing penetrated the tank but disagree how it got there during a minute sliver of time?" Judge Dunn suggested helpfully. "Yes, sir," Hill replied. The Fairs basked in the glow of Judge Dunn's approval, for about ten seconds.

"If the cage had been on, in your opinion, wouldn't the hanger bracket have just deflected off the vertical member and punctured the tank elsewhere?" asked Grubbs.

This pivotal question called to Judge Dunn's mind a judicial opinion about social costs and benefits, which he interrupted the questioning to share with everyone. The Kentucky precedent held that "you can't protect against all accidents," he said. "If Ford had surrounded the fuel tank with metal, maybe no one could afford the bus."

Since this pronouncement by the man who would decide the case translated roughly as, "The plaintiffs lose," it appeared that the Fairs' fortunes had suddenly hit bottom; but in fact that wouldn't happen until a moment later, when Hill answered Grubbs's question. "I wouldn't be surprised, if everything else was the same but the guard was on, if the hanger bracket might have deflected and punctured the tank," he said.

Grubbs did not pause to savor the moment, and the moment passed as he resumed his hypertechnical nitpicking. *How does the EDSMACK program figure the momentum change of the crash sector of the vehicle?* EDSMACK figures the momentum change by the speed before and after impact and also by the amount of crush. *What weight did EDSMACK use?* EDSMACK used the weight on the bus's right-front wheel. *How much weight was on the right-front wheel just before the impact?* Fourteen percent of the bus's weight. *How much was that?*

Judge Dunn broke in: "Take ten percent, add half, and deduct one percent. That's DUNNSMACK."

This jest occasioned hearty and protracted laughter, no lawyer wishing to fall short of any other when it came to appreciation for the judge's wit. When quiet at last returned, Dunn turned to Grubbs and asked, "What are you getting at?"

"We just want to establish some things so we can deal with them in our case, Your Honor."

"You don't want to tell me now. Okay," said Dunn. "It's your boat, you float it." (Dunn had already made clear his preference for well focused cases. "It's better to isolate one issue and beat it to death than try to shotgun the whole covey of quail," he'd told the lawyers.)

Grubbs with his hours of detailed questioning really may have been trying to prove something; or he may, as it appeared, have been trying to blow smoke, cloud the issues, bore the fact-finder into a somnolent state where emotions hold no sway, and run up the plaintiffs' expenses to the point where they would have no choice but to settle on Ford's terms. The next expert waiting to testify had to be paid to sit and wait while Hill was getting paid to sit and talk; meanwhile, it was costing the plaintiffs $4,000 a week for their two floors at the Carrollton Inn, and $15,000 a week for daily transcripts. Finally, Grubbs could hope to exhaust Murgatroyd and Robinson, who would be flying back and forth to their families in California each weekend for as long as the trial dragged on. But he may also have been wearing out the patience of Judge Dunn.

CHAPTER

54

Court began the next morning with a somber announcement by Judge Dunn. "My sister's daughter's child, while Rollerblading, was struck by an automobile yesterday, and died," he said. The judge explained that he had a great many nieces and nephews and had not known this grand-nephew well. (The twelve-year-old boy, whose name was Justin, was one of Dunn's sister Mary's twenty-seven grandchildren.) Dunn said he did not feel the need to recuse himself from this trial; the incident would not cloud his judgment. He invited the lawyers to speak up if they thought otherwise. Silence. This child's death did not involve drunk driving or a school bus. Back to the business at hand.

❏

If the lawyers had harbored any concern that personal history might impinge upon Dunn's judgment, it would have been about his first child, Billy.

Dunn cherished his three sons. They were born his flesh and blood, but it was through his time and trouble that they were imbued with his values, a reverence for the law being high on the list. "If you ever get stopped by a policeman, you better make sure you get a ticket," he warned them, abiding no trade on his position's influence. Once, when he and Laverne came home early from a night out to find the teenaged Billy running a beer-drenched poker game at the kitchen table, Dunn called the police and had his son arrested for underage drinking. Then he had him taken in handcuffs to the convenience store to finger the clerk who'd sold him the beer.

There was no alcohol involved when Billy agreed to time a classmate's

Super Sport 442 over the quarter mile some friends had marked off on a Glen Burnie, Maryland, street, one night just before his senior year in college was to begin. But he and the driver were unfamiliar with the course, ran it backwards, from the finish line to the starting line, and came full-speed to a T intersection. The car skidded into a tree, the roof was crushed, and Billy, in the passenger seat, broke his neck against the gear shift. A little cut on his finger was his only other injury. He was dead on arrival.

Twenty-six years had now passed. Billy had been dead for longer than he had been alive, but Dunn was still too devastated to visit the cemetery. "You never get over it," he'd tell you. "You live with it, but you never get over it."

❑

Redirect examination affords a lawyer the opportunity to repair the damage done on cross-examination, but always at the risk of calling attention to that damage. Grubbs had hit an artery when he got Hill to say that he "wouldn't be surprised" if the spring would have pierced the tank even if there had been a protective cage. Now Franklin tried to close the wound by giving Hill a chance to explain himself. "My opinion is very strong that *this* spring in *this* accident would not have punctured the tank with a guard on," Hill declared. "I meant that in *some other* accident the spring could hit the up-and-down piece in the center of the cage, glance off and still pierce the tank. But in *this* accident, it *could* glance off and still hit the tank, but could *not* pierce it, because of the orientation of the spring."

Oh.

Just in case Hill's explanation had evened the score, Grubbs availed himself of a re-cross-examination. (These volleys can go back and forth for as long as a judge allows.) Wouldn't the spring—with one end dug into the road and the bus impaling itself on the other—have penetrated the tank even *more deeply* if the tank had been held stationary by a cage guard instead of being knocked twenty-eight inches backward as it had been, away from the oncoming spring? Grubbs suggested.

"Not necessarily," Hill replied. "Possibly the spring would have vibrated and come out of the road."

"Anything is *possible,*" shot Grubbs.

"Anything is possible," Judge Dunn agreed, *"and you can't guard against all possibilities.* Maybe Kentucky opted against ordering the guard so the tank could move backward and not get penetrated."

The day ended on this bleak note, with the judge spouting defense maxims (You can't guard against all possibilities) and repeating defense theories (Maybe Kentucky chose not to have a cage, and for good reason).

The Fairs remained hopeful. "Sometimes the judge talks just to talk," Larry said.

"It's going as well as can be expected," Janey concurred.

"Of course it's going well," responded Larry. "It's our side of the case." There was a sobering thought. Their expert testimony had collapsed in a heap of contradictions; the judge was saying that leaving the cage off may have been *a really good idea,* and Ford had even't begun its case. "Our lawyers are getting on each other's nerves," Larry noted. (Mark Robinson was running out of ways to say *I told you so* regarding Hill's performance. "A lawsuit has to be precise," Robinson said. "It took me a while to learn that. I used to just put everything on.")

"They've each been the only child too long," said Janey understandingly, of the contentious legal luminaries. "This business about having to take turns is new to them."

There was one promising development. A state trooper had walked up to Mark Robinson's investigator, Gene Buhler, in court and asked, "Did the man call you about the leaf spring?"

"What man?" Buhler asked.

James Montgomery, a carpenter who had served as Carrollton's civil defense chief, had heard that there was a big disagreement at the trial about what had punctured the fuel tank. Montgomery remembered that, at the scene of the accident, he had seen the leaf spring's hanger bracket just a few inches away from the hole and pointing right at it. Realizing that he could answer a question that was apparently of great interest to both sides, he called the state police and said that if it would be of any help to anybody, he'd be glad to explain what had made the hole in the tank. They suggested that he contact the lawyers, which he found a shade beyond the call of duty. Now the plaintiffs' lawyers contacted him.

❏

First thing in the morning on Friday, February 21, James E. Montgomery, age sixty-two, took the stand. His gray hair, wire-rimmed glasses, and missing front tooth lent him the gravity of age, while his work boots, green pants, and flannel shirt bespoke the dignity of honest labor.

"What do you do for a living?" Franklin asked him.

"I'm self-employed," Montgomery replied. "My business card says 'Remodeling and Repair.' I'll make you a key or build you a house, or both."

Judge Dunn, like everyone else in the room, lit up. "Better give me one of those cards," Dunn said. Here was a man who could fix things. No job too small. Hallelujah.

"And where do you live?" Franklin continued.

Montgomery said he lived on Old Route 227, which lay between the big Route 227 and the Kentucky River.

Never one to let pass an opportunity to learn something, Judge Dunn leaned forward in his chair. "Where's 227 take you?" he asked.

"You can go anywhere in the world from there," Montgomery replied proudly.

What do you do? Where do you live? The attorney had scarcely cleared his throat and already the witness had established himself as the Zen master who lives by the side of the road. To pause and apprehend his wisdom would be to know all that there was to know.

On the night of May 14, Montgomery's story began, he was out for "a moonlight walk" with his wife when he heard sirens heading toward the I-71 interchange, three quarters of a mile away. Since he was the Disaster Emergency Services coordinator for Carroll County ("I had nineteen bodies out of the river in twenty-one years"), he rushed home and called the Carrollton dispatcher, who told him they had a bus wreck on I-71 near mile 40. It took him about forty-five minutes to fight his way through five miles of backed-up traffic to the scene. "I got on one knee and stuck my head under the bus with a flashlight to see if there was any more gas spilling out," he recalled. The bus was still hot to the touch. "I had my eye level with the gash, which was within arm's length. The hanger bracket was lined up with the gash, five or six inches from the gash. There was nothing else anywhere near as close."

In the center of the courtroom, the leaf spring had been placed atop the fuel tank like a sword lying on a coffin. It was about three feet long, made of five concentrically curved, three-inch wide, half-inch-thick rusty pieces of iron. Murgatroyd and Franklin lifted it with difficulty and held it up to the tank as Montgomery directed them, until it was just as it had been when he saw it that night.

"I saw on TV that there was a difference of opinion here," Montgomery said. "So I called. A lot of people said I was crazy to call." (Foremost among these had been his wife, Mary Lee, a nurse who was as sensible as most in her profession. She was worried that if Jim caused somebody the loss of a lot of money, someone might burn their house down. Montgomery understood her concern. "A company with the power of Ford, it makes me kind of leery to cross them," he recalled later, "because they can do anything they want to.")

❑

"When did you first talk to lawyers representing the plaintiffs?" Grubbs asked in an accusatory tone, as he began his cross-examination.

"I have no idea who's representing who," Montgomery replied, the very voice of disinterested reason. "I called the state police. They said no doubt Sonny Cease and some of the lawyers will want to talk to you. Then Gene Buhler [Robinson's investigator] spoke to me."

"When was that?"

"What day is today?"

Judge Dunn offered some help: "Last week was Valentine's Day."

"I remember that, because I didn't get my wife a Valentine," said Montgomery. "That's the reason I haven't been home since." Thus oriented to time, he recalled that he'd spoken to Buhler for about ten minutes two days ago. "I didn't know which side he was with," he asserted, improbably. "I still don't." He added that he had met with Mr. Franklin and his colleagues yesterday morning. Montgomery crossed his legs to get more comfortable, his pants riding up to reveal black, white, and gray argyle socks.

Because he had met with lawyers who must have introduced themselves, it seemed clear that Montgomery *did* know "who was representing who," yet he had claimed not to, escaped challenge by the otherwise vigilant Grubbs, and somehow maintained his aura of credibility. It was as though everyone in the room was wired into a simultaneous translator and understood him to mean, "I take no cognizance of who is representing whom; I am completely disinterested and therefore worthy of belief."

Grubbs motioned to his associate David Schaefer, who'd labored mightily on the pretrial briefs and been rewarded with Vanna White duty in the courtroom. Schaefer fired up the video player and began displaying color still photos of the crash scene. This was a juncture so clearly critical it prompted Judge Dunn to put in his second hearing aid. "It whistles a little," he apologized, "but then some of the ladies find that complimentary."

"The photos don't show what he thinks he saw," Grubbs told the judge, by way of introduction. (Not content with their mandated role of asking questions and arguing the law, all the lawyers were constantly testifying to an extent not seen since Perry Mason left the airwaves.)

Grubbs pointed at the murky photos and challenged Montgomery to name various pieces of mangled metal. Not surprisingly, in many cases he could not.

"I understand that, in all fairness, you just looked in quickly to see if there was any fuel coming out and got out of there," Grubbs said sympathetically. He pointed out another blurry form. "Is this the position of the hanger bracket as you saw it?"

"I can't see the hanger bracket in the picture," Montgomery replied, astutely. No, he replied to another question, he did not bother to look at the fuel tank again after the bus had been towed to the armory. "What I saw on the roadway was history as soon as they moved the bus the first inch." He knew not just his facts, but their significance, and he communicated both with absolute authority. (Said Montgomery later, "The lawyer [Grubbs], he was unruly about it, but not so it bothered me much.") If this had been a Grubbs-Montgomery boxing match, they would have stopped the fight.

At the lunch break, when Montgomery drove home in his dirty white Ford pickup truck, a Ford lawyer was right behind. "Mr. Schaefer came out here at lunchtime," Montgomery recalled later. "He was nice about it, but he tried real hard to sway me as to *maybe* I saw that. And I said, 'No, it's not like that. That's my testimony. That's the way it's going to be.' ...I seen what I seen."

CHAPTER

55

"**W**e are in Kentucky," Judge Dunn declaimed one morning in the trial's third week, "where one of the principal interests is horse racing, along with tobacco, and the surgeon general hasn't warned us about horse racing yet, though Pete Rose could attest to the evils attendant to it. . . ." As Dunn's disquisition tumbled on, the horse racing metaphor, whatever it was to have been, broke down. Mesmerized by his own words, he followed them this way and that until, ten minutes later, he arrived at his point, which was that the trial was taking too damn long: "What's wrong is wrong, and what's right is right," he said. "This court is beginning to think we could be making more progress."

The judge's languorous idyll seemed poorly calculated to kick an attorney into his homestretch sprint, but it mattered little, for neither whip nor spur was going to move Mark Robinson off his pace.

On Monday, February 24, Robinson had begun his examination of Larry Bihlmeyer, an apostate Ford engineer turned safety-engineering consultant whom Robinson himself had brought onto the Fairs' team. Bihlmeyer, a fortyish, slight, bald, stoop-shouldered man, nominally took the stand to offer his expert opinion on the design of the school bus's fuel system; but one of his principal tasks, as everyone could see, was to provide the requisite foundation for documents to be admitted into evidence. He would identify an exhibit, summarize its contents, explain that it had some relevance to this case, state that he had relied upon it as a basis for his opinions, and then Robinson would ask the judge to let it in.

For instance, he identified the NTSB report on the Baker, California, bus crash, a head-on collision, in which a bus's right-front leaf spring punctured its behind-the-front-door fuel tank.

"In the course of your work as a design engineer, is Exhibit 96 the type of document you commonly use and rely on?"

"Yes."

"And have you relied on this Baker report as the basis for your opinions in this case?"

"Yes."

"I move to admit Exhibit 96."

"Objection!" said Grubbs. The Baker crash involved a rear-engine Greyhound, not a front-engine school bus, and an aluminum fuel tank, not a steel one, so Ford's school bus engineers couldn't possibly have learned anything from that accident, he said. Dunn admitted the report, saying that if it turned out not to be relevant, he'd simply accord it no weight in his deliberations.

After Grubbs had lodged thirty-two objections to Robinson's first eighty-five questions—four were sustained— Judge Dunn's interest in the two lawyers' opposing views on admissibility rapidly dwindled. "Why don't you both shut up!" he shouted. To expedite matters, he devised a system: Grubbs's objections were deemed to be continuing, and meanwhile virtually all evidence was received with the proviso that Dunn would at some point hear argument on whether to un-admit it.

Dunn explained his system by an analogy to a putative local custom. "In Kentucky," he said, "a person who wants to get on welfare has to have no property, so he deeds it to his dad; but they call that 'a deed subject to recall,' because when he gets off welfare, he wants that property back. So these exhibits are subject to recall."

Thanks to this expeditious procedure, in the course of three days the court received into evidence fifty-six exhibits, including, notably, the minutes of several North American Automotive Operations (NAAO) executive committee meetings. These revealed that, contrary to the defense's insistent denials, Ford truck and auto executives at the highest levels really did share information, including in particular the results of Pinto crash tests; and that they had in fact on occasion explicitly expressed an intention to maximize profits at the expense of fuel system safety.

Especially damning was a series of memoranda to top management regarding the placement of the fuel tank in Ford's 1973 pickup trucks. Prior to that model year, the fuel tank had been located *inside the passenger compartment,* behind the seat. Ford's engineers had planned to relocate the tank between the frame rails in the 1973's. The change would add $5 to the cost of each vehicle, but was necessary, they said, "to remove objectionable gasoline vapors and sloshing noises from the cab area, and to improve driver safety."

After a draft of the tank-relocation plan was circulated for executives' comment, a memo stated: "Upon further review of the design cost and profit position of the 1973 Truck Program, Truck Operations intends . . . to revert to the present location for the fuel tank inside the vehicle as standard equipment and provide the outside fuel tank as an option at $15. . . . This change would improve profits by about $5 million. . . ."

In response, Ford's Central Product Planning Office had written directly to President Lee Iacocca, with a copy to Henry Ford, urging once again that the more safely located fuel tank be made standard equipment: Its $5 cost could be made up somewhere else, or the price of the truck could be raised without losing market share, the letter said.

On Tuesday, August 4, 1970, at 10:00 A.M., the North American Product Planning Committee met in the executive conference room at the Design Center in Dearborn. Those present included Iacocca and Henry Ford. According to the meeting's minutes, the pros and cons of making the outside-the-cab fuel tank location standard were discussed. "It was stated that the outside fuel tank would cost [the company] about $5.00 and could be successfully merchandised as an option." It was decided to make the outside tank optional, unless the competition made an outside tank standard, in which case Ford would follow suit.* The minutes noted: "The Chairman of the Board, being a member of the Committee and present at this meeting, approved the recommendations of the Committee with regard to the 1972–73 NAAO Truck Program Revisions."

"Obviously it's not Frank Sinatra," Judge Dunn interjected, "but what is the name of the Chairman of the Board?"

"Henry Ford II," replied Bihlmeyer. Based on his experience at Ford as a light truck engineer from 1972–86, Bihlmeyer said the memo typified the company's practice of making fuel tank safety optional, which he considered "unethical from an engineering standpoint." The plaintiffs had not uncovered any similar documentation of a decision to postpone the school bus fuel tank guard, but their point was that by then at Ford, such discussions were no longer necessary: Everyone knew what the men at the top wanted.

---

* As it turned out, Chevrolet did move its tank out of the cab, so Ford made a between the frame rails tank standard on *most* of its 1973 pickups, though the in-cab tank remained standard on some models.

Neither Iacocca nor Henry Ford was ever terribly interested in or knowledgeable about engineering. "I do not understand engineering so there is no point in cluttering up my mind with things I could not possibly understand," Ford stated under oath in 1979, after thirty-four years as the auto maker's chief executive. He concentrated on financial decisions— including whether a particular cost was going to go into a vehicle—and on the styling of the vehicle body, which he liked to call "the dress on the girl." Iacocca sat on the styling committee with him; their concern for the surface of things became apparent at this in-cab fuel tank meeting. After casually consigning some unknown number* of pickup truck drivers to incineration at the wheel, they moved on to a matter they deemed important. According to the minutes:

"At the conclusion of the scheduled business, there was a general discussion regarding . . . possible actions that could be undertaken by the Company to offset to some extent the unfavorable publicity the auto industry has been subjected to recently."

Robinson introduced through Bihlmeyer Ford's many petitions to NHTSA asking for the deletion, dilution, or delay of fuel system standards. But Dunn appeared unmoved by all this evidence of opposition to government regulation. "I take it any interested party has the right to comment on or ask for the delay of NHTSA regulations?" he remarked.

No party has the right to circumvent the public rule-making process and put the fix in, so Robinson hoped to get more reaction out of Dunn regarding the Nixon-Iacocca-Ford meeting. He showed Bihlmeyer the May 1971 letter in which Ford lobbyist R. W. Markley, Jr., reported on his "intergovernmental interface" with Ehrlichman shortly after that Oval Office meeting.

"Mr. Bihlmeyer," Robinson asked, "is this something you would rely on in forming your opinions?"

"As an *engineering* expert?" demanded Grubbs incredulously.

"This has nothing to do with engineering," Judge Dunn snapped.

Robinson asked Bihlmeyer to explain what it was in his background as an engineer that made him an expert on political maneuvering in Washington.

---

* The in-cab tank's problem was not the frequency of fires but the difficulty of escaping alive from those that did occur. Accurate data on lethal in-cab fuel tank fires were never compiled, and much of what does exist cannot be disclosed because of the confidentiality of settlement agreements. Mark Robinson believes there have been more in-cab lawsuits than Pinto lawsuits.

"It was my responsibility for several years to track proposed regulations," Bihlmeyer began. "I have experience with this kind of sequence and review—"

The response evidently struck Dunn as an insultingly transparent attempt to fashion some sort of legal justification for the offering of opinions he'd just said he didn't want to hear. The judge exploded. "Why don't you function as an engineer and not a lawyer, sir!" he bellowed at Bihlmeyer.

"I understand, Judge," Robinson said apologetically.

"You understand," said Dunn, "but *you"*—he shook his finger at Bihlmeyer—*"don't,* or you'd SHUT UP."

❑

Among the Ford documents Robinson introduced was the Fuel System Integrity Program Financial Review that recommended the delay of additional rear-impact protection on Ford cars "until required by law."

"The thought strikes this court," Dunn interjected, "that [delay] might be a prudent thing to do, because the government might change its mind [about the standards before putting them into effect]."

It was like throwing your best pitch right where you want it and seeing it pounded over the fence. What more could Robinson do? "If I had twelve average American jurors," he said during a break, "they would go along with the idea that the safety of children is more important than cost-benefit statistics, and that would be the whole case. The judge, with his logical, legal mind, he's seeing both sides of the issue like you have to on the bar exam. We have to crack through all that and find that Catholic heart beating in his breast."

CHAPTER

56

Karolyn Nunnallee told Janey Fair about a conversation she'd recently had with her surviving child, Jeanne, who had a birthday approaching.

" 'I can't believe you're going to be ten!' I told her. She looked down at the floor and just said, 'I know.' I asked her, 'What's the matter?' She said, 'Well, you know what happened to Patty when she was ten.' "

"Jeanne doesn't ride school buses if I can help it," Karolyn continued. "She walks to and from school—so she'll probably get hit by a drunk driver."

❑

In his fourth day on the stand, Bihlmeyer faced cross-examination by Grubbs. "This guard," said Grubbs, pointing at the cage holding the scorched fuel tank in the middle of the courtroom, "meets Standard 301, but you're not sure it would have prevented the tear in the tank?"

"That's right," Bihlmeyer replied.

"It can't protect against all foreseeable accidents?"

"Right. And the goal should be to protect against all foreseeable accidents, especially for school buses."

As he awaited the response to each of his thrusts, which he delivered with increasing force at a quickening pace, Grubbs stood with his hands clasped behind his back, to avoid a single unscripted gesture. He would remain in complete control all the way to the finish, as he proved once and for all that Ford had done nothing wrong by leaving off the cage.

"But this guard couldn't withstand the impact of a 60,000 pound tractor-trailer at 60 mph at 90 degrees?"

"No."

"Or the impact of an oncoming train?"

"No."

"Or if the Carrollton bus hits a concrete bridge abutment?"

"It would protect it," said Bihlmeyer, weakly. "It might not keep it from rupturing."

"If the bus rolls over several times, down an embankment, it wouldn't prevent the rupture or tearing of the fuel tank?"

"It wouldn't one hundred percent guarantee against it," Bihlmeyer conceded.

"Not even fifty percent?"

"I don't know."

"All of those hypotheticals are foreseeable hazards?" Grubbs insisted, building up to the crescendo.

"Yes."

"So you're saying you'd have to design a cage that could withstand all of them?" Grubbs demanded incredulously.

"No," replied Bihlmeyer. "I'd move the fuel tank."

Ooof! Grubbs rocked back on his heels and blinked. In hardly more than an instant he cleared his ringing head and pressed on gamely, but it was too late. He'd left himself open and the meek little witness had clocked him.

"The point is, Mr. Bihlmeyer, all of those occurrences are ones where there could be survivors on the bus," Grubbs went on. "So when you say you have to design for every conceivable accident, that's not possible, is it?"

"I said your goal for a school bus vehicle is zero children killed by the fuel system in a survivable accident. I'm not saying you can achieve the goal one hundred percent."

"Before this, the number of kids lost to fuel tank fire was zero, right?"

"Yes, and one accident changes it to a high number."

Karolyn Nunnallee began sobbing. "If I become an alcoholic after this trial, can I sue them?" she said through tears to her lawyer, and laughed, and began crying again. Janey Fair helped her from the courtroom. (Every time Nunnallee cried, she left the courtroom, out of embarassment, or a sense of dignity, or a need for privacy. If she'd been a little more calculating she might have seen the advantage in staying right where she was, so the judge could drink in her tears.) "I just hope if it ever happens to *their* kids," Karolyn said, nodding toward Grubbs and King, "that the kids can live through it."

❏

If there is a tide in the affairs of men, that afternoon it appeared to turn. Judge Dunn battered Ford with his rulings on the admissibility of some hotly contested documents. The Grush-Saunby Let 'Em Burn memo, which King had portrayed as a benign and by the way completely irrelevant example of constructive dialogue with the government, the judge admitted as evidence of Ford's opposition to fuel system regulation. The Nixon-Iacocca-Ford tape transcript, although it contained no reference to fuel systems or school buses, he admitted because "the gist of the whole thing tends to prove the policy of sacrificing safety to corporate profits," as did the Ford lobbyist's report on his followup meeting with Ehrlichman. Dunn took pains to note that he was *not* finding that the plaintiffs had proven such a policy existed; he was ruling only that this evidence was of value in settling the question of whether such a policy did exist. But the Fairs and Nunnallees found reason to believe he was seeing the case their way, and the Ford lawyers were commensurately disheartened.

CHAPTER
57

"In this part of the country," Judge Dunn lectured the litigants as court resumed the next morning, "until recently, a lot of people could not or would not avail themselves of the full services of a funeral parlor. The deceased would be laid out at home. Now, there was a gentleman whose wife had died, and according to this tradition her body was laid out in the parlor. To make sure that she was in fact dead, they put a mirror under the nostrils to see if it fogged up, and they put a feather under the nose to see if it stirred, and sure enough, there was no breathing. This woman had passed on."

Death and the thought of death were never far from this courtroom, and all present were especially attentive as the judge continued his grim narrative: "When the time came to remove the body, they took a door from its frame and placed the body on the door and carried it out that way. Now in the front yard there was a fine young oak tree, and as they were passing by with the body, they just bumped into it, and what do you suppose but the wife's eyelids flutter open and up she sits, alive as you and me. And, do you know, that woman lived on hale and hearty for twenty-five years, until one day she died. Once again she was laid out at home, and when the time came, they put her on a door, and they eased her out the doorway and as they carried her across the yard, the husband told them, *Watch out for that tree.*"

Everyone laughed together—the Ford lawyers, the Fairs, the Nunnallees, their lawyers—because the joke was funny and well told.

❑

Grubbs, knowing he had to make a come-back, resumed his cross-examination of Bihlmeyer with redoubled ferocity.

"Where is the normal location of the tank on a tractor-trailer?"

"On the left or right side, outside the frame rail."

"That is the accepted and customary location?"

"It's customary. I would not accept it from a safety standpoint."

"So," Grubbs suggested sarcastically, "all tractor-trailers should not be on the highways?"

"I'm not saying that," Bihlmeyer demurred. "But the safety factor should be addressed."*

Judge Dunn leaned forward. "Would it be just as safe or dangerous transporting people—as in a bus—as opposed to say, corn?"

"The school bus takes a higher order of engineering effort," Bihlmeyer replied.

The judge wasn't finished. "In fact," he mused, "is there a government standard for a people-transporting vehicle as opposed to a freight hauler?"

"Yes, there is," said Bihlmeyer.

---

* In 1984–86, tractor-trailers were involved in an average of 227 fatal fire-related accidents annually. Such trucks caught fire in 10 percent of all their fatal collisions with guardrails, concrete barriers, trees, and bridge-piers.

"The result [of a fuel tank breach] if carrying people would be more hazardous, more dire?"

Bihlmeyer agreed.

Grubbs was a quarterback who wouldn't scramble. He'd struggle to his feet after each sack more committed than ever to stay in the pocket. Slammed to the turf in mid-comparison of bus to truck, he pressed on with the next play in his book, which was to make the point that the accident was so freakish, so unforeseeable, that a manufacturer could not be faulted for failing to guard against it.

"Would you say a head-on collision with a closing speed of 110 mph is an ordinary event, likely to occur?" he asked.

Bihlmeyer said that it *was* likely to occur.

"You would call it usual and customary?"

"It's infrequent, but foreseeable."

"Ordinary or extraordinary?"

"Likely to occur."

"Likely to occur how often?

"With a school bus, one time is too many."

Grubbs couldn't seem to stop asking questions that elicited applause lines for answers. He had to get back in control, and it may have occurred to him that he should leave the accident alone and fall back to some tamer and more predictable topic, maybe something of a statistical nature. Bihlmeyer had earlier identified a 1967 UCLA school bus crash test report as one among many warnings of the danger of fuel tank fires. Now Grubbs would turn it against him and use it to show that the plaintiffs' suggested location, behind the rear axle, was itself dangerous.*

"At page 291," he began, "[the report] says, 'Owing to the many stops made each day by school buses, the rear-end collision is the most frequently occurring type of school bus accident.' Do you agree?"

"I don't know," Bihlmeyer said.

"Isn't that information one should have had in 1976 before deciding where the fuel tank should be?"

"Oh yes, and the information that helps me to know that is this document, dated July 17, 1971, 'Vehicle Fires' by Mr. John Habberstad," Bihlmeyer enthused, as he whipped out and waved the paper. Habberstad, as

---

* Herb Hill had testified that the tank should have been placed either between the frame rails behind the rear axle, or outside of the frame rail on the right but moved rearward four or five feet away from the doorway.

Ford's defense expert in this case, was going to testify that the fuel tank was fine right where it was.

"Does this paper relate to school buses?" Grubbs angrily demanded.

Bihlmeyer replied that it did.

"Does the word 'school bus' appear in it?"

"It says 'Vehicle Fires,' and a school bus is a vehicle," Bihlmeyer replied.

"That's not responsive to my question," Grubbs snapped.

Judge Dunn weighed in. "It's germane," he said.

Bihlmeyer began reading from Habberstad's paper. " 'Fuel tanks located near the perimeter of a vehicle are particularly susceptible to damage. . . . One of the better methods of limiting the possibility of tank cave-in or collapse during an accident would be to position it where considerable crushing of the vehicle structure would have to occur before the fuel tank would be deformed. One such choice is between the main frame members and a considerable distance ahead of the rear bumper—"

"I didn't ask you about that paper, did I?" shouted Grubbs, impotently.

"I think folks of ordinary ken would know that this paper has universal application," said Judge Dunn.

Grubbs had skidded off the road; the twisted, steaming wreckage of his case lay at the bottom of an embankment.

❏

Only Grubbs, to finish up the cross-examination, and Hance, to watch the store for the plaintiffs, returned to the courtroom immediately after the lunch break on that Friday, February 28. Grubbs stuck to his program, pointing out that various documents did not mention school buses, long after the judge had made it clear he agreed with the plaintiffs that fuel system design principles applied across the board. Meanwhile, the rest of the lawyers, spurred by the judge's pro-plaintiff tilt and the disastrous Bihlmeyer cross-exam, spent the afternoon's first hours in settlement talks.

❏

Mark Robinson returned to ask Bihlmeyer one question on redirect examination. "Why did Ford delay the installation of the cage for eight and a half months, once the body builders got a delay of the standard?"

"I object!" Grubbs shouted, his patience at an end. "That's not an engineering opinion!" The defense lawyer appeared to have a point.

Bihlmeyer certainly didn't *know* why Ford had acted as it did, and it was hard to see how his expertise as an engineer qualified him as a mind reader.

"In this world, you don't live in a vacuum," Judge Dunn told Grubbs. "You can't isolate things into little compartments." Alas, isolating things in little compartments was exactly what Grubbs had been paid to do for most of his life. "Go ahead," Dunn instructed the witness.

"In many instances," Bihlmeyer began, recalling his years as an engineer at Ford, "I attempted to have a safety fix made and I was told you don't do that, and you don't write it down, because it admits you have a defect. And if you *have* to have a fix, you delay it so it doesn't look like you're admitting a defect. So, for example, here, Ford would delay putting on the cage so they could say, 'We're not doing this to fix a defect; we're doing it because the government told us to.' "

Ironically, the plaintiffs' witness had just so much as said that plaintiffs' attorneys such as Mark Robinson and Skip Murgatroyd *themselves* had the effect of delaying safety improvements, because they scared companies out of fixing things lest the fix be used as evidence against them in a lawsuit like this one.

"You are saying," the judge said, "that over and above and beyond government standards, there's a Common Law duty to do things not to injure the public, and they violated that."

It wasn't clear that Bihlmeyer had said anything of the sort. The *judge* was saying it. It was a dark, dark day for King and Grubbs.

CHAPTER 58

Judge Dunn, as judges will, had early on encouraged both sides to settle. He had expressed increasing dissatisfaction as the trial, once slated for four weeks, showed every sign of stretching beyond twelve; and now as the litigants implacably plodded on, his short fuse burned to the nub. "You had better settle this case," he cautioned the lawyers in the latter days of February. "I am not going to die on this bench!"

Thus warned, a plaintiff who insisted on fighting through to a verdict could expect at best a meager reward; yet a recalcitrant defendant would be equally in peril of being punished by a whopping judgment. Though the judge would not be privy to the details of their negotiations, neither side could afford to be portrayed by the other as the unreasonable one, so a mutual accommodation had much to recommend it. All the same, Ford had from time to time disdained even to respond to a proposal from the plaintiffs. Then Dunn had suddenly embraced the once-despised Bihlmeyer as a prodigal son, and welcomed in all his evidence, too. To King and Grubbs, the notion of settling looked different now, viewed from over a barrel.

For their part, the Fairs and Nunnallees were reluctant to stand down from their oft-declared commitment to see this thing through to an official and public adjudication that Ford had done wrong. But they were prudent as well as principled, and inclined to heed the counsel of their counselors, with whom they had soldiered on now for four years. The advice came down to this: Things couldn't get much better, but they could get a lot worse, especially if the judge concluded that they were the ones who were refusing to settle.

The Fairs and Nunnallees had already won a great victory, their law-yers explained, by getting devastating documents into evidence. If there were a settlement, Ford would not admit fault, *but all of the evidence admitted at trial would remain on the public record.* The 200 plaintiffs' exhibits would be a godsend to people suing Ford in the future; rather than starting from scratch, they could copy Ford documents showing that car and truck operations were *not* completely insulated entities, that all parts of the company *were* aware of fuel tank dangers, that safety mea-sures had repeatedly been deferred until required by law, that Ford's president and chairman had pursued corporate policies putting the pub-lic at risk—evidence it had taken the Fairs' and Nunnallees' lawyers years to pull together.

Even if the Fairs and Nunnallees hung in and won a verdict, it would *not* serve as a precedent that could determine the outcome of another case: If a 1977 B-700 school bus were hit head-on and burned tomorrow, another judge or jury could find Ford blameless; for one thing, the details of two accidents were never identical.

A verdict *would* prove that Ford had been put on notice of the danger of perimeter-mounted fuel tanks, and provide a strong argument for punitive damages the next time such a fuel tank failed. A settlement, by contrast, would constitute just one more unproven claim. *But,* the lawyers cautioned, there was always the possibility that a verdict could go against them. Ford's contractor defense was troublesome: Kentucky *had* ordered the bus without a cage; Ford *had* met the state's specifications; and the fuel tank was hanging out there for all to see. The judge might not agree that Ford had a duty, because of its superior knowledge, to set Kentucky straight. Finally, even if Judge Dunn did find Ford liable, and did award substantial damages, Ford would probably file appeals that could take three years or more to work their way to the Kentucky Supreme Court.

The Fairs' legal expenses, which would come off the top of any award (or be absorbed by Murgatroyd's firm if they lost), were approaching $800,000, and were climbing, what with the experts' fees and the cost of transcripts, by thousands of dollars a week. (The Nunnallees' outlay was of the same magnitude.) Skip Murgatroyd renewed his assurances to his clients that, however much Ford dragged out the proceedings, his firm had the requisite resources to stay the course. But Janey Fair could not be dissuaded from her impression that, as she said later, "Ford had the financial ability to grind us into the ground. Settling then avoided the day when Skip might say, 'We have to settle. We've put out all we can put out.'" What she really dreaded above all was refusing to settle, losing, and leaving the lawyers, who were by now her friends as well as her champions, the worse for ever having known her. And finally, Dunn had *told* them to settle. "The judge made himself plain," said Janey, "and in the face of that, I don't know what else you do."

To Larry Fair, a change in tactics made sense. "We weren't getting what we wanted out of the trial," he'd explain. "There wasn't any press there. We wanted the publicity to promote legislation and regulation. It just didn't work, so you back up and punt. As far as driving to a final verdict of culpability, what difference does it make if no one knows about it?"

❑

The Nunnallees' attorney Mike Hance proposed to Ford's lawyers that the plaintiffs would drop their claims in exchange for payments of $3 million (which Ford had once offered) or $5 million (which Hance had earlier said would not be enough), with the parties agreeing to let Judge Dunn, acting as arbitrator, choose one of the two numbers. The defense did not like those numbers, but expressed interest, insisting however that Dunn should be able to choose any amount between the high and low figures that were eventually agreed upon. The talks continued by phone through the weekend, and resumed on Monday morning, while inside the court-room a gray-haired lady by the name of Neva Johnson took the stand.

King liked to joke that a plaintiffs' expert "is someone with a briefcase from more than fifty miles away." But Johnson was a fuel system design engineer of the first order. As a Goodyear Aerospace Corporation engineer during the Vietnam War, she had analyzed U.S. Army helicopter fuel systems to find out why post-crash fires were killing crews who'd survived being shot down. She had helped design a crash-resistant flexible fuel tank which, together with self-sealing breakaway valves, virtually eliminated post-crash fire deaths in survivable helicopter crashes. In 1975, under contract with NHTSA, Johnson oversaw the development of the compliance standard and test procedure for the very school bus fuel system integrity regulation that was central to this case. It was like calling Madame Curie as your expert on radiation, only better, because Johnson wasn't some foreigner but a cactus-tough Arizonan.

Johnson made clear that for a very long time it had been very well known that to put a fuel tank where Ford had put it was very dangerous. ("Fuel tank safety is like real estate," she always said. "The three most important considerations are location, location, and location.") In her opinion, there would have been no fire if the fuel tank guard had been installed. Using photos from Ford's own crash test of the cage, she showed that it would have withstood the Carrollton collision: The frame of Ford's test bus, hit by a 4,000 pound moving barrier, had bent just about the same amount as the Carrollton bus's frame had bent. This was to be expected, Johnson explained; the impact of a 4,000 pound moving barrier at 30 mph was just about the same as the impact of Larry Mahoney's pickup at 45 mph, because a truck absorbs energy by crushing, and the barrier does not. (The defense attorneys' ritual incantation of the phrase "110 mph combined speed" notwithstanding, it was undisputed that by the time the pickup had penetrated to the fuel tank area, the collision speed was probably much less than 45 mph.) The cage would have remained intact, Johnson said. It without question would have prevented penetration by the bus's front step, and it almost certainly would have blocked the spring.

(The plaintiffs did not concede that Ford would be any less culpable if the tank had been punctured by Sheller-Globe's step rather than by Ford's own spring. They argued that the step was just *one more* foreseeable danger that Ford had a duty to guard against.)

Without the guard, Johnson concluded, Ford's school bus fuel system design was defective; the defect was not obvious to people lacking expertise in fuel systems; the possibility and likely consequences of an accident such as the Carrollton crash were foreseeable; the school bus was extraordinarily dangerous, and a prudent manufacturer would have declined to sell it as it was.

For the rest of the week, Johnson patiently identified the documents that substantiated her opinions. All the while, the settlement negotiations continued. Ford came around to the position that Dunn should have to choose the high number or the low number, nothing in between. The plaintiffs offered to agree to a lower low ($2.7 million) in exchange for a higher high ($5.9 million), gambling that Dunn would consider the bottom number inadequate and perforce award the higher one. Ford didn't take that bet. Ford wanted the plaintiffs to agree never to write or cooperate with the writing of any books or articles about the bus crash or the litigation; the Fairs and Nunnallees replied that their refusal to be silenced on bus safety was not negotiable, though they agreed not to divulge the terms of any settlement. (Neither the Fairs nor the Nunnallees nor the lawyers representing them were the source of the author's information on the settlements.)

❑

Friday, March 6, was an unseasonably warm day in Carrollton. The steel-gray canopy that had been clamped to the hilltops gave way at the seams to reveal a surprising, pristine blue. Blazing yellow forsythia heralded the arrival of another spring. ("Spring is depressing because the world renews itself, and Shannon and her friends obviously don't renew themselves," Janey said.) At noon, after Neva Johnson concluded her direct testimony, the trial recessed for lunch. It never resumed.

Ford Motor Company had had enough. It agreed to a settlement, by the terms of which the Fairs and Nunnallees would drop their lawsuit in exchange for payments of either $3 million or $5 million, the amount to be decided by Judge Dunn acting as a private arbitrator; Ford would admit no wrongdoing.* For the moment, all that remained was for the lawyers to work out the wording of a joint press release announcing the suspension of the trial. It took them six hours, for the plaintiffs were content with full disclosure of what had happened and the defendant wanted anything but. In the end Ford was able to obfuscate even the fact that it had been a defendant, much less one that might pay the claimants who had sued more than thirteen times the amount it had given those who'd accepted the company's early offer.

The announcement to the press read: "In the interest of judicial economy and to achieve a prompt resolution, the parents of Shannon Fair and Patty Nunnallee and Ford Motor Company have agreed to resolve their claims through a private alternative dispute-resolution proceeding. . . . The resolution of this case through an alternative dispute-resolution proceeding will spare the emotional trauma, delay and uncertainties associated with the litigation, and is consistent with the manner in which other families' claims were resolved."

Judge Dunn would base his decision on the testimony he'd heard, the exhibits and briefs already submitted, and some depositions Ford would offer in place of the witnesses it had given up the chance to call. Dunn, who loved the written word, had found the live testimony for the most part dispensable, despite the lawyers' best efforts, as one put it, "to avoid being duplicative, repetitive and redundant." There was no time limit placed on Dunn. He might take two weeks, or two months. Larry and Janey hoped it wouldn't be two years.

---

* In a separate settlement, the $75,000 from Larry Mahoney's insurance company was paid out in equal parts to the survivors and the estates of the dead.

❏

The Fairs had scant opportunity to ponder the trial's sudden end. ("The lawyers are elated. We're not elated. We're not disappointed. It's just another step in the process of achieving school bus safety," Larry said. "Right now we're accumulating resources to pursue that goal.") Janey drove off with Karolyn Nunnallee to attend a MADD meeting in Nashville the next day, and that night, Janey's ailing mother died in her sleep. The Fairs hastened to Johnson City for the funeral, where Janey's sister Patty delivered a eulogy that began, "Frances Mullins came from a long line of courageous women. . . ."

❏

A month later, Judge Dunn called Ann Oldfather and informed her that he had "written an opinion" and was about to drive down to Louisville to drop copies off at Grubbs's office and at the office of Franklin & Hance, where she could meet him and get hers. On Tuesday afternooon, April 7, 1992, standing in the foyer at Franklin & Hance with a poker-faced Dunn, Oldfather ripped open an envelope to find a single sheet of paper whose two lines of print simply stated that he had awarded the Fairs and Nunnallees $5 million each.

Dunn told Oldfather he'd found that Ford had not taken any care at all in the manufacture of the bus. The company's behavior had been "abominable," he said. He'd concluded that the fuel tank failure had been preventable, and that Ford had had the capability and the opportunity to prevent it. (In subsequent conversations with others, Dunn suggested that all the evidence about Ford's alleged corporate policy of putting profits over safety had only complicated what for him was a straightforward case: Ford knew the fuel tank was vulnerable to puncture; the fuel tank was punctured in a foreseeable way; the resulting fire caused the deaths.)

Though it was technically true that the lawsuits had been settled without any finding of fault, the amount of the award left no doubt that Dunn—after considering all the evidence—had in effect found Ford so egregiously in the wrong that he'd hit the company with punitive damages. There was no other way to reach the $5 million figure. Compensatory damages are apportioned among all the defendants according to their share of responsibility for the deaths; there had been frequent references to Ford being assessed one half. Each girl's compensatory damages, even with Shannon's arguably high lifetime earnings, could not approach $10 million. The judge must have concluded not only that the bus was unreasonably dangerous, but that Ford had every reason to know it was and exhibited a reckless disregard for the lives of the children who would ride it.

Ford had ended up spending $5 million dollars each (not counting litigation expenses, which all together certainly surpassed $1 million) on two cases that might have been settled with some sort of good-faith commitment to contribute to the improvement of school bus safety.

That Ford executives had let that opportunity go by, said Murgatroyd, showed that "Ford doesn't take this kind of lawsuit very seriously. At the CEO level they talk only about $100 million items. They don't care. Unless we can get action from NHTSA, Ford just pays it off and goes on their merry way."

Certainly the $10 million settlement—which was either insured or tax-deductible for Ford*—would not constitute a major item on the company's ledger. A week after Dunn's decision, Ford announced a $3 *billion* investment in new plants and machinery, including $650 million to expand its Kentucky Truck Plant (and add 1,300 new jobs). But even for Ford Motor Company, the nation's third largest industrial corporation, $10 million was real money. Ten million dollars equaled 6.7 percent of Ford's $148 million earnings from U.S. automotive operations for the second quarter of 1992, the period during which the settlement payments were made.

Since this was a company that, in order to hold retail prices down 24 *cents* a vehicle, had fought a regulation requiring identification labels on brake hoses, one must assume that the costs of liability judgments and settlements were carefully scrutinized. And since those costs were not inconsequential, why would Ford refuse to get rid of a couple of lawsuits simply by meeting the plaintiffs' demands that it do something to enhance school bus safety? That refusal would seem to be attributable to some atavistic trait of the corporate culture. "Ford does not want to be dictated to," says Murgatroyd.

❏

Larry Fair drove to Oldfather's office on April 21 to endorse Ford's first check. The last installment arrived on May 5, just shy of the fourth anniversary of the bus crash.

---

* Litigation expenses, settlements and judgments (including punitive damages) arising from products-liability claims are tax-deductible to the extent that the corporation itself (rather than an insurer) pays them.

The $5 million came in addition to the $1.3 million that Sheller-Globe had paid to each of the two families. About $800,000 was deducted from the Fairs' $6.3 million to reimburse the lawyers for litigation expenses, leaving some $5.5 million. Retainer fees ate up 30 percent of that, the greater portion going to Murgatroyd's law firm, with Ann Oldfather, Mark Robinson, and consultant Byron Bloch dividing the rest. The Fair family ended up with roughly $3.8 million; a similar amount went to the Nunnallees.

Endorsing Ford's checks was "just one more step on the stairs to climb—nothing emotional," Larry observed at the time. "I signed my name. It's like the sun comes up and the sun goes down. I guess we should be excited about this, but we're not. When everybody's needs were in equilibrium, there was a settlement, with the terms decided by a third party. This wasn't a great victory. It's a battle to be continued. And we'll fight the battle again at a time and place of our own choosing."

EPILOGUE

JUDGE DUNN

Judge William R. Dunn died on Sunday morning, June 28, 1992, at the age of seventy, two months after rendering his decision in the bus crash lawsuit. Dunn, who'd had a heart bypass fifteen years earlier, had postponed a checkup until he could finish his work on the case. Admitted to the hospital for an angiogram, which revealed clogged arteries, he died the day before he was to have been evaluated for surgery.

"He was exhausted," his son Michael recalls. "He knew he was sick. But he knew he had to get through the Carrollton case. Of his whole career, he was the most proud of that case. He said, 'I was the only sonofabitch who could wade through the bullshit and tell the attorneys how it needed to be done.'"

LARRY MAHONEY

A huge gray tower rises ominously over the portal of a granite fortress set down on the fields of LaGrange, Kentucky. Chiseled in stark relief on this tower is one word: REFORMATORY. Here, a dozen miles from the spot where he crashed into the school bus, Larry Mahoney is being re-formed.

Before he was sent to the medium-security prison, Mahoney was, to all appearances, racked by remorse for what he had done and filled with compassion for his victims. ("If I could trade my life right now to bring every one of them back," he'd said, snapping his fingers, "I'd do it just that quick.") He had come to believe that he'd survived the crash for a reason, and he lived for the day when he could fulfill that purpose, whatever it might be—perhaps to lecture school children about drunk driving, "if that's what God wants me to do." But after a few years behind the walls, Mahoney has acquired an inmate's exquisite sense of grievance: Each prisoner compares his crime and his time to all the others' and finds that he's been shafted, he's the victim.

Mahoney's beef is that, thanks to a state law that went into effect in July 1986, prisoners in for specified violent crimes have to serve half their sentences—instead of Kentucky's usual one fifth—before becoming eligible for parole. He was convicted of, among other things, first-degree assault, for which he was sentenced to sixteen years, in 1989. Mahoney doesn't believe the legislators had drunk driving offenses in mind when they put Assault One on the list, but on the list it is. As a result, he has to serve the same minimum eight years as an ax murderer sentenced to forty years for a crime committed before July 1986, and he doesn't think that's fair.

Mahoney will come up for parole—and be turned down for parole—on July 20, 1997. Working very much in the public eye, the parole board will look at the gravity of his offense, listen to victim-impact statements from crash survivors and the families of the dead, and stamp his papers REJECTED. Then, unless he incurs a major infraction, with credit for good time he will be released no later than October 8, 2000.

Meanwhile, as a model prisoner Mahoney resides in an honor dorm in a one-man, 6' x 9' room with a door to which he has the key. His narrow window looks out on a field, a guard box, and another penitentiary. No pictures are allowed on the white cinderblock walls, but on top of his own thirteen-inch color TV—he likes to watch Andy Griffith and *The Beverly Hillbillies*—he keeps a photo of the woman he never quite made it up to see on the night of May 14, 1988, Kim Frederick; she still visits him. He has earned his high school equivalency diploma and is learning carpentry. He works as a clerk from 8:00 to 11:30 in the morning. Three days a week he lifts weights for an hour and a half. He's gained forty pounds of muscle, and his still quiet, almost girlish voice now comes out of a bull-necked, mammoth-shouldered two-hundred-pound body. He vows he'll never touch another drop of alcohol and, while denying he ever had a drinking problem, goes to Alcoholics Anonymous meetings, which in prison are not anonymous. (His attendance is the first thing the parole board will ask him about, he says. "If you don't go, they use it against you. If you do go, it doesn't help.") He lays awake nights and thinks about the bus crash, which he cannot remember happening. It takes him forever to go to sleep. Then, sometimes, he dreams that he is at home, and when he wakes up and looks around, he feels as though someone has hit him between the eyes with a sledgehammer.

Gone is the Harley Davidson cap that read "Ride Hard, Die Hard," which his prosecutor had portrayed as a declaration of extreme indifference to human life. Mahoney still insists that the hat "didn't mean anything," and maybe it didn't, or maybe it meant precisely that: Nothing means anything. In prison, Mahoney has two caps. One says "Kentucky"; the other, "World's Greatest Dad."

Spina bifida has consigned his daughter, Shawna, to a body brace that she must wear round the clock. Her mother, Mahoney's second ex-wife, Betty, brings her to visit every couple of weeks. Shawna has learned to walk a bit with the aid of a walker, and Mahoney beams as he describes her clacking across the shiny gray linoleum floor of the prison visiting room. "You should see her smiling, she's so proud of herself. She says, 'Daddy, when you get out, we're going to go fishing together!' She loves her daddy, that little girl."

Mahoney says he still prays every day for the Radcliff families, but he does not go to church services because once when he did, they showed a videotape about the school bus crash. "As of right now" he still hopes to do something to fight drunk driving when he's released. "But," he cautions, "this place gives you an attitude. By then I may be a completely different person."

LEE IACOCCA

"How can those board members sleep at night?" Lee Iacocca once demanded, speaking of Ford Motor Company's directors. He thought their consciences ought to have been tormenting them because they failed to resign in protest when Henry Ford fired him from the company's presidency in 1978. "The scars left by Henry Ford, especially on my family, will be lasting, because the wounds were deep," he wrote of his martyrdom. As it turned out, he looked as good as new a couple of weeks after getting sacked, when Chrysler Corporation offered him the positions of president and CEO.

Iacocca, whose incendiary Ford vehicles left so many people *really* scarred, evidently sleeps like a baby, blissfully ignorant of the meaning of the word "shame." Among the virtues he ascribed to himself in his 1984 autobiography was that of being "a safety nut." (*Iacocca* sold 6.5 million copies, and in a 1985 Gallup poll, Americans ranked Iacocca the third most respected public figure, after Ronald Reagan and Pope John Paul II; in 1986, there was serious talk of his running for president.) Chrysler in 1990 ran a series of advertisements consisting of letters to Iacocca from people crediting him with saving their loved ones' lives by putting airbags in Chrysler vehicles. ("I thank God for you and your deep appreciation for and dedication to automobile safety. Because of you I still have my little girl.") Of course Iacocca, the father of the Pinto and an opponent of safety regulations to the end of his career, had led the fight against airbags for twenty years, a fact he jokingly acknowledged in his autobiography: "I have the feeling that when I die—and assuming I go to heaven—St. Peter is going to meet me at the gate to talk to me about air bags."

Iacocca retired as Chrysler's chairman on Dec. 31, 1992, and was to receive $500,000 a year as a consultant through 1994. He divides his time between his villa in Tuscany and homes in Aspen, Colorado; Los Angeles, and Palm Desert, California. In 1993, Iacocca sold four-fifths of his holdings in Chrysler and netted $84 million.

FORD MOTOR COMPANY

In a moment of frustration, as he pleaded for the thousandth time that Ford Motor Company had simply built the school bus exactly as Kentucky had specified, Bill King, identifying with his client Ford, blurted out, "Are we the keepers of the American public? Are we the ones who are supposed to ensure that every little school child doesn't get hurt in an accident?" The questions were rhetorical, the answers clearly "No." Ford Motor Company is not and will never be its brother's keeper. It has no brothers. It is a corporation.

Man created the corporation in his own image. A "person" for legal purposes, a corporation is able to own property, to enter into contracts, to sue or be sued. The creation is an imperfect one, however; its similarities to the creator are limited. Whether or not Man has a soul, the corporation certainly has none; and it has no conscience, and it has no free will. A commercial corporation is constituted for the purpose of making a profit, and when presented with a choice between money and any other goal it will by its very nature go for the money, as surely as a plant grows toward the light. It is what it is. Men and women manage the corporation, and they have consciences and the freedom to choose, but those who rise to positions of influence accommodate themselves to the corporation's imperatives. Accordingly, it would be foolish to hope that automotive manufacturing corporations will ever make the safety of the public their top priority, unless compelled to.

The corporation is judged only by its bottom line. Ford Motor Company is doing splendidly. In 1993, in the biggest year-to-year financial turnaround in its history, it reported a profit of $2.5 billion.

SCHOOL BUSES

In 1989, after studying the Carrollton crash, the National Transportation Safety Board made three recommendations to NHTSA.

The first was that NHTSA should toughen up its standard for the flammability of interior materials in order to reduce the rate of fire spread in buses. NHTSA announced that it would consider a new rule, and industry comments generally favored the application of more stringent requirements to school buses of all sizes; only Ford argued that the rulemaking should exempt van-type vehicles (of which it is a leading manufacturer) because, Ford said, their smaller size makes them easier to evacuate.

NHTSA asked the National Institute of Standards and Technology (NIST) to investigate whether the flammability test should be revised. In 1990, NIST reported that NHTSA's horizontal flame test of material samples was completely inadequate, and recommended a full-scale test in which entire seats are burned in a simulated school bus interior. Applying such a test, NIST found that the still-prevalent untreated polyurethane and vinyl school bus seat ignites twice as fast and burns twice as hot as any of five readily available alternatives. NHTSA announced in 1991 that, in light of the NIST report, it would continue to consider suggestions for a new flammability rule. Three years later, no action has been taken.

The NTSB's second recommendation in 1989 was that school buses be required to have at least as many exits as nonschool buses had to have. In October 1992, NHTSA issued a rule requiring school buses built on or after September 1, 1994,* to have a number of exits that increases with the seating capacity. In addition to their front entrance and rear emergency exit, typical buses for forty-six passengers or more, for example, would have to add a side door or two exit windows; buses for sixty-three passengers or more would have to have those exits plus a roof hatch; those seating more than seventy would require yet another exit.

Finally, the NTSB recommended that NHTSA revise its fuel system

---

* If the bus chassis and body are built by different manufacturers, the deadline refers to the *chassis* completion date; bodies without the additional exits could continue to be mounted on pre–September 1 chassis indefinitely.

integrity standard to provide additional protection for school buses in severe crashes. In 1989, NHTSA announced that it was considering whether the performance requirements should be upgraded to guard school bus fuel tanks against such hazards as high-speed impacts and penetration by the bus's suspension; and also whether the standard's application should be broadened to include transit and inter-city buses. In 1991, NHTSA announced that it was still considering the school bus rule-revisions, but had decided against applying the standard to non-school buses because they are "much stronger structurally than school buses" and "fuel tanks on non-school buses are generally positioned between the front and rear axles and between the frame rails, and thus less susceptible to rupture from a collision."

In February 1993, the NTSB wrote NHTSA to ask whatever happened to the upgraded fuel system integrity and flammability requirements that it had recommended. More than a year later, there had been no reply.

The NTSB had also strongly suggested that all pre-1977-standard school buses should be taken out of service—not operated by churches, youth groups and summer camps, not exported to Central America, but taken off the road. By 1994, almost all public school systems had gotten rid of their pre-standard buses. However, as of May, at least 17,000 school buses in North America still did not meet the FMVSS 301-75 fuel system integrity standard; they still had not been brought in for modification after Navistar's pre-1993 design flunked NHTSA's impact test. In addition, many thousands of pre-1977 buses are presumably still in non-public-school use; there is no central registry from which to determine their whereabouts.

Since the disastrous gasoline-fed fire in Kentucky, nearly all full-size school buses have been ordered with diesel engines. Diesel fuel, less volatile than gasoline, reduces but does not eliminate the chance of a postcrash fire.

JIM AND KAROLYN NUNNALLEE

Jim Nunnallee took early retirement from the Air Force as a lieutenant colonel in the fall of 1992, after eighteen years of service, and he and Karolyn moved to Florida, to help run her family's cattle ranch and citrus groves. Karolyn has become a leader of Mothers Against Drunk Driving, starting up two new chapters, serving on the board of directors, and holding the office of vice president for public policy. "Janey Fair and I agreed we weren't going to take this lying down," she says. "If we had not done anything after the deaths of our children, then that would have been the tragedy."

The Nunnallees concentrate on fighting drunk driving in part because MADD provides structure and direction for their efforts; they weren't sure what to do next about school bus safety, or where to do it. "We thought we could get more bang for the buck with MADD," Jim explains, "rather than try to put our arms around the bus safety issue."

Reflecting on the court battle with Ford, Karolyn says, "I felt I was doing this for Patty. I loved her so much, I owed it to her to fight. But I realized in the last few weeks of the trial that I probably did it for me. I think, in a way, this was my way of keeping Patty alive. This was my way of holding on. When the trial ended and I drove past the crash site, I just realized it was over. You have to let go and get on with your life. It was like another funeral.

"Our focus for three years had been the trial. It's like a wedding. You plan and plan for months and then it's over and then what do you do? I guess I thought that at the end of the trial, if we win, Ford's gonna come down and do what we want them to. I guess I thought if you win you can force them to make their buses safer, or they would out of the goodness of their hearts. I felt in my naive way that they would be human enough to realize what they'd done to these families. But after seeing those Ford documents, I know they don't care about people. The bottom line is dollars. If it's going to make them money, they're going to do it. If it's not, they're not." But the legal effort was not in vain, she says. "We got documents out in the open, and if it ever happens again families will know where to get them. We've given Ford the opportunity to make things better, and if they don't, they're going to pay.

"I still think, 'When am I going to wake up from this and my life is going to be orderly and perfect and back the way it was?' I don't hear noises and think Patty's home like I did. But there's still part of you that wishes you would wake up, even though you're not going to.

"I remember when Patty died we told her little sister, 'Patty is in heaven and she's doing fine,' because you want to hear how safe people are, and that they're okay. We may meet again. I don't know. You can't spend your life dwelling on heaven and not doing anything to make this world better. As bad as the blows I've received, life has been good, and I want everyone else's to be good. Like the Girl Scouts: You leave a camping area cleaner than you found it. Life is that way: You leave it better than it was when you got there.

"Patty was named after my best friend in the military, Patricia Nicholson, and my college roommate, Susan Nobles. Patricia Susan. We always called her Patty. So on her headstone it says, 'Patricia Susan Nunnallee—Patty' and her birth date and her death date. She was never Patricia Susan to us. So two hundred years from now, if someone walks by, they'll know there was a little girl named Patty."

JANEY AND LARRY FAIR

The Fairs continue to live modestly in the same little tract house; the same old twelve-inch black-and-white TV monitors CNN on the cluttered kitchen table, and stacks of newspapers pile up on the den floor to be clipped for drunk-driving and school-bus stories. Still, however tenaciously the Fairs cling to their idea of themselves, the settlement money has changed their lives completely, from a financial standpoint. But the bus crash had already changed their lives completely from every other standpoint, so one more change hardly matters. It takes place on the surface, and they are living under water.

They have helped out their families in Tennessee, and made some charitable donations, and they will get around to endowing a scholarship in Shannon's name one day, when Janey gets two minutes away from her full-time volunteer work: Elected to MADD's national board of directors, she's also vice chairman of Kentucky MADD, on the board of the Kentucky Victims Coalition and a member of the Kentucky Highway Safety Coalition. Larry "minds the fort" at home, he says, and serves as Janey's de facto secretary—the most palpable impact of the settlement money is that neither has to hold down a paying job. "If you go to a MADD National victims' assistance workshop you'll see women who can afford to be there," Janey observes. She knows that the settlement has bestowed on her the greatest of luxuries—free time.

Some psychologists suggest that survivors who accept monetary compensation for the death of a loved one are often afflicted by guilt. Janey is grateful for the freedom of action the money gives her, but recognizes its emotional cost. "The money makes me feel guilty every time I'm around a victim who's struggling, and that's all the time," she says. The torments of Donald, who was close to Shannon as only army-brat siblings can be, are exacerbated by so-called friends who remark that he "lucked out." Larry alone feels no guilt whatsoever regarding the settlement. "We didn't accept money from Ford," he says. "We *took* money from Ford, because they knowingly built a killer bus."

Larry and Janey remain committed to improving school bus safety. The outcome of their often lonely battle with Ford gratified them not least, Janey says, because it showed that "somebody believed us." Now they have made it their goal to get fuel tanks moved away from the front door. In 1993, they and Murgatroyd sent out a couple of hundred information packets to the pupil transportation officials who buy school buses, as well as the buses' manufacturers, urging that the tanks be relocated. The replies were almost uniformly equivocal: The purchasers would look into the matter; the manufacturers would, as Navistar put it, make a change "if that's what the consumers want."* (Ford Motor Company did not reply.) The Fairs reacted with typical patience. In 1994, they sent out two hundred letters again. "We've planted some seeds," says Larry, "and they may take root sometime."

In the meantime, most of Janey's energy goes into MADD. Drunk-driving tends to outbid school bus safety for immediate attention, she explains. "All these victims are crying out. The bus fuel tank is silent, it's unseen, it's waiting to jump out at someboody else, but you go to what's at hand. I do some drunk driving victims' assistance—kids cut all to pieces like someone had taken a knife to their faces, fatherless children. The drunk-driving victim—that's the crisis at hand."

She labors for MADD with a desperate devotion. It is, after all, a matter of life and death; but there is more to it than that. "We think if we work real hard and get the drunk drivers off the road, we'll get our kids back," Janey confides. "But we won't."

Still, Janey Fair is sustained by "a sense that there has to be something more. I guess if I totally gave up on that idea then in the end I wouldn't see any use in working for MADD, I wouldn't see any use in just a lot of things, because if you get this drunk off the road, there's another one's gonna take his place. It's an uphill battle all the time.

"I want to see the people I love again. And every human being I know wants that. So that gives you the faith to think that surely there's a good possibility of that occurring or you wouldn't be born with such a desire, which is part of being human. So I live as if that possibility were true. And that is all we ever do in religion anyway, is we live as if certain things that are valuable to us are true.

"It's a conscious decision, because I do not want to live as if the world

* In 1994, Navistar began offering a fuel tank located aft of the rear axle between the frame rails as an option on its conventional school bus chassis.

does not matter and in the end it really makes no difference one way or another what you do: Your actions are never going to be called into account; you're gonna go right back to the dust that you came from and it's all over with. It is not valuable to human life to live that way. You have to be accountable for your actions, good and bad."

NOTES

The cases of *Janey L. Fair, individually and as personal representative of The Estate of Shannon Rae Fair, et al.,* v. *Ford Motor Company, et al.,* Civil Action No. 88-CI-101, and *James B. Nunnallee, Administrator, The Estate of Patricia Susan Nunnallee, et al.,* v. *Ford Motor Company, et al.,* Civil Action No. 88-CI-99, Commonwealth of Kentucky, Carroll Circuit Court, were consolidated for trial in 1989. Pretrial motions and depositions are cited as they were captioned when filed; they and their attached exhibits remain on file at the Carroll County Circuit Court. Plaintiffs' trial exhibits have been removed to the Attorneys Information Exchange Group, Inc., 651 Beacon Parkway West, Birmingham, AL 35209; (205) 945-4860.

PROLOGUE

9   Carroll County Coroner James Dunn: Author's interview, James Dunn.

11   Nichols was getting ready for bed: Author's interview, George Nichols.

CHAPTER 1

17   "Lord, as we make another trip": Author's interview, Rev. W. Don Tennison.

17   The eleven-year-old bus: For details of the bus crash, see National Transportation Safety Board (NTSB), *Highway Accident Report—Pick-up Truck/Church Activity Bus Head-on Collision and Fire near Carrollton, Kentucky, May 14, 1988,* Report No. NTSB/HAR-89/01 (Washington, D.C., 1989). Available from the National Technical Information Service, 5285 Port Royal Road, Springfield, VA 22161; phone (703) 487-4650.

18   Brother Wayne Spradlin kept a watchful eye: Author's interviews, Wayne Spradlin and Jerry Hardesty.

19   "Okay kids, bunch it up!": Author's interview, Janey Padgett. The description of events on the bus trip and at Kings Island is based on the author's

interviews with crash survivors Wayne Cox, Conrad Garcia, Sandra Glover, Jamie Hardesty, Joseph Percefull, Jennifer Scoville, Jim Slaughter, Katrina McNickle, Katrina Muller, Janey Padgett, Pam Uhey Flowers, David Walliser, as well as testimony at the criminal trial, *Commonwealth of Kentucky* v. *Larry Wayne Mahoney,* Case No. 88 C.R. 027.

19   black metal plaque: Author's inspection of exemplar 1977 Ford/Superior B-700 school bus.

19   By standard industry practice: Testimony of Thomas Dale Turner, Manager of Engineering Services, Blue Bird Body Company, Fort Valley, GA, in the Matter of The Investigation of the Highway Accident Involving Pickup Truck/Church Activity Bus Head-on Collision and Fire near Carrollton, Kentucky, on May 14, 1988. Docket No. HY-497-88, Volume II, p. 175, August 3, 1988.

20   Brother Brent Fischel: Author's interview, Brent Fischel.

CHAPTER 2

22   She and Mary Daniels: Author's interview, Diane Daniels.

22   "Nearly 15–20 million people die": Personal papers of Shannon Fair.

CHAPTER 3

29   John Jacobs and the Power Team: Details of performance from the videotape *Touches the World,* copyright 1991, John Jacobs Evangelistic Association, Dallas, Texas.

30   Pearman encountered his fourteen-year-old daughter, Christy: Author's interview, Dottie Pearman Williams.

31   His father, an army sergeant: Author's interview, Bill and Maddy Nichols.

32   Jack Armstrong, a sunburned: Author's interview, Jack and Joan Armstrong.

34   now traversed by 7,500 vehicles: NTSB Report, *Carrollton, Kentucky,* p. 21.

CHAPTER 4

37   James Carl Lucas had just lain down: Author's interview, James and Phyllis Lucas.

41   Carey Aurentz had been sitting: Testimony of Carey Aurentz at Mahoney trial. An excellent account of Aurentz's ordeal during and since the crash was written by reporter Gideon Gil, Louisville *Courier-Journal,* May 20, 1990.

42   After the doorway was clear: Author's interview with eyewitness Geoff Pinkerton supplements the Armstrongs' recollections.

CHAPTER 5

46   There must have been a hundred people: The description of events at the church is based on the author's interviews with Gary and Debbie Atherton, Diane Daniels, Janey Fair, Brent and Vicki Fischel, Janet Kytta, LuAnn and Kevin McNickle, Rosemary Martinez, Rev. W. Don and Martha Tennison, Glenn Grubbs, Radcliff police officer Roger Runyon, and WHAS radio reporter Mary Jeffries.

CHAPTER 12

73   Before Nichols and his team could count: The account of the identification process is based on the author's interviews with George Nichols, Steve Meadows, and Sonny Cease.

CHAPTER 13

79   supper club litigation, which led to $49 million in settlements: *Wall Street Journal,* June 26, 1992.

79   Chesley later recalled: Author's interview, Stan Chesley, Esq.

79   $155 million settlement: *Wall Street Journal,* June 16, 1992.

79   $3.7 billion settlement: *New York Times,* March 24, 1994.

79   When Ford engineer Robert Pelkey reported to work: Author's interview, Robert Pelkey.

80   Pat Butcher paid a visit: Author's interview, Pat Butcher.

80   Five years later, in 1993, Butcher's Family Worship Center: Carrollton *News-Democrat,* August 11, 1983, p. 6.

CHAPTER 14

83   Rosemary Martinez, who lost her only child: Author's interviews, Rosemary Martinez, Owen and Margaret Bennett.

CHAPTER 15

88   messages of condolence from President and Nancy Reagan and Vice President and Barbara Bush:
Reagan and Bush no doubt really did share the devastated families' sorrow. But neither thought hard enough, apparently, to make the connection between their own gutting of federal safety regulations and the suffering that follows. As chairman of Reagan's Task Force on Regulatory Relief, Bush had since 1981 worked manfully to delay, dilute, or altogether eradicate rules written by the agencies entrusted with protecting the health and safety of the public. Among the regulations the task force had helped stave off was

NHTSA's passive restraint requirement, which the Reagan Department of Transportation rescinded in October 1981. As president, Bush would intensify the anti-regulatory battle, declaring a moratorium on federal regulations across the board in 1992. "We're regulating ourselves to death!" he shouted to cheering supporters while campaigning for reelection in Michigan. *Wall Street Journal,* September 23, 1992, p. 1.

90   the case of Kevin Fitzgerald: Court papers, *Commonwealth* v. *Kevin L. Fitzgerald,* Carroll County, KY, Indictment, June 6, 1985.

91   "The offender by his act of murder...": Kentucky Revised Statutes 532.025.

92   The term "destructive device" is defined: Kentucky Revised Statutes 237.030.

CHAPTER 16

96   Thomas Huxley's essay "On a Piece of Chalk": *Lectures and Lay Sermons* by Thomas Huxley (New York: Dutton, 1938).

97   All the surface rocks of Kentucky: *The Geologic Story of Kentucky,* by Preston McGrain, Kentucky Geological Survey (Lexington: University of Kentucky, 1983).

CHAPTER 17

99   Dick Booher ... thought it would be a good idea: Author's interview, Dick Booher.

100   According to legal ethics: Author's interview, Professor Stephen Gillers, New York University School of Law.

104   Byron Bloch had observed over the years: Author's interview, Byron Bloch.

106   He showed her the National Transportation Safety Board Report on a 1972 accident in Reston, Virginia: National Transportation Safety Board, *Highway Accident Report, Schoolbus/Automobile Collision and Fire, Near Reston, Virginia, February 29, 1972,* Report No: NTSB-HAR-72-2 (Washington, D.C., 1972).

CHAPTER 18

108   John P. Coale, Esq.... felt as though he had been yelled at: Author's interview, John P. Coale.

109   for Coale, the first of three *People* stories he would score: The second was "In the Wake of a Tragic Hotel Fire, Disaster Attorneys Seek Compensation for the Victims—And for Themselves," by James S. Kunen, January 26, 1987. The third was "Two Families Fight to Make Ford Pay for the Kentucky

School-Bus Disaster That Killed Their Daughters," by James S. Kunen, October 31, 1988.

109 a gas leak at a Union Carbide pesticide plant killed more than 2,300: *Wall Street Journal,* November 24, 1986.

110 India settled for $470 million: *New York Times,* September 15, 1992, p. D-13.

110 Former Chief Justice Warren Burger denounced: *Wall Street Journal,* August 11, 1988.

111 Bronco IIs had a rollover death rate: Insurance Institute for Highway Safety figures, *New York Times,* June 15, 1992, p. 1.

112 Revenue from the 1991 marijuana crop: *Wall Street Journal,* December 24, 1992, p. 1.

CHAPTER 19

115 He said that the one third would cover those lawyers, too: Author's interview, Janey Fair.

117 $750,000 was paid out for each of the twenty-four children killed: The Louisville *Courier-Journal* reported the amount as $700,000, but the author is confident that his sources' figure is correct.

118 Ford had initiated settlement talks: Author's interview, Don Skeeters; and *National Law Journal,* July 18, 1988.

118 Ford associate general counsel Jack Martin did tell: *Wall Street Journal,* July 5, 1988, p. 21.

118 Ford spokesman Robert Waite: *News-Enterprise* (Elizabethtown, KY), July 3, 1988, p. 1.

119 Ford and Sheller-Globe paid them a fee of $4.6 million: Settlement documents obtained by the author.

119 Asked about allegations Don Skeeters replied: Author's interview, Don Skeeters.

119 That's not the way several of his clients remember it: Author's interviews, Gary and Debbie Atherton, Brent and Vicki Fischel, Kevin and LuAnn McNickle, Rosemary and Richard Martinez, Mickey Muller.

121 A Valley Coca-Cola Bottling Company truck with poorly maintained brakes: National Transportation Safety Board, *Highway Accident Report, Collision Between Mission Consolidated Independent School District School Bus and Valley Coca-Cola Bottling Company, Inc., Tractor-Semitrailer, Alton, Texas, Sept. 21, 1989,* Report No. NTSB/HAR-90/02 (Washington, D.C., 1990).

121 Seventeen families of the children who died: *New York Times,* September 19, 1992, p. A-22.

CHAPTER 20

123   The Nunnallees met on July 8 with Grubbs: Louisville *Courier-Journal,* July 9, 1988, p. 1.

124   The *Courier-Journal* editorialized: Louisville *Courier-Journal,* August 28, 1988.

CHAPTER 21

127   The National Transportation Safety Board's investigation: National Transportation Safety Board, *Interstate Bus–Automobile Collision, Interstate Route 15, Baker, California,* Report No. SS-H-3 (Washington, D.C., 1968).

CHAPTER 22

132   Motor Vehicle and School Bus Safety Amendments of 1974: Public Law 93-492, October 27, 1974.

CHAPTER 23

135   49,163 deaths in 1965: National Safety Council, *Accident Facts* (Chicago, 1992).

136   *Unsafe at Any Speed:* (New York: Grossman Publishers, 1965, 1972).

136   May 9, 1973 . . . hearings on the school bus safety bill: 93rd Congress, 1st sess., Subcommittee on Commerce and Finance, Serial No. 93-98.

139   a 1970 report on inadequate bus body strength: National Transportation Safety Board, *Special Study, Inadequate Structural Assembly of Schoolbus Bodies—The Accidents at Decatur and Huntsville, Alabama,* Report No. NTSB-HSS-70-2 (Washington, D.C., 1970).

141   the regulatory agency stated, "It is obvious": 39 Fed. Reg. 27585 (July 30, 1974).

CHAPTER 24

141   Notice of Proposed Rulemaking: Docket 73-20, Notice 4, 40 Fed. Reg. 17036. Comments on the proposal are on file in the docket at NHTSA, Department of Transportation, Washington, D.C.

142   Ford's Automotive Safety Office (ASO) sent the proposed rule: Depositions of John Durstine and Edward Mabley, *Fair* v. *Ford* No. 88-CI-101, Carroll Circuit Court, Carroll County, KY.

144   A 1976 letter from NHTSA administrator James Gregory to Lee Iacocca: *Hearings, Subcommittee on Consumer Protection and Finance,* 94th Cong., 2nd sess., Serial No. 94-96, p. 282.

145 Ford was directed to recall: NHTSA Identification 78V-176.

145 Safety Standard 301-75: Docket 73-20, Notice 8, 40 Fed. Reg. 48352.

CHAPTER 25

146 Henry Ford II declared: *The Struggle for Auto Safety,* by Jerry L. Mashaw and David L. Harfst (Cambridge: Harvard University Press, 1990), p. 71. The initial regulations closely tracked existing General Services Administration and Society of Automotive Engineers standards.

146 The initial safety standards: Docket 3, Notice 1, 31 Fed. Reg. 15212. Ford's comments on the initial proposals are on file in the docket at NHTSA.

148 A pre-meeting briefing memo: *Nunnallee* v. *Ford,* No. 88-CI-099, Carroll Circuit Court, Carroll County, KY, exhibits to the deposition of John Ehrlichman, December 19, 1991.

149 An April 21 memo: Ibid.

149 The National Archives official transcript: "Part of a Conversation Among President Nixon, Lido Anthony Iacocca, Henry Ford II, and John D. Ehrlichman in the Oval Office, on April 27, 1971," The Nixon Project, The National Archives, Washington, D.C.

154 Volpe produced a Memorandum for the President: Ehrlichman deposition exhibit. See note for p. 148.

154 GM equipped 1,000 1971 Chevrolets with air bags: *Hearings, Subcommittee on Consumer Protection and Finance,* 94th Cong., 2nd sess., Serial No. 94-96, p. 435.

155 a May 5, 1971, letter from Ford's lobbyist Markley: *Fair* v. *Ford,* Plaintiffs' Exhibit 151.

155 General Motors chairman Jim Roche had his at-bat: Ehrlichman deposition exhibit. See note for p. 148.

156 NHTSA officials later confirmed: "Report by the Subcommittee on Oversight and Investigations of the Committee on Interstate and Foreign Commerce," House of Representatives, 94th Cong., 2nd sess., October 1976, C.I.S. No. H502-40, p. 187.

156 NHTSA amended its passive restraint standard: FMVSS 208, Docket 69-7, Notice 12, 36 Fed. Reg. 19254.

156 the appeals court ruled: *Chrysler* v. *Department of Transportation,* 472 F.2d 659 (6th Cir. 1972).

156 NHTSA . . . reissued a proposed passive restraint standard: The subsequent history of FMVSS 208 is recounted by Mashaw and Harfst, *Struggle for Auto Safety,* p. 205ff.

157 NHTSA later estimated: Subcommittee on Oversight Report, p. 183. See note for p. 156.

CHAPTER 26

158 Office of Science and Technology: Author's interview, Lawrence A. Goldmuntz, former chairman of the ad hoc committee.

158 Its report: *Final Report of The Ad Hoc Committee,* Prepared for Office of Science and Technology, February 28, 1972. Provided to author by Clarence Ditlow, director, Center for Auto Safety, Washington, D.C.

159 "You can always prove that two things aren't different": Robert Brenner, president, Institute for Safety Analysis, 1976 House Hearings, Serial No. 94-96, p. 456. See note for page 144.

159 Program Plan: NHTSA "Program Plan for Motor Vehicle Safety Standards," October 1971, DOT/HS 820-163; as opposed to "National Highway Safety Bureau Program Plan for Motor Vehicle Safety Standards," June 1970, DOT/HS 820-083.

160 suspending the rule making: 37 Fed. Reg. 1120.

160 the Seventh Circuit Court of Appeals struck down: *H & H Tire Co.* v. *U.S. Department of Transportation,* 471 F.2d 350 (1972).

161 Twenty-nine standards were issued: 1976 Oversight Report, p. 175. See note for p. 156.

161 "Most of the political opposition": Ibid., p. 157.

161 "safety shall be the overriding consideration": Ibid., p. 175.

161 Ford Motor Company objected: Ford Motor Company letter to NHTSA, October 28, 1975, re: Docket 75-25, Notice 1, on file at NHTSA.

CHAPTER 27

162 NHTSA, in February 1975, proposed an amendment: FMVSS 217, Docket 75-3, Notice 1, 40 Fed. Reg. 8569.

162 The prior FMVSS 217: Docket 2-10, Notice 3, 37 Fed. Reg. 9394.

162 Robert B. Kurre ... wrote to NHTSA: The letters of Kurre, Crampton, Thomas-Built, Sheller-Globe, and the National School Transportation Association are in the NHTSA Comment File, Docket 75-3, Notice 1.

163 Robert L. Carter ... stood prepared to deliver: *Fair* v. *Ford,* Sheller-Globe Corporation's Disclosure Pursuant to C.R. 26.02 (4) Regarding Anticipated Expert Testimony at Trial.

163 Carter ... wrote to Senator Robert Griffin: The letters of Carter, Bursian, Gregory and the Physicians for Auto Safety are in the NHTSA Comment File, Docket 75-3, Notice 1.

164 The regulatory agency's written submission: Hearings, Subcommittee on Consumer Protection, Serial No. 94-96, p. 278. See note for p. 144.

165 NHTSA finally amended FMVSS 217: Docket 75-3, Notice 2, 41 Fed. Reg. 3871.

165 NHTSA subsequently amended FMVSS 217: Docket 75-3, Notice 4, 41 Fed. Reg. 22356.

165 The School Bus Manufacturers Institute opposed the schedule: Hearings, Subcommittee on Consumer Protection, Serial No. 94-96, p. 470. See note for p. 144.

165 at a 1973 hearing SBMI had proudly cited: Subcommittee on Commerce and Finance, Serial No. 93-98, p. 1041. See note for p. 136.

165 Wayne Corporation had asked for a delay: Robert B. Kurre's May 13, 1975, letter to NHTSA, in Comment File, Docket 73-20, Notice 4.

166 Congressman John Moss . . . explained: Author's interview, John Moss.

166 SBMI lobbied the House Commerce Committee's subcommittee: House Committee on Interstate and Foreign Commerce, 94th Cong., 2nd sess., Report No. 94-1148.

166 SBMI's expression of indifference regarding the fuel system standard: Hearings, Serial No. 94-96, p. 470. See note for p. 144.

166 The subcommittee, voting in closed, executive session: 94th Cong., 2nd sess., Report No. 94-1148. See note for p. 166.

166 Representative Preyer spoke in support of H.R. 9291's postponement: Debate on H.R. 9291 is in *Congressional Record—House,* June 11, 1976, p. 17,776ff.

168 Richardson Preyer . . . found himself consistently in agreement: Author's interview, Richardson Preyer.

168 Delay was the universally agreed upon price: Author's interview, Michael LeMov, former chief counsel Subcommittee on Oversight and Investigations, House Interstate and Foreign Commerce Committee.

168 Ford Motor Company alone would build: *Fair* v. *Ford,* Ford's Answers to Plaintiffs' Interrogatories.

168 Eckhardt felt truly discouraged: Author's interview, Bob Eckhardt.

168 the Senate passed the House Protection Act: The Senate's actions and debate are at June 24, 1976, *Congressional Record—Senate,* p. 20,160ff.

169 School Bus Vehicle Safety Report: U.S. Department of Transportation, Washington, D.C., January 1977, Document No. DOT HS 802 191

169 the House concurred: June 29, 1976, *Congressional Record—House,* p. 21,106.

CHAPTER 28

170   Heavy Truck Product Letter 76HT77: Plaintiffs' Exhibit 106.

170   As a result of the product letter: Ford's preparations to meet FMVSS 301-75 are described in the following depositions of Ford engineers: *Fair* v. *Ford,* Robert Pelkey, Feb. 12, 1991; D. J. Karalash, March 15, 1990; Keith Lewis, Aug. 14, 1990; Robert Kraemer, July 17, 1990; John Durstine, May 16 and Aug. 7, 1990; and Edward Mabley, May 29, 1990, Aug. 9, 1990, and Feb. 13, 1991. (Unless otherwise indicated, all subsequent citations are to *Fair* v. *Ford.*)

170   Product Change Request Number 785037: Plaintiffs' Exhibit 102.

171   A steel cage guard was the only means: Ford's Answers to Plaintiffs' Interrogatories.

171   Kraemer never thought that: Deposition of Robert Kraemer, pp. 74, 88.

172   Karalash had never heard of the Reston NTSB report: Deposition of D. J. Karalash, p. 220.

172   he was "just curious": Ibid., p. 63.

172   John Durstine . . . appeared equally disinclined to brood: Deposition of John Durstine, August 7, 1990 pp. 22, 75.

173   product verification plan: Plaintiffs' Exhibit 106.

173   Crash Test No. 3241: Deposition of Edward Mabley, August 9, 1990, Exhibit 14.

173   The final engineering sign-off: Plaintiffs' Exhibit 106.

173   the Kentucky Truck Plant completed a "functional build": Plaintiffs' Exhibit 107.

173   Product Change Request directing the assembly plant *not* to install: Plaintiffs' Exhibit 108.

174   A Product Letter signed by Kraemer's superior: Deposition of Robert Kraemer, Exhibit 11.

174   "I didn't want to offend anybody": Keith Lewis deposition, Aug. 14, 1990, p. 76.

174   "That someplace else is a management decision.": Deposition of John Durstine, May 16, 1990, p. 213.

175   "I don't know of any documented system": Ibid., p. 220.

175   "I concurred in the consensus": Deposition of Edward Mabley, Aug. 9, 1990, p. 11.

175 "so we all consensed": Ibid., May 29, 1990, p. 151.

175 "This was clearly within my responsibility": Ibid., Aug. 9, 1990, p. 70.

175 "The reason it was delayed": Deposition of John Durstine, May 16, 1990, p. 183.

175 "the balance of the industry downstream": Deposition of Edward Mabley, May 29, 1990, p. 174.

176 Superior's bodies . . . would have fit: Deposition of Richard Premo, Nov. 14, 1990, p. 84.

176 Sweet never heard of any manufacturer: Author's interview, Berkley Sweet.

176 William King was prepared to argue: Author's interview, William King and Robert Pelkey.

176 Mabley, who could see the carcasses: Deposition of Edward Mabley, Aug. 9, 1990, p. 96.

176 "If we had a standard, we had to meet it": Ibid., p. 169.

CHAPTER 29

177 the annual specification revision meeting: Information about the meeting, the specifications, contracts and bids, and Jones and Jackson themselves is drawn from *Fair* v. *Ford,* Deposition of Paul E. Jones, July 12 and 13, 1990, and the exhibits thereto; and Deposition of Samuel G. Jackson, July 13, 1990.

178 *Ford Truck Data Book:* See *Nunnallee* v. *Sheller-Globe Corporation, et al.,* Appendix to Ford Motor Company's Memorandum in Support of Its Motion for Partial Summary Judgment.

178 "For the most part," the Ford man replied: testimony of Keith Lewis, National Transportation Safety Board, *In the Matter of the Investigation of the Highway Accident Involving Pickup/Church Activity Bus Head-on Collision and Fire Near Carrollton, Kentucky, on May 14, 1988,* Docket Number HY-497-88.

179 Minimum Standards for School Buses: *Minimum Standards for School Buses, 1970 Revised Edition, Recommendations of National Conference on School Transportation,* available from State of Florida, Department of Education, Bureau of Curriculum and Instruction, Publications and Textbook Services, Tallahassee, Florida 32304.

180 Frank W. Cyr . . . initiated that 1939 conference: Author's interview, Frank W. Cyr.

181 standards adopted at the 1939 conference: M. C. S. Noble, Jr., *Pupil Transportation in the United State,* (Scranton, PA: International Textbook Co., 1940).

181 the conclusion that the National Safety Council had reached: National Safety Council, Inc., *School Buses, Their Safe Design and Operation* (Chicago, 1933).

181 The standardization process: *School Bus Standards, 1945 Revised Edition,* on file with author.

182 a Heavy Truck Product Letter: Plaintiffs' Exhibit 212.

183 On the frame-assembly line: Tours of Ford's Kentucky Truck Plant are conducted by appointment; phone (502) 429-2146.

183 March 23, the completed chassis rolled off the line: Ford's Answers to Plaintiffs' Interrogatories.

183 the Pinto's history: Gary T. Schwartz, "The Myth of the Ford Pinto Case," 43 Rutgers Law Review 1013 (1991).

184 In his autobiography: Lee Iacocca with William Novak, *Iacocca, an Autobiography* (New York: Bantam paperback, July 1986).

184 "Even Joan Claybrook": ibid., p. 171.

CHAPTER 30

185 "Sell-O-Gram": On file with author.

186 Sheller-Globe's vehicle safety director, Richard Premo, could write: Deposition of Richard Premo, Nov. 13, 1990, Exhibit 24.

186 FMVSS 302: 49 CFR Section 571.302.

187 Brady Williamson and his associate Fred Fisher: Author's interviews, Brady Williamson and Fred Fisher.

187 federal guidelines: Neoprene is one material used to pass the flammability test recommended by the Federal Transit Administration. See note for p. 221.

CHAPTERS 31 AND 32

191 This account of Shannon's last months is based on the author's interviews with Anita Ardisson, Tanya Blair, Wayne Cox, Stacy Crump, Autumn Dempsey, Donald Fair, Josh Groomes, Tommy Hill, Kari Knight, Pat McKinney, Brian and Leeann Morrison, Angela and Roger Norton, Jim, Tim, Kenny and Kevin Yelton, Billy Shutts, and Brian Stinnett.

CHAPTER 33

203 Information about Mahoney and his actions comes from the author's interviews with Mahoney, his son, Tony, and ex-wife Janice King, Taylor Fox and Dennis Mefford, as well as police reports and testimony at Mahoney's trial.

CHAPTER 34

212   C. S. Lewis, *A Grief Observed* (San Francisco: HarperCollins, 1989).

CHAPTER 35

213   the National Transportation Safety Board convened: see note for p. 179.

214   according to Pelkey's notes: On file with author.

CHAPTER 37

221   Urban Mass Transportation Administration (UMTA), had Recommended Fire Safety Practices: Recommended Fire Safety Practices for Rail Transit Materials Selection, 49 FR 32482, referencing test procedure FAR 25.853. The Federal Transit Administration, successor agency to UMTA, recommends the same standard for transit buses and vans, 58 FR 54250.

223   NTSB had recommended five times since 1969: NTSB Report, *Carrollton, Kentucky,* p. 70.

223   an accident that had occurred near Rustburg, Virginia: National Transportation Safety Board, *Highway Accident Report, Tractor-Semitrailer/Schoolbus Collision and Overturn, Rustburg, Va., March 8, 1977,* Report No. NTSB-HAR-78-1 (Washington, D.C., 1978).

CHAPTER 38

225   The NTSB in its final report stated: NTSB Report, *Carrollton Kentucky,* p. 68.

CHAPTER 39

227   John C. Eckhold once described the office: *Grimshaw* v. *Ford Motor Company,* Superior Court of the State of California for the County of Orange, Case No. 197761, Deposition of John C. Eckhold, Dec. 9, 1976, p. 6.

CHAPTER 40

233   Ford had "voluntarily" recalled 16,000 ambulances. NHTSA Recall Identification Number 87V-113.

233   and 188,000 heavy vans: NHTSA Recall Identification Number 87V-144.

233   Ford recalled 15,000 ambulances again: NHTSA Recall Identification Number 88V-133.

237   Aaron lay in a hospital bed: Author's interview, Larry Conyers.

238   Roever's stump speech: As heard on *The Dave Roever Story,* audio cassette, Roever Evangelistic Association, P.O. Box 136130, Fort Worth, TX 76136; (817) 238–2000.

240   the Roever Evangelistic Association took in $2,078,302: Figure from the REA's filing with the Evangelical Council for Financial Accountability; phone (800) 3BE-WISE.

Chapter 41

242   *Our Precious Loss:* Available from Roever Evangelistic Association.

Chapter 42

246   The State Supreme Court had ruled: *Ewing* v. *May,* 705 S.W. 2d 910 (1986).

246   one of the five firms most utilized by Ford: *National Law Journal,* July 8, 1991.

246   the then-296-lawyer firm: In 1988 McGuire, Woods, Battle & Boothe was the nation's sixty-sixth largest law firm, *National Law Journal,* September 24, 1990. By 1992, it had risen to thirty-eighth, with 380 lawyers, *National Law Journal,* September 27, 1993.

246   He had set six Ivy League records: King's exploits were chronicled in "Master in the Ivy's Den of Virility" by John Underwood, *Sports Illustrated,* December 3, 1962. The title refers to Dartmouth coach Bob Blackman.

248   "I've seen this picture before": Nina Walfort, "Judge, Citing Caseload, Retirement Plans, Benches Himself," *Louisville Times,* January 27, 1983.

249   But, as he explained to a reporter at the time: Richard Wilson, "Judge Walks Away from Trial and Career," Louisville *Courier-Journal,* January 27, 1983.

249   Ford's recalcitrance in discovery: See for example, Milo Geyelin and Neal Templin, "Ford Attorneys Played Unusually Large Role in Bronco II's Launch," *Wall Street Journal,* January 5, 1993. The article describes how, when the Bronco II showed stability problems during its development, Ford lawyers quickly rounded up all pertinent engineering documents. "More than 50 documents that should have been included in the 1982 round-up were instead destroyed. . . ."

250   intracompany presentation by an engineer: "Product Liability, Rough Draft." On file with author.

250   Ford could act as though they did not exist: See, Connie Bruck, "How Ford Stalled the Pinto Litigation" *American Lawyer,* June 1979.

CHAPTER 43

257 "his BAC . . . must have been at least .21: Estimated by the prosecution's alcohol expert, Dr. Kurt Dubrowski, professor of medicine, University of Oklahoma.

CHAPTER 44

261 Said Lee Williams: Author's interview, Lee Williams.

264 "I told the Lord": Williams's account of his epiphany is taken from the Dave Roever video *Our Precious Loss.* See note for p. 238.

265 He calls his speech "From Pain to Promise": Available on audio cassette from Lee Williams's Ministry to Families, P.O. Box 925, Radcliff, KY 40160.

CHAPTER 47

275 His family was inclined to agree: Author's interview, Laverne, Michael, and Patrick Dunn.

CHAPTER 48

278 for about $125 apiece: Assuming free labor. Author's interview, Bobby Sheroan, Director of Pupil Transportation, Hardin County, KY.

CHAPTER 49

283 a $15 million verdict against Hyundai: *Ketchum* v. *Hyundai,* VC 004170 (Superior Court, Los Angeles County, 1993).

283 Fuel System Integrity Program Financial Review: Ford Motor Company Safety Planning, Car Product Planning, April 22, 1971, *Nunnallee* v. *Sheller-Globe, et al.,* Plaintiffs' Opposition to Ford Evidentiary Motions in Limine, Exhibit 5, January 1992.

284 A California appellate court: *Grimshaw* v. *Ford Motor Company,* 119 Cal. App. 3d 757 (1981).

285 the Let 'Em Burn Letter: Ford Motor Company letter to NHTSA, September 19, 1973, petitioning for reconsideration of FMVSS 301, Docket 70-20, Notice 2, on file at NHTSA.

285 "The Societal Costs of Motor Vehicle Accidents": NHTSA, Preliminary Report, April 1972.

286 number of fatalities . . . was more like twenty-seven: Gary T. Schwartz. See note for p. 184.

287 $12 million for one year: *New York Times,* March 29, 1993.

CHAPTER 50

289   calling for a payment of $1.3 million: This figure was not announced. Neither the Fairs nor the Nunnallees nor any of the plaintiffs' attorneys were the author's source.

293   "Nineteen fifty-eight: twenty-six children are trapped and drowned": On February 28, 1958, a Floyd County school bus carrying forty-seven children aged six to eighteen skidded into the Big Sandy River near Prestonsburg, Kentucky. Twenty-six and the bus driver drowned as the bus sank in thirty feet of water.

293   "Nineteen sixty-seven: UCLA crashes two school buses": See Derwyn M. Severy, Harrison M. Brink, and Jack D. Baird, "School Bus Passenger Protection," Society of Automotive Engineers, Inc., New York, 1967, Report Number 670040.

293   "Nineteen sixty-eight: nineteen are killed in Baker, California": NTSB Report, *Baker, California*. See note for p. 127.

293   "April 1972, the Reston crash": NTSB Report, *Reston, Virginia*. See note for p. 106.

293   "Nineteen seventy-five: NHTSA runs an Impala": The National Aviation Facilities Experimental Center (NAFEC) ran a 1971 Chevelle into a school bus in a crash test conducted for NHTSA. *Fair* v. *Ford*, Plaintiffs' Exhibit 195.

CHAPTER 53

308   *Dulieu* v. *White & Sons:* [1901] 2 K.B., 669, 679.

CHAPTER 54

316   Foremost among these had been his wife: Author's interview, Jim and Mary Lee Montgomery.

CHAPTER 55

320   the minutes of several North American Automotive Operations (NAAO) executive committee meetings: *Fair* v. *Ford*, Plaintiffs' Exhibits 136, 137, 155.

320   a series of memoranda: Ibid., 148, 149.

322   Ford once stated under oath: *Frank A. Fisher* v. *James Schultz*, SWC 29079 Superior Court, Los Angeles County, Deposition of Henry Ford II, Dec. 14, 1979.

CHAPTER 57

327   In 1984–86, tractor-trailers: NHTSA, *Heavy Truck Fuel System Safety Study*, Report No. DOT HS 807 484 (Washington, D.C., Sept. 1989).

328   a 1967 UCLA school bus crash test report: Severy et al., "School Bus Passenger Protection."

CHAPTER 58

333 Johnson was a fuel system design engineer: See, for example, *Crash-worthy Fuel System Design Criteria and Analyses,* USAAVLABS Technical Report 71-8, Eustis Directorate, U.S. Army Air Mobility Research and Development Laboratory, Fort Eustis, Virginia, March 1971.

333 Johnson oversaw the development of the compliance standard: NHTSA, *Development of a School Bus Fuel System Integrity Compliance Procedure,* Report No. DOT HS 801 529 (Washington, D.C., April 1975).

335 "to avoid being duplicative, repetitive and redundant": *Fair* v. *Ford,* Sheller-Globe Corporation's Trial Brief, p. 6.

337 Ford announced a $3 *billion* investment: *New York Times,* April 14, 1992.

337 the nation's third largest industrial corporation: Ford trailed General Motors and Exxon, *Fortune,* April 22, 1991.

337 Ford's $148 million of earnings: Ford Motor Company, Second Quarter Report to Stockholders, Summer 1992.

337 a regulation requiring identification labels: In 1975, Ford successfully petitioned for the amendment of FMVSS 106-74. Subcommittee on Consumer Protection, Hearings, Serial No. 94-96, p. 347. See note for p. 144.

EPILOGUE

LEE IACOCCA

341 "How can those board members sleep": *Iacocca,* p. 138. See note for p. 184.

341 "The scars left by Henry Ford": ibid., p. 146.

341 in a 1985 Gallup poll: *Current Biography Yearbook 1988* (The H. W. Wilson Company, New York 1988, 1989).

341 "a safety nut": *Iacocca,* supra, p. 313.

342 "I thank God for you": Chrysler ad, *People* magazine, July 30, 1990.

342 an opponent of safety regulations to the end of his career: See, e.g., *Fortune,* Feb. 12, 1990, p. 72; ABC News "Nightline" #2622, June 11, 1991.

342 "St. Peter is going to meet me": *Iacocca,* supra, p. 316.

342 and netted $84 million: *Automotive News,* Aug. 16, 1993; *The New York Times,* Nov. 20, 1993.

FORD MOTOR COMPANY

343 it reported a profit of $2.5 billion: *The New York Times,* Feb. 10, 1994.

SCHOOL BUSES

343   Industry comments in response to NHTSA's announcement: 56 FR 7826

343   a study by the National Institute of Standards and Technology: Department of Commerce, National Institute of Standards and Technology, Center for Fire Research, "Assessment of the Fire Performance of School Bus Interior Components" (Gaithersburg, MD 1990), Document No. PB90-265307.

343   In October 1992, NHTSA issued a rule: Docket 88-21, Notice No. 3, 57 FR 49413.

343   the deadline refers to the *chassis* completion date: Author's interview, Patricia Breslin, Office of Vehicle Safety Standards, NHTSA.

343   NHTSA announced that it would consider a new rule: Docket 89-04, Notice 01, 54 FR 13082.

343   NHTSA announced in 1991: Docket 89-04, Notice 02, 54 FR 20408.

344   the NTSB wrote NHTSA: Feb. 18, 1993, letter from NTSB Chairman Carl W. Vogt to Mr. Howard Smolkin, Acting Administrator, NHTSA, on file with author.

344   at least 17,000 school buses: Author's interview, Navistar executive.

INDEX

accidents, *see* bus accidents; Carrollton
    bus crash; school bus accidents
Ackman, John, Jr., 76, 89, 90
Adams, Brock, 156n
air bags, 152, 154–55, 157, 342
aisles, narrowness of, 36, 123, 163, 165
Alcohol Driver Education, 207, 217–18
Allen, Phil, 174–75, 246, 250–51, 253
Alton, Tex., school bus accident in, 121,
    268
ambulances, Ford's recall of, 233
American Motors, 149n, 156n
Amtrak-Conrail crash, 110
Angel, Frances, 130, 131, 198, 277, 336
Angel, Sarah Isabelle Hite (Granny
    Angel), 130, 131
Angel, Thomas, 130
Ardisson, Anita, 191–93
Armstrong, Jack, 32–33, 38, 42
Armstrong, Joan, 33, 38, 42
Arnett, Jennifer, 22, 44, 46, 68
Arnzen, Mark, 276
Aspin, Les, 132, 136–37
Atchley, Dennis, 278
Atherton, Cynthia, 46, 47, 119–20, 192,
    194, 197
Atherton, Debbie, 119–20
Atherton, Gary, 119, 120
Aurentz, Carey, 26, 31, 32, 41–42, 236
autopsies, 74–76

BAC (blood alcohol concentration), 76,
    216, 257
Baker, Calif., bus accident near, 127–28,
    293, 299, 319–20
Baldani, Russell, 257–58

Banciu, Lou, 306
Belli, Melvin, 109
Bennett, Kay, 77
Bennett, Margaret, 83
Bennett, Owen, Jr., 83
Bennett, Terry, 77, 100–103, 114–15, 117,
    119–20, 240
Bernstein, Mark, 73, 74
Best Western Gold Vault Inn, media
    center in, 232–35
Beverly Hills Supper Club fire, 78, 79
Bhopal gas leak, 109–110
Bickers, Roy, 90–91
Bickers, Ruby, 90–91
Bihlmeyer, Larry, 319–25, 327–31
Birch, Frank, 195
Birky, Merritt, 221, 225–26
Blair, Tanya, 197
Bloch, Byron, 104, 106–7, 306–7, 338
blood alcohol concentration (BAC), 76,
    216, 257
blood tests, 76–79
Blue Cross/Blue Shield of Maine, 109
BMCS (U.S. Bureau of Motor Carrier
    Safety), 144, 160
Boehly, William, 219–20
Booher, Dick, 99–101
Booher, Jason, 34, 42, 99, 195
Boston Bag Test, 234–35
Boyle, Tom, 79–80
Bradley, Clint, 30–31, 32
Brittain, Neil, 13
Brotherhood Mutual Insurance Co.,
    101–2
Bryant, Milo D., 236
Buhler, Gene, 315, 317

Burger, Warren, 110
Burnett, Jim, 214–15, 222, 228–29
Bursian, Robert, 163
bus accidents:
  near Baker, Calif., 127–28, 293, 299,
    319–20
  see also Carrollton bus crash; school
    bus accidents
Bush, Barbara, 88, 240–41
Bush, George, 88, 148, 240–41
Butcher, Pat, 80–81

Campbellsburg Volunteer Rescue Squad,
  56–57
carbon monoxide (CO), 76, 78
Carroll County Circuit Court, 123
Carroll County District Court, Mahoney
  arraigned in, 89–90
Carrollton armory:
  autopsy and identification work at, 73–
    76
  school bus remains brought to, 13–14
Carrollton bus:
  gas tank of, 76–77, 103, 107, 166*n*, 225,
    226, 230, 244, 292–93, 310, 311,
    334
  inspection of, by Fairs and their
    lawyers, 231–32
  locking up of, 80
  maintenance of, 17, 18
  number of people on, 18
  purchase of, 17
  Richwalsky's views on, 308–9
Carrollton bus crash:
  cause of deaths in, 76
  computer simulation of, 310–12
  deaths in, 9–14, 50, 69, 71, 73–76; *see
    also specific people*
  description of, 9–14, 34–43
  emergency door opened in, 36
  explosion in, 39, 55
  fire in, 10–13, 35–43, 62, 69, 71, 187,
    221–23, 235, 294
  hospitalizations in, 73, 76, 80–81
  Kentucky's official investigation of,
    304–5
  lack of impact injuries in, 76
  Lewis's investigation after, 174
  news reports on, 66, 71
  NTSB inquiry into, 178, 213–31, 242,
    299*n*
  removal of remains in, 13–14
  rescue efforts in, 38–42

resentment of name of, 291
rumors about, 67, 112
Carrollton Holiday Inn, 68–70, 73, 74
  Ford team at, 79–80
Carrollton *News-Democrat,* 90
Carter, Robert L., 141, 159, 163–64
CBS Evening News, 233
Cease, Henry, Jr. (Sonny), 73, 74, 231,
  290, 317
  testimony of, 304–5, 307–8, 310,
    311
Center for Auto Safety, 142
Chandler, Jean, 204
Chesley, Stan, 79, 110
Chevrolet, 178, 321*n*
chlorine, 78–79
Chowning, Sam, 259–60
Chrysler, 149*n*, 156*n*, 341–42
Church Day, at Kings Island, 9, 17, 21–
  27
Claybrook, Joan, 184
Claybrook, Karen, 92
CNN, 71
Coale, John P., Esq., 107–17, 232, 233,
  244, 282
  background of, 108–10
  as media-master, 109, 110, 115–16,
    268
  settlement denounced by, 122
Coale, Kananack & Murgatroyd, 108
Coleman, William, 156*n*, 169*n*
The Commonwealth of Kentucky v. *Larry
  Wayne Mahoney,* 256–62
compensatory damages, 244, 279–82,
  306, 336–37
  lost lifetime earnings and, 272, 279–
    280
  psychological evaluations and, 280–
    282
Congress, U.S.:
  safety standards and, 132, 136–39, 148,
    157*n*, 161, 164, 166–69, 214, 299
Constance, Amy, 30
Conyers, Aaron, 19–20, 236–37
Conyers, Josh, 19–20, 32, 87
  in crash, 39, 56, 236–37
  death of, 56
  at Kings Island, 22–25
Conyers, Rebecca, 19–20
Corboy, Phil, 110
Court of Appeals, U.S., 156*n*
Cowan, Fred, 91
Cox, Ron, 99

Cox, Wayne, 28, 30, 34, 99, 197
  in crash, 40
  at Kings Island, 24, 27
Crampton, Byron, 163
Cranston, Alan, 169
crash tests, 173, 222*n,* 245, 294, 299*n,*
    300
  Pinto, 184, 296, 320
  UCLA, 293, 328
Craycroft, Rev. Leo, 87–88
Crowley, Monica, 157
Crump, Stacy, 197
Cummings, John III, 110
Cumulative Regulatory Effects on the
    Cost of Automotive Transportation
    (RECAT), 158–59
cyanide, 78
Cyr, Frank W., 180–81

Daniels, Diane, 47, 66, 99, 112, 117
Daniels, Dominick V., 164
Daniels, Lisa, 25
Daniels, Mary, 32, 47, 99
  in crash, 39, 46
  funeral of, 87–88
  at Kings Island, 22–25
Darnell, Tammy, 28, 37
Davidson, Al, 101–2
Davidson, John, 78
Davis, Betty, 205, 207, 341
Dealer Transport Company, 183
death penalty, 76, 89–92
Dempsey, Autumn, 193, 197, 198
Dennis, Harold, 236
dental identification, 74, 75
destructive device, use of term, 92
Dickinson, Teddy, 111
Dodge, 178
DOT, *see* Transportation Department,
    U.S.
Dow-Corning, 79*n*
Dowie, Mark, 286
Downey, Phil, 215, 216, 217
Drifter's Tavern, 204
drunk driving, 156, 324, 339, 341
  near Baker, Calif., 127–28
  death penalty and, 89–91
  destructive device and, 92
  Ford's contribution to fund against,
    118
  impairment and, 216–17
  MADD and, 118, 243, 267–68, 336,
    344–47

of Mahoney, 32–35, 76, 91, 217, 209–
    210, 215–19, 243, 257–62
  NTSB hearings and, 215–19
  penalties determined for, 91
  pre-crash witnesses to, 32–34
  Roever and, 238–40, 242
  safety regulations against, 233, 235–36,
    238, 242–43, 258–59, 278
Dulieu v. *White & Sons,* 308*n*
Dunn, Billy, 313–14
Dunn, Cheryl, 9, 11
Dunn, James, 9–13, 82
Dunn, Laverne Jobert, 275
Dunn, William R., 274–77, 279, 310–17,
    319–23, 326–37
  death of, 339
  first day of trial and, 289–92, 295–99,
    301
  second day of trial and, 305–7
  settlement encouraged by, 331–33
  third day of trial and, 307–9
DuPont Plaza Hotel fire, 110
Durrance, Jess, 37
Durstine, John, 143, 172–75

Earnest, Julie, 87
Echols, W. G., 181
Eckhardt, Bob, 166–68
Eckhold, John C., 143, 144, 227*n,* 285
*Economic Cost of Motor Vehicle Crashes,
    The* (NHTSA), 285*n*
Edelen, Don, 79
EDSMAC (Engineering Dynamics
    Simulation Model of Auto Crashes),
    310–12
Education Department, Kentucky,
    Division of Pupil Transportation of,
    176*n,* 177–79, 182, 186, 187, 228
Ehrlichman, John D., 149, 150, 154–57,
    326
Etheredge, Kashawn, 30, 38, 46, 192
evacuation-time regulation, 222–24
Evans, Richard T., 173–74
Ewbank, Weeb, 246
exits, 132, 236
  evacuation-time regulation and, 222–
    224
  insufficient, 103, 123, 127, 187, 293
  NTSB's recommendation on, 343
  rear, 36, 37, 39–42, 162–65, 187, 278
  testing of, 128
  window, 37, 39, 137, 163, 165*n,* 186–
    187, 233, 236, 278, 289

Failure Analysis Corporation, 300
Fair, Donald, 45, 46, 96, 202, 268, 273, 346
   birth of, 131, 132
Fair, Hazel, 44, 70–71, 125–26
Fair, Janey Mullins, 43–48, 65–70, 72, 99,
     104–7, 124–32, 197, 201, 231–36,
     241–43, 267–73, 277–81
   background of, 128–30
   Bloch's meeting with, 104, 106–7
   childbirths of, 131–32
   Coale and, 112–17
   Commonwealth of Kentucky v. *Larry*
     Wayne Mahoney and, 256, 261
   courtship and marriage of, 126–27
   death penalty and, 92
   deposition of, 269–73
   funeral and, 83, 96, 97
   grief of, 211–13, 267, 280–81
   group counseling of, 131
   at Holiday Inn, 68–70
   legal work of, 114–15, 126, 269
   in MADD, 243, 267–68, 336, 346, 347
   on Mahoney's drinking, 208
   need to know truth and, 104–6
   NTSB hearings and, 213–14, 215, 219–
     221, 225, 230
   post-trial life of, 346–48
   settling as viewed by, 332–33
   testimony of, 303–4
   TV appearances of, 268
   see also Fair v. *Ford;* trial
Fair, Lawrence, 44, 47, 68, 70–72, 96, 104,
     124–28, 201, 232–36, 242, 243, 267–
     269, 275–82
   background of, 125–26
   Coale and, 107–8, 111, 112–17
   death penalty and, 92
   deposition of, 272, 273
   Family Support Group and, 99, 100
   in Korea, 71–72
   memorial service and, 235–36, 238,
     240
   NTSB hearings and, 213–14, 215, 219,
     220, 223, 225–27, 230
   post-trial life of, 346–47
   retirement of, 277
   self-control of, 281–82
   settlement and, 337, 338
   Shannon's birth and, 131–32
   tactical change as viewed by, 333
   TV appearances of, 268
   see also Fair v. *Ford;* trial
Fair, Ray Chase, 125–26, 132

Fair, Shannon Rae, 32, 43–48, 112–13,
     191–202, 235
   baptism of, 97, 197, 198
   birth of, 131–32
   blood test of, 76–79
   carbon monoxide level of, 76
   in crash, 39, 44–48, 187, 304–5
   crepe dress of, 83
   death of, 65–72, 76, 82, 113, 304–5
   fourteenth birthday of, 191
   funeral of, 83, 95–99
   Hill and, 193–96
   identification of, 76
   justice for, 123, 243
   at Kings Island, 22–25
   life dedicated to Jesus by, 198
   lost lifetime earnings of, 272, 279–80
   maturity of, 193, 200
   mother's deposition and, 269, 271–72
   near death of, 124–25
   personality and activities of, 191–202
   pets of, 201–2
Fair, Stefan, 273
Fairfax, George William, 129
Fairfax, Lord, 129
Fairfax, Sally, 129
Fairfax v. *Hite,* 129
Fair v. *Ford,* 123, 149, 154–55, 178–79,
     211, 231, 269–338
   Aug. 11, 1989 hearing and, 244–54
   compensatory vs. punitive damages in,
     244–45, 336–37
   depositions taken by Ford's lawyers in,
     269–73
   Ehrlichman's deposition in, 155
   Grush-Saunby report and, 285–88
   Kraemer's deposition in, 172
   Pinto and, 183–84
   replacement of judges in, 248, 274,
     297
   see also trial
Family Support Group, 99–104, 108, 117,
     238, 243
   Davidson's presentation to, 101–2
Family Worship Center, 80
Farmer, Kim, 38
Federal Aviation Administration, 221
Federal Motor Vehicle Safety Standard
     (FMVSS) 217, 162, 165, 186–87, 223,
     230
Federal Motor Vehicle Safety Standard
     (FMVSS) 301–75, 141–43, 145, 170–
     176, 182, 222*n,* 230, 344

Federal Motor Vehicle Safety Standard (FMVSS) 302, 221
fires, 110, 219–20, 233, 234–35, 327–29
  in Baker, Calif. bus accident, 127, 299
  Beverly Hills Supper Club, 78, 79
  in Carrollton bus crash, 10–13, 35–43, 62, 69, 71, 187, 221–23, 235, 294
  in Reston crash, 106, 172
  safety standards and, 141–43, 186
  in tractor-trailer accidents, 327*n*
Fischel, Brent, 20, 49
Fischel, Dwailla, 49, 93
Fischel, Lee, 49
Fischel, Sammy, 49
Fischel, Vicki, 48–49, 50, 62
Fisher, Fred, 187
Fitzgerald, Kevin, 90–91
flammability tests, 234–35, 268, 343
Flanigan, Peter, 148*n,* 149, 155, 156
Foran, Ciaran, 41, 42, 306*n*
Ford, Christina, 149
Ford, Gerald, 141
Ford, Henry II, 14, 146, 148–55, 184–85, 321–22, 341
  Nixon's meeting with, 149–55, 158, 250, 293, 326
Ford, William, 185
Ford Motor Company, 14, 103, 132, 140, 142–55, 166*n,* 170–76, 182–85, 258
  ambulances recalled by, 233
  Automotive Assembly Division of, 174
  Automotive Safety Office (ASO) of, 142–43, 146, 227–30, 285
  Broncos of, 111, 147
  Central Product Planning Office of, 321
  Cost Information Reporting as viewed by, 161
  crash tests of, 173, 184, 245, 294, 296, 299*n,* 320
  defense team of, 79–80
  Design Analysis Activity of, 250
  Docket 3–2 opposed by, 160
  Durstine's Product Letter and, 174–75
  Econoline Club Wagon of, 147
  export witnesses of, 277
  Fairs' lawsuit against, *see Fair* v. *Ford*
  FMVSS 301–75 and, 142–43, 145, 170–176, 182
  Fuel System Integrity Program Financial Review of, 283–84, 323
  fuel tank safety and, 106–7, 122, 123–124, 132, 142–45, 170–76, 178–79,

183–84, 244–45, 250, 285–87, 319–330, 333–34, 336
Grimshaw v. *Ford Motor Company,* 282–84
  Heavy Truck Product letter 76HT77 of, 170
  Henry Truck Operations of, 143, 147, 170–76, 244
  Kentucky Division of Pupil Transportation and, 177–79, 228
  Lewis's investigation in, 174
  local influence of, 114
  Material Control System of, 171
  Mercury Capris recalled by, 145
  nondisclosure policy of, 249–50, 279
  North American Automotive Operations (NAAO) of, 279, 320–21
  North American Product Planning Committee of, 321
  NTSB hearings and, 213–14, 220–21, 224–31
  Nunnallees' counteroffers to, 122–24
  Nunnallees' lawsuit against, *see Nunnallee* v. *Ford*
  Pelkey's Product Letter at, 182
  Pinto of, 143, 151, 183–84, 244–45, 250, 251, 282–84, 286, 296, 320
  Preproduction Control Activity of, 171
  Product Development Group of, 283
  Purchasing Activity of, 171
  Skeeters & Bennett and, 112, 116–21
  Test Operations and Engineering Services Office of, 173
  after trial, 342–44
Ford Truck Data Book, 178
Fox, Taylor, 209, 215–16, 217, 258
Franklin, Larry, 116, 236*n,* 287*n,* 304, 305, 311
  opening statement of, 292–94
Frazier, Michael, 33
Frederick, Kim, 205, 207–10, 258, 340
"From Pain to Promise" (Williams), 265–267
fuel system, 296–301
  of Carrollton bus, 76–77, 103, 107, 166*n,* 225, 226, 230, 244, 292–93, 310, 311, 334
  crash test simulations and, 173, 296
  Docket 3–2 and, 160
  in Ford's 1973 pickup trucks, 320–21
  of GM pickups, 107*n*
  Habberstad's view of, 225
  in-cab, 320–22

fuel system (*cont.*)
  location of, 103, 106–7, 160, 172, 178,
    179, 181–82, 186, 226, 230, 233,
    236, 293, 296–98, 320–22, 327–29,
    333–34
  NTSB's recommendation on, 343–44
  of Pinto, 183–84, 244–45, 250, 296
  in Reston crash, 106, 172, 229
  safety and, 76–77, 106–7, 122, 123–24,
    132, 141–46, 165, 166, 170–76, 178–
    179, 182–86, 222*n*, 230, 244–45, 250,
    278*n*, 285–87, 319–30, 333–34, 336,
    343–44
  standardization of, 181
  testing of, 128
  as trial evidence, 292–93, 316
  of U.S. Army helicopters, 333
funerals, 83–88, 92–93, 95–99

Garcia, Conrad, 31, 36, 48, 63, 310
Garcia, Mr. (Conrad's father), 48
gas tanks, *see* fuel system
Gauthier, Wendell, 110
General Motors (GM), 107, 136, 154,
    155–56, 177–78, 299
Gill, Jeffrey, 259
Glover, Kim, 37
Glover, Sandra, 28–29, 37, 58
Gohn, Richard, 83–86, 92–93, 120
Graham, Carroll, 10
Green, Brown, 103–4, 110
Gregory, James, 144–45, 164
Grief Observed, A (Lewis), 212
Griffin, Robert, 163–64
Grimshaw v. *Ford Motor Company,* 282–
    284
Grubbs, Bill, 80, 123, 269, 270, 276
  Aug. 11, 1989 hearing and, 246–49, 252
  trial and, 289, 290, 299–300, 302–5,
    310–12, 314, 317–18, 320, 322, 324–
    325, 327–31
Grush, Ernest, 285–87
Grush-Saunby report (Let 'Em Burn
    Letter), 285–88, 326

Habberstad, John, 80, 221, 224–26, 229*n*,
    328–29
Haddon, William, Jr., 143–44
Haldeman, H. R., 149
Hance, Mike, 116, 123, 182, 270, 276, 294,
    333
  background of, 270
  Banciu's settlement offer to, 306

Hard Copy (TV show), 268
Hardesty, Jamie, 36, 37, 40, 41
Hardin, D. J., 185–86
Hartke, Vance, 169
Hebert, Mark, 309
Hendricks, Todd, 268
Herman, Ray, 13
Hews, Arthur, 282
Higgins, Scotty, 198–99
Hildebrand, Jack, 257–58
Hill, Herb, 309–12, 314, 328*n*
Hill, Tommy, 193–96
Hitchcock, Ralph J., 220–24
Hite, Andrew, 129, 130
Hite, Great Granny, 129–30
Hite, John, Jr., 129
Hite, John, Sr., 129
Hite, Joist (Johann von der Heydt), 128–
    129
Hite, Sarah Isabelle, 130, 131
Holt, Juan, 57
homicide, reckless, 256–57, 259
horizontal flame test, 221, 343
House of Representatives, U.S., 132, 136–
    139, 166–69
  Commerce Committee of, 156, 166
  H.R. 9291 and, 166–68
  Oversight Committee of, 161
Howard, Stephanie, 36, 51
Huxley, Thomas, 96

Iacocca (Iacocca), 341, 342
Iacocca, Lee, 14, 184–85, 321–22, 341–42
  Gregory's correspondence with, 144–
    145
  Nixon's meeting with, 149–55, 158,
    250, 254, 293, 326
insurance, insurance companies, 156*n*-
    157*n*
  of Mahoney, 101*n*, 207, 301, 335*n*
  of Radcliff First Assembly of God,
    101–2
Insurance Institute for Highway Safety,
    184
International Harvester, 145, 177–78, 299
Interstate Commerce Commission (ICC),
    298
Interstate 71, description of, 34
Ireland Army Hospital, 131

Jackson, Sam, 177–79, 182
Jacobs, John, 29
Jacques, Grace, 109

Japan, economic competition from, 149, 152, 153
Jefferson, Michael, 193, 195
Jeffries, Mary, 66
Jobert, Laverne, 275
Johnson, Neva, 333–34, 335
Jones, Howard S., 109
Jones, Paul E., 177–79, 182

Kananack, Michael, 111
Karalash, D. J., 171–72
Keith, Roy, Jr., 237*n*-38*n*
Kentucky:
    destructive device in, 92
    Division of Pupil Transportation in, 176*n,* 177–79, 182, 186, 187, 228
    Division of Purchases in, 177
    legally drunk in, 76
    reckless homicide in, 256–57
    school bus ordering in, 177–79, 182
    State Police in, 177
    supper club fire in, 78, 79
Kentucky Association of Funeral Directors, 82
Kentucky Correctional Psychiatric Center, 90
Kentucky Rule of Civil Procedure 26.02, 252
Kentucky school bus crash, *see* Carrollton bus crash
Kentucky Truck Plant, 147, 173, 183, 293, 337
Khomeini, Ayatollah Ruhollah, 109
King, Janice, 203, 204, 205, 207, 208
King, William Haven, Jr., 176*n,* 279, 342
    Aug. 11, 1989 hearing and, 246–47, 249, 252–53
    background of, 270
    depositions taken by, 270–72
    trial and, 289, 290, 297–99, 325, 326, 331, 333
Kings Island amusement park, 17–27, 265
    Church Day at, 9, 17, 21–27
    departure for, 17–21
Knapp, William, 206–7
Knight, Kari, 87, 195, 197
Koeppel, Bill, 80
Korea, school bus accident in, 71–72
Kraemer, Robert, 171–72, 174
Kurre, Robert B., 162
Kytta, Charlie (son), 59, 60, 61, 64, 94, 95

Kytta, Chuck (father), 28–29, 30, 59–64
    burning of, 35, 38, 76, 94–95, 187, 289
    bus's departure and, 18–19, 21
    death of, 62–64, 69, 76, 92–93
    funeral of, 92–93
    passenger list of, 49, 50
Kytta, Janet, 59–64, 69
    on husband's death, 93–95
Kytta, Mandy, 59, 60, 61, 64, 95
Kytta, Mr. (Chuck's father), 63

Labor Statistics, U.S. Bureau of, 158
lap belts, 158
lawsuits:
    Family Support Group meetings and, 99–104, 108, 117
    Grimshaw v. *Ford Motor Company,* 282–84
    Pinto, 183, 286
    settlement and, 116–22
    see also Fair v. *Ford; Nunnallee* v. *Ford;* trial
Lester Motors, 182
Let 'Em Burn Letter (Grush-Saunby report), 285–88, 326
Lewis, C. S., 212
Lewis, Keith, 173, 174, 230
Lincoln, Abraham, 201
Lincoln, Thomas, 201
Louisville *Courier-Journal,* 103, 106, 124, 179*n,* 238*n,* 269
Lucas, James Carl, 37
Lucas, Phyllis, 37

Mabley, Edward, 175, 176
McCollister, John Y., 137–38
McGuire, Woods, Battle & Boothe, 246
McNickle, Katrina, 21, 30, 35
    in crash, 38–39, 54–55, 57
McNickle, Kevin, 102
Maguire, Andrew, 166
Mahoney, Betty Davis, 205, 207, 341
Mahoney, Janice King, 203, 204, 205, 207, 208
Mahoney, Judy, 81
Mahoney, Larry W., 89–92, 203–11, 236, 248
    arraignments of, 89–90, 206
    arrests of, 76, 80–81, 205–6, 207
    bankruptcy of, 207, 208
    blood alcohol concentration of, 76, 216, 257

Mahoney, Larry W. (*cont.*)
  Butcher's visit to, 80–81
  charges against, 76
  Commonwealth of Kentucky v. *Larry
    Wayne Mahoney* and, 256–62
  death penalty and, 76, 89–92
  depression of, 90
  drinking of, 204, 207–10, 215–18, 340
  drunk driving of, 32–35, 76, 91, 207,
    209–10, 215–19, 243, 257–62
  Fair v. *Ford* and, 289, 291, 292, 297,
    300–301, 305, 308–9
  hospitalization of, 73, 76, 80–81
  insurance of, 101*n*, 207, 301, 335*n*
  marriages and divorces of, 205, 207
  post-trial life of, 339–41
  pre-accident activities of, 203–5, 208–
    210
  protection of, 89
  sentencing of, 260–62
  supporters of, 90, 236
  Webb's finding of, 56–57
Mahoney, Makayla, 259
Mahoney, Mrs. (Larry's mother), 89, 208
Mahoney, Shawna, 205, 206, 207, 341
Mahoney, Tony, 203, 204, 205, 208
manslaughter, second-degree, 257, 260
marijuana, 112
Markley, R. W., Jr., 155, 322
Marks, Anthony, 92–93
Martin, Bill, 76
Martin, Jack, 118
Martinez, Richard, 121
Martinez, Rosemary, 83–86, 92–93, 102,
    120–21
Maryland Court of Appeals, 108
mass fatalities, problem in, 12
May, Robert Mahoney, Esq., 126
Meade County School District, 17, 18, 177
Meadows, Steve, 74, 75, 291
Mefford, Dennis, 207, 209
memorial services, 88–89, 93, 232, 235–
    241
  unveiling of monument at, 237
MGM-Grand Hotel fire, 110
Michigan Alcoholism Screening Test
    (MAST), 218
Michigan Fleet Equipment Company,
    182–83
Mills, April, 27, 196
Minimum Standards for School Buses,
    179
Monk, James, 90

Montana crash (1984), 220
Monte Vista Burial Park, 98–99
Montgomery, James, 315–18
Montgomery, Mary Lee, 316
Morgan, Phillip, 23, 32, 93
Morris-Baker Funeral Home, 97
Morrison, Brian, 199
Moskowitz, Herbert, 216–17
Moss, John, 132, 138–39, 143, 161, 166
Mother Jones, 286
Mothers Against Drunk Driving (MADD),
    118, 243, 267–68, 336, 344–47
Motor Carrier Safety, U.S. Bureau of,
    (BMCS), 144, 160
Motor Vehicle and School Bus Safety
    Amendments (1974), 132, 136–39,
    141, 161, 162
motor vehicle deaths, statistics on, 135
Motor Vehicle Manufacturers Association,
    143
Muessle, Steve, 33–34
Muller, Katrina, 19, 30, 40–41, 54–55,
    120, 236
Muller, Mickey, 19, 120
Mullins, Frances Angel, 130, 131, 198,
    277, 336
Mullins, Gloria, 43–47, 66, 70–71, 128,
    130, 235, 237
Mullins, Janey, *see* Fair, Janey Mullins
Mullins, Patty, 96, 98–99, 125, 130, 198,
    336
Mullins, T. R., 130
Munson, Robert H., 227–30
Murgatroyd, George W. III (Skip), 111,
    272–74, 282, 283, 291
  Aug. 11, 1989 hearing and, 244–48,
    250, 251, 254
  background of, 254–56
  trial and, 291, 302–3, 306–7, 312, 330,
    332–33, 337
Murgatroyd, Tracy, 255, 256
Mustain, Tina, 87

Nader, Ralph, 136, 150
Nall, Joseph, 76–77
National Accident Sampling System
    (NASS), 220
National Archives, Nixon tapes in, 149–
    154
National Center for Voluntary Action
    (NCVA), 148
National Conference on School
    Transportation (1945), 181, 298

National Conference on School
   Transportation (1970), 179, 298
National Council of Chief School
   Officers, 180
National Education Association (NEA),
   179, 182
National Highway Traffic Safety
   Administration (NHTSA), 135n,
   136–45, 147, 148, 156, 159–66, 184,
   233, 283
   cost-benefit analysis and, 157–61
   crash tests of, 222n
   Docket 3–2 of, 159–60
   Environmental Impact Statement of,
      142
   Fatal Accident Reporting System
      (FARS) of, 179, 219n
   Ford's petitions to, 322
   fuel spillage standards and, 141–45,
      171
   Johnson's contract with, 333
   National Center for Statistics Analysis
      of, 219–20
   NTSB hearings and, 219–24
   NTSB's safety recommendations to,
      343–44
   Pinto lawsuits and, 183, 286
   Program Plan of, 159
   societal costs study of, 285, 287
National Institute of Standards and
   Technology (NIST), 343
National Organization for Victims
   Assistance, 267
National Safety Council, 181n, 219n
National School Bus Standards
   Conference (1939), 179–82, 298
National School Transportation
   Association, 163
National Traffic and Motor Vehicle Safety
   Act (1966), 135, 136, 152, 160, 161
National Traffic Safety Bureau, 135
National Transportation Safety Board
   (NTSB), 76–77, 80, 127–28, 139–40
   Carrollton crash inquiry of, 178, 213–
      231, 242, 299n
   reports of, 106–7, 139, 179n, 223, 225,
      230, 242
   safety recommendations made by,
      343–44
Navistar International school buses,
   222n, 344, 347
NCVA (National Center for Voluntary
   Action), 148

Nelson-Edelen-Bennett Funeral Home,
   83–85
neoprene, 187
News Democrat, The, 90
NHTSA, *see* National Highway Traffic
   Safety Administration
Nichols, Bill (father), 261
Nichols, Billy (son), 31–32, 41, 93, 261
Nichols, George, 11–13, 73–76
   at Holiday Inn, 69, 73
Nichols, James L., 218–19
Nichols, Maddy, 31–32
Nichols, Mr. (Billy's father), 31, 32
Nicholson, Patricia, 345–46
NIST (National Institute of Standards and
   Technology), 343
Nixon, Pat, 148
Nixon, Richard, 14, 148–59, 250, 254, 293,
   326
Nobles, Susan, 346
North Hardin High School, awards
   ceremony in, 238–40
North Hardin Memorial Gardens, 88,
   235–37, 238n
Northwest Airlines, 110
Notice of Proposed Rulemaking for
   Federal Motor Vehicle Standard
   (FMVSS) 301–75, 141–42
NTSB, *see* National Traffic Safety Board
Nunnallee, Jeanne, 324, 345
Nunnallee, Jim, 52, 104, 112, 116, 232,
   234, 236, 276, 290
   counteroffers to Ford and, 122–24
   retirement of, 344
   testimony of, 303
   see also Nunnallee v. *Ford;* trial
Nunnallee, Karolyn, 104, 112, 113, 116,
   232, 234, 236, 238, 290, 324, 336
   bus remains viewed by, 302
   counteroffers to Ford and, 122–24
   post-trial life of, 344–46
   testimony of, 303
   see also Nunnallee v. *Ford;* trial
Nunnallee, Patty, 25–26, 51, 52, 232, 303,
   345–46
   in crash, 55, 187, 305
   personality of, 113
Nunnallee v. *Ford,* 123, 124, 178–79,
   276–77, 282
   see also trial

Obergone, E. J., 36
Office of Management and Budget, 161

Office of Science and Technology, 158
Oldfather, Ann, 115, 282, 283, 336–37, 338
  Aug. 11, 1989 hearing and, 246, 247, 249, 253
"On a Piece of Chalk" (Huxley), 96
One More for the Road (video), 238
Our Precious Loss (video), 242
Our Times (TV magazine show), 233–35

Padgett, Brittany, 25–26, 57–58
Padgett, Janey, 20, 25–26, 29, 32, 52
  in crash, 35–36, 55, 57–58
Page, Donald R., 71–72
passive restraints standard, 152–57
Pearman, Cheryl, 34, 42
Pearman, Christy, 24, 30, 34, 40, 192–193
Pearman, Dottie, 264–65
Pearman, John, 265
  bus's departure and, 18–21
  in crash, 35, 40
  death of, 50, 61, 62, 63
  lawsuits against estate of, 66, 100
  return trip and, 27–30, 34
Pelkey, Robert, 79–80, 176*n*, 182, 214, 253
People, 109, 110, 115*n*
Percefull, Joseph, 19, 22–25, 32
  in crash, 39–40, 56
perceptual impairment, 217
Percy, Charles, 138
Peterson, Pete, 153
Pfizer, Inc., 79*n*
Physicians for Auto Safety, 142, 164
"Pinto Madness" (Dowie), 286
Points of Light Foundation, 148
polyurethane, 187, 343
Premo, Richard, 176, 186
Preyer, Richardson, 166–68
Preyer amendment, 166–68
Product Change Request (PCR), 170–71, 173–74
psychological evaluations, 280–82
psychomotor impairment, 215, 217
public health, auto accidents and, 135–136
punitive damages, 244–45, 336–37

Raby, Byrd, 214, 225
Radcliff, Ky.:
  description of, 111–12
  return of bodies to, 82–83

Radcliff First Assembly of God, 17–22, 268
  bus purchased by, 17
  insurance of, 101–2
  lawsuits against, 100, 102, 236
  Martha Tennison's leading of service at, 66–67
  official notification of deaths at, 82
  post-accident bus purchase of, 278
  shared funeral at, 92–93
  worried families assembled at, 44–51, 53, 60–63
Raskin, Larry, 280–82
Rather, Dan, 233
Reagan, Nancy, 88
Reagan, Ronald, 88
Rebozo, Bebe, 156
Redmond, Robert F., Jr., 158
release system, 170–71
Reston, Va., school bus accident in, 106, 172, 179*n*, 229, 299, 301
Reston Report, 293
retread tire performance, 160
Richards, M. A., 170
Richwalsky, Paul, Jr., 91–92, 232, 258–59, 308–9
Riley, Leeann, 202
Ritter, Barbara, 73
Rivera, Geraldo, 101
Robinson, Mark, Jr., 282–85
  background of, 282–83
  opening statement of, 295–96
  trial and, 288, 295–96, 306, 311, 312, 315, 319–20, 322–23, 329–30, 338
Robison, Procter, 80, 123, 247
Roche, Jim, 155–56
Roever, Dave, 238–40, 242–43
Ruckelshaus, William, 151
Runyon, Roger, 50
Rustburg, Va., school bus accident near, 223

SAE (Society of Automotive Engineers), 103, 139
safety, safety standards, 103–4, 132, 135–187
  air bags and, 152, 154–55, 157, 342
  cost-benefit analysis and, 103, 136–40, 153, 157–61, 283–88
  Cyr's study of, 180
  drunk driving vs., 233, 235–36, 238, 242–43, 258–59, 278
  Fairs' interest in, 116, 123

fuel system, 76–77, 106–7, 122, 123–124, 132, 141–46, 165, 166, 170–76, 178–79, 182–86, 222*n,* 230, 244–45, 250, 278*n,* 285–87, 319–30, 333–34, 336, 343–44
  in 1966, 135–36, 146–47, 152, 160, 161
  passive restraints, 152–57
  NTSB hearings and, 219–30
  Preyer amendment and, 166–68
St. Christopher's Roman Catholic Church, 87–88
Satterwhite, Charles, 246, 247, 248, 259, 260
Saunby, Carol, 285–87
SBMI (School Bus Manufacturers Institute), 143, 163, 165, 167, 168, 179*n*
Schaeffer, Donald, 289, 317, 318
school bus accidents, 132, 293
  in Alabama, 139
  in Alton, Tex., 121, 268
  in Korea, 71–72
  statistics on, 179*n,* 219–20
  in Virginia, 106, 172, 179*n,* 223, 229, 299, 301
  Yuba City High School, 169
  see also Carrollton bus crash
school buses:
  Boston Bag Test and, 234–35
  color of, 180
  Fairs' purchase of, 268
  Green's view of dangers of, 103
  Kentucky's ordering of, 177–79
  recall offer and, 122–24
  safety standards for, *see* safety, safety standards
  as trucks, 147–48, 251–52
School Bus Manufacturers Institute (SBMI), 143, 163, 165, 166, 167, 169, 179*n*
School Bus Vehicle Safety Report, 169*n*
Scott, Will, 146–47
Scoville, Jennifer, 26, 28–31, 34
  in crash, 41, 55, 56
seatbelts, 152, 153
seats, flammability of, 103, 123, 186, 187, 268, 343
second-degree manslaughter, 257, 260
Senate, U.S., 136, 168–69, 174
Sergent, Gary, 289, 300–301, 305–306

Seventh Circuit Court of Appeals, 160
Sharon, Jim, 304
Sheller-Globe Corporation, 163, 258, 276, 334, 338
  Carrollton bus body of, 80*n,* 103, 169, 176, 182
  Carter as witness for, 163
  exit requirements and, 163
  expert witnesses of, 277
  Fair v. *Ford* and, 123, 186, 211, 231, 289–90, 292, 305
  Hardin's "Sell-O-Gram" at, 185–86
  Nunnallees' lawsuit against, 186
  plaintiffs' settlement with, 289–90, 305
  settlement and, 112, 118, 119, 243
  Superior Coach Division of, 80*n,* 176, 180, 182, 183, 185–87
Siegel, Harvey, 217–18
Simpson, Jinky, 204
Skeeters, Don, 77, 117, 119
Skeeters, Mike, 77–78
Skeeters, Sandy, 77
Skeeters & Bennett, 77, 79, 100–101, 110–11, 114–15, 240
  rumors about, 112
  settlement arranged by, 112, 116–122
Slaughter, Jim, 19, 22–25, 32
  crash and, 35, 39–40, 55–56, 304
slumber parties, 191–93
smoke inhalation, 76
"Societal Costs of Motor Vehicle Accidents, The" (NHTSA), 285, 287
Society of Automotive Engineers (SAE), 103, 139
Sowder, Tanja, 33–34
Spradlin, Wayne, 18
steering column, collapsible, 158
Stithton Baptist Church, 197, 198
Strong, Robert, 56, 304
Summers, William L., 257–58
Superior Coach, 80*n,* 176, 180, 182, 183, 185–87
Supreme Court, U.S., 157*n*
Sweet, Berkley, 169, 176

Tedescucci, Linda, 60, 61
Tennison, Allen, 36, 49, 52, 58, 63
Tennison, Martha, 49, 50, 52, 58, 278
  worship service led by, 66–67

Tennison, Rev. W. Don, 52, 53, 238, 241, 264, 278
  Bennett's no-sue policy and, 100
  bus's departure and, 17–19
  concerns of, 66
  first report of accident and, 48–50
  gratitude of, 49, 58
  lawsuits and, 66, 100, 101
  at memorial service, 88
  settlement and, 118–19
"thin skull doctrine, the," 308*n*
Thomas Built bus company, 163, 166
Thompson, Emillie, 26, 31–32, 41
  funeral of, 92–93
Thompson, Eric, 31
Toms, Douglas, 149, 151, 152, 156
toxic fumes, 78–79, 103
Toyota, 80*n*
tractor-trailers, fuel tank of, 327
Transportation Department, U.S. (DOT), 136, 140, 169, 180
  under Nixon, 149, 151–56, 158
  under Reagan, 156*n*-57*n*
trial (*Fair* v. *Ford; Nunnallee* v. *Ford*), 288–338
  Bihlmeyer's testimony and cross-examination at, 319–25, 327–330
  Cease's testimony at, 304–5, 307–8, 310, 311
  dates set for, 276–77, 279
  Dunn's encouraging of settlement at, 331–33
  first day of, 288–301
  fuel system as evidence at, 292–93, 316
  Hill's testimony at, 309–12, 314
  Johnson's testimony at, 333–34, 335
  Montgomery's testimony at, 315–318
  nonjury, 290–92, 297
  opening statements at, 292–301
  photographic evidence at, 304–5, 317–318
  Richwalsky's views on, 308–9
  second day of, 302–7
  Sergent's shuttle diplomacy and, 305–306
  settlement of, 335–38
  third day of, 307–9

Tubby's Tavern, 204–5, 208
Tunney, John, 169

UCLA crash test, 293, 328
Uhey, Crystal, 93
Uhey, Pam, 58
Union Carbide, 109
Unsafe at Any Speed (Nader), 136
Urban Mass Transportation Administration, 221

Valley Coca-Cola Bottling Company, 121
"Vehicle Fires" (Habberstad), 328–329
Voglund, David, 112
Voglund, Denise, 46, 87–88
Volpe, John, 149, 152, 154–56
von der Heydt, Johann (Joist Hite), 128–129

Waggoner, Rev. Gene, 67, 82
  at memorial services, 88–89, 93, 235
  at Shannon Fair's funeral, 97–98
Waite, Robert, 118, 122
Walliser, David, 30, 57
Wall Street Journal, 118
Wall Tube & Metal Products Company, 171
Ward bus company, 137, 176*n*
Washington, George, 129
Washington Post, 148
Waxman, Henry, 166
Wayne Corporation, 137, 165
Weaver, Jerry, 240
Webb, Tommy, 56–57
We Care Fund, 265
Wheelock, Amy, 23, 46, 192, 195, 196, 199
  funeral of, 87–88
Wheelock, Janet, 46, 47
White, Juanita, 90
Wilkinson, Wallace, 87, 88, 236, 241
Williams, Dottie Pearman, 264–65
Williams, Joy, 20, 25–26, 32, 51–53, 55, 66, 262–66
  identification of, 75
Williams, Kristen, 20, 25, 51, 53, 55, 66, 262–66
Williams, Lee, 20, 26, 51–53, 66, 67, 94, 261–67

"From Pain to Promise" speech of, 265–67

Mahoney's sentencing and, 261–262

marriages of, 262, 264–65

Williams, Robin, 20, 25, 51–53, 55, 66, 262–66

Williamson, Brady, 187

Williamson, George, 247–49, 252–54, 273–74, 297

Wilson, James E., 137–39

Witt, Chad, 27, 87

Woodward, Hobson & Fulton, depositions taken at offices of, 269–273

Worcester (Mass.) Polytechnic Institute, 234

Wright, Debbie, 90

Wunderlich, Joe, 66

Yuba City (Calif.) High School bus accident, 169

ABOUT THE AUTHOR

James S. Kunen, at the age of nineteen, wrote *The Strawberry Statement,* the bestselling account of Columbia University's 1968 student strike against the Vietnam War. His reporting from Vietnam for *TRUE* magazine led to his second book, *Standard Operating Procedure.* He later became a defense attorney in the criminal courts of Washington, D.C., and recounted his experiences in *"How Can You Defend Those People?"* Kunen's articles have appeared in *The New York Times Magazine, People, Esquire, GQ, Harper's, Newsday,* and many other newspapers and magazines. He lives with his wife and two children in Brooklyn, New York.